IKKI

IKKI

SOCIAL CONFLICT
AND POLITICAL PROTEST IN
EARLY MODERN JAPAN

James W. White

Cornell University Press
Ithaca and London

The publisher gratefully acknowledges grants from the Japan Foundation and the University Research Council at the University of North Carolina at Chapel Hill, which aided in bringing this book to publication.

The maps of Japan used in this book are adapted from Herbert Bix, *Peasant Protest in Japan, 1590–1884*, and are used by permission of Yale University Press.

First published 1995 by Cornell University Press
First printing, Cornell Paperbacks, 2016

Library of Congress Cataloging-in-Publication Data

White, James W. (James Wilson), 1941–
  Ikki: social conflict and political protest in early modern Japan
/ James W. White.
    p. cm.
  Includes bibliographical references and index.
  ISBN: 978-0-8014-3154-8 (cloth : alk. paper)
  ISBN: 978-1-5017-0443-7 (pbk. : alk. paper)
  1. Social conflict—Japan—History. 2. Peasant uprisings—Japan—
History. 3. Japan—Social conditions—1600–1868. 4. Japan—
Politics and government—1600–1868. I. Title.
  HN723.W56   1995
  303.6'0952—dc20   95-16279

Cornell University Press strives to use environmentally responsible suppliers and materials to the fullest extent possible in the publishing of its books. Such materials include vegetable-based, low-VOC inks and acid-free papers that are recycled, totally chlorine-free, or partly composed of nonwood fibers. For further information, visit our website at www.cornellpress.cornell.edu.

CONTENTS

FIGURES

TABLES

Appendix

NOTE ON ORTHOGRAPHY

Macrons have been used over long vowels in Japanese words, except when the word is the name of an author writing in English or a word of common use, such as *Tokyo* or *shogun*.

IKKI

INTRODUCTION

In the early nineteenth century the village of Higashi Zenyōji lay in the Maebashi district of Kawagoe domain, overseen from a distance by a county magistrate (*kōri bugyō*) and a smattering of samurai administrators located in the domain's castle town.[1] Though it was sited in a fertile region near the Tone River, Higashi Zenyōji had fallen upon difficult times. The whole Kantō region, around present-day Tokyo, was undergoing rapid economic change. People were moving out of farming into commercial and small-scale industrial activities and out of the villages into the bustling and more prosperous towns. Those who remained in the village saw their fortunes declining, and the exactions of village officials and incursions of landlords and moneylenders drove even more people from the villages.

Kawagoe domain was sensitive to these problems, and unsurprisingly so: its revenues depended upon the annual rice tax, and the decline of the farm economy struck directly at the administration's bottom line.[2] Thus in 1820 the domain established the Agricultural Promotion Office to subsidize farming, hire agricultural workers, attract farm families from outside the district, and supervise the cultivation of disused land. Many of its activities were actually carried out by local landlords and officials, one of whom was Hachiemon of Higashi Zenyōji.

Hachiemon had led a rather checkered life. In 1784, when he was only eighteen, the death of his father and the collapse of family businesses forced him to wed and set up his own household. He lived through the crop failures and famine of the 1780s and the peasant protests that accompanied them, including one riot in a village near his own, and in 1791 he left for a stint of work in Ise,

---

[1] I am indebted to Fukaya Katsumi (1978) and to Daishiro Nomiya (1992) and the Hyakushō Ikki Kenkyū Kai (1980) for the tales of Hachiemon, Hyōsuke, and Bansuke.

[2] The mainstay of both domain and shogunal governments was an annual tax (*nengu*) levied on whole villages based on their agricultural productivity (in all products) and assessed in units of rice.

1

in south-central Japan. Returning to Higashi Zenyōji, he served as a village official for over a decade. By 1808, however, he was bankrupt; so he left rather precipitately for the capital city, Edo, where he earned enough to pay off his creditors. By 1819 he had risen to the position of village headman. His record was hardly unblemished: he had done a bit of time in jail, had spent 170 days in manacles for another offense, and was reprimanded by the authorities at least once. Nevertheless, 1821 found him recruiting settlers on behalf of Kawagoe domain.

It was not a good year. Drought, wind, and frost damaged the crops—especially the mulberries on which sericulture depended—and the domain, hit with a state imposition for coastal defense, decreed a tax increase: village officials were to survey and assess the crops, subject to a check by domain officials. Hachiemon sent a request to the domain for a temporary exemption because of crop conditions, but it was denied, and when he and his colleagues submitted their crop surveys the domain raised the assessments, amounting in the case of Higashi Zenyōji to a two-thirds increase in the tax bill. At the behest of his villagers Hachiemon appealed again—not against the policy or the principle of the tax but simply for a one-year extension of the old system. He received no response.

At this point the farmers began to get together. Two subheadmen of groups of farmers within the village came to see Hachiemon, and seven other villages met to plan a collective plea, though such a meeting could be officially labeled a conspiracy (*totō*). The farmers sent representatives to the Agricultural Promotion Office. The head of the office agreed to pass on their petition but told them it should come only from the poor of the villages. The farmers were undeterred; indeed, the core of the movement was not the poor but those of modest means whose economic viability was threatened by the tax increase. In the eleventh month a group left the Maebashi district to lodge a protest directly with the lord of the domain in Edo.

Although representatives of Higashi Zenyōji were not part of this group, Hachiemon wanted both to aid the farmers and to avoid an overt and illegal appeal. So he and two other headmen pursued and caught up with the Edo-bound group and persuaded them to hold off while the village officials tried one more time. Domain officials then solicited a petition from the people, ostensibly cooperating, although their primary motive might well have been the fear that an open appeal in Edo would cost them all their jobs. When the petition was in hand, however, and the people dispersed to their respective villages again, the domain officials rejected and confiscated it, accused the seven villages of conspiracy, illegal flight, and illegal appeal, and launched an investigation.

In the first month of 1822 Hachiemon and fourteen others were arrested. The investigation—a somewhat euphemistic term for a process based largely on torture—lasted almost the entire year, and one alleged leader died in the course of it. In the end Hachiemon alone was sentenced to life in prison, where he died in 1830 at the age of sixty-four.

The 1830s were a time of dire hardship and famine in much of eastern Japan, and the Gunnai region of Kai province, just west of Edo, was no exception. A mountainous area that imported rice and depended for its well-being on wheat, tobacco, sericulture, and weaving, Gunnai was economically and commercially innovative by necessity and economically unstable by nature. It was also doubly hit by hard times: its own poor crops cut its income and its usual suppliers of rice raised prices and cut shipments. The inequality of supply and the merchants' right to profit were not issues; what was unacceptable was the hoarders' unwillingness to share.

The people at first responded legally, with requests for aid from the intendant (since Gunnai was shogunal territory) and demands that local merchants sell rice at reasonable prices. When these attempts failed, the people began to organize, largely under the guidance of local officials, one of whom was Hyōsuke of Inume village. Hyōsuke was born in 1797 into a traditionally elite family and was the head (*kumigashira*) of an intravillage group of families. Amid an air of simmering incipient conflict, he was one of the farmers who drew up a list of rules to govern the behavior of those participating, prepared flags for village groups, and obtained some swords. He was also shrewd enough to foresee the consequences of the growing popular movement: he divorced his wife, settled his debts, and arranged for his family succession before the people took action.

Action began in the eighth month with assaults on the shops of several rice-hoarding merchants in Gunnai; on the twenty-first there was more desultory destruction, and a paper circulated calling for the people to assemble and march on the Kuninaka Basin to demand price reductions and loans of rice. The response was immediate, and a movement of several thousand small and large farmers and their village officials moved down from Gunnai. The movement was not theirs for long, however: no sooner did they hit the village of Kumayado than their ranks were swelled—eventually to perhaps thirty thousand or more—by an influx of the local poor, vagabonds, and others. Discipline was lost; forced sale and loan of rice gave way to simple destruction of buildings, food, and pawn and land records; and the village basis of organization evaporated.

At this point Hyōsuke and his colleagues—and indeed most of the Gunnai people—withdrew, leaving the field to a rampaging wave of rioters, who in the last week of the month destroyed over three hundred shops and storehouses throughout Kuninaka and the provincial capital of Kōfu. This violence, though disorganized and unfocused, was not indiscriminate: the targets were rice merchants, moneylenders, landlords, and pawnbrokers. The intendants were helpless, their stations simply bypassed; with no armed force of their own, they could only appeal to neighboring lordly domains to send soldiers. When the lords responded, the rioting was quelled. Arrests followed, and eventually some three hundred participants were punished. Of those punished, only 10 percent were from Gunnai, and Hyōsuke was not among them, although a death penalty was imposed on him in absentia.

In some ways the most noteworthy stage of Hyōsuke's activities began here. In the ninth month he fled Gunnai and spent the next several months in a peripatetic flight that belies the conventional notion of nineteenth-century Japan as a closely governed society. He crossed the mountains to the shore of the Japan Sea, then headed west to Tango province and back over to Bizen province on the Inland Sea, crossed to the island of Shikoku, traveled west through Shikoku, and then crossed back to Aki province on Honshū. He continued westward to Suō province at the end of Honshū and then turned eastward again, going through Ōsaka, southward into Yamato province, northward to the city of Kyoto, and finally to Ise province near Nagoya, where his diary ends in the eighth month of 1837. Family records suggest that he then made his way to the Edo area and eventually returned to Gunnai sometime around 1845 (Fukaya 1978). He appears to have died peacefully in 1867 at the age of seventy-one.

Hyōsuke's skill in avoiding the executioner commands our respect. It is equally striking that he moved with almost complete freedom around Japan for at least a year, supporting himself largely with such skills as abacus, mathematics, and divination. Clearly there was a demand for Hyōsuke's skills in almost every village, and a clientele able to pay for them, sufficient to keep him in food, clothing, and lodging. The poor of Kuninaka, who snatched the Gunnai protest out of the hands of Hyōsuke and his neighbors, were obviously a major sector of society, but not all of society.

Bansuke, of Yonekawa village in the Nanzan district of Shinano province, was a reprobate. His family, once aristocratic, had long since fallen into the ranks of the common people. Bansuke's generation had also slid from the status of village elder, and the expulsion from the inner circle apparently rankled Bansuke. His elder brother achieved a measure of success, but in 1838 (when Bansuke was forty-two) the family was bankrupt and moved from the village. In 1850 they returned, landless, poor, and possibly unwelcome. Obstreperous and hostile to village rules, Bansuke had been arrested some half dozen times for gambling and assorted offenses. In 1835 he had instigated a dispute over the collection of local taxes. The dispute had been resolved through negotiations, but Bansuke disagreed with the outcome, and it was not until the local intendant leaned on him, at the behest of his fellow villagers, that he had acquiesced.

When Bansuke returned to Yonekawa in 1850 he found a situation much to his taste. The people of mountainous Nanzan had long enjoyed a favored administrative status, being located in relatively lightly ruled (the intendant's office was distant and understaffed) and undertaxed shogunal territory. They also benefited from being able to pay their taxes in coin, exchanged for the official assessment in rice at a locally set rate. But in 1843 it had been announced that the district was going to be assigned to neighboring Iida domain. The locals were perfectly aware that Iida taxes were heavier and paid in kind, and that the corvée was heavier as well. Village officials appealed both to Iida domain and

ACKNOWLEDGMENTS

Along the path of the project of which this book is the outcome I have incurred intellectual debts and have been the beneficiary of assistance from many collegial and institutional sources. This brief note cannot begin to describe them in all their deserved detail, but each merits credit for whatever strengths the book possesses.

The original intellectual stimuli for this book came from the seminal work of three individuals. The work of Charles Tilly, which has shaped recent American research on popular contention more than any other scholar's, both drew me into the subject and provided, in its ever more sophisticated evolution, the theoretical perspective that decisively organizes this book. In view of the historical span of my own study I had occasionally thought to entitle this book *Three Rebellious Centuries*, to show that in some respects at least I had gone beyond Tilly's *Rebellious Century*. In the meantime, however, *The Contentious French* appeared, in which Tilly analyzes four centuries of popular contention in France and in this respect, as in others, puts me back in my place.

My second inspiration is Thomas C. Smith, unquestionably the premier quantitative historian of Japan the United States has yet produced. His *Agrarian Origins of Modern Japan* must still—thirty-five years after publication—be addressed by any serious student of Japanese modernization or early modern Japan. It certainly influenced my own view of socioeconomic change during that era. And until I read his *Nakahara* I would never have believed that demographic history could actually be exciting.

My third source of stimulation was Hayami Akira, whose contributions to Japanese economic and demographic history parallel those of Tilly to the history of popular contention. He has amassed a data set on the demographic history of dozens of Japanese villages of a richness probably unmatched in the world, has been a leading light of the quantitative economic history movement in Japanese academia, has argued persuasively for significant revision of conventional images of Japan's population history and its relationship to economic growth and popular living standards, and at the same time has graciously responded to the demands of any number of obtrusive foreign scholars who appeared at his door.

Once the project was under way, while I was a visiting scholar at Keiō University, I soon learned the value of the guidance and data-gathering suggestions of Nishikawa Shunsaku and Saitō Osamu. Nishikawa taught me my most valuable methodological lesson of the year. Whenever I lamented the gap between Tokugawa-era statistics and my statistical ideals, "Kore shika nai," he would say to me: It's all there is. Use the data carefully, prudently, within their limitations, and triangulate your answers with varied data, but don't run away from an important question because the data are less than ideal. And my only regret about Saitō's excellent comparative history of Japan and Europe, *Puroto-Kōgyōka no Jidai* (The age of protoindustrialization), is that he has not yet translated it into English, thus depriving a foreign audience of the knowledge and enjoyment I derived from it.

The staff, librarians, and graduate students at Keiō were unfailingly helpful, and a troupe of the latter, under Hamano Kiyoshi, coded the Aoki Kōji data set used so frequently in this book. During that same year at Keiō I also benefited mightily from the knowledge and criticism of established scholars in the field of early modern popular contention, among them Fukaya Katsumi, Aoki Michio, Yamada Tadao, and Yasumaru Yoshio. The members of the Quantitative Economic History Group were a willing and helpful audience for a presentation of my research plans and progress.

Back in the United States, Ishimitsu Akiko, J. P. Kim, Barry Ottman, and Hamano Kiyoshi assisted with everything from coding and data entry to data management and analysis. As I began to write, William Kelly, Stephen Vlastos, Richard Smethurst, Ronald Rindfuss, Stuart MacDonald, George Rabinowitz, Tim McKeown, and the Comparative Politics Discussion Group of the Political Science Department at the University of North Carolina read articles and chapters and provided both methodological and substantive suggestions, as did anonymous referees from several journals. Part of the material in this book first appeared as "Cycles and Repertoires of Popular Contention in Early Modern Japan," in *Social Science History* 17 (1993). Finally, Tilly, Marius B. Jansen, and Mark Ramseyer read this book in its earlier (and much longer) entirety, and saved me from errors of both fact and interpretation.

Of course, I could not carry through this entire project on my own. The Carolina Population Center, the UNC University Research Council, the Social Science Research Council, the Fulbright Commission, the National Science Foundation (SES-8308413), and the Z. Smith Reynolds Foundation all supported various stages of the research, though none is responsible for any of the ideas expressed here. Ideas, money, research assistance, and collegial critique are all essential to any project of this scope; I have been fortunate to enjoy all in generous measure, and I extend my appreciation to all my benefactors and coconspirators accordingly.

J. W. W.

to the local intendant for continuation of the previous tax system. Failing in both attempts, they appealed directly to one of the shogun's elders (*rōjū*) in Edo. This appeal failed also, but in 1845 the district had again become shogunal territory.

Relief was short-lived. In 1846 Nanzan was assigned to Shirakawa domain. Again local officials appealed, and Shirakawa agreed to allow payment in coin until 1855, although at a new exchange rate that amounted to a tax hike. By 1852 the farmers were organizing, and in 1855 a petition went to the domain from village leaders and better-off farmers. The appeal was rejected and a number of the petitioners were chained or jailed; retraction and apology were demanded; and the district was hit collectively with an additional exaction. The domain also postponed in-kind payment until 1859, but the people regarded this outcome as a failure and continued to plan. Since officials' overtures didn't seem to be working, attention began to move down the social ladder, and it wasn't long before eyes fell on Bansuke, if only as a fall guy.

Thenceforth, activities ran on two tracks: higher-level elements considered various appeals, and smaller farmers and tenants kept local feelings fermenting, partly by circulating the tale of Sōgorō, a legendary protest leader in days gone by. In the twelfth month of 1859 village representatives went to the market town of Haramachi to protest the exchange rate. The intendant agreed to listen, but the poorer farmers pushed the representatives to do more. More people gathered in Haramachi, and on the twenty-fourth, some one hundred of them called on the magistrate in Ichida with a further petition. His response was an abusive rejection. On the twenty-seventh most of the petitioners returned home, but some one thousand—mostly tenants and poorer farmers, including Bansuke (if he knew he was being used, he didn't seem to mind)—regrouped. By this time village officials, fearful of an illegal appeal that would expose them to the wrath of the domain, were trying hard to control events.

Angered upon learning of the rejection of the petition at Ichida, the crowd headed off to present its own demands to the domain, now not only calling for restoration of shogunal rule but also denouncing domain cuts in irrigation and ferry subsidies, double standards in administration, punishment of previous pro-testers, unresponsiveness, and the appointment of oppressive officials. This kind of action was serious stuff, as a party of Iida domain officials the petitioners encountered in Chayamachi informed them: they were in conspiracy to appeal illegally and should return home immediately. The petitioners asked the officials to transmit the petition to Shirakawa domain. When the domain officials refused, the credibility of the village officials cracked, and Bansuke and his poorer allies took over.

On the twenty-ninth Bansuke's group met with officials of Shirakawa domain. Harsh words were exchanged, and Bansuke, true to form, tried to lay hands on the magistrate. Surprisingly (or perhaps unsurprisingly, for official prestige had come to a sorry pass by the 1860s), Bansuke got away with this assault and even came away with an oral agreement to fix the tax situation as under shogunal rule. The domain's word was hardly trustworthy, and although the protesters withdrew, they followed up in 1860 with many petitions. But the domain did as it pledged, giving in on the tax issue, replacing the magistrate, and further aiding Nanzan with cash.

Bansuke was not appeased. Perhaps he was simply angry at being eclipsed (once the protest was over, leadership reverted to the village officials), or perhaps he really did feel that the aid was insufficient. In any case, 1860 found him stirring up the smallholders, and the new magistrate let the village headmen know that this agitation had better stop. Bansuke was told that his activities jeopardized the district's gains. Thus recognized (and paid off), Bansuke cooled his followers, but in the spring he was briefly jailed anyway.

By autumn Bansuke was at it again, arguing that the tenants and smallholders had been overpaying their taxes for several years. In the tenth month a tenant gathering brought the division between tenants and landlords out in the open. The plan was to present the landowners with a set of demands, but domain officials, alerted by the landowners, arrived and arrested Bansuke and four others. The officials patrolled the villages, and the tenants caved in. The landed had won, the landless lost, and Bansuke got life in prison for his efforts. His eventual fate is unknown, but he was transferred to domiciliary confinement back in Yonekawa in 1863, at the age of sixty-eight, and freed in 1870 (Yasumaru 1975: 206).

Popular Contention in Early Modern Japan

The three stories just recounted are parts of a richly variegated text of conflict that runs throughout the early modern history of Japan.[3] This period (1600–1868), during which Japan was ruled by the shoguns of the Tokugawa family, was one of state building and economic development, social change and cultural transformation, and it is hardly surprising that patterns of conflict among the common people, and between the people and those who ruled them, are closely intertwined with these phenomena. The intimate connection between text and context is exemplified by the generic term for popular contention during the era: *ikki*, usually translated as "peasant rebellion" and often defined explicitly in terms of the Tokugawa political and social system. Such contention, it can be argued, had a powerful effect on the policies, personnel, and institutions of Tokugawa-era government. Of revolution we see nothing, but the cumulative effect of the sorts of political concessions seen in the preceding stories proved decisive for the viability of the Tokugawa state. Furthermore, the prevalence of conflict belies the

---

[3] The concept of popular contention is discussed in, inter alia, Oberschall 1973: 3, 6; Olson 1971; Tilly 1981: 9; Tarrow 1989; White 1984: 54; Goldstone 1991: 40ff.; and March and Olsen 1989. My usage of the term *popular contention* is derived primarily from the work of Charles Tilly; to paraphrase him (1986: 3–4), it refers to the banding together of groups of common people to act (offensively or defensively) on their interests, making claims in ways that directly, visibly, and significantly—and disruptively or obstructively—affect other people's realization of *their* own interests. Such action may be legal or illegal, violent or nonviolent, legitimate or illegitimate, but to some extent it contravenes the conventions of everyday life. See also page 323 below.

old stereotype of a uniquely harmonious Japanese society. Indeed, although contention waxed and waned, varied from place to place, took multiple forms and metamorphosed over time, and was throughout intimately enmeshed in contextual changes, it appears to have been almost ubiquitous in the Tokugawa era.

This book describes types and repertoires of Tokugawa-era contention, the rise and fall of great waves of conflict and protest, the actors in the drama and their targets, their organizations and motivations and tactics, and the magnitude and intensity of their efforts. It maps the distribution of conflict across counties, provinces, and domains, and across the early modern era, tracing the evolution of forms, magnitudes, and other dimensions of contention from before the Tokugawa era began until a decade after it gave way to the modern era.

Though the focus of the book is narrow, my investigation may cast light on the nature, causes, and meanings of popular contention in general. The sorts of popular contention represented by ikki are in many respects neither uniquely Japanese nor uniquely early modern. Similar phenomena have occurred and do occur in other societies and at other times. In fact, the prevalence of this sort of behavior prompts general questions: Is contentious behavior rooted in human reason or emotion, in social relations, in the actions of rulers or exploiters, or in the workings of the system of national states and economies around the globe? What does the level of conflict—low or high—say about the quality of life in a society? Is conflict a cultural interloper and solvent, or does it reflect and perhaps even cement dominant cultural patetterns? In short, what is the nature, cause, and meaning of popular contention?

Such general questions lead us back to the specific: Why this? Why them? Why here? Why now? and How? This book explores these questions by considering the structural and cultural context of Tokugawa society; the conjuncture of weather and events, man-made and natural incursions on popular livelihood; the attitudes and ideologies of rulers and ruled; and the nature of leadership in Tokugawa society. From these factors it identifies the *reasons* why people contended either with each other or with the authorities (their grievances, frustrations, selfless ideals and selfish interests, goals, indignations), the *means* of contention at their disposal (weapons, symbols, numbers, leaders, organizations, and other resources), and the *opportunities* for contention available to them under the status quo.

The combination of reasons, means, and opportunities explains both the quantity and quality of popular contention, although I am also concerned with which of the three is most important in which situations. Much of my attention is directed toward the forms contention took, the participants, and others of its aspects. Many previous studies have described the relationships between, for example, the behavior of state officials and frequency of political protest, and such studies provide us with expectations about the sorts of relationships likely to be found in Tokugawa Japan. I test these expectations against the Tokugawa experience.

Another sort of explanation is also called for: explanation of the consequences of conflict for Tokugawa society. Popular contention had implications for those who participated (on both sides), for the structures, policies, and personnel of government, for the subsequent course of Japanese history, and for the growth of theory in the social sciences. By looking at the implications of contention for its setting and by evaluating the interpretations offered by others, this book assesses the meaning of popular contention.

A Model of Popular Contention

This excursus takes us farther than I like from individuals such as Hachiemon, Hyōsuke, and Bansuke, but it is an essential step in making them larger—or at least more exemplary—than life. They are interesting figures in their own right, but they are also data. And data, by themselves, tell us little. To become the building blocks of understanding they must be set in context and bound together by theory.

Figure 1 sets forth the theoretical framework of this book. I do not actually "test" the model here; rather, I maintain that this model does in fact represent the causal process behind popular contention in early modern Japan. Indeed, I could not test the entire model at one time even if I wished, for quantitative data are lacking for some parts of it—notably interests and individual and collective decisional calculi. In these cases, we must infer what is going on. Interests are expressed in popular statements of intention and justification, but they are only stated reconstructions (sometimes with tendentious purposes) of intention and justification and not necessarily the original attitudes at all. I try to bridge these inferential gaps from both sides.

I have already noted the relevance of the institutional and structural context to popular contention; indeed, many analyses of contention remain on this level, associating overall levels of conflict in societies with the macrolevel characteristics of those societies.[4] I am more interested in context as a determinant of interests, opportunities, and resources, but the indirect influence òf context on contention is of great help in inferring the nature of this determination.

As noted in Figure 1, context can be viewed analytically as having political, economic, social, and ideological or cultural dimensions. The primary aspect of the political context is the state, and the early modern Japanese state occupied an inherently contentious position vis-à-vis the people.[5] The people constantly attempted to broaden the scope of their freedom of action and minimize their

---

[4] See, e.g., Skocpol 1979; Goldstone 1991; Tong 1991; Hibbs 1973; Gurr 1968; Muller 1985; Huntington 1968; Olson 1963.

[5] State is defined here as "a relatively centralized, differentiated, and distinct organization that controls the principal concentrated means of coercion within a contiguous and clearly bounded territory" (Tilly 1989b: 165). See also Weber 1947: 154; Gerth and Mills 1981: 78ff. I have argued elsewhere (White 1988c) that it is unhelpful to think of Tokugawa Japan as a feudal system; efforts to place the Tokugawa state in a comparative context are significantly enhanced if one analogizes it instead to the early modern states of Europe.

Figure 1. A model of popular contention

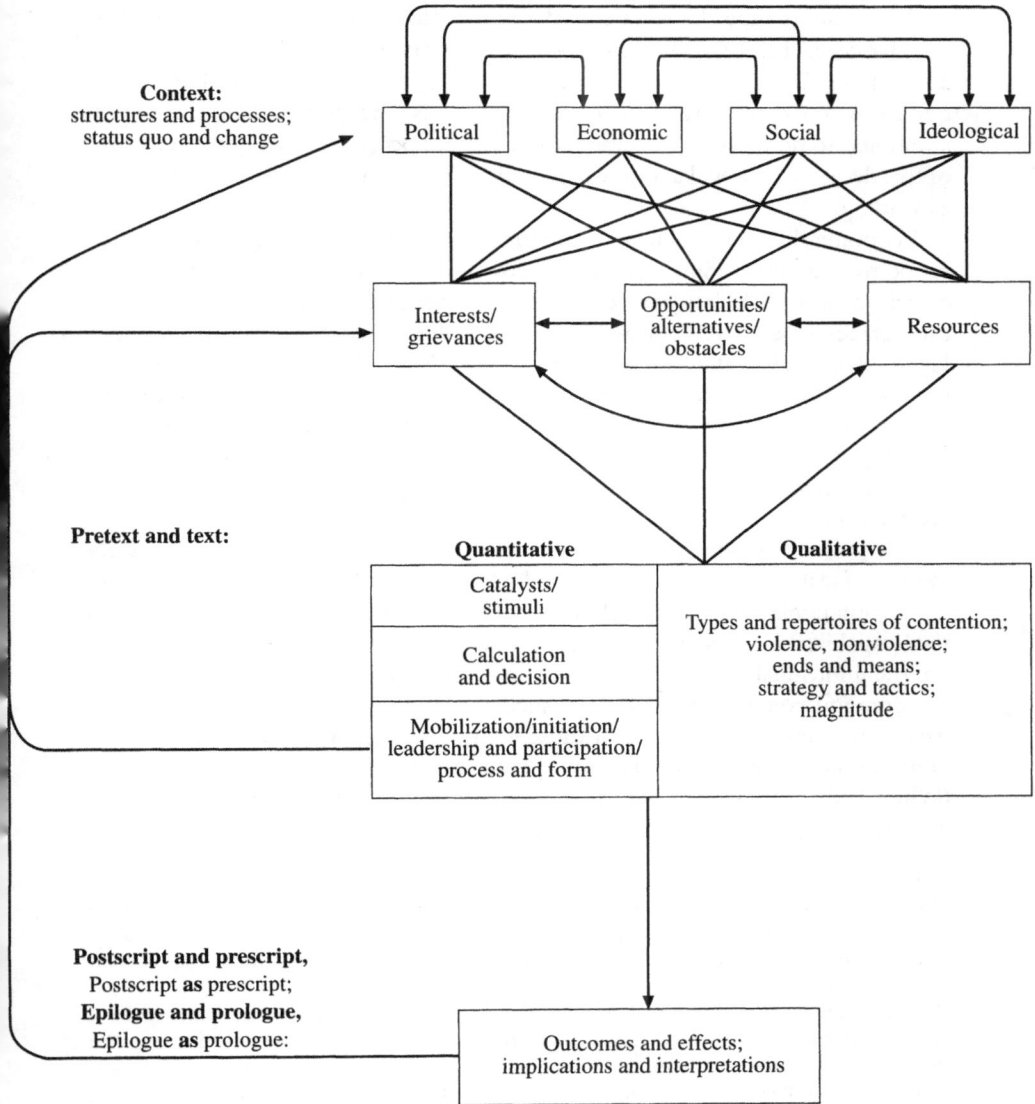

obligations, while the state attempted to regulate them more effectively and provide less to them in return. Moreover, in the early years the scope of state activity grew dramatically, provoking repeated confrontations both with the common people and with their intermediate overlords. Nevertheless, to the extent that the state was willing to repress them consistently it was able to reduce both popular and aristocratic resistance.[6]

After a short time the state ceased to grow (for reasons I shall discuss), but popular conflict did not diminish, because over time the capacities and consistency of the Tokugawa state decayed, but its aspirations did not.[7] The consequence was a condition of "overreach." That is, the government chronically attempted to do more than it was capable of, and people such as Bansuke, aware of this decay of both will and power, could see their opportunities for contention expanding.

Economically, the Tokugawa context was agrarian, although the agrarian economy was undergoing significant growth, commercialization, and protoindustrialization.[8] Scholars have documented a positive relationship between the early stages of economic growth and sociopolitical conflict.[9] In early modern Japan, too, this was the case, although I maintain that the path of causation ran not through the socially traumatic effects of rapid change or the immiseration of development's "losers" but rather through the proliferation of interests resulting from social differentiation and through the attempts of better-off commoners to abdicate their historical role as patrons and protectors of the less well-off.

The political economy, too, played a role. Its most significant aspect in early modern Japan was state extraction. Higher rates and new media of taxation always antagonized the people, but over the long run, extraction contributed to state capabilities. Consequently, I see a positive macrolevel relationship—driven on the individual level by opportunities, not grievances—between *declining* taxation and contention. As for the social economy, the preponderance of the data—including the prosperity of those who supported Hyōsuke in his travels—indicates that the lives of the Japanese people improved during the Tokugawa era (White 1989). Because of the vagaries of climate and (increasingly) the market, however, their vulnerability did not diminish. In consequence, the people did not

---

[6] Although repression appears to stimulate contention in the short or even medium run, the Tokugawa and Meiji experiences indicate that when applied consistently and heavily, it reduces popular insubordination—and vice versa (Gurr 1980: 215, 439–40; Hibbs 1973; Muller 1985; Charles Tilly, personal communication 1993).

[7] It is important not to confuse state growth or development—that is, the emergence of more modern state institutions and practices—with state capability or performance, which involves balancing what the state wishes to do or must do against its ability to extract the necessary resources and put them to effective use. See White 1988c; Weiner and Huntington 1987: 353–89; Brown 1991; Evans et al. 1985: 350ff.; Powell 1982: chap. 1; Almond and Powell 1966: chap. 11; Kimmel 1988: 17ff.; Tilly et al. 1975: 35.

[8] Protoindustrialization refers to the increasing production of nonagricultural products or processed agricultural goods for increasingly distant markets by small productive units predominantly located in the countryside. See Tilly 1983; Mendels 1982; Saitō 1983; Bohstedt 1983: 215ff.

[9] The relationship is not completely clearcut (Zimmermann 1983: 95; Gurr 1980: 176ff.), but for the early stages of modern economic growth it does appear to be the case: Wolf 1969; Calhoun 1982; Thompson 1966; Scott 1976.

become fat and contented as living standards improved but remained anxious and extremely protective of whatever gains they had made.

With regard to contention, the most important aspect of the social context in early modern Japan was neither a sweeping abstraction such as class nor a micro-unit such as the family but rather the community, the primary locus of loyalty for most of the common people.[10] Community norms demanded contention under some circumstances—especially by community leaders such as Hachiemon and Hyōsuke—and demanded respect for collective interests, which, if ignored by the better-off, were seen as grounds for contention by Bansuke and his ilk. Communities possessed collective interests that crosscut class; to the extent that communities remained cohesive—and many did, even amid rapid economic growth—their capacity for contention was enhanced. And the Tokugawa state, which removed the samurai from the land and left local administration in the hands of commoners, provided the people with extraordinary opportunities to plot away from official eyes (see also Skocpol 1979).

Yet, despite the overarching influences of government, economy, and society, popular contention is the result of individual decisions, and it is only through individual perceptions and calculations that context begins to matter. We cannot often measure popular consciousness directly, although we do have contemporary diaries, manifestoes, official analyses, and the observations of scholars then and now.[11] I have tried to characterize these attitudes broadly; among those of greatest relevance are popular evaluations of the propriety and efficacy of contention per se and of rights, reciprocity, and the proper nature of authority.

Along with these, I believe, the aspects of popular consciousness most relevant to contention are two. First, the common people were never "mystified," or persuaded by the elites that uncomplaining subordination was right, proper, and eternally ordained. They saw through the ideology of domination and on occasion turned it against the elites themselves.[12] Second, the people were (though not narrowly rational utility maximizers) able to reason and to calculate the costs and benefits of their own behavior *and also* acutely moralistic in their judgments and capable of a high degree of indignation and passion, as the grimly calculating Hyōsuke and irrepressible Bansuke both suggest. Whereas rational thinking was common in the economic sphere (see T. Smith 1977), people tended to see community and polity in highly moral terms of rights and justice, contract and reciprocity. Rationality and morality, moreover, were sequenced (March and

---

[10] Magagna 1991; Calhoun 1982; Manning 1988. On the limited utility of class, see Kelly 1985.

[11] All these sources must be used with care. The language of the Tokugawa people was often part of a negotiating strategy, intended more to influence others than to represent their real feelings (Ravina 1992), and many scholars of our own day—such as typically Marxist Japanese historians—adopt approaches in which analysis appears tendentious.

[12] See in this regard Scheiner 1973; Scott 1976, 1985; Tilly 1986; Tilly et al. 1975; Fukaya 1978, 1983.

Olsen 1989, esp. chap. 3). Such ideals as morality and justice established limits of acceptability on elite activity and propriety of popular response, and it was *within* this framework that individuals calculated the costs and benefits of their action.

I am suggesting, it should be clear, that the different aspects of context are interrelated. In Tokugawa Japan the economic and social systems were the direct result of political decisions and were integrated with the polity; the long-term protoindustrialization and short-term fluctuations of the economic system and the consequent stratification, differentiation, and dislocation of the social system had far-reaching implications for the government. A social factor—socioeconomic differentiation—progressed faster in the cities than in the villages, and the implied proliferation of potentially conflicting interests, combined with the economic factor of market vulnerability and the resource of dense settlement and communication, seems to have outweighed the heavier urban administrative hand *and* the socially disintegrative effects of stratification, producing higher levels of contention in the city than in the countryside.

The ideological-cultural context was to some extent a pre-Tokugawa given, but the Tokugawa adopted certain ideological and philosophical principles designed to legitimate their rule. As with every ruling ideology, these principles were a two-edged sword (Kertzer 1988). Elites used them to rationalize their actions, but they were also a popular resource when government did not live up to them. And like the economy and society, the milieu of consciousness slipped out of the hands of the elites as the Tokugawa era drew on, until the polity was more at odds than in synchronization with all three.

On the level of interests, opportunities, and resources, the model moves from the outside world to individuals' and groups' perceptions of it. Indeed, much of my emphasis on the outside world derives from my view that the social institutions within which individuals lead their lives involve roles that entail certain expectations (March and Olsen 1989), and these roles and role expectations generate individual beliefs and behavior—behavior that, absent institutional considerations, can appear to fly in the face of individual self-interest, almost suicidally so in the case of Hachiemon and Hyōsuke. Individual beliefs or interests include anger, profit seeking and utility maximization, survival, institutionally imposed obligations and imperatives, and so forth.

Interests present a major problem in this book, inasmuch as they are individual characteristics, whereas the data are overwhelmingly aggregate. Many studies have successfully inferred interests from aggregate data (Gurr 1970; Hibbs 1973), but theirs were more extensive and reliable than those available for Tokugawa Japan. I have had to rely on relatively gross characteristics of individuals and groups for my inferences about their views on contention. Still, I was not without guideposts: several such characteristics have been found to be systematically related to interests, and I have approximated them here, especially when it was possible to check them against individual-level data.

The first is social class.[13] Without reifying or homogenizing, one can see in Tokugawa society large, albeit highly internally variegated, groups who stood in more or less the same relationship to the major concentrations of wealth and power in society. They were in a common legal and economic position vis-à-vis the elites, and they were treated uniformly by the elites in ways that stimulated grievances or indignation. Consequently, common (albeit restricted) discontents and common reactions to economic or policy change can be inferred.

The second basis of inference is community. Community ways of life, autonomy, prosperity, and survival constituted common interests, from which I have inferred what sorts of government actions would be seen as threats. I have inferred interests not just from the relationship between community and outside world but also from the position of individuals and groups within the community. Degrees of economic well-being, political enfranchisement, and social integration and patterns of landholding varied greatly within communities, and so did interests. A marginal scamp like Bansuke was free to do largely as he pleased, while the obligations of leaders like Hachiemon and Hyōsuke could lead ineluctably to participation in conflict, even if the scaffold loomed beyond.

A third basis of inference is local history and culture (Yokoyama 1977, 1986). I found the concept of "cultures of contention" helpful. Certain localities were characterized over the years by far more conflict than others, and although I am unsure of the mechanism of transmission (I suspect local legends, songs, chronicles, and martyrs [Walthall 1986, 1991]), it does seem clear that there is a continuity of contention in some places which is not fully explicable by the ecological or political context.

But context is central, with regard to opportunities also. They are what the outside world appears to offer or withold, and some maintain that the "opportunity structure" for contention can in fact be more important than either interests or resources (Calhoun 1983: 898). I have found all to be important, but four types of opportunities in particular appear singularly closely associated with popular contention in early modern Japan.

Coerciveness is the first important aspect of the opportunity structure, and Tokugawa Japan illustrates the importance of consistency and time. Inconsistently coercive regimes—sometimes lax, sometimes repressive—invite more contention than consistently permissive or draconian regimes,[14] and whereas repression may simply stir people up in the short run (Gurr 1980: 52–54; Hibbs 1973), in the long run it appears to work (Tilly et al. 1975; Wortman and Brehm 1975; Rothbaum 1980). In their early and most coercive years both the

---

[13] Thompson 1966: 9–11; Tilly 1980: 40ff.; Wolf 1969: xii; Sasaki 1973: 193ff.; Bix 1986.
[14] This conclusion parallels those of Zimmermann 1983: 199; Muller 1985; Muller and Weede 1988; and Hirsch and Perry 1973.

Tokugawa and Meiji regimes successfully reduced levels of contention nation-wide; in the interim decades the progressive ineptitude and inconsistency of the Tokugawa regime invited steadily increasing levels of contention.

Apart from coercion, the simple absence of agents of government also invites contention.[15] The autonomy of the Tokugawa village gave the people much more room for maneuver than some students of the period have suggested. Lack of supervision implies high overall levels of contention. I have found that, other things being equal, communities in less tightly and coherently administered regions were more prone to conflict.

A third aspect of opportunity of which the people took advantage was elite vulnerability. Succession, fiscal crisis, or factional division often spurred the people to action, as did failures of the elites to live up to their own principles of rule.[16] Finally, the context presented the people with alternatives to and objects of contention. Among the alternatives were disaster relief and the provision of petition boxes and judicial redress; where these were used adroitly the regime escaped considerable conflict. At the same time, government offices and mer-chants' homes and shops were lightning rods for dissent, and their presence goes far to explain the spatial distribution of contention.

The availability of courts thus constitutes an opportunity. Having a lawyer, that is, a tool or weapon in one's own possession, constitutes a resource. Numbers, organization and cohesion, and leadership were the resources of greatest value to the Tokugawa common people. They always outnumbered the elites (DeNardo 1985), although the fact that they were essentially unarmed dictated circumspection. The gathering of large numbers of people in cities and towns greatly facilitated the inception of contention. And particularly at the inception, the prior gathering of a crowd—at, say, a market or festival—made it far safer for a potential leader to stick his neck out with minimal fear of being singled out.[17]

Bonding, either psychological or social, was another crucial resource (Tilly 1978: 60ff.). The people adopted a variety of rituals of bonding—oaths, peti-tions, or a common cup—which no doubt bucked up their courage and demon-strated collective resolve. The units of mobilization were usually whole communities, but one must not overestimate the unity of communities—espe-cially cities and villages where socioeconomic differentiation was well advanced. Nevertheless, the *higher* levels of contention in cities and in more economically advanced regions suggest that common community interests—or at least cohe-sion and common interests among groups *within* the community—survived the developmental process.

---

[15] Skocpol 1979: chap. 3; Brustein and Levi 1987; Oberschall 1973: chap. 4; Perry 1980: 40; Wakeman 1977.

[16] Brustein and Levi 1987; Kelly 1985; Bix 1986; Scott 1985; Ravina 1992; Walthall 1986.

[17] See also Bercé 1980, 1990. In this book masculine pronouns are the rule, given the predominance of men in contention in early modern Japan.

There were two common types of leaders in popular contention, institutional and entrepreneurial. Hachiemon and Hyōsuke personify the institutional; Bansuke, the entrepreneurial. The formal positions of institutional leaders entailed the obligation to lead their communities in time of crisis; in light of the personal cost of inaction, leadership even in the face of severe punishment was a completely rational path (White 1988b). Entrepreneurial leaders were a much more fluid type, emerging from society's margins in time of turmoil and motivated more by conviction or impulse than by obligation. I believe (see also Fukaya 1978) that the very process of socioeconomic change which corroded the cohesion of communities also produced more "Robin Hoods" like Bansuke, who lived by their wits on the edge of the law and the community. Their presence provided the common people with sufficient leadership to make contention possible.

This realm—of interests, opportunities, and resources—is the level of the model on which the clearest theoretical confrontation takes place, the most problematic stage of the causal process. It is here that those who espouse deprivation, normative, moral-economy, or value-, justice-, or indignation-driven explanations of contention confront those who espouse resource-mobilization, utilitarian, decision-focused, or rational-choice explanations.[18] As noted, I consider both. This strategy is not novel, the confrontation notwithstanding; such participants in the debate as Ted Gurr and Charles Tilly (1993: 36) have acknowledged that both grievances and opportunities play a part; Edward Muller has systematically built both into his own model of aggressive political participation (1979), and modeler Jon Elster too (1989: 14, 20) has asserted that human actions in general are determined by desires (what one *wants* to do) and opportunities (what one *can* do or, more accurately, what one *perceives* that one is able to do). The acknowledgment of the multidimensionality of causation has in fact become general.[19]

Simply accepting all three dimensions, of course, begs the question of their interrelationships. I maintain that in early modern Japan interests led to opportunities (if you *want* to hit someone you will look for a chance to do so) and to resources (you will look not only for a chance to hit him but for something to do it with); opportunities influenced interests (on the one hand, consistent repression leads, over time, to lower aspirations; on the other hand, if you need money and the county magistrate leaves the vault open, why not grab some?) and resources (repression reduced the number of willing protesters; yet government

---

[18] The former school is epitomized by the work of Ted Gurr (1970) and James Scott (1976, 1985). The latter school may be divided between those—such as Charles Tilly (1975, 1978, 1986) and Anthony Oberschall (1973)—who emphasize the importance of the resources the people are able to mobilize and those—such as Mancur Olson (1971) and Samuel Popkin (1979; and summarized in White 1988c and Lichbach 1991)—who stress the rationality of popular decisions to participate in contention or not.

[19] Oberschall 1973: 27ff.; Kriesi n.d.; Gurr and Duval 1976: 140ff.; Tong 1991: 17ff., 199; Little 1989: 23; Siverson and Starr 1990; Rule 1988: chap. 8.

establishment of a petition system transformed individuals into signatures, a new resource); finally, resources influenced both interests (if you have a hammer, suddenly a lot of things seem to need pounding) and opportunities, in that, for example, an official might become marvelously more open to a group whose unity was clear (Elster 1989: 17).

The final question to be asked about these three dimensions regards relative weight. In my view,

1. interests, or sudden changes in interests, were by themselves unlikely to lead to contention except in desperate, any-port-in-a-storm situations. The only common exception was when the obligations of the role one occupied (e.g., village headman) dictated action regardless of the probability of success.[20]

2. Changes in opportunities alone *could* lead to contention, since all individuals have preferences and, everything else being equal, if the opportunity to achieve a preexisting goal presents itself, someone will take a shot at it.

3. Resources alone were highly unlikely to lead to contention; even if provided with a gun, one is unlikely to shoot if there is no desirable target in view.

4. Interests and opportunities, opportunities and resources, and all three together could lead to contention, but

5. interests and resources together were unlikely to lead to contention by themselves. Regardless of all else, one had to have a chance of success (except when one's role required one to participate). Very few people, however angry or well armed, wanted to play Don Quixote. Some observers of popular contention have presumed the participants to be mindless bundles of impulse; neither leaders such as Hachiemon (and even Bansuke) nor even the urban rabble in a food riot fits this image. Desperation, perhaps; death wish, no.

To some extent individuals and groups continuously calculate interests, opportunities, and resources, and rarely does the calculation lead to contention. Some sort of catalyst or "last straw," which generates a sudden change in interests, opportunities, or resources (or in the numbers of people in certain interest-opportunity-resource situations) is necessary to make individuals and groups suddenly adopt unconventional, contentious means. The sorts of stimuli of greatest importance in early modern Japan included natural disaster or dearth (particularly when combined with elite unresponsiveness); sudden changes in levels of deprivation (most Tokugawa commoners lived pretty close to the bone even in good times); inflexible imposition of old policies or adoption of new ones;

[20] There is an additional instance in which interests alone might lead to action, and this is the case of expressionistic contention. In some contention success and failure are not major considerations; indeed, Japanese history is replete with examples of going heroically (and vainly) down in flames for the sake of a glorious principle (see Morris 1975; Scott-Stokes 1974; Najita 1974; White in Gordon 1993; inter alia) Such expressionistic action was not a significant component of popular contention in Tokugawa Japan.

unilateral elite violations of what I shall argue amounted to a social contract between elites and people; failure of elites to fulfill their obligations vis-à-vis the people; sudden threats to the subsistence or economic viability of individuals, families, or communities; and the appearance of division or indecision among elites.[21]

Given such catalysts, how did people decide whether or not to act? Dividing the normative and rational aspects of the decision is vain (Migdal 1988: 26ff.), for values, myths, symbols, and morals interact with rewards, sanctions, material constraints, and opportunities. Moreover, what was reasonable or rational depended on an individual's or group's position in the social hierarchy of wealth, prestige, and power; whether one was a potential leader or follower; the cultural context of the decision; and the stage of the conflict process at which the individual or group was faced with a decision. There was a big difference between stepping out to confront a phalanx of armed samurai and falling in with a rioting mob passing boisterously by.

My challenge was to avoid completely particularistic explanations of the decisional calculus of contention. At some level, every single such decision was sui generis, but my goal was generalization. I maintain that the decision to contend—either as leader or follower, initiator or joiner—had four general characteristics: it was rational, public, strategic, and institutional.[22] I have already argued for rationality. Contention was also the pursuit of "goods," such as tax cuts, that benefited the entire public, whether participants or not. This quality no doubt tempted some to sit back and let others take the risks, but this temptation was reduced by the fact that it was in everyone's interest to participate because the bigger the incident the fewer the risks and the greater the odds of success, and because the price of failure could be survival.[23] Behavior was also strategic; that is, it depended on people's expectations of others' (allies' and antagonists') behavior, and in a society as densely organized as Tokugawa Japan, people could predict with great certainty that they would not be alone and make fairly confident predictions about many official responses too. Finally, the ability to predict was largely institutional in origin: people would do thus and so because they were embedded in cultural and organizational contexts that dictated certain responses to certain situations and defined standards of justice and redress. Even when people desperately grasped at straws, what could be thought of as a straw was determined by experience.

---

[21] Such factors are not uniquely significant in Japan (Shingles 1987; Zimmermann 1983: 162ff.; Bercé 1980: 17–18, 256; 1976: chap. 1; Popkin 1979: 28), nor do they necessarily occur singly: Tilly 1990b.
[22] On its rationality, see White 1988b; on "publicness," see Chamberlin 1974; Oberschall 1973: 113; Hardin 1982; Runge 1984b; Grafstein 1989; Muller and Opp 1986; Finkel et al. 1989b; Little 1989: chap. 2; on strategy, see Mason 1984; Chong 1989; Dion 1986; Schelling 1978: 213; on institutionalism, see March and Olsen 1989; Moore 1978: 5.
[23] In other words, collective interests coincided with individual interests, in contrast to the usual contradiction of interests posited by the "prisoners' dilemma" metaphor of the decision process: White 1988b.

Of course, these considerations did not operate similarly for all. Leaders and followers decided in different ways, as did those who initiated contention and those who fell in later on. Both risks and potential benefits loomed larger for leaders; their motives were more individual and less collective; and they were more often constrained by institutional context (see also Oberschall 1973: 116, 159; Frohlich et al. 1971: 6–7, 42ff.). The risks were also much higher (and probable benefits lower) at the beginning of an incident; accordingly, it seems that strategic expectations, public benefit considerations, and institutional factors were far more important to those taking the first step than to latecomers. But this step was not out of the question, since the frequency of prior *non*contentious gatherings and the "building-block" entry of whole villages into events (rather than the recruitment of individual contenders) reduced risks acceptably.

Such combination of factors continued in the penultimate stage of the conflict process in early modern Japan: mobilization and action. Leaders interacted with potential followers, actions began and ended, individuals joined and withdrew, and the action drew to a successful or unsuccessful close. At this point the interaction of quantitative considerations (action or inaction) gave way to qualitative. What sequences of catalysis, calculation, and mobilization led to big or small outbursts, appeals or assaults, immediate or distant goals, economic or political goals, commoner or elite targets, urban or rural arenas of contention, reform, repression, or revolution, and so forth?

In early modern Japan the government's extractive policies made popular resentment endemic; attempts to regulate or tax new economic activities were seen as new provocations; and long-term changes further differentiated economic groups and interests *and* diminished the capacity of the state to work its will. Consequently, there was in almost any time and place a significant number of people with an interest in contention. Moreover, they lived in cohesive, largely autonomous communities with many occasions for public gatherings, dense networks of communication, and ongoing arrangements for many types of collective action—circumstances that enhanced the safety of prior planning and mobilization. And these communities were endowed with leaders obligated to defend them.

Finally, although socioeconomic and attitudinal changes during the era reduced the solidarity of community leadership, they also diminished deference to authority and fostered the growth of the social elements from which entrepreneurial leaders emerged. Thus in Tokugawa Japan there was a built-in set of stimuli to contention and built-in facilitating factors that made both participation and leadership relatively low—and falling—in cost, and nonparticipation singularly "costly." The process of contention was characterized by a swift transition from widespread grumbling to mobilization of large numbers of socioeconomically similarly situated people. And it was dynamic: in extended incidents leadership gave way, relatively, to the shaping of contention by the interactions of the contenders, and to the later entry of participants with less commitment to community norms or to the original goals of the conflict and more inclination to loot and carouse, as we have seen in Gunnai.

PART I

THE CONTEXT OF
CONTENTION

In assessing how various factors intertwined, I have differentiated in several ways between types of popular contention (see Appendix 2). Contention took many forms, from petition and grumbling to full-scale insurrection, and I fit the sorts of activities in which Hachiemon, Hyōsuke, Bansuke, and others engaged into this larger framework. I also differentiate between social contention among the people and political contention between the people and the state and between incidents of different magnitudes of size and intensity. I do so because different types of events had different causal antecedents, resulted from differential reasoning by different groups and individuals, and followed different trajectories from inception to resolution. But the text of contention had three additional aspects of note which also interacted with those mentioned so far: its goals, its degree of radicalism, and its distribution across time and space.

The goals of contention in early modern society—including Japan—most often addressed administrative and fiscal burdens, maladministration, or injustice, although many incidents involved multiple issues (Yokoyama 1986: 161ff.). But overarching the content of goals was their pervasive moderation and conservative presupposition of the status quo. Granted, revolutions may begin with simple goals, and even modest objectives may have profoundly radical implications; indeed, many of the claims advanced by the common people were incompatible with the status quo. Nevertheless, the striking thing about Tokugawa contention in general is the utter lack of radical, much less revolutionary, popular intent or any attempt by the elites to mobilize the people in their struggles.[24]

Nonradical ends were matched by nonradical means. Popular contention could be highly destructive of property, but it was overwhelmingly nonviolent against people. Aggressiveness was variable, however: when the people confronted the state, they tended to mobilize in large numbers but (with good reason) to exercise considerable deference; when they contended among themselves they did so in smaller numbers but with greater intensity.

That political protest differed from social conflict reflects the variation of the intensity of contention with the state's presence in different times and places. Peripheral regions and more administratively fragmented ones saw more contention, and it was disproportionately social and thus more intense. Regions undergoing economic development also saw more contention and, other things being equal, more social conflict. Over time, I found a high magnitude of overall contention—especially political protest—at the beginning of the Tokugawa era, which declined (and became more social) as the polity became institutionalized

---

[24] Magagna (1991: 23, 113, 140ff., 258) and Calhoun (1982: 60, 97) stress the question of implications, but even if Tokugawa contention contravened the status quo its participants denied that it did, and no reading of the theoretical literature (Lenin 1952: 16–17; Yamada 1984: 275; Brinton 1965; Perry 1980: 2; Trimberger 1978: 2–3; Zimmermann 1983: 298; Zagorin 1982, 1:17ff.; Walton 1984: 6ff., 13; Johnson 1964: 16–17; Weller and Guggenheim 1982: 168; Skocpol 1979: 4) makes their activities look revolutionary, as we shall see. The Meiji regime may have imposed a revolutionary transformation on Japan, but the Restoration itself was not a revolutionary transfer of power (Tilly 1993: 240). Indeed, the key aspect of a revolutionary transfer of power which was missing in Japan was, as we shall see, an active role by the people (Tilly 1993: 10).

and its popular salience diminished. Contention rose again and once again became more political as the Tokugawa state disintegrated and the Meiji regime took over.

Such interactions help explain the occurrence and "life course" of contentious events, but they leave the picture incomplete. The lowermost level of Figure 1 completes it.

The first component of this level is the response to contention—efforts by the elites to maintain public order, protect their own interests, and uphold their principles. In early modern Japan this response tended to be first conciliatory and then repressive (especially with respect to political protest). Often the state let an incident run its course and then brought in the troops and rounded up suspects. Concessions most often took the form of concrete accommodation of popular demands, but never, never any acceptance of the notion that popular contention was legitimate (Gamson 1975). Indeed, contention was often followed by substantive concessions *and* severe repression.

The extent of repression varied with type of behavior and magnitude. Big political conflicts were dealt with most harshly, small social conflicts least so. Overall, repression was severe but inconsistent; the severity decreased and the inconsistency increased over time, until the Meiji regime reestablished a consistent pattern of coercive response. But at no time—until the Meiji era, that is— were repression and refusal to legitimate popular contention sufficient to support the argument that contention was a failure overall: the cases in which the people explicitly received what they sought were simply too numerous.

These outcomes lead us to the systemic component of the outcome of contention: its feedback effect on context and on interests, opportunities, and resources. This component is difficult to assess, since specific effects are difficult to trace to specific conflicts. Nevertheless, popular contention in early modern Japan had a significant influence on its context: officials were rewarded or punished; policies were beefed up, revised, or junked; and institutions were abolished, strengthened, or created.[25] Economic or social arrangements successfully resisted or gave in to challengers; old hierarchies gave way to new; new groups gained entry into the community. Contention left a cultural and psychological residue as well. Traditions were born or extinguished; the blackened become "bandits" and the eulogized became "martyrs;" the community was reaffirmed or it gave way to new ideologies. These effects varied with the type of contention involved, but overall they seem clear.

The same goes for effects of contention on interests, opportunities, and resources. The dynamic here was relatively consistent: successful contention enhanced popular assessment of opportunities and resources and strengthened at least the utilitarian (if not the moral) justification of contention. Unsuccessful

[25] McKean 1981; Gurr 1980: 249ff.; White 1984; Reich 1982. George Wilson (1992: 129) goes so far as to maintain that elite response to popular contention late in Tokugawa times made a major contribution to the radicalism of the Meiji regime.

responses, and outcomes. To these data I added, from various sources, roughly 150 measures of the contextual arenas I have described and the years in which the events occurred. The Tokugawa era is singularly rich in quantitative data from multiple sources, though some of them are biased and must be used carefully.[27] To these quantitative data I add the stories of Hachiemon, Hyōsuke, and Bansuke and other case studies; secondary studies of popular contention in various places and times during the era; and theoretical overviews of contention from different perspectives.

None of these data is unimpeachable. When possible I focus on the lowest level, the county, to minimize homogenization and put us on the level at which the political and economic factors that affected the common people are best studied.[28] I also adduce data from different sources on the provincial, domainal, and regional levels in search of corroboration. The analysis is not integrated until the conclusion; rather, it is layered and cumulative, as I seek congruent findings at various levels of analysis. And quantitative data must always be complemented by qualititative and contextual information.[29]

Throughout, my purposes are explanatory: my typologies of contention and of turbulent times and places imply constellations of interests, opportunities, and resources, and Part II concludes with an interpolative thrust from context and text toward cause. At this point we have a phenomenon in its setting, a text in its context, and the task is to explain the link between the two. The first step in this direction is taken in Chapter 10, in which a variety of quantitative indicators of contextual characteristics is brought to bear to discover correlates of contention: What sorts of times and places, characterized by what political, social, demographic, economic, climatological, geographical, fiscal, coercive, religious, and quality of life properties, are distinctively high or low in what types of contention? My examination of context and content has generated many expectations about patterns of causation—that is, answers to the questions Why

---

[27] For example, the shogunate's periodic provincial population censuses included only commoners. The samurai exclusion reduces all figures comparably; moreover, the biases in these data are consistent through time. The data were gathered from administrative units (domains and shogunal territories) and aggregated at the provincial level; since most provinces were mixes of the two types of units (including multiple domains), the bias also tends to be consistent across provinces. Nevertheless, the census data were recoded into quintiles, reducing the probability that any province is incorrectly coded (see Saitō 1988: 31). Except for a few instances (as noted), all quantitative data are recoded into quintiles for analysis. Data are lost thereby, but error is also reduced: just because the data say that Province A had a population of 600,000 and Province B had 650,000, the numbers are not necessarily accurate. In fact, it is possible that B was smaller than A. But quintile coding is likely to assign them the same value, which is safer than relying on the raw data.

[28] Mendels 1982: 77; Hasegawa 1977: 31; Nakamura 1964b: 190; Ragin 1987: 25. Aggregating quantitative data also has an artificial inflationary effect on the strength of the statistical relationships found (Tong 1991).

[29] Moreover, I restrict myself to statistical methods that are relatively robust and forgiving (most ambitiously, OLS regression) and interpret statistical measures of association broadly: a gamma higher than 0.60 or a tau higher than 0.40 is high; a gamma lower than 0.20 or a tau lower than 0.15 is negligible; and multicollinearity is considered problematic when independent variables intercorrelate at 0.70 or more (Asher et al. 1984: 202, 255)

them? Why this (and Why in this way)? Why here? Why now? In Chapter 11 I identify correlations among context, conjuncture, and conflict which corroborate these expectations.

In a sense, I have now explicated the forest, the fuel, tinder, and high temperatures, but I still have to justify inferring causation from these factors. Measurement of the magnitude and shape of the ensuing conflagration helps, but where is the spark? Chapter 12 tackles this question: How, and over what, does conflict actually begin? My preliminary expectation is that the spark is to be found in changes in, and in the balance among, the perceived interests, opportunities, and resources of individuals and groups. New grievances, new chinks in the government's armor, new weapons can separately or together turn passive people into active contenders.

There is yet another consideration: Who strikes the spark? I have looked at the leadership roles of community officials and at the emergence of less institutional (and less savory) leaders such as Bansuke. I now ask why anyone would want to take the lead. After all, look what happened to Hachiemon. If it does in fact appear that someone might rationally do so, what sorts of persons might make what sorts of first moves, and how might they lead others to follow?

To pursue my metaphor to its end, what of the firemen? In Part IV I go from asking, Why? to asking, What then? and So what? That is, what were the outcomes, consequences, feedback effects, and implications of popular contention? Here I consider the state's response in terms of behavior, structure, policy, and personnel. Repression and conciliation, punishment and concession, reform and reaction were all apparent at different times. And what of the people themselves? Did they benefit from contention? Did they learn anything new? Or were they simply cowed into quiescence? Some assert that contention was epiphenomenal and the people mindless rioters; I present contrary evidence on both scores.

The question of the implications of past for subsequent conflict is considered as well. Did the political and social movements of the Meiji Restoration and the Meiji era owe much to Tokugawa-era contention, or were they new phenomena in a new age? Just how important was Tokugawa-era contention after all? How significant was conflict and with regard to what? What did it mean? What does the pattern of popular social and political contention tell us about the history of this era in particular and of Japan—and other early modern societies—in general? Have we come away from this exercise with any new understandings or with any new—or old but newly refined—analytical or theoretical tools? Hachiemon, Hyōsuke, and Bansuke are fascinating in their own right, but do we now also better understand why thousands like them did what they did? I hope that we do, but as always, the reader is the final judge.

1

THE POLITICAL CONTEXT

Popular contention in Tokugawa Japan was not a violent eruption from a staid and stable context, nor was it born from an archaic and stifling context as the precursor or agent of new identities and world views.[1] Contention flowed from context, and without an understanding of context no understanding of contention is possible.

My treatment of context is selective. I am interested in aspects of the overall Tokugawa context conducive to stability and order or to contradiction, instability, and conflict. I am also arbitrary. My division of context is artificial, for the Tokugawa polity was a political economy, and society and culture were also part and parcel of the polity; but I hope that analytical clarity justifies the distinction. Some factors of interest have multiple relevance. For example, the official ideology of "benevolent government" was embedded in both policy and popular culture. I treat these separately in each context.

The Institutional Structure of Tokugawa Politics

For several centuries prior to the establishment of the Tokugawa regime Japan had been governed under a series of *bakufu*, or quasi-feudal systems featuring a nominal emperor at the top, a supreme warlord/aristocrat, or shogun (nominally the emperor's vassal, but actually the ruler of the country), and a hierarchy of enfeoffed vassals and their vassals under him (Mass and Hauser 1985). The last of these systems disintegrated into civil war in the late fifteenth century, and for

---

[1] The first view is that of the "mass society" theorists in particular and of those who see contention as pathological in general (see Kornhauser 1959; Rule 1988; Tilly 1978, 1978a). The second view is that of the "new social movement" theorists (see *Social Research* 1985). Their argument is based entirely on contemporary analyses, but there is good reason to doubt that it holds in modern times, much less in early modern society (see Tarrow 1989).

a century government was in the hands of regional powerholders. In the last half of the sixteenth century a series of leaders unified progressively larger pieces of the country, and in 1600 Ieyasu of the Tokugawa house defeated the last rival coalition and asserted military control over the entire country. A bit of pressure on the imperial court led to his appointment as shogun; thus empowered, he proceeded to divide up the country into Tokugawa house lands and fiefs allocated to allied lords, former enemies, Buddhist temples, and Shinto shrines. At the top he built his own bakufu, designed both to govern the house lands directly and to maintain control over all the lords.

The Tokugawa regime was an unprecedentedly centralized form of government, but it did not spring full-blown from the hand of Ieyasu. The previous bakufu had already built "power analogous to the power of a state" (Wakita 1982: 346), and Ieyasu's immediate predecessors had taken major steps to dissolve independent guilds and free cities; impose national land surveys; disarm the common people and fix them on the land as a closed social class; make, unmake, and move lords around and raze their castles; move the samurai off the land and transform them from landed warriors to stipended urbanites; and establish new local-level political structures and revenue systems (Hall 1981: 15ff., 194ff.; Wakita 1982).

Nor did the regime reach maturity under Ieyasu. It was consolidated during the first half of the seventeenth century under his successors (Nakane and Oishi 1990: 22) and continued to grow in institutional sophistication into the first half of the eighteenth century (Nakai 1988: x–xi), achieving a level of bureaucratic impersonality, legalization, administrative rationality, and central control which, compared with early modern European states, is impressive (Mass and Hauser 1985; Totman 1967; White 1988c). The institutionalization of the regime continued throughout the era; the most important such developments for us were the Tribunal, a supreme judicial structure established in 1635; the Magistracy of Accounts, which also assumed judicial functions; roving inspectors and censors; and a substructure of lawyerlike roles and officially designated litigants' lodgings in the shogun's capital of Edo.[2]

The power to invade the jurisdictions of the lords had initially been coercive; after the imposition of Tokugawa rule it became increasingly administrative, founded on Tokugawa house lands (*bakuryō* or *tenryō*), which accounted for roughly one-quarter of the country's total productive capacity (Kitazawa 1982),

---

[2] The Tribunal, or Hyōjōsho, whose jurisdiction was national, was somewhat similar to the English Star Chamber. It was made up of representatives from the three major magistracies: City Government (Machi Bugyō), Temples and Shrines (Jisha Bugyō), and Accounts (Kanjō Bugyō). See Totman 1967: 187; Nakane and Oishi 1990: 30; McEwan 1962: 109; Hall 1991: 447. The inspectors, or *junkenshi*, were teams of bakufu officials who toured both house lands and lordly domains at will to check on the quality of administration, domain finances and coercive resources, and popular living standards and grievances (Hall 1966: 364; Totman 1967: 59; but see also Brown 1991). The censors (*metsuke*) were bakufu officials with similar functions and prerogatives, but they more often operated individually and covertly.

although gifts of territory to retainers shrank this resource base during the era (Tokyo Hyakunen Shi 1973, 1:1352). Control of the house lands, too, became increasingly administrative: roughly 40 percent were parceled out as domains to two thousand plus immediate retainers of the Tokugawa, or *hatamoto*, while 60 percent (the *chokkatsu-chi* or *okurairi-chi*) remained under the jurisdiction of the Magistracy of Accounts, which administered them through some fifty intendsants (Nakai 1988: 117ff.; Kitazawa 1982: 36–37; Hall 1991: 169–71). The intendants, however, were transferred frequently, and most lived in Edo and delegated to assistants; grass-roots control was in the hands of the village headmen. There were usually only a few dozen assistants, in territories equivalent to medium-sized lordly domains governed by a thousand officials or more (Totman 1967: 62–73; Rekishi Kagaku 1974: 75–76). The bakufu never possessed, and never tried to possess, enough officials to govern the house lands closely; it remained a weak presence and frequently entrusted its lands to the administrative control of nearby lords (Hall 1991: 205).

Tokugawa Ieyasu distributed fiefs to a variety of lords and retainers; these domains were often fragmented, and many parts of Japan were patchworks of jurisdictions with few or no coercive resources. Holding the top status were the lordly houses related to the Tokugawa family.[3] Then came the immediate vassals, the hatamoto, followed by some 150 "hereditary lords" (*fudai*) who had been on Ieyasu's side at the decisive battle for control in 1600, and finally about a hundred "outer lords" (*tozama*) whose houses had been on the losing side in that battle (Hall 1991: 152; Totman 1967: 111ff.). But status did not correlate with capabilities: the related houses held big domains but had no tradition of strength, being basically creations of the state; the hatamoto were fragmented and underadministered; and the hereditary lords' domains were often widely dispersed in small parcels. The outer lords, by contrast, often remained in control of the large holdings they had held before 1600.

Thus status and power were dissonant, but what are of more interest to us are the fragmentation of jurisdictions and inconsistency of administrative practice and capability across jurisdictions. At one extreme, entire provinces were under the rule of a single lord; at the other, single counties bore literally dozens of separate bakufu, lordly, hatamoto, and clerical jurisdictions. In fact, sometimes single villages were divided among a dozen or more rulers, each of whom was entitled to a portion of the village taxes and often had a headman in his part of the village; unsurprisingly, no single lord was eager to take responsibility for social control in the village as a whole.

All lords were themselves under the thumb of the bakufu. After the battles of 1600 the Tokugawa eliminated or reduced the holdings of almost a hundred lords; the first five shoguns together eliminated 200 lords, created 172, transferred 280, and increased the size of 200 holdings, reallocating in the process

---

[3] These included, in Japanese, the *go-sanke*, the *shimpan*, the *sankyō*, and the *kamon* houses, of which there were roughly twenty (Hall 1991: 152).

roughly half of the country's entire productive capacity (Hall 1991: 150–52; Aono 1988: 23). One family was moved ten times in four generations; one lord was moved three times in twenty-nine years (Aono 1988: 30). Additionally, each lord was limited to one castle in his domain; new lords had to be invested by the bakufu; weddings linking lordly families had to be approved by the bakufu; and all the lords were required to live in alternate years in Edo and, when absent, to leave their families hostage there. Clearly, when all these measures were in place the Tokugawa house had little to fear even from its old enemies, much less its vassals. The administrative prerogatives of the lords were limited by Tokugawa laws or *hatto* (Hall 1991: chaps. 4, 5; Harafuji 1978); every domain's fiscal, economic, and social data were at the disposal of the state (Hall 1991: 158–59; Iinuma 1991: 102); and when the lords gathered in Edo there was "not a whisper of parliament" about them (Totman 1967: 36).

The Tokugawa state was in control: the autonomy of the domains was "as good as nil" (Iinuma 1991: 102). Most bakufu offices were occupied by hatamoto, though hereditary lords held those at the top; nevertheless, the hereditary lords saw themselves more as lords than as bakufu officials, and the Tokugawa reciprocated: they showed them no special favors, moved them more frequently than they did the outer lords, and exempted them from no regulations (Bolitho 1974: chap. 2, 116–18). Lordly domains possessed more extractive and coercive capabilities than did the house lands, though the hereditary domains were more poorly staffed, dependent, and smaller than the outer (Hall 1966: 357; 1955: 23; Bolitho 1974: 46). And the hatamoto lands practically invited dissidence: small to begin with, they became smaller and smaller until not one in ten was an economically and administratively viable unit.[4]

The Tokugawa polity was both cause and effect of popular contention. And one prime aspect of the polity was the balance of power between the bakufu state and other political elites. In the case of Japan the others were the lordly domains, or *han*—hence the common appellation, the *bakuhan* system. In each of the bakufu states that had ruled Japan since the twelfth century the center was limited, but it was also able to establish checks between the lords and manipulate the fragmentation inherent in the feudalistic structure (Mass and Hauser 1985; Berry 1987; Maruyama 1974).

The two questions to be asked about all such systems were What was the bakuhan power balance? and Why was it what it was? I maintain, first, that the Tokugawa state was unquestionably supreme and, second, that the limitations on state power were largely voluntary, in that the Tokugawa government decided

---

[4] In 1705 there were 2,354 hatamoto domains, accounting for about 10% of the nation's productive capacity, or 2.7 million *koku* of a total of 25.9 million (for an explanation of *koku*, see note 6), but averaging less than 1,200 koku apiece. By the 1790s their numbers had grown to 2,908, but their average size had shrunk to 940 koku. By this date only 8% of them had lands of greater than 3,000 koku; 45% held lands of less than 500 koku (an average of only 242 koku). Kodama 1967: 198; Fukawa 1976: 283; Suzuki 1962.

early on not to attempt to build a fully centralized modern state, not to try to force the biggest domains to obey every one of its edicts (Brown 1993).

Concerning the first question, observers such as Harold Bolitho (1974: 38), Albert Craig (1961: 4, 36), and Mary Elizabeth Berry (1986) have stressed the nondevelopment of institutions typical of modern states and the breadth of domain autonomy and concluded that, with the exception of establishing "a monopoly of war" (Berry 1986: 245), the Tokugawa took few steps beyond a basically feudal distribution of power. I and others, however, have held that the bakuhan system was at least as centralized as any of the so-called absolutist states of early modern Europe.[5]

In the first place, a statistical profile of relative power bases is instructive: the Tokugawa house lands accounted for roughly 15 percent of the nation's total productive capacity, and the hatamoto for another 10 percent.[6] The related houses occupied roughly 15 percent, the hereditary lords 25 percent, and the outer lords roughly 35 percent (Totman 1967: 33; Craig 1961: 15; Murakami 1965). Thus the lords far outweighed the bakufu and its retainers, but there were some three hundred of them; they jealously protected their prerogatives vis-à-vis one another, and none posed any sort of a threat to the Tokugawa during the formative seventeenth century. I have already mentioned some of the state restrictions on lordly power and domain autonomy. Others include the requirement that bakufu law be incorporated into domain law; state regulation of currency, religion, and commerce; precedence of bakufu over domain courts; state-approved trusteeship, rather than ownership, of domains by lords; and frequent (albeit irregular) extractions from the lords by the state.[7]

But a taxonomical question remains: Of the different familiar types of states, which did the Tokugawa state most resemble? There are those who term it feudal,[8] but I find the category of limited help (Murakami 1985: 403). It seems to me that the closest analogue to the Tokugawa state was the "absolute" state of early modern Europe—not because either was in fact absolute but because they exercised strikingly similar degrees of control over rival elites and their own common people and because the "statelike" attributes missing from the Tokugawa state were *also* missing from the European. The developmental level I

---

[5] White 1988c; Hall 1966, 1981; Vlastos 1986; Maruyama 1974; Nishikawa 1979.

[6] Throughout this book I speak of productive capacity, or assessed agricultural capacity, because that is how administrative units all the way down to the village were measured. The unit of measurement was the *koku*, the amount of rice (about five bushels) needed to feed one person for one year; throughout the era there was a close correlation between assessed capacity (or *kokudaka*) and the population of provinces, domains, and counties (with the exception of a small number of highly urbanized counties).

[7] Hall 1966: 374; 1981: chaps. 8, 9; Hall and Jansen 1968: 205; Bendix 1978: 431ff.; Yoshizumi 1967. The absolute fiscal reliance of the state on the lords was not as great as in early modern Europe; it was the prerogative that mattered.

[8] Bloch 1964, 2:447; Anderson 1979; Bix 1986: xxvff.; Wakita 1975; Ishii 1978: 29.

have in mind is that of France immediately before Louis XIV, Prussia before the Great Elector, Russia before Peter, and England before Henry VIII.[9]

None of the "absolute" states of Europe could dispose at will of the property or liberties of nobles; the Tokugawa had unlimited power of attainder. The bakufu never had to buy the nobles off as did Frederick William of Prussia in 1653, trading state military and fiscal rights for nobles' autonomy within their estates; the Tokugawa never achieved such fiscal authority, but they could intervene in a variety of ways between a lord and his people, as we shall see. Tokugawa Japan had no body equivalent to the French *parlements* or the English parliament, able to check the state; Japan after 1600 certainly never saw anything resembling the noble revolts of the Fronde and the English Revolution. One of the defining trends of the early modern state was the separation of state sovereignty from the ruling class, on the one hand, and the person of the monarch, on the other; I have already noted the separation of the bakufu from the lords, and by 1600 the notion of the ruler as an absolute and impersonal "public authority," or *kōgi*, subordinate neither to lords nor to monarch was already current (Hall 1991: 89, 94; Berry 1986).

I have drawn a fragmentary picture, to be filled out hereafter, but the parallels between state structure and performance and popular contention in Tokugawa Japan and early modern Europe are sufficient to recommend the analogy. My framework of comparison is limited to but one period of European history, however. Why did this comparability not continue? That is, why did the Tokugawa state, after attaining ascendancy in 1600 and unquestioned national jurisdiction by 1650, not continue to centralize?

There is nothing inevitable about governmental growth. In the development of European nation-states the incentive for growth most often cited is defense against rivals both foreign and domestic. In the words of Charles Tilly (Evans et al. 1985: 170), "War makes states."[10] But Japan faced no foreign threats until the mid-1800s, and thus no pressure to maintain a large standing army or develop an all-encompassing taxation system. In light of the threats to civil order posed by armies themselves (Bercé 1980: 147) and the near-universal resistance to enhanced revenue measures, it seems quite plausible that the Tokugawa state opted to forgo full centralization once its own security was assured. It is possible, in turn, that the low military and extractive posture of the Tokugawa state contributed to its longevity. The state enjoyed the luxury of simply backing off when new revenue initiatives stimulated resistance, of letting the economy go its own way, and of leaving the lords alone as long as they kept their own domains quiescent and did not defy Tokugawa authority. The contrast to England and

---

[9] White 1988c. The discussion below draws also upon Tilly 1986; Beloff 1962; Williams 1970; Bendix 1978; Totman 1967; Dorn 1963; Kiernan 1980; Gagliardo 1967; Iinuma 1991; Rebel 1983; Mousnier 1970; Evans et al. 1985; and even Anderson 1979, which describes "absolutism" in a way that sounds very much like Tokugawa Japan.

[10] Kiernan 1980; Gilbert 1975; Tilly 1986; Kimmel 1988.

France, where fiscally desperate states pushed their countries clear to revolution, is sharp. So is the situation in Japan in the mid-1800s, when one can see a hint of how the Tokugawa state might have developed in a context of war. In the mid-nineteenth century foreign states began to nose around Japan's shores, and the bakufu in response began to impose coastal defense burdens on the lords; these burdens were reflected in fiscal strain and heavier domain taxes, which in several instances provoked popular resistance.

A plausible alternative motive force for state building is domestic political competition, and here again the mid-nineteenth century offers a telling example of what the early Tokugawa had been lucky enough to escape. In the mid-1860s the domain of Chōshū rebelled against the bakufu, and the state ordered a number of lords to launch a military campaign against Chōshū. The resulting mobilization brought increased taxation, inflation, food shortages, squeezing of merchants (who responded by witholding commodities)—as well as a rash of popular contention (Arakawa 1964; Totman 1967; Aoki M. et al. 1981, 2:287ff.) which hastened the downfall of the Tokugawa state.

But the events of the nineteenth century do not explain those of the seventeenth. In the seventeenth century the lords were an administrative aid (Hall 1991: 156), not a threat (Totman 1967: 253). It is true that the outer lords retained significant political and military power. Ieyasu had subdued but not eliminated them, for elimination would have taken far more military exertion, and he was satisfied with professions of loyalty (Wilson 1992: 36). In light of the blood shed in Europe to secure centralization, again, Tokugawa self-restraint appears not only understandable but perspicacious. In some ways the Tokugawa state acted decisively: power centers such as free cities, religious institutions, and coalitions of lords were destroyed and some individual lords were cultivated.[11] But in no case were the pressures toward state building as great as they were in early modern Europe. Still, there *is* one area—popular contention—from which pressure did come, and the growth of the Tokugawa state in this sphere suggests that, where the need arose, the state was both able and willing to expand.

The Tokugawa era came to an end in 1868 when a coalition of dissident outer lords extracted from the emperor a decree dismissing the Tokugawa shogun and authorizing the coalition to realize this measure. In the face of this fait accompli (and the superior military strength of the coalition) the shogunate caved in almost immediately. The regime that replaced the Tokugawa state was nominally simply a restoration of the emperor to direct rule after centuries of usurpation of his prerogatives by the bakufu. In fact, it was dramatically new in that its objective was to make Japan into a modern state able to withstand the threatening imperialistic currents swirling through Asia at the time.

---

[11] Indeed, the primary significance of the bakufu's powers vis-à-vis the lords lay not in their use but in their being unquestioned: it was unlikely that the bakufu would or could have insisted on obedience to each by such great outer domains as Satsuma or Chōshū. See Brown 1993.

From our perspective the Meiji Restoration—so named because it was the Meiji emperor who was putatively restored to his rightful position of rule—has two aspects of primary importance. First, the Restoration ushered in a period of intense, purposive political centralization and economic development. The economic system that underpinned the Tokugawa regime was obliterated, and an economy based on modern principles was put in place quickly, although the period of really rapid development postdates this study. The 1870s, however, did see the demolition of the bakuhan system and the emergence of a highly centralized bureaucratic state. In light of the intense popular opposition that similar state building and economic transformation encountered in Europe, it is unsurprising that popular contention during the first decade of the Meiji era is worthy of notice.

The second important aspect of the Restoration was that it had almost no popular dimension whatsoever. W. G. Beasley (1972) and Conrad Totman (1980), among others, have painted comprehensive pictures of the fall of the Tokugawa with almost no attention to the commoners at all. No groups or classes previously excluded from a meaningful role in politics actively participated in the Restoration, or gained such a role by virtue of participation therein (Skocpol 1979: chap. 2). Popular contention in the 1860s, by distracting the bakufu and draining resources from it, clearly weakened it in the face of elite challengers, but despite small-scale mobilization of commoners into domain forces under samurai command, there was no autonomous popular component in the Restoration itself at all. Moreover, there was significant "participation" in the Restoration by merchants who bankrolled the anti-Tokugawa coalition, but their contributions were minor and neither collective nor autonomous, and there was no place for this group in the new regime either.[12]

I discuss the Meiji regime's orientation toward popular contention later. At this point a summary of overall structural change will suffice. Between 1868 and roughly 1870 the situation was one of disorder. Old structures, whether of articulation or repression, had ceased to exist, and new officials—often inexperienced, zealous, and in charge of repeatedly changing institutions and policy—took office throughout the country (Tozeren 1981). The period was highly politicized, but what the new political rules (and payoffs) were to be was as yet unclear. Both in Tokugawa Japan and elsewhere (Calhoun 1983: 899) popular interests, resources, and opportunities have proven extraordinarily responsive to changes in the context of contention. One might therefore expect a sudden rise in conflict in the late 1860s, but contention grows out of convention, and it is unsurprising that new *forms* of contention were slow to appear, awaiting as they did the emergence of a coherent new institutional context.

---

[12] Even George Wilson (1992), who stresses the psychological involvement of the common people in the instability of the last years of the Tokugawa and the influence of their ideas on the leaders of the Meiji state, sees no real political participation by the people in the Restoration.

This initial period of upheaval and rapid institutional flux was replaced during the 1870s by a two-pronged institutional thrust. By 1870 it was clear that the Tokugawa *koku*-based revenue system (see note 6) would have to be replaced by something more effective. Moreover, for efficient extraction of the resources needed to build a powerful state, a unified administrative system was essential. First, the institutions of the bakuhan system were replaced by national and local political institutions directly subordinate to Tokyo. Local autonomies of all kinds were formally abolished, although informal autonomies, of course, persisted for many years (Fraser 1981: 15). Second, in a modernizing thrust, imperial appointees loyal to the new state took over structures explicitly modeled on the nation-states of Europe and North America. The organizing principles and behavioral maxims of premodern government went out, new ones came in, and the result was a nation-state that deployed far greater coercive resources than its predecessor.

The Ideological Foundations of Tokugawa Politics

Tokugawa Ieyasu's intention was to establish a polity that would endure forever. Shrewd enough to realize that military might was not enough to ensure longevity, he and his successors worked diligently to devise ideological justifications for Tokugawa authority. Imperial investiture of each shogun was but the beginning; a variety of sources—Confucianism, familism, Shinto—were blended to convince both elites and masses that the politicoeconomic status quo was both inevitable and legitimate. From our perspective the ideological underpinnings of the Tokugawa system were most significantly autocratic but contractual, secular and agrarian, and increasingly national.

Autocracy was the most obvious characteristic of Tokugawa ideology. The people had no formal, justiciable rights whatsoever. Tokugawa rule has been accurately described as exploitative, arbitrary, and oppressive. The consequence, however, was not popular inertness, and not simply because the degree of coercion was insufficient to cow the people. There was much in the Tokugawa ideology which gave the people not only wiggle room but justification (at least in their own eyes) for dissent. Moral justification of rule began even before Tokugawa: the disarming of the populace in the late sixteenth century was justified by its supposed contribution to public order (Elison and Smith 1981: 20). But as the elites soon learned, the morality they invoked was a two-edged sword.

In fact, the Tokugawa system relied in the last analysis on the consent of the governed, notwithstanding the denials of both sides and the propensity of each to interpret the "social contract" according to its own interests (Moore 1978). In the case of Tokugawa Japan three contractual factors stand out: the exchange of reproduction for revenue, the government's obligation to rule benevolently, and the people's entitlement to relief and redress.

The people were obligated to offer up a variety of taxes; in exchange they expected unequivocally, and the government acknowledged in practice, that the government would guarantee the reproduction of the populace—more collective than individual, but not only physical but as freeholding farmers.[13] The people were entitled to material relief or political redress. Relief could take the form of tax cuts or grants or loans of seed, food, or money; redress included the protection of the people from arbitrary (as defined by the bakufu) or (excessively) rapacious rule. Again, no popular rights were ever acknowledged by the elites, but a never-ending stream of popular appeals, acts of relief, and formal channels of petition make it quite clear that both sides recognized the contract in principle.

If relief was the particular manifestation of the contract, benevolent rule (*jinsei*) was the general. The concept itself was Confucian, although it strikingly resembles the "seigneurial munificence" of an earlier European day (Duby 1974: chap. 3). The concept was hardly altruistic: the Tokugawa recognized that an exploitative agrarian political economy required ideological reassurance, guarantees of moderation in extraction, and concrete provision for coping with the inevitable crop failures (Vlastos 1986; Harootunian 1970). Agriculture was the basis of rule, and both economic failure (due to climate) or fiscal failure (due to excessive extraction) threatened the basis of Tokugawa rule. Individual lords, moreover, understood that such failures (and the contention they induced) invited punishment by the bakufu. A ruling class with very little regard for the people had no choice but to be solicitous of them.

Equally fortunate for the people, the concept of jinsei was so broad and vague that popular interpretations—imaginative, to say the least—were impossible to reject in principle. At the same time, jinsei was a contradictory concept: the need of lordly houses to balance their books often came into conflict with the requirement to guarantee popular reproduction (Nishikawa 1979). As the era wore on the concept became a weapon in the hands of people who tried to play their own lord off against the bakufu.

This manipulation of ideology was made possible by the contradictory dictates of the feudal and central elements of Tokugawa rule. Nominally, each lord was autonomous within his domain; in fact, by 1600 the concept of *kōgi*, or "public authority," had been developed in reference to the shogun as a supreme national figure (White 1988c; Berry 1986; Mass and Hauser 1985: 151). By the end of the era the term had come to signify an impersonal central government with clear (at least to the people) precedence over any individual lord (see also Maruyama 1974). The Tokugawa saw kōgi as a tool for enhancing shogunal legitimacy and overcoming the centrifugal tendencies of the system; the people saw it as an avenue of appeal. Moreover, lordly violations of benevolent rule, combined with the notion of kōgi, provided the people with opportunities for contention of which Ieyasu never dreamed.

---

[13] Fukaya 1979: 202ff. I am loosely translating the Japanese version of the exchange of *naritachi* (to come into being) for *toritate* (the collection of taxes).

The last two features of Tokugawa ideology of relevance to popular contention were its secularism and its agrarian core. The secular nature of Tokugawa
rule markedly affected popular contention, primarily, I maintain, by moderating
it. It is no accident that Tokugawa Japan saw nothing remotely resembling the
religious revolutions, wars, and chiliastic movements of Europe, with their sanguinary pursuit of virtue and equally sanguinary repression.

Japan did resemble Europe in another respect: its emphasis on agriculture as
the font of virtue, the heart of the economy, and the source of revenue. By far the
major revenue source was the *nengu*, or annual tax paid on the productive
capacity of the land. The condition, and control, of the agricultural population
thus became major political concerns, and anything that jeopardized either
production or population elicited immediate government response.

Physiocracy thus colored the issues, physical arenas, actors, and resources of
popular contention, especially in one aspect and one consequence. The aspect
was mercantilism or autarky. Each domain sought economic independence and
viability and a positive "balance of trade" with other domains. The result was
economic fragmentation and noncooperation. There could be acute famine in
one domain and none next door, but the aid that might reduce one's neighbor's
chances of a food riot were infrequently forthcoming. The economic and fiscal
results of, for example, natural disaster were highly localized, and contention
varied accordingly.

The consequence of agrarianism became visible only as the Tokugawa era
wore on. After extraordinary growth during the seventeenth century, agricultural
output leveled off, and thereafter the real economic action—and the growth
potential for revenue—was in the nonagricultural sector, especially protoindustry
and commerce. The ruling class, however, could never free itself from its agrarian
fixation, and nonagricultural activities were never fully encouraged or exploited
(Aono 1988). Isolated domain development programs were tried, and at times
the bakufu itself toyed with the idea of protoindustrial development; moreover,
attempts to tax nonagricultural pursuits were a perennial bone of contention
during the latter years of the era. Nonetheless, the taxation efforts were ad hoc
and aimed at what already existed, not linked to encouragement of the
nonagricultural tax base. Moreover, it was difficult for the regime to proclaim the
supremacy of agriculture and simultaneously to justify fiscal reliance on industry
and commerce. The regime's own ideology expanded the opportunity structure
for popular contention.

I shall not systematically examine the dominant political ideology of the Meiji era,
although it also heavily influenced frequencies and patterns of popular contention
during the era.[14] During its first decade the regime had no coherent ideological
basis. It did renounce Tokugawa practices and ideals, but exactly which ones, and
how completely, were still unclear to both elites and people. Popular attachment

---

[14] Smethurst 1986; Bowen 1980; Ike 1950; Akita 1967.

to Tokugawa ideology—whose opportunity structure was familiar—continued, and it was the new government's renunciation of this ideology, more than the content of a new one, which contributed to contention in these years. Still, a few discernible aspects of the emerging Meiji ethos can be related to popular contention.

The first was imperialism and nationalism. The justification for the Restoration was imperial—the emperor had commanded the insurgents to eliminate the shogunate and restore him to his rightful position of rule—and national—the reason for eliminating the Tokugawa was their manifest inability to protect the nation and the throne from foreign incursion. It is impossible to assess the extent to which average Japanese felt allegiance to the throne, but to the extent that they did, it was probably a dampening factor in popular contention, since all the dislocating reforms of the Meiji era were carried out in the name of the emperor.

The second aspect was statism, and it probably had the opposite effect. The Meiji state, in its first years, was primarily concerned with survival, and it was inclined to brook no dissent while consolidating its position. It wanted to cut off the Tokugawa past, and if concepts such as jinsei appeared to provide dissenters with opportunities, then they were renounced. The people continued to see the care of the people as the state's duty; the state saw its mission as the care of itself, and it conceded only where necessary. Elsewhere, its attitude toward popular contention was hard-nosed.

Thus the ideological implications of Meiji rule for popular contention have less to do with the content of this ideology than with the new regime's intolerance of dissent and failure to follow traditional governmental precepts regarding treatment of the people. Relief, yes—indeed, with central control of the economy and the ability to import foreign food supplies food riots disappeared almost immediately. Redress, no—indeed, a number of the regime's new prefectural governors won promotions for their draconian ways. Revenue, yes—a new land survey and tax and a host of additional taxes made it clear that the new regime was going to be unprecedentedly extractive. And reproduction, yes—but it was the reproduction of the state, not the people, which took precedence. The Meiji state unilaterally abdicated traditional state obligations to the people, and in the short run its coercive posture and imperial legitimacy were sufficient to defuse contention. In the long run state and people worked out a new contract; the state developed a new ideological basis and the people developed new means of pushing their interests, and a new world of popular contention emerged. But that is another story.

Structure in Practice

The autocratic impulses of the Tokugawa state bespoke close regulation of the people, the samurai, and the lordly domains. The last decades of the sixteenth century saw the development of two major policies upon which the Tokugawa regime built its regulatory strategy: the *kokudaka* system and the separation of the samurai from the people.[15] And throughout the Tokugawa era the major characteristics of regulatory policy were, first, its increasingly national tone and, second, its diminishing effectiveness.

The kokudaka system was on the surface an extractive policy, involving the surveying of the entire nation and the assignment of a productive capacity measured in rice to each piece of land upon which the tax payable by the holder of that land was based. The basic unit of measurement was the koku of rice (the amount needed to feed one person for one year, or about five bushels); the capacity of a piece of land was its kokudaka. But the system went far beyond taxes. In the first place, it required national land surveys, that is, control of the entire national territory by the state and suppression of those who resisted. The power of lord and shogun now penetrated down to the last rice paddy, and with detailed knowledge of each lord's resources the shogunate's power was significantly enhanced (Iinuma 1991: 94–95).

Second was the question of who was going to hold the land. The answer was, a new class of farmers, or *hyakushō*, created by the state as freeholders by right (but permanently bound to land registered nontransferably to their families, and to their closed social class) with the obligation to pay taxes and corresponding rights of political participation in village affairs.[16] A large unfree class of serflike agricultural workers was abolished, and its members leveled upward, while small-scale local magnates and many landed samurai were simultaneously pushed down into the hyakushō class. The result was a huge, relatively homogeneous farming population clearly demarcated from the remaining samurai, with the responsibility for tax payment and the size of that responsibility made quite clear.[17]

The final consideration in the new system was what the lowest unit of administrative responsibility—individual, family, community, or domain—would be. The answer was, the village; the result was an extensive system of collective administration and responsibility (the *murauke* system). Land was registered to hyakushō families; each family held its land and exercised its rights within a particular village. Kokudaka were aggregated by village, and the village allocated its tax obligation internally and paid as a unit. The village was also collectively responsible for civil order and for the punishment of crime within its borders. The principle of collective responsibility was extended downward to subvillage

---

[15] On the kokudaka, see Wakita 1982; Fukaya 1979: 116ff.; Vlastos 1986: 21; Hall 1966. On the separation, see Wakita 1982; Birt 1985; Kaikyū Tōsō 1981.

[16] One should differentiate this de facto ownership on the family level from de jure landownership. All land ultimately belonged to the emperor; his subordinate, the shogun, allocated it for the time being to the lords. On the farmer's level, however, the family to all intents owned its land, having unequivocal rights to hold it, till it, and dispose of its after-tax product.

[17] The transformation did not take place overnight: it was the middle of the seventeenth century before all the ambitions of those moving upward and the resistance of those pushed downward were fully resolved. Upward mobility into the hyakushō class did not cease—clearing a piece of land usually brought ownership and hyakushō status—but upward mobility *out* of the class did.

groups, which were in turn accountable for the behavior of their members. Thus the kokudaka system, devised to generate revenues, also became part of the social control system.

Complementing the restructuring, organization, and—it was hoped—neutralization of the populace was the neutralization of the samurai as a possible source of dissent. Commoners were forbidden to possess arms, but in the late sixteenth century the country was still heavily populated by landed warriors who had in the past organized the people against the lords. Hideyoshi, Tokugawa Ieyasu's predecessor, issued a decree commanding the samurai to reside in the castle towns of their respective lords. Many lords had already taken steps to sever their retainers' ties to the land; the decree completed the process. The warriors' fiefs were transformed from landed properties to accounting devices, stipends calculated in koku of rice amounting to the kokudaka of their old territorial fiefs. The warriors were thus placed under the eye of the lord, the people were deprived of leadership and arms, and the samurai could be more easily mobilized in the case of popular insurrection. The strength of the samurai vis-à-vis the people and their integrity and independence as a class were enhanced; vis-à-vis the lord and the shogun their strength was eroded. At the nexus of elites and people the separation had one further consequence, which contradicted the subordination of the people: the countryside was now a power vacuum, essentially self-policed by the people and under the discretionary powers of autonomously chosen village leaders. To prevent chaos the state pursued three strategies: incorporating village leaders into the formal government as its lowermost agents, ruling through the medium of the written word, and providing avenues of redress in the hope that they would prevent dissatisfaction from becoming contentious. Over time none of these measures sufficed, and coercion became more necessary; unfortunately, it was applied neither consistently nor effectively.

While regulating both samurai and people, the state never forgot to keep the lords themselves in line. Specific measures included the requirement of alternate-year residence in Edo; the shogun's power to transfer, confiscate, and alter fiefs (Craig 1961: 18); and the leveling of excess castles. In the latter half of the era the bakufu thought little of sending its own officials into the domains to enforce the law (White 1988c) or even to lead a program of domain reform (Shōji 1981: 476). The overall policy was summed up in the *buke shohatto*, or codes governing the warrior houses, first issued by the bakufu in 1615 and revised several times during the next hundred years. The codes detailed the restrictions on interactions among the lords, their obligations to the bakufu, and the shogun's prerogatives in regard to the lords (Nakai 1988: 202ff.).

Thus, not only de facto incursions but legal prerogatives as well characterized the Tokugawa state. That this state was comparable to early modern European states is ever clearer (Anderson 1979: 95ff.). Ieyasu and his immediate predecessors extirpated religious competitors, never even contemplated anything like the

French estates, executed lords and eradicated their houses, leveled castles, and banned vendettas, in addition to other regulatory measures.

Extraction is a different story, but not dramatically so, although extraction from the people was less direct than in Europe, and state extraction from the elites was less regularized. Extraction from the people took three primary forms: the "land tax," or nengu, a percentage of the kokudaka of a piece of land; miscellaneous other taxes (*komononari*), including those levied by the village to support its officials; and the corvée.

The land tax was in principle an in-kind tax, with the actual rate based on annual preharvest surveys of crops in the field, but provision was made for part or full payment in cash and special reductions were made (or at least expected) in instances of crop failure. When agricultural conditions were especially poor the rice-cash equivalency rate was set so as to lower the real tax rate. Over time, the government's desire for fiscal predictability led to the widespread adoption of a new system in which previous years' average production was used to calculate a permanent tax rate (Aoki M. et al. 1981, 5:212). The government made provision for reductions in time of dearth (Aoki M. et al. 1981, 2:211ff.; Tozeren 1981: 104). The result was incessant popular demands for such reductions, which, if unanswered, could lead to conflict.[18]

Simultaneously, the people's desire for flexibility led to increasing monetization of tax payments. This allowed the people to go into more profitable cash crops and economic pursuits while continuing to pay at the old tax rate. The result was greater popular income taxed at a fixed rate, that is, a lower real tax rate and a reduced share of the economic product for the government (Smith in Hall and Jansen 1968; Chambliss 1965: 99). The costs of government rose, however, during the era—often led by the lords' immense cost of maintaining their residences in Edo—creating fiscal distress, and every measure designed to relieve it antagonized the people.

One measure was resurvey of the land to reflect increased productivity, but the people were perfectly aware of the purpose of surveys and resisted them whenever possible. Another measure was a higher tax rate, but this was even more provocative. A third measure was to tax previously untaxed activities, especially protoindustry; one can imagine the reaction of the people. A related tactic was to establish domain monopolies or monopsonies in protoindustrial products; this strategy pushed popular resistance one step away, but eventually, private producers could be expected to object to this competition and regulation.

The result of this situation was fiscal expediency bordering on chaos.[19] Some domains simply fell further into debt. Some imposed austerity programs, often

---

[18] Fixed rates per se, however, did not become a major source of contention, as found by Scott (1976, 1985).

[19] Aoki M. et al. 1981, 1:141; Fukaya 1979: 85–86; Fukawa 1976: 169; Nishikawa 1985: 136; Nagasu 1986.

cutting the stipends of their samurai to balance the books (one can imagine the effect on samurai morale). A host of nontax revenue measures were tried: land reclamation (but this often involved a corvée), forced loans from merchants (no need to guess to whom these costs were passed on), protoindustrial development strategies, compulsory collective saving schemes, and debasement of the coinage or issuance of paper currency. Some domain strategies worked (Craig 1961), and it is no accident that the domains that led the Meiji Restoration had built stable fiscal bases. The overall picture, however, is one of increasing fiscal distress, largely because the elites were reluctant to extend exploitation in the face of popular resistance. The upshot of this floundering was economic instability, which might increase the probability of contention just as much as a tax increase.

Most extractions were domainal, but the bakufu also extracted income, from both elites and people. State extraction was less individualistic and direct than in contemporary Europe, and extraction from the lords by the state was not so regular or heavy, but both expanded. The people living in the Tokugawa house lands were of course subject to all the customary taxes. People throughout the country, however, regardless of domain, were also subject to the *sukegō*, a corvée of manpower and horses imposed on villages along the major post roads (Vaporis 1986). And given the bakufu's exclusive control over the coinage, the repeated debasements toward the end of the era amounted to a tax on everyone.

Vis-à-vis the lords, also, the bakufu's extractive prerogatives were unquestioned. Edo, like Versailles, functioned as a massive regulatory and extractive mechanism, keeping the nobles under the shogun's eye and separating them from their wealth. Additionally, the bakufu imposed ad hoc levies on the lords. One such was the *agemai*, a commutation into cash of the lords' original military service obligation to the Tokugawa (Shimbo and Saitō 1989: 152ff.). Another was the *otetsudai-fushin*, a demand for labor, materials, and money for bakufu construction projects (Yoshizumi 1967, 1968). Well over a thousand such impositions were made on the lords during the era, expressly (if only partly) for the purpose of weakening affluent domains. And finally, as foreign ships began nosing about Japan's coasts in the nineteenth century, the bakufu assigned coastal defense duties to the lords—at their own expense (Rekishigaku Kenkyū 1985: 279ff.). Extractions from the lords were, of course, not direct causes of popular contention, except when the domains passed the burdens directly on to their people or when the impositions disrupted domain economies.

The Tokugawa era witnessed a striking growth in state power during the seventeenth century, followed by a leveling off and then progressive decay, interrupted by successively less efficacious bouts of reform, until the end of the era. In analyzing this process one must, however, take care to differentiate the dimensions of state development or stateness from state capability. State development involves the acceptance of the state by major political actors. In the field of popular contention it additionally involves the acceptance of state prerogatives regarding social control and order and the state's role as an avenue for the redress of popular grievances and the focus of national political identity.

The capability of the state to devise and carry out policies that realize the goals it sets for itself is a matter quite separate from its acceptance by other actors. The two do tend to covary over the long run. Thus, modern states tend to be both legitimate *and* potent. But disjunctions are both possible and, historically, amply evident (Bercé 1980: 110). Effective but unaccepted states are able and willing to rule primarily on the basis of coercion; the Tokugawa state represents the opposite condition: it was unquestionably accepted but limited in capabilities (Brown 1991).

The Tokugawa state, especially in the realm of social order, continued to grow in "stateness" throughout its life, while its capabilities glacially declined. When the Tokugawa commanded overwhelming military power in the seventeenth century, they chose not to use it; at the end of the era, when they needed such power, they didn't have enough to prevail (Ooms 1975). Two hundred years of peace utterly eroded both the martial skills of the samurai and the military organization of the state, which by late in the era had become what some describe as "an unorganized rabble" (Totman 1967: 45; Rekishi Kagaku 1974: 41), thus broadening the contradiction between state ends and means.

A brief review of state performance under the Tokugawa clarifies this view. The first half of the seventeenth century was the time of state centralization, with the lords subordinated to the bakufu and the economy largely removed from their control (Bolitho 1974). The thirty years centering upon 1700 were the high-water mark of bakufu centralization (Nakai 1988) and the first of several periods of ostentatious luxury in both public and private spheres. The centralization scared the lords, and the luxury symbolized moral decay, fiscal irresponsibility, and popular transgression of the status hierarchy (Hall 1955; Nishikawa 1979). Retrenchment followed, both fiscal and political, and was relatively effective (Hall 1991: 458ff.). Economic growth had driven down the price of rice and thus the value of government revenues; Shogun Yoshimune (1716–1745) imposed a price-support program that succeeded only too well. The price of rice was rising nicely, as planned, when a plague of locusts in 1732 destroyed the rice crop in western Japan, driving the price out of control. Political retrenchment in the context of the 1720s and 1730s meant reversion away from a monarchical shogun, but even in this case nominal state prerogatives were unhindered. In response to the 1732 famine the bakufu ordered lords to ship rice to affected areas in order to contain social disorder—a transgression of lordly autonomy which elicited no opposition (Yamada 1984: 209ff.).

During the mid-eighteenth century bakufu prerogatives and finances continued to erode, except in the area of social control, while the economy continued to diversify and grow. The two trends were related: a prosperous class of rural landlords-moneylenders-protoindustrialists began to appear, but the bakufu was never able to exploit them for revenue purposes because it relied on them, as village officials, for political control and relief activities (Shimbo and Saitō 1989: 140). The economy continued to slip out of government control as the official grip on markets weakened and domain currencies appeared. In the 1760s a bakufu official named Tanuma Okitsugu began an attempt to capture its potential. His tenure in office was characterized by heavier taxation; by promotion, regulation, and taxation of commerce and protoindustry; and—perhaps inescapably, given the imbrication of politics and money—by rampant corruption.[20]

Tanuma's program was attacked not only for its corruption but also for its assertion of bakufu powers and for its infidelity to physiocratic principles. Unfortunately, it coincided with a series of disastrous crop failures in the 1780s, and Tanuma was fired in 1786 and followed—again—by a period of conservative reform. Demands for Confucian virtue in public life, price cuts, sumptuary regulations, the abolition of licensed merchant associations, and edicts ordering migrants to return to their villages and attempting to take land out of the hands of landlords were issued. Meanwhile, the state retreated once more to a lower-profile role. The bakufu partially balanced its budget with exactions from the lords (Hall 1991: 495ff.), and many of them—driven to the wall by financial deficits—no longer had the luxury of practicing agrarianism. They opted instead for a wide variety of programs of domain development (*kokueki*): agricultural commercialization and protoindustrialization aimed at domain solvency, autarky, and extradomain sale of their products (Rekishigaku Kenkyū 1985: 270ff.; Aoki M. et al. 1981, 2:256ff.; Ooms 1975: chap. 4).

These policies accelerated the incorporation of the rural rich into public structures of control and exploitation. Unfortunately for the government, this group was also accountable to the people and possessed of its own political and economic motives. Thus, this incorporation did not necessarily enhance the performance of the state. Nevertheless, a succession of good crop years contributed to political and social stability throughout the first quarter of the nineteenth century.

This lull did not represent greater state capability, however. On the contrary, it was partly due to a sequence of devaluations of the coinage beginning around 1820, which increased bakufu revenues while initiating an inflationary trend. In the 1830s the roof fell in with another series of disastrous harvests and skyrocketing prices; the bakufu responded with (by now) utterly ineffective price cuts, guild dissolution, ideological rectification, and reagrarianization decrees that lasted only two years before their failure was clear and their proponents dismissed from office (Hauser 1974; Shimbo and Saitō 1989: 159ff.). The early eighteenth-century reform period had lasted some fifteen years; that of the late eighteenth century, less than ten; this one began in 1841 and ended in 1843. As in the 1780s, a few individual domains carried out effective reforms—for example, Chōshū (Craig 1961)—but the case of Akita domain (Hyakushō Ikki 1980: 23ff.) was probably more typical. The harvest failed in 1833 and urban food prices (and unrest) rose; the domain tried to extract more rice from the countryside but in January 1834 producer protests swept from the villages right into the castle town, and the domain canceled this effort. In February riots occurred

---

[20] Hall 1955; Ooms 1975; Harootunian 1970; Sasaki 1974.

again, aimed at rice stocks earmarked for shipment to domain mines, but popular demands proliferated, with people attacking a variety of domain policies and institutions. The domain responded by importing some 130,000 koku of rice from Osaka (and incurring a debt of over 200,000 *ryō*)[21] and "borrowing" from its own retainers' stipends.

The 1834 harvest was good, but 1835's failed again, and further domain relief led to further debt, aggravated by bakufu imposition of a coastal defense obligation. The image is of a domain unable to perform, to extract resources from its populace, or to effect its will. And the state wasn't much better off: divisions within the bakufu, bakufu-lord opposition, and government demoralization doomed the state's own initiatives. The last straw was the reversal, in 1841, of a state edict transferring a lord from one domain to another (Hyakushō Ikki 1982: 119; Kelly 1985). Elite and popular resistance on the local level combined with intrastate splits to frustrate the decision, the first recorded instance of successful defiance of such an act of state. Clearly, poor performance had by this time begun to affect state acceptance, and the Tokugawa state was beginning to slide toward both impotence *and* illegitimacy.

In retrospect the writing was visible on the shogunate's wall after the crisis of the 1830s and its abortive reforms. But from the perspective of contemporary actors the decisive point was 1853, when American Matthew Perry arrived to demand that Japan open its doors to international diplomatic and commercial intercourse. Rapid deterioration of economic and political stability ensued: humiliating governmental concessions to the foreigners; an unprecedented "retreat from centralized authority" into consultation with the lords over foreign policy (Mass and Hauser 1985: 173ff., 185ff.); court criticism of the bakufu; fiscal distress caused by the need to purchase arms, pay indemnities for violence against foreigners, protect foreign diplomats, and support foreign missions; and rampant inflation following the opening of Japan to foreign trade in 1858.

The bakufu made two stabs at reviving its credibility and authority, in the late 1850s and the mid-1860s. Both were too little and too late: in the mid-1860s the bakufu launched an attack on the domain of Chōshū (one of the losers in 1600, and of dubious allegiance ever since) for its now-overt opposition to Tokugawa rule; the revenues needed for the operation drove inflation even higher and caused acute hardship for both domains and people; and failure to bring Chōshū to heel destroyed what was left of Tokugawa legitimacy.[22] Elite-level politics consumed the attention of state and domains, and the welfare of both samurai (whose stipends were targets of domain "revenue enhancement") and people (even after the poor harvest of 1865) took a back seat. By the time the Restoration coalition—with Chōshū among its leaders—toppled the Tokugawa government, both its capacities and its acceptance were things of the past.

---

[21] One ryō equals about sixteen ounces of silver.
[22] Totman 1980; Jansen 1961; Beasley 1972; McClain 1988; Motoyama 1962.

The Meiji Restoration raised popular hopes for a lighter administrative and fiscal hand and national salvation. What the people got was centralization, nationwide standardization, and state extraction and regulation.[23]

The immediate aftermath of the Restoration was a brief period of administrative disorder, during which popular expectations of respite and autonomy seemed fulfilled. But soon the new regime began to replace domain authorities with prefectural governors and national officials, to tighten and standardize tax collection (national revenues more than doubled between 1870 and 1872 according to Beasley 1972: 381), and to beef up the military. Then came a blizzard of reforms: state-supported education, conscription, construction of railroads and telegraph, abolition of the domains and of the Tokugawa class system in toto, freeing of occupations, and a land reform in which tillers became owners of their land and, simultaneously, subject to a new nationwide land tax.[24] The new educational structures introduced a Westernized curriculum; conscription was widely termed a "blood tax"; telegraph lines were rumored to be tubes carrying Japanese blood for foreign consumption in the seaports; the old domains and their officials—often the object of considerable loyalty—gave way to unknown outsiders and unfamiliar offices; and the samurai were cast adrift. The new land tax meant higher taxes for some regions and lower for some; nationwide, it didn't change the tax burden much. It involved a new survey, however, which revealed that roughly 30 percent of the nation's farmland had previously eluded the eye of the revenuers (Yamamura 1981), and it was rigid, due on a nonnegotiable date, and payable entirely in cash. It broke the link between economic and political rights (as epitomized in hyakushō status), and fully commodified a factor that had previously possessed a social quality, thus dramatically and unilaterally redefining the relationship among state, people, and market.

Popular antagonism to these reforms is easy to imagine. They redefined even the nature of "the people," who were no longer retainers or peasants of such-and-such a lord but subjects of the emperor.

Public Order, Contention, and Control

The final aspect of the political context regards social control and dissent, a delicate, frequently contradictory policy sphere. In principle no official or act of government could be questioned, no commoner had any "legally justiciable right" vis-à-vis the state (Hall and Jansen 1968: 209), and resistance to just about any official act was punishable by death. It is not in fact true, however, that the "authorities strictly prohibited anyone appealing to any authority superior to the local feudal official, against whose exactions and brutality the people were left

---

[23] The following discussion draws heavily on Beasley 1972; Norman 1965; Hayashi 1976b; Irokawa 1966; Tozeren 1981; Dower 1975; Rekishi Kagaku 1974; Sasaki 1979.
[24] Beasley 1972; Tokyo Hyakunen Shi 1973: vol. 2; Chambliss 1965; Uesugi and Ishitaki 1988; Yamamura 1981.

defenseless" (Dower 1975: 330; Walthall 1991: 5) or that dissent was unfailingly followed by bloody retribution.

In practice, the state "pledged itself implicitly to offer redress when merited to all the people of the nation, including those under the immediate jurisdiction of the daimyō [lords]" (Nakai 1988: 130), and regardless of what the state acknowledged, the people perceived a traditional right to appeal on a variety of grounds. Tokugawa elites were perfectly at home with cruelty and rapacity, but they had built a system that forced them to respond to popular entreaties.

From the beginning, the Tokugawa state recognized the need for channels of popular contention if order were to be maintained in the countryside in the absence of the samurai. It also recognized that the officials responsible for these channels might not be impeccable. Indeed, at first the bakufu sided with the people against what they saw as their primary threat: the local authority of lords and residual powers of pre-Tokugawa notables (Aoki M. et al. 1981, 4:54ff.). Initially, collective flight from misruled domains was permissible for farmers whose taxes were paid up, and even "end-run" appeals (*osso* or *jikiso*) to officials above one's immediate superior were acceptable when an appeal was repeatedly rejected or when the superior himself was at fault (Rekishi Kagaku 1984: 14–15; Aoki M. et al. 1981, 1:126ff., 5:170ff.). Additionally, injunctions to honesty and attention to popular grievances were issued to local officials, and the people were thus aware that misrule, although it did not violate any "rights" of their own, was illegal in the state's eyes.

Tokugawa laws governing contention were extensive and detailed, but their core principles were straightforward. Appeals to authority which were deferential and supplicatory rather than confrontational or demanding, which were within official channels, unorganized, directed to immediate superiors, lodged by an official rather than by the people, and focused on the application of the law or the behavior of officials rather than the legitimacy of the law or the officeholder were likely to be entertained. Moreover, contention among commoners which did not involve the government was likely to be left to the resolution of the people themselves (Aoki M. et al. 1981, 4:176; Aoki K. 1966: 6; Vlastos 1986: chap. 2).

These principles were elaborately specific. If one participant in an appeal carried even a farm implement, the action was illegal. Prior assembly, calculated mobilization, and oath taking all constituted illegal "conspiracy" (*totō*). Likewise, challenging the right of the state to do whatever it wished was illegal. But far from being signs of exceptional brutality, such definitions are quite similar to those found in other early modern states.[25]

On the punishment front, also, there was less than meets the sanguinary stereotype. Tokugawa elites, like contemporaries in Europe (Bercé 1990: 146ff.; Bohstedt 1983: 64–65), were perfectly aware that they could never corral all the

---

[25] Bohstedt 1983: 4ff.; Manning 1988: 55ff., 80–81; Magagna 1991: 106; Stevenson 1979: 5ff. Indeed, the definition of riot in sixteenth–eighteenth-century Britain was so vague that it could plausibly be used against any contentious collective gathering at all.

miscreants in a riot or impose tight control on the entire society. Therefore, punishment—albeit frequently vicious—was exemplary and deterrent, following the dictum of *ichibatsu hyakkai*, "warning one hundred by punishing one" (Shigematsu 1986: 208). It tended to follow four additional principles as well: it was initially minimal and decentralized, substantively post facto, and penetrative (Kitazawa 1982).

While events were actually in motion the authorities tended to stand back. Official response came late, avoided direct confrontation, and tended to be nonviolent, relying rather on admonition and intimidation. Suppression was left in the hands of village headmen, intendants, and other lower-level officials as much as possible. Real enforcement waited until the dust had settled and the people had returned home (they were, after all, tied economically and politically to their villages), at which point officials fanned out over the countryside, interrogating people by the score. Actual punishment was informally harsh and formally rather light. Interrogations were lengthy and brutal, and in many incidents more people died in the investigation than after it.[26] But punishment was, as noted, largely didactic; the massive Demma Rebellion of 1764, which involved over a hundred thousand people, resulted in one execution and three remote banishments, plus a host of fines and minor punishments. In cases involving matters of principle or seen as threatening by the regime, wholesale executions were carried out. For example, when the people of Shiraiwa domain stormed their lord's castle in 1638 and killed one of his high officials, the bakufu executed 130 of them.[27] I shall look further at this type of event later; at this point it is necessary to note that it was the exception rather than the rule.

Finally, although immediate suppression was left to local officials, subsequent investigation was often handled by the bakufu, whose agents penetrated into the countryside with little regard for domain autonomy. Arrests were made on the authority of the kōgi, and bakufu courts often dealt with the accused. After the Kamo Uprising of 1836, which involved over ten thousand participants and spread across six lordly domains and fifteen Tokugawa vassal domains, all those arrested were taken by the bakufu to Edo, and it was the bakufu that announced the subsequent sentences (Shōji 1981: 478). There was little question in the minds of either elites or people as to who was in control. The whole process, moreover, was quite transparent to the people, and they could calculate accordingly.

Calculation was further facilitated by the fact that, although the entire governmental system of bakufu and domains operated in secret, the local and national agents of redress of grievances were known to all. Local avenues included one's

---

[26] This pattern was to the domain's advantage, since punishment of commoners required, in principle, consultation with the bakufu, and this, of course, opened the door to the possibility of punishment of the domain by the state. See Kaikyū Tōsō 1981: 229.

[27] Vlastos 1986: 37. One should note—as other lords probably did—that the bakufu also abolished the domain.

immediate political superior, who was bound by the dictates of benevolent rule to tend to the needs of the people. (Inasmuch as punishment of miscreant officials was at least as bloody as that of commoners, officials were not unconcerned with popular critique of their performance.) Another avenue was petition boxes, established in bakufu territories after the 1720s. Anyone could insert a petition on any subject, and the contents were periodically reviewed by the shogun (Nakai 1988: 147).

The right of petition accorded by the petition box was generalized by the people to the bakufu's inspectors (*junkenshi*), who toured both Tokugawa and domain lands to investigate the quality of government and remind officials of their responsibility to rule benevolently. The legality of petitions to these officials was questionable, but they were sufficiently effective that they became very popular (Yamada 1984: 24ff.).

National institutions were problematic, since the very act of appeal was a violation of the legal hierarchy, and no plea in Edo was legal without the permission of both the claimant's village and his lord (Hall and Jansen 1968: 227). But in practice national arenas, too, became important in popular contention. The two most relevant structures were the Magistracy of Accounts and the Tribunal; the magistracy had jurisdiction over cases originating in Tokugawa house lands, and its members also sat on the Tribunal, the bakufu's "supreme judicial body" (Nakai 1988: 65; Aoki et al. 1981, 4:174ff.), which respected no jurisdiction but its own.

The importance of these judicial bodies can be estimated from the number of cases they heard and the magnitude of the infrastructure they spawned (Aoki M. et al. 1981, 4:61ff., 174–215; Shigematsu 1986: 15–16). Certain inns were officially designated as lodgings for litigants, and the owners of these inns gradually took on lawyerly functions, preparing briefs and documents, instructing litigants on substance and procedure, playing a role in court-ordered mediation, and apparently passing out bribes when called for. This last was not the only reason the government looked askance at these amateur solicitors. They were criticized for fomenting contention and facilitating frivolous litigation, but they played an apparently essential role, for nothing the government did obviated them. The bakufu had overseen the transformation of coercion and contention into national phenomena by exercising coercion and substantively inviting contention.

In the early years of the Tokugawa era coercion was directed mainly at the elites, and the people were permitted a variety of avenues of protest and redress by the bakufu at least partly as a weapon against these elites (Aono 1988: 216ff.). Popular petitions also facilitated the efforts of lords to reduce the power of their own vassals (Yokoyama 1986: 86). An edict of 1603 formalized this channel: direct appeals to the shogun or his officials and flight from one's village were permitted in the case of local or domain misrule (but *not* in protest of tax rates or assessments or the content of policy). Another of 1633 further detailed procedures for remonstrance by different social groups (Aoki M. et al. 1981,

1:121ff., 5: 194–95; Yamada 1984: 35, 42; Fukaya 1979: 185–86). Rule by law was replacing arbitrary rule, and in 1643 village headmen were given the duty of reading the relevant laws to their villagers at stipulated intervals.

The obverse of institutionalizing contention was the proscription of contention outside of legal channels, especially organized contention. The limitations on direct, or "end-run," appeals were tightened in 1633 and illegal petitioning was made a capital crime (Vlastos 1986). The bakufu issued a series of bans on prior concert and congregation, oath taking, and conspiracy which became basically universal by the end of the century (Yamada 1984: 35ff.). Controls on vagabonds and the unemployed were simultaneously tightened (Aoki M. et al. 1981, 5:197ff.). But a relative leniency continued. It was illegal for any lord or intendant to interfere with legal flight (Maruyama 1974: 127); punishments tended to be limited to a few ringleaders; and official corruption, especially among local officials, was dealt with harshly (Hayashi 1976a: 87ff.; Sasaki 1974: 142, 151).

This situation changed during the first quarter of the eighteenth century. The people had begun to demand not just honest rule but lighter rule, seeking not only policy change but also structural change, including the elimination of certain official positions (Hayashi 1976a: 87ff.). Moreover, the early eighteenth century was the period of the Kyōhō reforms—standardized tax systems, new taxes on by-employments, and reduced relief (Fukaya 1979: 222ff.). Popular resistance rose, and at this point—partly because by this time the lords and samurai had long ceased to be a threat—the state stiffened. The judicial system was streamlined, bans on contention broadened, punishments tilted increasingly against the people, intravillage mutual surveillance and collective responsibility systems strengthened, and the domains instructed to repress contention (Fukaya 1979: 216ff.; Aono 1988: 216ff.; Sasaki 1974: 151). In 1721 protest against one's lord—always legally dubious and always risky—was explicitly banned (Bolitho 1974: 189); in 1734 the lords were instructed to provide, if asked, military forces to nearby intendants for repressive purposes; and in 1638 the permissible limits of dispatching domain forces outside the domain were widened (Yamada 1984: 51ff.). In 1698, 1716, 1721, 1742, and 1750 additional forms of contention were banned, conspiracy and forcible petition defined with increasing severity, and punishments toughened (Aoki M. et al. 1981: 4:59ff.; Vlastos 1986: chap. 2; Hall 1991: 447–54).

The state was not blind to the causes of contention and took compensatory measures. Laws of 1712 and 1713 were designed to speed the processing of popular grievances; a variety of offices were eliminated; and edicts of 1694, 1713, and 1744 ordered village headmen to open their books to the people.[28] Nevertheless, the overall trend was toward severity. Headmen and group leaders in contentious villages were to be dismissed and the villages fined collectively; the merits of irregular appeals were to be disregarded; and repressive edicts were to

---

[28] See Fukaya 1979: 216ff.; Aoki M. et al. 1981, 1:136, 140.

be read to the villagers more often (Aoki et al. 1981, 4:60; 5:219; Yasumaru 1975: 151; Vlastos 1986). In 1771 peaceful demonstrations outside the gate of a lord's Edo mansion were banned, and the possession of so much as a hoe or sickle made the action illegal (Yamada 1984: 71ff.). In such incidents, if the leaders were indeterminable those participants who came first in the village population register would be punished; to drive the point home, a gateway appeal in 1773 was punished with twenty-four executions and a number of banishments (Aoki M. et al. 1981, 5:236ff.). In 1769 the use of firearms against protesters was legalized, and beginning in 1772 they were in fact used (Aoki et al. 1981, 5:225ff.; Rekishi Kagaku 1974: 17). A previous system of rewards for headmen who kept their villages *out* of incidents was supplemented in 1770 by a program of rewards for those informing on, and accusing, plotters and participants in popular contention (Aoki M. et al. 1981, 5:230).

But this tightening could not overshadow two concurrent trends: nationalization and destabilization. The emergence of contention as a national political phenomenon was a major trend during the eighteenth century. Repressive edicts increasingly covered both Tokugawa house lands and domains, and the state began to veto domain concessions to popular contenders. The lords were only too happy to cite bakufu edicts in deterring or suppressing dissent (Hayashi 1976b: 170–71; Yamada 1984: 53ff., 71ff.; Ooms 1975: 8–9). And the people drove the whole process. The gateway appeals just mentioned were just one aspect of a popular tendency to seek conflict resolution, and targets, in the capital.

Destabilization was less visible, but just as significant. The developments of the eighteenth century seem to represent a crackdown on contention; in fact, they were more of a response to the spread of popular contention out of control. The fragmentation of authority and lordly self-absorption under the Tokugawa made concerted repression difficult, and even with the new measures firmly in place, the famine of the Temmei period (the 1780s) was accompanied by an unprecedented wave of contention. The recession of this wave, although partly due to controls (Bix 1986; Jansen 1989: 71–84), seems to owe as much to the Kansei reforms and to an upturn in the agricultural economy.

The period between the 1790s and the 1830s was one of relative popular quiescence, and during the remainder of the era the state took few new legal or procedural initiatives. There were some—in the early nineteenth century the Osaka city magistrate began to accept petitions by leagues of merchants (*kuniso*) for relief from official restrictions on trade (Shimbo and Saitō 1989: 42)—but most such actions were indirect. The Tempō reforms of the 1840s were designed to reinvigorate the rural economy, and an edict of 1843 forcing migrants to Edo and Osaka to return to their origins was intended to reduce the number of (presumably uncontrolled and turbulent) transients in the cities. The institutional framework of coercion was fully developed by this point, however, and the most instructive focus of attention is thus the performance of that structure in action, especially as politics became more elitist, more national, and eventually mortal for the regime in the mid-nineteenth century.

The image of the Tokugawa regime with regard to social control is severe. "Protest action never passed unpunished," writes Anne Walthall, and "leaders were invariably executed" (1983: 571). Indeed, the regime had at its disposal a wide variety of gruesome punishments, including crucifixion, drawing and quartering, and decapitation, and it applied them not only to culprits but to relatives, neighbors, officials, and acquaintances. Moreover, any count of punishments undercounts the actual toll of deaths in prison and under interrogation. For example, a riot in Kai province in 1750 involving over ten thousand people resulted in property confiscations, banishments, manacles, and fines. These punishments sound lenient until one notes that over fifty of those detained died in jail between their arrest in 1750 and the announcement of the verdicts in 1753 (Yashiro 1989: 241–42).

But the state also provided for banishment (to places of varying distance for varying periods), imprisonment, flogging, pillorying, confiscation of property, variable detentions and domiciliary confinements, chains and manacles, and fines. This finely graduated continuum warns us against easy generalization, and a closer examination of the reality of enforcement reinforces this suspicion. Many government edicts were in fact hortatory and were neither enforced nor intended for enforcement by all domains. The state's posture, notes Philip Brown, was one of "imperious decrees and lax enforcement" (Brown 1991: 16). When the common people fought each other the state often stood aside. Even when punishment ensued, there was limited correspondence between the magnitude of contentious events and the severity of resulting punishments. The Tokugawa state, like the seventeenth-century French state, "had a taste for concealing its ultimate weakness by an occasional dramatic display of punitive justice; and anyone wishing to escape such justice had only to survive the odd burst of severity" (Bercé 1990: 91).

This tendency toward the "burst of severity" and how ineffective it was as intimidation may be seen in the twenty-year running battle between the people of Hida province and two generations of Tokugawa intendants (Yashiro 1989: 78ff.). Intendant Ōhara Hikoshirō, appointed in 1766, antagonized the people by eliminating woodcutting rights, tax discounts, and a floating cash-rice exchange rate and by imposing new extractions and moving up the tax payment date by two months. In 1771 village officials met to discuss his depredations, and a popular riot spurred them to remonstrate with him formally. A few of their requests were accepted, but one participant was executed and three were banished.

In 1773, with this resolution still in process, Ōhara announced a new land survey. Two representatives met with him and requested that the survey be limited to newly reclaimed lands; Ōhara reported this meeting to the Magistracy of Accounts, received permission to classify it as a conspiracy and coercive appeal (*totō gōso*), and launched an investigation. The people, no doubt knowing what form an investigation was likely to take in Ōhara's hands, responded with appeals to one of the shogun's elders in Edo, to the Magistracy of Accounts itself, and (thrice) to neighboring Owari domain. Not to be upstaged, Ōhara rounded up 283 village officials and demanded that they sign affidavits saying that the petitioners were not legitimate representatives of the people. Several refused, organized a coalition of villages, and instituted an economic blockade of the intendant's seat, Takayama, and then demanded that Ōhara write a letter of authorization for a group of petitioners to take to Edo. In the face of this action Ōhara called in the eleventh month on the neighboring domains for military help; several responded and the protesters were dispersed, and some five hundred were arrested. In 1774 the bakufu sentenced sixteen to death and twenty-four to exile; almost ten thousand others received everything from lighter exile to fines.

This settlement could hardly have contributed to popular confidence in the efficacy of protest, especially since the land survey went ahead, the assessed value of the district's land rose 25 percent, and Ōhara was promoted. His successor, in 1781, was his son Kamegorō, a chip off the old block, who "borrowed" money without repayment and refused to repay tax overpayments. These sorts of practices led in 1788 to an appeal by two representatives before the gate of the top bakufu official, Matsudaira Sadanobu. Ōhara Kamegorō's attempt to have these representatives repudiated by local officials failed. In 1789 a new shogun, as was customary, announced a grand tour by an inspector. Ōhara moved quickly to round up the sorts of people likely to make an appeal to the inspector, but one local resident went to neighboring Noto province and lodged an appeal there. The inspector agreed to accept an appeal from the people of Hida upon his arrival.

In the fifth month the inspector arrived in Hida, and representatives of thirty-two villages petitioned him for relief from Ōhara's misrule. An inspection by the Magistracy of Accounts followed, and in the eighth month Ōhara was summoned to Edo. In the twelfth month he was exiled to remote Hachijō Island; two of his lieutenants were executed; and 70 percent of the county officials in his district were fired. The protesters received no punishment.

This sort of performance may well have puzzled the people, but it obviously did not cow them. The scope of legal petition and appeal narrowed, the severity of control techniques increased, and the state's jurisdiction over social control expanded, but the state's capacity to do its will decayed. One envisions an ever more grasping state hand that withered even as it reached farther and farther. Over the course of the Tokugawa period the average contentious event *grew* in numbers of participants and villages involved, in duration, in intensity, and in destructiveness, and yet individuals were punished in smaller and smaller percentages of these incidents, punishments involved fewer and fewer individuals, and the proportion of heavy punishments (death and severe exile) diminished. Concessions and amnesties became more common over time, and ultimately in the 1860s the state lost its monopoly of coercion, both to elite rivals in the domains and to commoner militias (*nōhei*), which were organized by local notables. In Ōmi province in 1842 the people chased a bakufu land survey team from their district (Borton 1938). Things had come a long and sorry way since Intendant Ōhara launched his survey in 1773.

The Meiji state took an exceptionally dim view of popular dissent, although in all fairness I must note that repression was less a predilection than an imperative of a regime hard pressed to modernize and defend the nation. The policy provoked much dissent. Contentious events during the first decade of the era became longer, bigger, and more intense and destructive than they had been during the Tokugawa era, but the Meiji regime didn't dally with the contenders. Punishments were applied in more incidents, more people were punished per incident, and punishments became much more severe.

The people at first expected administrative relaxation; they were quickly disabused. Flight and forcible appeal were banned in the first months of the era (Kajinishi 1978: 287), and an edict of 1871 declared: "To make an appeal by gathering a large mob of people is termed a *totō gōso*. . . . It is strictly outlawed" (Tozeren 1981: 520). Ōkuma Shigenobu, one of the new regime's leaders, was of the opinion that "when people resist violently they should be rigorously suppressed; if it is inescapable that as many as a thousand are killed then no one should be reprimanded" (Sasaki 1972: 117). And his government practiced what it preached. One insurrection in 1873 was followed by no fewer than 63,947 convictions, including four death sentences, and another in 1876 incurred 50,733, including one sentence of death and three of life imprisonment (Yasumaru 1975: 283).

That part of the Meiji era under inspection here is too short and too fluid to permit comprehensive characterization. The establishment of a nationwide police force and a coherent judicial system, for example, postdates my study. Insofar as the combination of policy and practice combined to shape popular interests, opportunities, and resources in regard to contention, however, we can note the rapid creation of a Western-style army with modern weapons, which could be deployed by rail and steamship and coordinated by telegraph; of a network of nationally appointed prefectural governors with this force behind them; and of a regime intent on hurling the country into the modern world—on its terms—and indisposed to brook any obstruction. The people, for their part, were during this era still resident in small villages that increasingly came under direct government scrutiny. The old basis of community mobilization was undermined by the new land tax, which was assessed and paid individually (Jansen 1989: 430), and new bases for community autonomy and popular mobilization expanded far more slowly than the official system of social control.

Political Context and Contention

It is my argument that the aspects of political context emphasized here—institutions, ideology, policy and performance, and social control—had a direct effect on popular interest in and opportunities and resources for contention. They also had an indirect, and highly contingent, influence on the stimuli to contention, on the nature of leadership and participation, on the quantity and quality of contention, and on its outcomes.

Institutionally, the Tokugawa state was characterized by autocracy and fragmentation. The polity was despotic, at least in principle. To the extent that it was so in fact, it generated innumerable popular grievances, more so in the more tightly regulated and more extractive domains than in the Tokugawa house lands, and more so during the periods of intensive state building in the seventeenth century and the early Meiji era.

The degree to which such grievances were transmuted into contentious behavior depended on opportunities and resources. The Japanese people, perceptive and rational, were more likely to act where and when institutions were more fragmented and less effective either at fulfilling expectations of good government or at repressing dissent. That is, we find more contention in Tokugawa house lands than in the domains, more in unstable domains than in stable ones, more in regions that were divided among a variety of jurisdictions, and more later in the era.

The Meiji regime, of course, generated a wide variety of new and different grievances in a (short-lived) administrative vacuum, and we see an upsurge of contention during the new era. The regime acted quickly, however, to reduce institutional opportunities for contention, and this policy soon reduced contention. How the two factors interacted we shall see.

I have also asserted that institutional arrangements put sufficient resources in the hands of the people to make contention thinkable, despite the disarming of the people. Foremost among these were the administrative autonomy of the village and the absence of any armed military or police force in the countryside. Again, it is in those areas where the distance between the government and the village was greatest—the Tokugawa lands—that we find the most contention, as we do also at times—such as later in the era—when government and its agents of coercion were less effective.

One seldom thinks of institutional structures as stimuli to specific episodes of contention, but in Tokugawa Japan, as elsewhere, even autocratic structures were familiar and provided opportunities of one kind or another. Specifically, any institutional change such as a redrawing of domain boundaries, the transfer of a lord, the establishment of a new office (especially a local one, which would be supported by a new exaction from the locals), might be expected to catalyze existing discontent. And even the day-to-day workings of the system, with its built-in tension between bakufu and domains, could stimulate conflict by suddenly creating opportunities or generating grievances.

Institutions might also be expected to produce leadership. As I have noted, the village headman was not only empowered to rule authoritatively but also obligated to mediate his village's relations with the outside world, whether in his role as tax collector or as protest leader. At the same time, the headman was integrated into higher structures of power and was expected by them to keep his people quiet. Thus the position was highly ambiguous and tension filled. A headman who refused to stand up for his people would forfeit his respectability; one who didn't might forfeit his head. As the Tokugawa era wore on and the headmen were increasingly integrated into the power structure, leadership accordingly became more diverse.

I have already suggested that the frequency of popular contention was greater when and where institutions were less coherent and effective. The institutional context also had a qualitative effect. Specifically, the disarming of an essentially rational people reduced violent contention; the absence of religion as a factor meant less chiliastic and fanatical conflict; the separation of samurai from people deprived them of the sorts of leadership most necessary to widespread popular insurrection; and the refusal of the Tokugawa to push through to full centralization of the state spared the country the sorts of penetration and extraction that gave rise to out-and-out warfare in early modern Europe.

Finally, institutions imply outcomes. Suppression of contention, harshness of punishments, and frequency of success varied systematically across time and space. Specifically, a weaker bakufu was more likely to cave in, more likely to leave popular contention to popular resolution, and less likely to deal harshly with contenders than the domains. Overall, institutional decay over time was associated with more successful outcomes, in terms of substantive concessions and popular survival, with two exceptions. The first involved contention seen as a real threat to basic values of the regime. Incidents involving samurai or religion, for example, elicited repression on a scale similar to that in Europe. The second involved the Meiji regime, which early on set up administrative and coercive institutions that significantly reduced the odds of successful, or unpunished, contention. The Meiji state also took a firm stand against those who questioned its basic values and goals, although its posture was inflexible primarily because it, unlike the Tokugawa state, was intent on mobilizing and transforming—not simply running—the country.

The major aspects of Tokugawa political mores dealt with here include benevolent government (that is, autocracy with reciprocity), agrarianism, secularism, and the growing concept of kōgi, or national authority. It was benevolence that had the greatest explicit influence on popular interests. Over and over, contentious groups expressed discontent with official failures to reciprocate submission and deliverance of taxes with guarantees of subsistence. Such manipulation of ideals presupposed the political status quo. Unsurprisingly, the decay of the status quo—in this case, the increasing inability of the government to live up to its own standards—led to greater popular discontent toward the end of the era. Contention also increased after the Meiji Restoration, when the new regime reneged altogether on the principle of benevolence and simultaneously enhanced the autocratic quality of rule.

Ideology also created opportunities to contend. It divided the elites, between those who espoused agrarian ideals and those who saw protoindustrial growth as the solution to their problems, between lords and the bakufu officials who backed the kōgi of the state, and between those at the grass roots, who often ruled rapaciously or incompetently, and those above, who felt obliged to protect the system by maintaining some semblance of benevolence in government. The shrewd selection of issues, targets, and venues of contention shows the people at their most calculating (Ravina 1992), and we can see a diversification in all these areas later in the era, when ideology increasingly lost its power to unify the elites. These divisions, of course, were rapidly eliminated after the Restoration. During the early Meiji era a short period of upheaval and chaos in the political culture opened the opportunity structure, but even though an upsurge of contention ensued, it came to an early end as the elite got its ideological ducks in a row in the 1870s.

The ideology of benevolence and reciprocity was a powerful tool in the hands of the people. It guaranteed nothing, of course, but it seems clear that the common people felt what amounts to a traditional (and universally recognized, if only de facto) right to minimally effective and honest government, relief in time of dearth, and subsistence at least as franchised hyakushō. The currency of this resource continued throughout the era. After the Restoration this social contract was unilaterally abrogated by the state, which recognized no popular ideological justifications for remonstration upon which broad sectors of the people could base contentious behavior with predictable consequences. Indeed, though contention soon became less frequent, it became more violent, since neither partner to conflict was playing by mutually accepted rules.

In addition to playing an overarching role in shaping interests, opportunities, and resources, ideology was the source of myriad stimuli to specific episodes of contention. Violations of the social contract set the people off as often as anything, and one finds such stimuli becoming more intense in the Meiji era after wholesale revocation of the contract by government. No single violation need have set off action—causation was much more complex than that—and in many incidents the people (once catalyzed) composed long lists of grievances that had piled up over years. Still, the last straw was very often such a violation, and when the stimulus or provocation in question was entwined with ideological principles, contention became more likely, for even if leaders might expect to be punished for their actions, the likelihood of substantive redress of grievances was greater. Such calculation, which divided individual outcomes from and subordinated them to collective ones, was typical of the leaders of popular contention.

Rank-and-file contenders, on the other hand, were likely to be influenced by ideology only when they were of hyakushō status; to the extent that ideological factors mattered, such franchised freeholders played a larger role in contention than tenants or the landless. The reason is that status, more than physical survival, defined the core of "subsistence" as a guarantee of benevolent government, at least in the countryside. Urban food riots involved physical subsistence, but as we shall see, it was not the very poorest elements in either city or country who rose but rather those who had more than simple physical subsistence at stake.

This expectation suggests the complexity of popular contention. The ideology that guaranteed status was subject to decreasing observation by elites over time. Accordingly, one would expect the role of hyakushō in contention to increase.

But I have also noted an increasing role for *lower* social elements in contention over time. It may be that the overall role of ideology, consequent on its observation by the elites, diminished over time and thus the ideologically motivated came to play a smaller role. But at this point we cannot tell.

I can, nevertheless, say that to the extent that ideology mattered it is unsurprising that there was more contention later in the Tokugawa era. Contention became progressively more focused on national targets and venues as the notion of kōgi spread and the state took ever greater resonsibility for both the causes and the consequences of contention. Nevertheless, throughout the era the intensity of conflict was less than it was in early modern Europe, perhaps because of the secular ideology of the time. Religion seems, in comparative perspective, to inspire extremes of brutality next to which (relatively) simple contention over tax rates, corruption, and disaster relief pales. That far and away the bloodiest insurrection in Tokugawa history—the Shimabara Rebellion of 1637–1638— was also the only one with significant religious overtones suggests what Japan escaped by its secularism.

Finally, ideology seems to have had an influence on the outcomes of contention—not individual outcomes, for people were punished more on the basis of elite confidence and of the extent to which substantive popular demands questioned the status quo, but collective ones. The realization of popular demands was more likely where the regime recognized the validity of popular grievances. Indeed, in many instances elites used redress didactically, pointing out that they were doing something or other for the people out of the benevolence of their hearts. Such outcomes were most likely when appeals had leapfrogged over immediate local or domain officials (who were usually the target of the grievance), and their superiors could throw these subordinates to the wolves in putting themselves forward as champions of the people. After the Restoration the entire regime was focused on the emperor, and it was far more likely that superiors would back subordinates. Indeed, the relationship between the invocation of ideology and outcome faded after the Restoration, only to be restored after the new state and society cobbled together their own social contract.

The overall policy thrust of the Tokugawa state was one of tight regulation and heavy extraction; over time, state development accelerated and then leveled off (except in the area of social control, where it continued to expand), while performance rose, leveled off, and then declined. The result, in terms of resources, was beneficial for the people. As state extractions became less effective, more of the economic surplus remained in the hands of the people. How prosperity may have specifically affected political resources (the people's were, of course, officially nil) we cannot say, but it is not unlikely that, given grievances and opportunities, having more time and money made contention more probable.

The result, for the state, was overreach, an attempt to do more with less. Overreach was one of the commoner causes of large-scale political instability in the states of early modern Europe as well. We can see the condition in Tokugawa Japan, and we can see contention vary in response.

Overreach can be investigated in three ways. The first is macrolevel. As state capabilities dwindled, opportunities for contention increased independent of grievances, but in fact grievances also increased as the result of less and less effective administration. As noted, in the area of social control the Tokugawa state continued to expand even after it ceased its centralizing efforts in other sectors. Thus the regime was attempting to do more with less, a recipe for trouble. The second way to get at overreach is at the domain level. That is, we can differentiate domains that tried to regulate and exploit their people to varying degrees, and also domains with differing degrees of structural stability and coherence. What we find is that those attempting to do more with less were more contentious. The third way is ecological: counties and provinces can be characterized by varying degrees of institutional coherence and effectiveness and by regulative and extractive activities. Areas with overreaching administrations (of whatever type—domain, vassal, bakufu) were indeed plagued with more contention.

This exercise is valuable as well because it enables us to compare the relative importance of interests and opportunities. In addition to aggressive but incapable—that is, overreaching—regimes, there were also heavy-handed and capable and lax and inept ones. Lightly governed areas generated fewer grievances, but if they were lower in coercive force they were also higher in opportunities for contention. Aggressively ruled areas generated more discontent but, if effectively run, provided fewer opportunities. We can pursue this exercise into the Meiji era, when, after initial vacillation, the course of policy and performance was decisively in the direction of greater penetration and regulation, and state capabilities were growing. One can infer both escalating grievances and declining opportunities, and I shall examine their interaction later.

Policy and performance are both relevant to the catalysis of contention as well. New policies of whatever type frequently spurred resistance. What was established might not have been pleasant, but it was familiar and the people in most cases had adjusted to it, if not taken advantage of it. Many popular manifestoes called for a return to the "old laws" and "old ways" of administration, sometimes invoking concrete precedent and sometimes an idealized time when governmental burdens were light, popular autonomy was complete, and harvests were perennially bountiful. The result was an official wariness of policy change which grew into outright reluctance in the later years of the era, although the fiscal crises of most domains cried out for innovative policy. Unfortunately, the cry was answered most often in years of dearth, when domain revenues were suddenly threatened, but a new exaction at such times was likeliest to elicit a contentious popular response.

Decaying political performance, though less provoking than policy change, could also be a catalyst for conflict. Most often it took the form of failure to respond to sudden worsening of the popular condition. A bad harvest, say, would bring rural calls for a tax cut and loans or grants of food, seed, or money;

indirectly, it would lead to urban demands for cheaper food, money, or soup kitchens. Such steps were the bottom line of benevolent government, and failure to perform invited popular action. But more than a catalyst for contention, decay influenced the cast of contentious characters. The impact of decay was greater on the lower orders, and we accordingly see an increasing frequency of plebeian contention. Moreover, the thrust of Tokugawa policy over time was to incorporate village leaders into the higher power structure, further fragmenting rural society and producing larger numbers not only of participants but of entrepreneurial leaders as well.

The overall quantitative effect of policy and performance, as noted, varied across regime types. Over time, however, the opportunities for contention grew, and grievances, if they did not increase absolutely, diversified across the social spectrum. Thus we find more contention of all kinds during the later years of the era. Qualitatively, fragmentation (exacerbated by the socioeconomic diversification discussed in the next two chapters) led to a higher proportion of contention among the common people and relatively fewer instances of political protest.

Such a trend had distinct implications for the outcomes of contention. Policy became tighter over time, but enforcement relaxed; we are therefore unsurprised to find that punishments declined even as contention became more intense across the era, and more successful too. These developments occurred not simply because the government was more likely to give in where it could not prevail but also because, if social conflict did become relatively common, then the substantive outcome was the result of interactions between the people and did not depend on a less and less reliable regime. Therefore we find that the people contended with increasing impunity and success as the era drew to a close. And once again, we see a sharp reversal after the Meiji Restoration.

The implications of policies and performance in the area of social control closely parallel those in the policy area in general. Harsh but increasingly inconsistent control reflected expansive but increasingly inept government: it was provocative but not deterrent. As personal calculations discounted punishment, the cost-benefit balance and the frequency of contention shifted significantly. Resources were of little moment, for only rarely during either the Tokugawa or early Meiji eras did the people possess tangible resources with which to resist the official forces of coercion. Nevertheless, opportunities for contention expanded dramatically after the first century of Tokugawa rule regardless of interests.

The declining certainty of punishment had a glacial effect on the background of contention, but specific government regulations played a catalytic role in specific incidents. Direct appeals to higher echelons of government were often the result of nonresponse at the local level; indeed, we shall see over and over how overt contentious action occurred only after repeated rebuffs by local officials. I shall also look at the role of coercion in the conflict process. In some instances it acted as an accelerator, enraging previously deferential contenders; in others it influenced tactics, as when amnesty was one of the contenders' demands; in still others it was a factor in the outcome of contention, as when official forces dispersed contentious gatherings.

Coercion also influenced the tactics and composition of leaders and participants. Tactics focused on efforts to achieve anonymity (leaders were often difficult to discern because they tried to obscure their role) and to avoid provoking the state when possible. Composition was influenced by the likelihood that punishment would probably be limited to—and was indeed always probable for—leaders. Thus village officials, already likely to be natural leaders, were by far the most likely organizers of contention. It was relatively rational for them to play this role despite the odds of punishment. Over time the diminishing probability of punishment made leadership rational for others as well, and the social variety of leaders increased.

Finally, the decreasing probability of punishment helps to explain why contention increased during the Tokugawa era. Popular grievances were a more or less constant feature of politics; the less dangerous contention was, the more of it appeared. The fate of leaders was always in question, but it became brighter over time. Substantive success was highly unpredictable, but (especially in the realm of social conflict) its odds were greater than zero and rising. At given moments we should also find lax jurisdictions more contentious than others, that is, bakufu territories more contentious than the domains. Yet, bakufu territories were more lightly taxed, and the people by inference more contented. Once again, the contradictory implications of different aspects of the political context push our expectations in different directions, and a conclusion must await direct examination of contention itself.

2

THE ECONOMIC CONTEXT

The economic history of Tokugawa Japan was one of growth, with contradictory qualities of its own and contradictory implications for both the people and the government. It was a dynamic era, a time of land reclamation, technological and botanical innovation, extensive education, and increasing production and productivity in agriculture; sophistication in financial practices; protoindustrialization in commerce and manufacturing; and expansion and nationalization of markets.

Economic growth—albeit regionally variable—was both absolute and per capita. The distribution of its fruits also was more egalitarian than the feudal characteristics of the political economy would suggest. At the same time, the economic situation of both domain and bakufu governments deteriorated. They extracted less effectively, saw revenues decline both relative to national product and absolutely, and their administrative capabilities shrank as a result. Thus, contradiction was an important economic theme.

In this chapter I address the economic context of popular contention, to which this contradiction is key. I set out the basic principles on which the economy was based and then look sequentially at the quantity and quality of economic change and its implications for the people, for government, and for popular contention.

The Political Economy of Tokugawa Japan

Economic activities during the Tokugawa era were in the first place political. The state did not concern itself with all aspects of economic behavior, but the class structure, the structure of commerce and its relationship to agriculture, and the size and form of cities were all determined by policy. This policy was feudal in its ethos. Agriculture, exploitation, and domain autarky were its ideals, under the rule of a parasitic samurai aristocracy antipathetic to economic pursuits. Autarky, nevertheless, did not imply either domain independence or bakufu withdrawal from the economy. Bakufu maintenance of roads, elimination of trade barriers, and monopolization of currency amounted to a significant regulatory capacity over the economy.

The grass-roots ideal of the Tokugawa political economy was the freeholding farmer or hyakushō, a full-time cultivator living in and paying taxes through the village. Ideally, taxes accounted for the entire surplus. Yet to say that the Tokugawa ideal was physiocratic is not to say that commerce was completely discouraged. Rather, it was designed to serve the state. Like the samurai, commercial activities were in principle restricted to the cities and placed primarily in the hands of merchant guilds chartered by the government. Their purpose was to keep the cities fed and clothed, to control economic activities outside the cities, and to keep the national economy—especially the flow of tax rice—running smoothly. To this end the rulers tended to keep urban taxes lower than rural (Aono 1988: 178ff.; Hall 1991: 122–23, 177). The immediate result of the concentration of samurai consumption and its economic supporters and agents was an extraordinary burst of urbanization during the seventeenth century. For the remainder of the era Japan rested at what was for a preindustrial society quite a high level of overall urbanization (Rozman in Jansen and Rozman 1986), and Edo was the biggest city in the world. Farmers tilled diligently, lived frugally, and paid responsibly; artisans kept up the supply of commodities; merchants made sure the tax revenues ended up in the government's coffers and the commodities in its storehouses and clothes closets; and the domain was at peace—so at least was the theory.

The reality was more complicated. According to Hayami Akira (1982a), Japan underwent just before and during the Tokugawa era an "industrious revolution," a cultural transformation in which popular orientations toward economic diversity and betterment and toward the necessary sorts of rational calculations became culturally dominant. Efficiency and profit increasingly supplanted effectiveness and survival in the calculations of producers (Nishikawa 1985: 34); attitudes secularized, and popular definitions of utility superseded other definitions. The origins of this revolution—which Hayami dates from roughly 1600, albeit with great regional variation—are beyond the scope of this book. What concern me here are two of its effects on the Tokugawa economy: growth and deagrarianization.

We cannot calculate the growth of the gross national product of Tokugawa Japan, but we can document it. During the Tokugawa era cultivated land doubled in area and agricultural output increased fourfold, whereas population only tripled (Hayami 1982a). The most spectacular growth in production and land cultivation took place during the seventeenth century, and it was a good thing it did, since the extraordinary growth of population in general and cities in particular during that century could have sunk the Tokugawa regime had not the food supply kept pace (after Goldstone 1991: 24ff.). Cultivated land increased by roughly 80 percent, output by 40–60 percent, and population 2.5

times.[1] During the eighteenth century all these rates of increase fell off, but that of population went to near zero, resulting in stable or falling prices during the century (Nishikawa 1979: 117). One aspect of continuing growth was agricultural, the result of improved seeds, fertilizers, tools, and knowledge. The overall rate of agricultural development in the eighteenth and nineteenth centuries actually exceeded that of the seventeenth (Nakamura 1964a: 134; Hall 1966: 420–21; Umemura 1965: 143).

The other aspect of growth was commercial and protoindustrial. This cannot be quantified nationwide, but considerable anecdotal data suggest a booming volume of goods available after the middle of the eighteenth century, and in two well-documented regions in western Chōshū domain and central Kai province agricultural activity seems, by the mid-nineteenth century, to have accounted for no more than 50 percent or 60 percent of all economic activity.[2] The nineteenth century—at least after 1820—was in general a period of inflation, but this was sparked not by a falloff in economic production but by currency debasements carried out by a regime attempting to increase its revenues but unable, because of popular resistance, to tap into the increasingly dynamic protoindustrial sector.

Agricultural growth was not simply a matter of more arable land and more rice. It was intimately related to the social structure, especially the elimination of local political powerholders in the agrarian sector, the supersession of cooperative by family farming, and the creation of the upwardly mobile hyakushō class, for whom the rewards accruing to individual effort under a system of fixed tax rates were clear.[3] Some scholars have asserted that the increased production was the result of desperation in the face of rapacious taxation and imminent dispossession and that it went to the rulers. In fact, it was the result of social and political stability, the enormous demand for food in the cities, and market opportunities, and a good share of the proceeds stayed in the commoner class (Hanley and Yamamura 1977; T. Smith 1959: chap. 6; Umemura 1965: 145ff.). Moreover, agricultural growth drove up demand for labor (and thus wages) and also increased the supply of labor available for off-season protoindustrial activity.

Increasing demand for labor and increasing agricultural surplus in the villages point toward popular contention. Surplus in the hands of the commoners opened the way to moneylending, land concentration, and protoindustrial entrepreneurialism (Rekishi Kagaku 1974: 61ff.; Sasaki 1974: 101). The demand for labor meant that anyone becoming landless might find work and thus remain in the village rather than be driven to the cities. Urbanization was thus dampened, but village social stratification became more complex, including everyone from

---

[1] Hall 1981: 334–36; Nakane and Oishi 1990: 62; Nishikawa 1979: 9ff.; Kitō 1983b.

[2] Nishikawa 1979; Nishikawa in Jansen and Rozman 1986; T. Smith 1969; Saitō 1985; Shimbo and Saitō 1989; Tōkei-in 1968: 69, 89–131, 148.

[3] Hall 1981: chap. 11. As James Scott (1976) has pointed out, peasants often prefer high but flexible tax rates to low but inflexible ones, but this preference presupposes more effective tax collection than Japan's.

landless agricultural laborers through tenants and marginal part-tenant smallholders to freeholders of all scales who enjoyed the "de facto, unconstrained
private property" rights that the system evolved (Wakita 1975: 301).

In the first place, this transformation resembles in broad outline the privatiza-
tion and technological modernization of agriculture which in other early modern
societies has been associated with extraordinary levels of conflict (see, e.g.,
Manning 1988). In Japan, however, the whole process did not take place as a
top-down mercantile or governmental imposition but was opportunity driven,
spontaneous, bottom-up, and popular. It happened because the people benefited
from it. Second, agricultural growth was diverse. In some cases events such as the
introduction of the sweet potato dramatically increased the noncommercial carrying capacity of the land. In other cases agricultural growth was commercial,
based on cotton and other labor-intensive, tenant-raised lowland crops; on silk
and other upland crops grown primarily by freeholders; or on rice. Each implied
a different labor force, different types of market integration, different social
results, and—at least hypothetically—different patterns of popular contention
(Nakamura 1964a: 136ff.). Thus we are not surprised to find in early modern
Japan only a weak relationship between commercialization of agriculture per se
and contention.

The era of protoindustrialization in Japan—roughly the eighteenth and nineteenth centuries—followed Europe's by about a century (Saitō 1985: 16–24).
Economic development in general and protoindustrialization in particular were
further advanced in southern Japan and lowland areas about 1600, driven by
agricultural development and market penetration. During the Tokugawa era
protoindustrialization moved gradually toward the east and into the mountains in
a context of rapid population growth. This pattern of demographically driven
protoindustrialization (to which a large pool of cheap labor is essential) was also
seen in Europe, but in Japan, unlike Europe, the development was sufficient to
absorb the available labor pool without massive social dislocations (Saitō 1983,
1985: 184ff., 219ff.; Bohstedt 1983: 132; Manning 1988: chap. 10). Therefore
it was compatible with the dominant pattern of smallholding agriculture and the
village structures that encompassed it.

Nevertheless, change did occur, primarily in the relationship between tenancy
and protoindustrial by-employments. Both increased during the Tokugawa era,
but the connection was not a simple one. Initially the economy grew as the result
of both commercialization of agriculture and protoindustrialization (which were,
of course, intimately related in that much protoindustry involved the processing
of agricultural products). Wages went up, and the surplus in the hands of some
commoners did also. Increased wages made farm labor less attractive than tenancy to large landowners, and many turned in this direction (Smith 1959:
126ff.). Sometimes tenantization involved downward mobility, as in the case of
farmers who pawned and lost their land but stayed on to till it for someone else.
But often it constituted *upward* mobility, a chance for the landless to get back
onto the land. Adding a small tenancy to a freehold might allow marginal farmers

to stay on an otherwise nonviable piece of land and keep their treasured hyakushō status. Thus, tenancy might mean not failure and misery but survival or even improvement.

Protoindustrial pursuits were another attractive way for prosperous commoners to use their money. They were a money-maker, being relatively untaxed and utilizing labor during the agricultural off-season. They were even more attractive to marginal farmers and tenants, especially those who could at least feed themselves from their own land.[4] They were also attractive to the landless (Fruin 1980: 262 n. 3), since they allowed families to stay in the village and keep alive the dream of reattaining landed status. They often paid better than farming (Aono 1988: 201ff.). Unsurprisingly, complex combinations of freeholding, tenancy, agricultural labor, and by-employment grew up in the villages.

Thus, facile equation of either tenancy or protoindustrialization with popular impoverishment or class polarization is mistaken. Tenancy and protoindustrialization clearly advanced; poverty was highly variable across time and space; polarization is simply not proven by the available data (White 1989). What took place, on the contrary, was increasing pluralization and heterogenization of rural society (Smith 1959; Tozeren 1981). Either polarization or pluralization could have led to contention, but polarization simply did not occur with sufficient uniformity to be the sole cause. In fact, we find regionally variable combinations of landholding, commercialization, and class change interacting to explain the patterns of contention.

Flows, volumes, and processes of trade are not of primary interest here; I take note only of its ruralization and its nationalization. The economic center of gravity moved toward the countryside during the era as the cities and their merchant guilds lost ground to innovative and unregulated rural entrepreneurs. The government did not intend this trend; indeed, it attempted to forestall it and then to exploit it. But such attempts were largely in vain, and their primary effect was to provoke popular opposition. Moreover, after the sixteenth-century burst of urbanization, which was driven by the relocation of the samurai to the cities, the cities were more or less on their own, and most stagnated economically (Hauser 1974). Urban living standards became problematic, and official assistance became increasingly necessary to the maintenance of both living standards and social order in the cities.

Commerce also became national during the era. Commodities of countless types were traded nationwide, and the diminishing regional variation in the price of rice (Iwahashi 1981) reflects the central role the Ōsaka rice exchange came to play in assuring commodity flow and price balances. Another index of nationalization of commerce was the increasing transformation of taxes from kind into cash. More and more people were earning a living outside agriculture. Their incomes were in cash; they needed cash to buy the commodities neither they nor their regions produced; and they became increasing hostile to manipulations of

---

[4]Tozeren 1981: 136; Saitō 1983, 1985; Saito in Jansen and Rozman 1986; Katō 1990.

the rice-cash exchange rate by hungry revenuers and crafty brokers. The "industrious revolution" was also a market revolution; by the end of the era few regions of the country were immune to the forces of monetization, commodification, and economic interdependence. Consequently, when Japan's ports were opened to foreign trade in 1858, the impact was nationwide. Export products shot up in price (benefiting their producers but punishing Japanese consumers and contributing to runaway inflation), domestic industries that competed with cheap imports went into a tailspin, and the entire economy became vulnerable to overseas economic fluctuations. It is to be expected that economic volatility would contribute to popular contention, and indeed, contention rose sharply after the opening of the ports.

Economic Change and Standards of Living

Economic growth during the Tokugawa era, together with population stability from the end of the seventeenth until the early nineteenth centuries, meant that at least on the macrolevel things were getting better. Government revenues declined both absolutely and as a proportion of the economy. The contradiction between maximum extraction and social order gave the people considerable leverage vis-à-vis the elites. Thus there were more resources in the hands of the commoners as time wore on; the question is, which commoners?

Many assume it was commoner elites, because of the increase in tenancy and concentration of landholding, a Marxist conviction that the higher-ups always get everything, and the clear increase in popular contention as the era wore on. But this view is not necessarily accurate. Living standards that improve, or fluctuate around a stable axis, can be associated with the high levels of contention seen. Tenancy, also, did not necessarily mean immiserization: some have asserted that rising nonagricultural wage levels forced landlords to drop their rents, thus making tenancy more attractive. Even the inflationary rise in the price of rice in the nineteenth century meant a profit for anyone paying rent in a fixed amount of cash (Nomiya 1992: 191, Craig 1979: 295ff.).

Indeed, anecdotal evidence argues for rising standards of living for much of Tokugawa society. Cityward migration (mostly among the lower elements) declined toward the end of the era, suggestive of rising wages and employment opportunities in the countryside (White 1992b). Also, demographic indicators of rural distress in other early modern societies, such as increasing marriage age, are missing in later Tokugawa Japan (Goldstone 1991: 252; Kitō 1983b; Hayami 1973, 1988b). Thomas C. Smith (1959: 141) has found a leveling of size among units of farm management in the later Tokugawa period, leading to the emergence of an increasing pool of cultivators with roughly equal resources. Selcuk Tozeren (1981: 211–12) has documented at least one case of relatively equal distribution of the increasing surplus. Susan Hanley (1983: 190–91) asserts that commoners' incomes, too, became more level over time.

Contemporary anecdotes suggest the same. The injunctions of the Tempō reforms against extravagant living in the countryside revealed the problem (Tokyo Hyakunen Shi 1973, 1: 1342–43). Susan Hanley (1983: 191) has characterized living standards as "relatively clean and hygienic." Fukuzawa Yukichi, writing in 1863 (cited in Tussing 1966: 80), noted that economic change had benefited the people even amid galloping inflation because wages had also increased dramatically; indeed, he attributed the inflation partly to popular demands for more and better products and cited the disappearance of miscellaneous service workers and day laborers as evidence of betterment. And finally, William Kelly's (personal communication, June 1990) work on the fires that repeatedly laid waste to Edo throughout the era conjures up an image of frequent programs of public assistance and an almost constant construction program, both signifying a downward redistribution of food and money. I have already noted the relatively lower urban tax rates.

None of which is to say that everyone was prosperous, or even that most were stably so. Macrolevel development is quite compatible with increasing microlevel poverty (Thompson 1966: 203ff.), and a slight improvement in the living standards of most can be accompanied by increasing misery, expoitation, and insecurity for the rest. Some (Harootunian 1988: 454–55) have suggested that Smith (1959) and Hanley and Kozo Yamamura (1977) simply overestimated the improvement in living standards, and others (Walthall 1986: 6ff., chap. 4; Sasaki 1979: 17) have asserted that commoner elites raked off the profits at the expense of both government and people. Neither argument is quite on target, even though poverty was indeed widespread in Tokugawa Japan, especially in the cities (Hall 1991: 591).[5] Isabella Bird (1880), a traveler in Japan in the late nineteenth century, reported scenes of extreme dearth and squalor in northern Japan (along, it must be added, with rhapsodies about the pastoral beauty of other regions). It could well be that half or more of the urban population was poor, as indicated by social status, occupation, or housing situation and by the frequency of public relief programs.[6] The issue is not whether or not poverty was common; it is the tie between poverty and contention. Hayashi Motoi (1976b: 70) maintains that poverty was a constant during the Tokugawa era and therefore cannot explain any specific "struggle at this time, in this place." In fact, poverty did vary in time and space, but as we shall see, contention was not necessarily most common in places or times of greatest poverty. The explanation lies rather in the combination of absolute need, structural vulnerability to markets and food supplies, economic fluctuations, and political stimuli and responses to economic and social change and to contention itself (see, e.g., Tilly 1978: 185ff.).

---

[5] Harootunian's evidence of misery and economic distress is popular contention; we shall see further on that the corollary—that the poorest regions are the most contentious—does not hold. In Walthall's case, Smith's (1959) evidence for relative leveling, inter alia, is simply more compelling.

[6] White 1992b; Minami 1978; Sasaki 1972; Fruin 1973.

My impression of popular living standards in the Tokugawa period is, first, that life was fairly close to the bone. Data suggest a per capita caloric intake of fifteen hundred to seventeen hundred per day, of which between 75 percent and 90 percent came from rice and other grains and sweet potatoes.[7] Such figures, of course, mask the difference between some metropolitan areas, which produced essentially no food, and areas that produced several thousand daily calories per capita of food.[8]

Second, over the era there was nevertheless a secular rise in living standards. It was not linear but ratchetlike, with repeated market-induced and climatic setbacks. Given the growth of markets and of populations not producing their own food, the effects of such setbacks may, if anything, have become more severe as the era wore on.

Third, the poverty of some regions has perhaps been overestimated, along with the influence of living standards on contention. In northern Japan and in central Shinano, both known for their popular contention, the hardness of life appears less than moralistic Confucian observers of that day or Marxist observers of our own have asserted, and conflict there is linked more clearly with market integration and, by implication, with economic growth than with absolute poverty.[9] In the absence of extraordinary official extractions and climatic reversal, a hardworking farmer could make it (Nagasu 1986: 38ff.). To say that he could survive, however, does not necessarily imply that he had much margin, was satisfied with his lot, or would tolerate official actions that jeopardized his situation.

Economic Fluctuations and Vulnerability

I maintain that it is economic change more than economic condition that conduces toward contention. Preindustrial societies are intrinsically vulnerable to such change, especially those with feudal political economies that permit one domain to ignore famine in its neighbor. And protoindustrializing societies are more so, since they are home to increasing numbers of people who no longer produce their own food, either because they have moved to urban areas or because, though still in the village, they are in nonagricultural pursuits. In my view all three types of vulnerability and reversal—ecological, market or producer, and urban or consumer—play a role in contention.

Of course, economic factors did not operate in a vacuum. The government's response to reversal—tax and rent cuts for producers, price cuts for consumers—

---

[7] Nishikawa in Jansen and Rozman 1986; Mosk and Pak 1977; Kitō 1983a; Ōkawa 1976; Kagaku Gijutsu Chō 1967.

[8] Where this food was consumed cannot be determined, but if the people of a locality faced dearth they could always seize what was produced locally.

[9] Nishikawa 1979: 146ff.; Yokoyama 1986: 12ff., 211ff.; Vlastos 1986; Kozo Yamamura, personal communication, August 1981; Tozeren 1981.

was key, and the government knew it (Kelly 1985: 46ff., chap. 3). But some policies accentuated natural reverses. Repeated devaluation of the coinage and issue of domain paper currencies in the nineteenth century increased economic instabilities of all sorts. The aim of devaluation was to push up the price of rice (in which taxes were denominated); that of the money printing was to suck up specie from society for revenue purposes. There was always a temptation to overdo both, and both increased in frequency, with inflationary and contentious consequences, after the first major devaluation in 1818 (Shimbo and Saitō 1989).

Ecological vulnerability was inescapable. Frost, wind and hail, rain and flood, drought, volcanic eruption, insects—the Tokugawa farmer faced them all. Figure 2 shows the relative frequency with which each province was hit by natural disasters during the era.[10] The northeast certainly appears to deserve its reputation as climatologically cursed, although this vulnerability extends throughout the Kantō region and down the central mountain spine to Shinano. Two regions of secondary affliction are Kyūshū and western Shikoku, and the central Kinai, which are usually thought of as relatively blessed weatherwise and low in contention. They were, of course, as vulnerable to drought and rain (especially typhoons) as any region, and their putatively low levels of contention bear scrutiny.

But disaster is not the whole picture, and adding Figure 3 gives us some hints about the full scope of ecological vulnerability. The figure combines modal county frost-free days per year and altitude, on the assumption that colder highland regions are more chronically vulnerable to the weather, and that making a living from the earth is harder even in the best years than in the warmer lowlands. In general, the two figures are similar: the northeast, the central mountain core, central Kyūshū and western Shikoku, and the Kinai have their vulnerable parts. The only striking difference is the rugged region in the western interior of the main island of Honshū, which appears to be surprisingly free of natural disasters; I shall look at this area later in comparing the effects of long-term and short-term economic conditions.

A final point to be made from Figure 3 is the presence of ecologically vulnerable regions scattered throughout the Japanese archipelago. As my analysis of contention will make clear, the facile equation of tough conditions and contention in the east and easy living and quiescence in the west is questionable. Counties with no recorded contention at all during the 288-year period sometimes abutted endemically contentious ones, even within single political jurisdictions. From Figure 3 we can also see how the most ecologically favored areas were in places contiguous with the least favored. The parallel bears investigating.

Another parallel is the correspondence between the periods of greatest turbulence and periods of most intense dearth during the Tokugawa period. The four greatest famines of the era were the Kyōhō, in 1732–1733, the Temmei, in 1782–1787, the Tempō, in 1833–1839, and the Keiō, in 1866–1969 (Arakawa 1964, 1967: 57). Questions of policy intertwine. The Kyōhō famine was largely

---

[10] For a discussion of the coding of these data see White 1992b.

The Context

Figure 2. Total natural disasters, by province, 1590–1877

1 Ōsumi		
2 Satsuma		
3 Hyūga		
4 Higo	**Kyūshū**	
5 Chikugo	**region**	
6 Hizen		
7 Chikuzen		
8 Buzen		
9 Bungo		

10 Tosa	
11 Iyo	**Shikoku**
12 Awa	**region**
13 Sanuki	

14 Nagato	
15 Suō	
16 Aki	
17 Iwami	
18 Bingo	**Chūgoku**
19 Izumo	**region**
20 Bitchū	
21 Hōki	
22 Mimasaka	
23 Bizen	
24 Inaba	

25 Harima	
26 Tajima	
27 Tango	
28 Tanba	**Kinki**
29 Ōmi	**region**
30 Iga	
31 Ise	
32 Shima	
33 Kii	
34 Awaji	

35 Settsu	
36 Izumi	**Kinai**
37 Kawachi	**region**
38 Yamashiro	
39 Yamato	

40 Mino	
41 Owari	
42 Mikawa	
43 Tōtōmi	
44 Suruga	**Chūbu**
45 Izu	**region**
46 Hida	
47 Kai	
48 Shinano	
(Shinshū)	

49 Wakasa	
50 Echizen	
51 Kaga	**Hokuriku**
52 Noto	**region**
53 Etchū	
54 Echigo	
55 Sado	

56 Kōzuke	
57 Shimotsuke	
58 Musashi	
59 Hitachi	**Kantō**
60 Shimōsa	**region**
61 Kazusa	
62 Awa	
63 Sagami	

64 Iwashiro	
65 Iwaki	
66 Uzen	**Tōhoku**
67 Rikuzen	**region**
68 Ugo	
69 Rikuchū	
70 Mutsu	

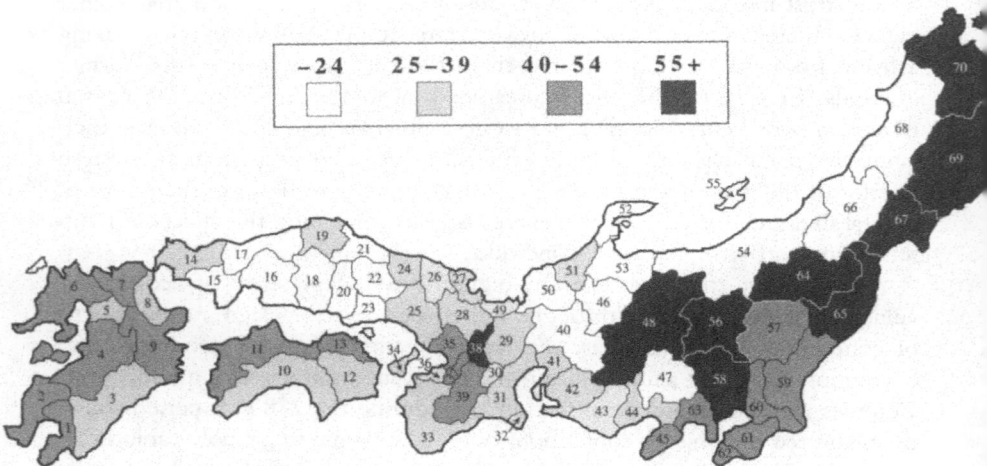

Source: Arakawa, 1964: 248–62.

Figure 3. Ecological vulnerability

1 Ōsumi	25 Harima	49 Wakasa
2 Satsuma	26 Tajima	50 Echizen
3 Hyūga	27 Tango	51 Kaga
4 Higo	28 Tanba	52 Noto **Hokuriku region**
5 Chikugo **Kyūshū region**	29 Ōmi **Kinki region**	53 Etchū
6 Hizen	30 Iga	54 Echigo
7 Chikuzen	31 Ise	55 Sado
8 Buzen	32 Shima	
9 Bungo	33 Kii	56 Kōzuke
	34 Awaji	57 Shimotsuke
10 Tosa		58 Musashi
11 Iyo **Shikoku region**		59 Hitachi **Kantō region**
12 Awa	35 Settsu	60 Shimōsa
13 Sanuki	36 Izumi	61 Kazusa
	37 Kawachi **Kinai region**	62 Awa
14 Nagato	38 Yamashiro	63 Sagami
15 Suō	39 Yamato	
16 Aki		64 Iwashiro
17 Iwami	40 Mino	65 Iwaki
18 Bingo **Chūgoku region**	41 Owari	66 Uzen
19 Izumo	42 Mikawa	67 Rikuzen **Tōhoku region**
20 Bitchū	43 Tōtōmi	68 Ugo
21 Hōki	44 Suruga **Chūbu region**	69 Rikuchū
22 Mimasaka	45 Izu	70 Mutsu
23 Bizen	46 Hida	
24 Inaba	47 Kai	
	48 Shinano (Shinshū)	

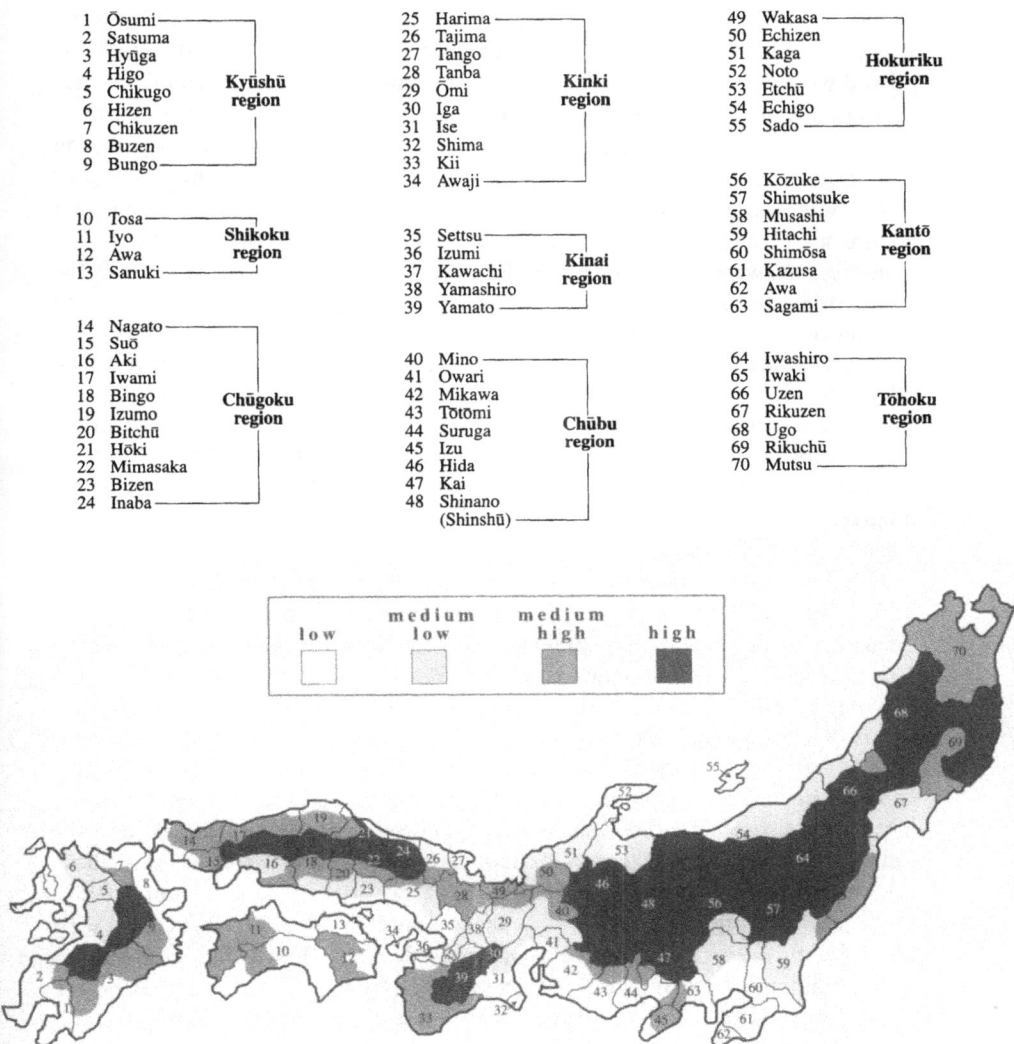

Sources: Geographical Survey Institute, 1977;
International Society for Educational Information, 1974.

the result of Shogun Yoshimune's efforts to raise the price of rice, combined with
an insect plague in western Japan (Harada 1982: 92ff.). In Temmei government
profligacy and incompetence aggravated the results of a series of bad harvests.
Personnel and policy reforms were launched to remedy both, and (amid improved weather) a major wave of contention came to an end. In Tempō another
series of crop failures were followed by famine and another wave of contention,
which were in turn followed by political reforms (and better weather). Again, the
contention came to an end. When the Keiō famine occurred, the Tokugawa
system was wheezing toward collapse. The western domains were insurgent, the
bakufu was decrepit, and inflation was raging. In 1866 the harvest failed, and
many regions were swept by famine. By 1869 Japan again had credible government, domestic peace, good weather, decent food prices, and falling rates of
contention. As these last three episodes all suggest, a constellation of factors was
probably at work, but in every case economic reversal also appears independently
related to high rates of contention.

The penetration of markets added to nature a vulnerability to the profit
motivations of unknown persons far removed from one's own village. It added
the need to come up with cash tax payments. It added income elasticity to
relatively fixed costs. And as producer units grew smaller and agricultural labor
became commodified, it weakened the cooperative "safety net" that James Scott
(1976) has found so important to stable rural life in agrarian societies (T. Smith
1959: chap. 11). Economic life became more volatile—a phenomenon found
elsewhere at similar developmental stages (Wolf 1969; Rebel 1983: 93ff.; Huang
1985: 293)—and even those who opted to stay in agriculture were drawn toward
new equipment, fertilizers, and technologies, which in turn drew them into the
hands of moneylenders (Vlastos 1986).

The overall contours of market conditions, as they impinged on producers
and consumers, are visible in Figure 4. The rice price index shown (Iwahashi
1981) is the mean of the annual price in Hiroshima, Ōsaka, Edo, and Aizu,
four cities spanning the length of Honshū, with 1840–1844 = 100. These
prices intercorrelate at r = 0.81. The Kyoto retail price index (Umemura 1961:
175) is a composite of the prices of several staple consumer goods, with
1801–1810 = 100. Kyoto builders' wages (Umemura 1961: 175) are real wages
in the building trades in that city, with 1801–1810 = 100. The bakufu land tax
rate is Hara Akira's (n.d.) estimate of the tax rates levied in Tokugawa house
lands. Except for the rice price index, none of these indices is valid nationwide.
the Kinai region, however, in which Kyoto lies, had by the middle of the
eighteenth century become the central node in the national economy, and broad
economic trends there can be taken as general indicators of the state of the
whole (Saitō Osamu, personal communication). Similarly, the tax rate, albeit
nationally applicable, does not apply to domain lands; in particular, the rate
was lower in the Tokugawa lands than elsewhere. Still, there is good reason
to believe that the trend shown did apply nationally (Hara Akira, personal
communication; Hall and Jansen 1968: chap. 15). Bakufu finances (Shimbo

1978) are shown as surpluses or deficits in millions of gold ryō (1 ryō = about 0.5 oz.).

Figure 4 shows, first, the long-term rise in prices over the entire Tokugawa era, reflecting a secular process of growth. Second, the eighteenth century was in general a period of stability, until about 1825; in particular, 1790–1820 provided a whole generation with falling prices and enhanced well-being (Nishikawa 1985: 127). Third, the period after 1825 was one of rising prices and falling real wages (Umemura 1961: 173). My wage data are urban, but real agricultural wages similarly increased up until the 1820s and then, at least in some areas, decreased (Saitō 1973c). Toward the end of the era this effect became regionalized. After the opening of the ports silk-producing areas in central and eastern Japan enjoyed a boom, but the cotton-producing areas in western and southern Japan were hard hit by cheaper imported cotton (Saitō in Jansen and Rozman 1986). And even in many of the sericultural regions consumer prices went up faster than producer (Vlastos 1986).

Fourth, the entire era, particularly after 1700, was characterized by sharp fluctuations. Five stand out: the 1710s, 1740s, 1780s, 1830s, and 1860s. Market penetration grew throughout the era and, as expected, we find successively greater magnitudes of contention in the later cycles of rising prices and falling wages. Also, in line with so-called J-curve models of contention, we see that cyclical reversals following long-term economic growth were accompanied by more contention than cycles occurring earlier in the era. Thus, the important aspect of these five cycles is not simply the height of the price curve, and we shall therefore not necessarily expect to find more contention in, for example, 1715 than in 1785.

The final measures in Figure 4 are official, not market. The first is the real land tax rate in bakufu-administered territories, and it shows a secular decline throughout the era. It in fact overestimates the tax rate, since a calculation of Japan's GNP during this period, were it possible, would show a diminishing share for agriculture. Overall, this estimate suggests a tax burden falling by almost 50 percent during the era, and contributes to a picture of economic improvement for the people, while the state's budget fell into chronic deficit in the later eighteenth century. So the questions remaining include: Did the fruits of betterment go to exploiters, implying more contention? Why did changes not better everyone's lives and lead to less conflict? Or whatever else may have occurred, do the repeated reversals of fortune independently explain the cycles of contention?

Some 10–15 percent of the Japanese population, including over a million in Edo alone, lived in cities during the Tokugawa era. They produced for markets and were more vulnerable to the price and wage fluctuations shown in Figure 4 than villagers. Indeed, they were more likely to be vulnerable as consumers than anyone else. In other protoindustrializing societies a large stratum of landless agricultural and protoindustrial laborers—a proletariat—appeared (Saitō 1986, esp. 12), but in Japan so many rural laborers managed to hold onto a piece of

Figure 4. Economic trends in Tokugawa Japan

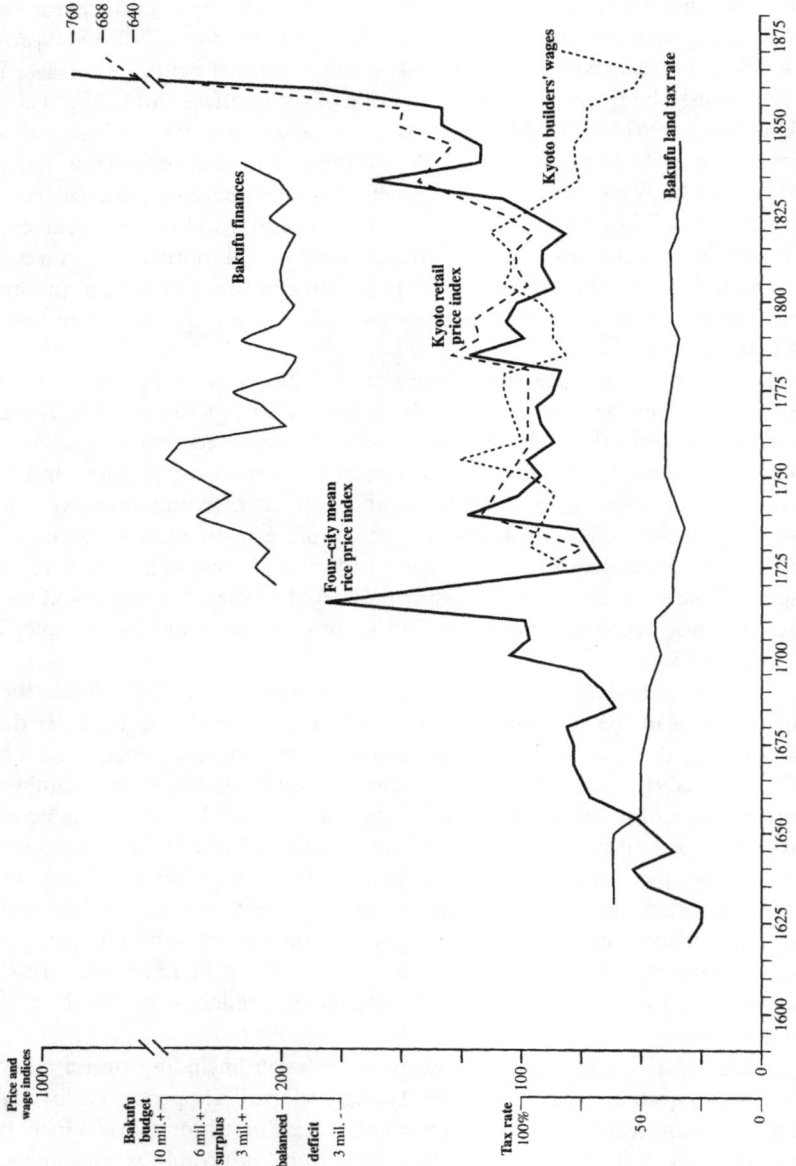

land, even if only as tenants, that true proletarianization occurred on a significant scale only in the cities.

Does proletarianization explain the higher levels of contention we find there? Not necessarily; I reject any exclusively economic causation of conflict. There are, of course, other factors that suggest higher levels of contention in the city. Certainly we expect qualitative differences in urban contention—most particularly, if Europe is any example, food riots—and perhaps a different causal pattern as well. The causation of urban contention should stem more directly from urbanites' lives as consumers, whereas rural conflict should more often focus on what farmers get for their labor, how they deal with those who provide them with credit (and thus threaten their land), and how much of their product the state and its minions try to wrest from them.

The Economy and the Government

Economic change during the Tokugawa era redounded to the detriment of government. Neither bakufu nor domains rested inert in the face of these changes; the problem was that every remedy was contentious. Increased taxes, new taxes, forced loans from merchants and communities, regulation of merchants, debasement of the coinage, official monopolies and monopsonies, manipulation of rice-cash exchange rates, early collection of taxes—everything made someone mad. The only immediately cost-free remedies were (for the domains) to reduce samurai stipends and (for the state) to raise exactions from the domains and to borrow, both of which only postponed the day of reckoning.

The outlines of fiscal decay were apparent by the late seventeenth century, when the burgeoning of popular culture made it clear to all that the common people were enjoying a degree of wealth wholly out of line with official principles of frugality. Rising costs and fixed revenues had already pushed many domains into debt, and a 1695 debasement of the coinage set a new and ominous precedent (Maruyama 1974: 119ff.). The Kyōhō period of the early eighteenth century saw reforms aimed at increasing revenues (Aoki M. et al. 1981, 2:209ff.) through new and increased taxes and trade regulations, but even the new taxes and regulations amounted to an admission that the official policy of control of commerce and industry by official, monopolistic urban guilds and chartered merchants was a failure (Sheldon 1958: 168).

This weakness of will was evident elsewhere. In 1721, in an attempt to stem the trend toward concentration of landholdings, the shogunate ruled that interest on loans for pawned land was to be limited, that repayment was to be stretched out, that land forfeited during the previous five years could be redeemed upon repayment of principal, and that land was not henceforth to be forfeited through pawn (Yashiro 1989: 191–92). One village headman in Uzen province hid this decree from his villagers, but they found out about it, and in early 1723 some hundreds of them descended on forty-six local creditors, demanding recalculation and repayment of excess interest, seizing records, and taking their land back.

The local headmen and creditors called for help and the bakufu summoned ten popular leaders, ten creditors, and a number of village officials to Edo. In the seventh month of 1723 the bakufu announced the outcome: 114 individuals were punished, including six executions and nine remote exiles, and the state revoked the whole set of decrees in which it had placed such hope. It was simply one early example of reform attempts that proved to cause more problems than they solved.

Bakufu revenues reached their historical high in 1744 (Aoki M. et al. 1981, 2:209ff.), but did so amid a flood of petitions for revision, relief, and recission. Moreover, as shown in Figure 4, despite this peak the state's financial picture soon turned gloomy.[11] By the middle of the century the state had for all purposes capitulated to popular resistance; thenceforth its efforts focused on indirect levies, extractions from the elites, and taxation of nonagricultural activities. Some of these—for example, attempts in the 1780s to control the Ōsaka rice exchange and establish a "national property tax"—were in fact efforts at further state building and at harnessing rather than denying market and manufacturing development, but they failed (Ooms 1985: 9–10; Hall 1955: 18, 63).

By the nineteenth century the state was in disarray. The Tempō reforms of the 1840s dissolved the chartered guilds, which were accused (unjustly) of responsibility for inflation; their demise demonstrated the basic nonviability of the Tokugawa political economy and led to even greater price instability (Sheldon 1958: 161; Toyoda 1962: chap. 8). Vain attempts at central control followed. The chartered guilds were revived in 1851, and an edict of 1860 specified five major commodities whose trade was to be channeled through Edo (Tokyo Hyakunen Shi 1973, 1:1461–64). The inflation of the 1860s and the crop failure of 1866, which hit hardest in eastern Japan, center of Tokugawa power, while leaving the state's western adversaries unaffected were merely the last blows to state finances (Arakawa 1967: 121–25).

In contrast to the state, many of the domains recognized the nonviability of physiocracy. They moved increasingly during the eighteenth century to stimulate saving and to lead and guide investment and economic growth in all sectors, seeking autarky and solvency.[12] They traded with other domains directly, bypassing Ōsaka, and by the second quarter of the nineteenth century over half had established official monopolies or commercial organs of their own (Yoshinaga 1973). Success was striking in some domains. By 1854, 45 percent of the revenues of Nambu, for example, were derived from commerce and protoindustry (Hyakushō Ikki 1980: 104ff.). And the fruits of the initiatives of several domains became the economic basis upon which opposition to the Tokugawa state was built. In only a few dozen domains, however, did extraordi-

---

[11] One should note that of the subsequent surplus years, most were related to crop failures, when rice prices rose (Nishikawa 1985: 62). Also, an 1830 ryō was worth less than a 1730 ryō.

[12] On this topic, see Jansen 1961; Craig 1961; Nishikawa 1979; Tokyo Hyakunen Shi 1973, 1: 1304; compare with Rebel 1983: 22ff.

nary, nonagricultural revenues ever amount to more than 15 percent of the total (Beasley 1960). Even where they did, there was no free lunch: many domain initiatives involved the co-optation of rural elites, both forcing the people to develop new leadership resources and providing them with new grievances. The people recognized clearly that all these reforms had basically one objective—more revenue (Aoki et al. 1981, 2:221ff.).

The Meiji Economic Context

The economic context of the first decade of the Meiji era was one of turmoil without resolution. By the late 1880s the outlines of the modern Japanese economy were clear, and industrial strikes, workers' movements, and tenancy disputes were coming to the fore, but in the 1870s the government was experimenting. By the end of the first decade several important measures were in place, and the decks had in many ways been cleared for modern economic growth, but the economic, political, and social implications were as yet by no means clear and the people had still to figure out how to push within the new system for collective gain. In popular social behavior continuity was more striking than change during these early years.

One deck-clearing operation the Meiji regime executed quickly was the abolition of the closed class system and the chartered guilds and the freeing of economic pursuits. Another was the complete commodification of land with the extension of title, with complete freedom of transfer, to the previous de facto owner.[13] Former samurai were now free to enter business, and farmers to leave the land; those with money were free to consume lavishly, invest productively, or buy land. Family fortunes fell and rose dramatically. Collectively, the people were affected most strongly by the social differentiation that followed and by two other phenomena: price stability and the new land tax.

As one can see in the last years of Figure 4, real wages turned upward soon after the Restoration, prices dropped (Nishikawa 1979: 127), and popular livelihood rapidly became significantly more predictable and manageable, although growth rates did not soon change. Unfortunately, government extraction quickly became more predictable too. In the early 1870s the state calculated what revenues it would need for financial viability, carried out a land survey, and figured backward to arrive at a tax rate of 3 percent of the value, not the productive capacity, to be applied nationally to the new owners of the land (Yamamura in Jansen and Rozman 1986; Kajinishi 1978). An effective tax rate of approximately 25 percent of yield took hold. For hitherto heavily taxed regions, especially in the south and west, this constituted a tax reduction (of fully 37 percent in Kōchi prefecture); for the previously undertaxed north and east, a hefty hike (of 38 percent in Iwate prefecture and 71 percent in Tokyo [Yamamura in Jansen and Rozman 1986: 395]). In at least some regions we may

---

[13] Hirschmeier 1964: 10–11; Toyoda 1962: 293–94; Honjō 1972: 355; Yamanashi-ken 1978: 40.

infer intense grievances, and yet overall, the Restoration was followed by a rapid dropoff in conflict. Of course, the Meiji pacification was the product of multiple factors—stable, effective, and capably coercive government not least among them—but the distinctive implications of economic transformation for contention between people and state also demand our attention.

This overview of the Tokugawa economic context gives rise to several observations regarding popular contention. The economic structure, as noted, was political and feudal; therefore, I suspect that politically focused grievances and political stimuli played a greater role than in more laissez-faire economies. The exploitativeness of the system provided no lack of contentious interests, but the system was in fact so pervasively exploitative that we may wonder whether they were variable and thus able to explain differences in contention across time and space. Moreover, given the integration of polity and economy, it is possible that economic contention was *more* likely to incur the wrath of the authorities in Japan than elsewhere; that is, the opportunity structure may have been severely constrained.

The economic structure, in addition to suggesting the constellation of interests, opportunities, and resources involved in contention, also suggests the major actors. On the challenging side, the major actors were, first, freeholding farmers, the predominant, and leading, element in the countryside; second, the rural poor and tenants, to the extent that they were present, usually in a subordinate role; and third, middling and lower-strata urbanites. Against them were arrayed the officially privileged merchants, which were simply targets, and the governments of domains and state, which could be either targets or active adversaries or both.

Most of the internal variation in the Tokugawa political economy was not built-in. Rather, it resulted from the wide-ranging economic changes that characterized the era. Tokugawa Japan "economized" and grew, and such changes are associated with an increase and diversification in popular contention. Economic interests and expectations multiplied, and there was more exclusively economic and less political contention over the course of the era. Moreover, the absolute level of contention increased. Socioeconomic differentiation led to diversification of actors and targets and opportunities. What it did to resources is unclear: the question is whether the new resources went into the hands of those who considered themselves part of the status quo or not. Certainly some resources remained in the hands of the lower strata, and many of the upper commoner strata were co-opted into target status, and we thus see more participation by, and even leadership among, the lower strata. In other words, economic change generated more leaders, more followers, and more interests, opportunities, and resources for contention. It also led to more economically oriented contention and relatively less political protest. When moneylenders and landlords are more salient in local society than tax collectors and intendants, one may expect that they will bear the brunt of popular ill will. This choice of targets may explain why the outcomes of contention became more successful and less punitive, since intimate state interests were less likely to be threatened.

Still, we must not rush to the conclusion that economic development universally leads to more contention. There may have been less market- and development-linked contention in Japan than elsewhere since these changes were most frequently the product of spontaneous popular entrepreneurship, not the sort of top-down compulsion commonly associated with such contention elsewhere (Magagna 1991). Moreover, if economic change had proceeded too rapidly, it could have created forms of social instability which would militate against the degree of organization and coordination essential to collective action (Tilly et al. 1975; Bohstedt 1983: chap. 3). In particular, great economic flux combined with tight political control might have constrained contention significantly, which again recommends the first decade of the Meiji era to our attention.

During the Tokugawa era, however, economic change did not approach this pace. Consequently, I focus on the relationship between differentiation and contention. There is disagreement here, but it provisionally appears that differentiation entailed greater interclass and interstratal antagonism, and thus more conflict, rather than diminished social cohesion, and therefore less conflict. I am aware of commodity- and region-linked differences in protoindustrial development. In lowland and more western regions market development was based on land-extensive and tenant-produced cotton and rapeseed; in upland and eastern Japan it was more often based on labor-intensive sericulture, pursued as an agricultural by-employment by freeholding farmers (Wigen 1990; Vlastos 1986). The latter areas were more contentious, although there are those who assert that the greater socioeconomic differentiation of the lowlands created at least the potential for contention there too (Rekishi Kagaku 1974: 87ff., 305ff.; Hayashi 1976b).

The regional and commodity characteristics of protoindustrialization must be further linked with economic conditions. I have asserted that living standards in general improved during the Tokugawa era, but they did not do so uniformly. Rapid development is quite compatible with both increasing living standards and increasing poverty (Nomiya 1992; Walthall 1986), and neither is incompatible with increasing contention (Craig 1979: 319 n. 84; Barnes, Kaase et al. 1979). To the extent that living standards improved, we see more contention aimed at asserting new claims and protecting new gains and less in regard to subsistence demands. We also see more contention absolutely to the extent that the fruits of development were relatively widely distributed.

I doubt that enhanced living standards could have "bought off" contention, for in autarkic, agrarian, preindustrial societies economic downturns are endemic, and during protoindustrialization their effects are magnified by the increasing numbers of the economically vulnerable. I have noted the growth of two vulnerable populations: farmers, particularly those enmeshed in market relationships, and city dwellers. Producer vulnerability, we may presume, was linked primarily to ecological and climatic conditions and secondarily to policies and markets; urban contention was probably the reverse because elites could intervene between crop failure and urban dearth.

Vulnerability to short-term economic fluctuation is, in all likelihood, more intimately connected to the catalysis of contention than are more long-standing interests, opportunities, and resources. I shall investigate the relationship between economic and political fluctuations—that is, periods of reform—but I still expect to see an independent tie between economics and conflict. One need not adopt an exclusively economistic posture to agree that a sudden increase in one factor can, *ceteris paribus*, lead to a sudden jump in contention. Nor can we fully address the role of vulnerability until we look at the politicoeconomic connection, since whether contention takes a political or social form was influenced not only by the type of vulnerability involved but also by perceptions of the responsibility of government for the reversal and of its capability to remedy the situation. To the extent that economic development proceeded outside the ken of the state, and to the extent that the state was unable to exploit development and maintain its capabilities, the state became a less salient actor, a less likely target, and a diminished threat to contending commoners.

This is what happened in Tokugawa Japan. The economic context of the Tokugawa state was debilitating, but the government was not content to slide gently into oblivion. Rather, it attempted, halfheartedly and inconsistently, to penetrate and exploit the economy even as its resources dwindled. The result was overreach. Government actions were sufficient to stimulate popular grievances but not enough to close the opportunity structure for contention. State actions could always stimulate mobilization, but they became less important relative to the actions of commoner agents of the market. What are the implications for the overall magnitude of contention? Too soon to tell, but I expect to find that political protest varied with state activism and salience, and thus declined relative to social conflict during the Tokugawa era.

The Meiji Restoration, of course, restored the centrality of the state, and there was a resurgence of political conflict after 1868. Economically, the first decade of the Meiji era brought rapid social and economic flux and dramatically enhanced mobility opportunities, combined with the rapid imposition of a no-nonsense, coercive state. State penetration also proceeded apace, especially in the form of the new land tax. Some contention was aimed at this and other economic reforms, but it tended to be regionally specific. No explicit trends in economic interests, opportunities, or resources were yet visible. The consolidation of the new political economy and a new socioeconomic structure in the 1880s preceded either qualitative or quantitative change in contention. The economic context of the first years of Meiji was open-ended; our expectations must be also.

3

THE SOCIAL AND
DEMOGRAPHIC CONTEXT

The structures of Tokugawa society with the greatest relevance for the study of popular contention were the class system and the village. The class system differentiated among four closed orders—samurai, peasants, artisans, and merchants. The samurai monopolized political power, social status, and (at least initially) wealth. The peasants were the economic foundation of the regime, the virtuous embodiment of hard work, frugality, and submission. Artisanal pursuits did not have the moral cachet of agriculture but were at least productive. Merchants were considered parasites, producing nothing and profiting from simply passing commodities around, and they stood at the bottom of the status hierarchy.

Thus Tokugawa society resembled early modern European societies of orders (Zagorin 1982, 1: chap. 3; Mousnier 1970: 5ff., 234), although the division was actually simpler than the four strata suggest: the only really significant division at the beginning of the Tokugawa era was between the samurai and everybody else. Despite the vast gulf between samurai and commoners, elites had certain obligations toward the people, though downward obligations were weaker than in Europe (Bloch 1964, 1:219; Elison and Smith 1981: 10).

The formation of the Tokugawa class system had its own logic, some stages of which are extremely important to our interest. The first stage was the national land survey, or *kenchi*, carried out in the sixteenth century, which assessed the productivity (or kokudaka) of each unit of land. The kokudaka system enabled the shogun to allocate fiefs to retainers, the retainers to allocate stipends to their retainers, and all government units to allocate revenue obligations to the taxpayers.

But who should the taxpayers be? The government did not directly tax the feudal lords, nor they their samurai retainers. So the burden fell on the producers,

who were tied to their communities by being given de facto land titles and rights
of political and social participation in their villages as hyakushō, or farmers.
Hyakushō status entailed tax-paying obligations but was coveted because of the
accompanying rights, and it constituted dramatic upward mobility for those who
had previously been quasi serfs. Indeed, the establishment of the system has been
described as a "pro-peasant . . . revolution" (Elison and Smith 1981: 10).

But the hyakushō were not quite individual freeholders. The final component
of the social structure was the collective responsibility, or *murauke*, system, under
which the tax-paying units were villages, not families or individual farmers
(Nishikawa 1985: 23–24). Villages allocated their tax obligations internally in
accord with the kokudaka of each hyakushō family, and neither family status nor
landholding had any meaning outside a specific village.

The key components of the kenchi-kokudaka-hyakushō-murauke system for
us are the freeholding farmers and the collectivist village. Each step of the system
holds implications for conflict. Land surveys and assessments were a perennial
bone of contention; hyakushō status was avidly sought and vehemently protected; and both the distribution and exercise of rights within the village and
collective rights vis-à-vis other villages and the state generated innumerable
conflicts. The farmers became a socially and economically defined stratum with
common rights, norms, and interests, resources, and opportunities; it would be
naive not to expect to find them at the center of much popular contention. And
the village is the same: it was the context within which rights and privileges held
meaning; it was a unit of mutual assistance; and it created the possibility of
defense (or pursuit) of interests in a way that no other social unit could.

The family was a key focus of identity in Japan also, but family status and
identity existed within the village, and neither families nor clans nor individual
family members served as nuclei in Tokugawa-era popular conflict. Even village
headmen could not let family override community, as we have already seen in the
saga of Hyōsuke.

Another social structure of relevance elsewhere was the secret society or
heterodox religious group, found in both Europe and China.[1] In Tokugawa
Japan quasi-underworld groups of gamblers, local bosses, marginal workers, and
general-purpose ne'er-do-wells like Bansuke produced a number of leaders of
contentious action (Fukaya 1978), but they seldom became units of either dissent
or mobilization. Religious groups, as political actors, were essentially obliterated
before the Tokugawa era began.

Thus, for many of our purposes, social structure boils down to community.[2]
Communities in Tokugawa Japan were basically urban or rural. Cities accounted
for perhaps 15 percent of the total population. There was in each domain a castle
town, seat of the domain (or, in the case of Edo, the shogun's) government and

---

[1] Cohn 1961; Chesneaux 1972; Naquin 1976, 1981; Goldstone 1991.
[2] This conclusion may seem simplistic, but at least it thus far corroborates the far better documented
conclusions of, inter alia, Victor Magagna (1991) and Roger Manning (1988).

home to its samurai population and all the retainers, producers, merchants, and service personnel essential to its operations and their lives.[3] Government tried to restrict commercial activity to the castle towns by chartering and privileging merchant groups and tried to keep the urbanites in line with a variety of social control measures, but the basic vitality of the castle towns was political. With the waning of the capacities of both shogunate and domains it is unsurprising that the populations of the castle towns stagnated after their burst of growth in the seventeenth century.

The other type of town took several forms: some grew up around post stations on the roads, some around frequently visited temples, some at seaports, and some around periodic markets. With the exception of Ōsaka, the economic heart of the country, they were smaller than the castle towns and less well regulated, either economically or politically. The authorities ignored them at first and never really came to grips with their role or potential until the very end of the era. Such towns linked country and city as exchanges for goods and services, manufactured and agricultural goods, and tillers and merchants. The state was far less intrusive and its minions less in evidence, and unsurprisingly, contention in this arena revolved far more around nonpolitical than political issues.

Indeed, we shall see that urban size, political or economic qualities, and internal organization were, as in other early modern societies, linked to the causation, magnitude, and process of contention (Bohstedt 1983: 37ff., 202ff.). There was also a simpler relationship between urbanism per se and conflict. Cities have contradictory characteristics, and lower taxes and tighter administration suggest less contention, but their vulnerability, population density, communication, and the protective anonymity of urban life seem to count for more.

I shall, however, spend more time looking at the villages, home to over four-fifths of the Japanese people. Research on a wide variety of preindustrial societies has shown that the village is a major factor in popular contention.[4] Threats to the autonomy, viability, and cohesion of the village were threats to all, especially to the better-off farmers, who tended to dominate the village and benefit most from its viability. The village context provided its members with interests, resources, definitions of friend and enemy and allies; unsurprisingly, it was "natural soil for rural protest" (Zagorin 1982, 1:86).

These generalizations also apply to Tokugawa Japan. I have already noted the autonomy enjoyed by the village. Its separation from the elites was exacerbated by the nature of the exploitation by these elites, which focused on the village and not the individual (Vlastos 1986: 11–14) and which was open, easily measurable, unilateral, and zero-sum, as opposed to exploitation within the village, which was

---

[3] On the castle towns and their legacy, see Hall and Jansen 1968: chap. 10; Tsuda 1977: 75; Morikawa 1962: 393–94; Sekiyama 1958: 237ff.; Kurasawa 1968.

[4] This discussion draws heavily on Magagna 1991; Manning 1988; Calhoun 1982, 1983; Zagorin 1982, 1:86; and Perry 1981.

befogged by kin and ritual relationships. Moreover, the hyakushō stratum fused a classlike commonality of status, interests, and relationship to the means of production with communal identity. Hyakushō status entailed de facto rights vis-à-vis elites, legitimated remonstration, and was an intrinsically collective concept. Each farmer was concerned with the survival of every other, for the failure of one did not reduce the village's tax obligation: others simply had to make up the difference (Aono 1988: 132ff.).

Indeed, some believe that popular contention was continuous with quotidian village activity (Tilly et al. 1975; Calhoun 1982: 41). Tokugawa villages were living networks of ongoing cooperative, collective actions—economic, social, religious, and political—of which contention was simply one type, under extreme conditions (Aoki M. et al. 1981, 3:65). Even though special rituals—oath taking, passing a ritual cup, and composing a self-righteous manifesto—were involved in contention, at base it was simply a mobilization of existing social collectivities for a particular purpose.[5]

The necessity of acting collectively does not, imply that the Tokugawa village was unchanging, uniform, or completely harmonious. One can easily imagine the implications of protoindustrialization for socioeconomic (and psychological) differentiation, community solidarity, and conflict. In Japan, however, nonagricultural by-employments *combined* with the hyakushō ideal; they made it possible for those with otherwise nonviable holdings to stay on the land and for the landless to stay in the village with the hope of regaining landed status (Vlastos 1986; Saitō in Jansen and Rozman 1986: 400). Thus, protoindustrialization did not lead to large-scale rural depopulation and did not erode village solidarity as much as one might imagine.

Nevertheless, protoindustrialization was an important source of economic variation from region to region (Tilly 1982, 1983). I shall look also at the type of commodities on which modern economic activities were based, in particular sericulture and cotton. Village sociopolitical organization is also relevant. Some villages were fiscally beholden to and controlled by a single lord, whereas others paid taxes to as many as a dozen overlords (Sasaki 1972: 323ff.; Hyakushō Ikki 1980: 364ff.). Each lord had administrative prerogatives with regard to those on "his" land, and these created vertical administrative channels within the village. Additionally, the village had its own comprehensive structures for administering pan-village functions. Some have predicted that such areas would exhibit less contention due to social fragmentation; I believe that there was more, because administrative responsibility was so muddied and social control so tenuous.

The same concept—fragmentation—has social implications. How did village structure and changes in it influence solidarity and the degree of internal conflict as opposed to the capacity for conflict with outsiders? There was much conflict in the Tokugawa village, over everything from a neighbor's wandering livestock to

---

[5] Although before the Tokugawa era the ikki was a special-purpose collectivity (Katsumata 1982; Aoki et al. 1981, 1:25–97, 2:29–136).

religious and social privileges. Temple and shrine groups, young men's associations, and subvillage administrative units; tenants, small farmers, and the landless—all had distinctive interests, and each could feel threatened by others in the village. The extent of such division and conflict is a matter of historiographical debate. Some see the Tokugawa village as repressive, divided, and hostile; others, as egalitarian, voluntarist, and cohesive.[6] The ingredients of internal conflict were, of course, present even if the more positive view of the village is accurate. In the first place, the creation of the Tokugawa political economy created a considerable number of basically nonviable hyakushō; thus, from the very beginning the potential for bankruptcy existed (Sasaki 1974: 18ff.). Moreover, those who began in a favored position arrogated to themselves village office, access to common land, and other privileges, which quickly became flashpoints as those below improved their economic positions. And many did so, as agricultural and protoindustrial growth shook up the economic hierarchy; indeed, so systematically did pressures for openness and participatory rights issue from the previously lower orders that some observers have described the process as the "democratization" of the village (Shōji 1970: 86ff.; Tozeren 1981; Rekishigaku Kenkyū 1985: 109ff.).

Thus inherent potential for intracommunity conflict grew as the era wore on. Even the broadening of participatory rights did not quiet things down. Indeed, now people could fight over new issues such as qualifications for office, the number of participants per household, and recall of officials (Shōji 1970: 96ff.), and even those still at the bottom of the heap began to assert their interests (Aoki M. et al. 1981, 4:82ff.; Rekishigaku Kenkyū 1985: 109ff.). Simultaneously, the village was fragmented by incursions from without by landlords and moneylenders from other villages and by the state, which increasingly tried to co-opt village officials into its structures of exploitation and social control. But we still do not know what the consequences of these changes were. It is easy to expect more internal and less external, more social and less political contention, but the co-optation of local leaders might make the state itself more salient and more a target of grievance. And what of the overall level of contention in society? Would it subside from a high magnitude of major challenges to the state to a grumbling undertone of innumerable petty social squabbles? Or might social conflict escalate into wholesale intraclass hostility? A more detailed look at the governance, structure, and control of the village clarifies things.

Community Governance

Most villages in Tokugawa Japan were subdivided administratively into groups of households (*kumi*), each with a resident leader (*kumigashira*); the village had its headman (most commonly *shōya* or *nanushi*), who in most cases governed with the assistance of a council of resident leaders or elders and was accountable to the

---

[6] For a brief introduction to this debate, see Koschmann 1978: 254ff.

assembly (*yoriai*) of village hyakushō and, in some areas, a farmers' representative (*hyakushōdai*), chosen by the freeholders for the purpose of restraining abuses of authority. The village was itself usually one of a group of villages headed by an overheadman (*ōjōya*). Up to this level all officials were commoners, and the headmen were almost always well-off and literate; all except the overheadmen were chosen by the villages themselves through family status, rotation among eligible families, discussion, or election.[7] Overheadmen were appointed by the domain or the shogunate (although the approval of their subordinate villages was sometimes required), and they enjoyed many of the privileges of the samurai. As the contact point between people and domain or state, the overheadman is an important focus of attention.

Above this point all officials were samurai: subintendants (*tedai*), intendants (*daikan*), and magistrates (*gundai* and *bugyō*) of the domain or the shogunate. But the key nexuses were between the villagers and their headman and between the village (or group of villages) and the intendant. Both headmen and intendants stood between state and society, integrated to varying degrees in each and subject to demands from both. The headmen easily lost touch with government; the intendants, with the people. Both were constantly tempted to abuse their roles for political or personal gain, and both sometimes colluded to defraud both people and regime (Hall 1955: 118; Vlastos 1986). Yet ultimately the government needed the people more than it needed any one of these officials, making end-run appeals to higher levels of government an effective threat (Aoki M. et al. 1981, 1:135–37).

Many such officials went to no little personal risk to pass on the grievances of those under their jurisdiction to higher levels of government, but for every Hachiemon there was probably one like the shogunal subintendant of Shindatsu, who, importuned in 1729 by the people for tax relief, pointed out that old people and children were unproductive and their deaths were therefore not cause for concern. The farmers were unpersuaded by this logic, and even when warned that if they did not subside he would see that *all* of them were executed, some two thousands of them went to the castle town to pursue their petition. The shogunate rejected their plea, defined it as illegal, and punished 93 of them, of whom two were in fact executed (Sasaki 1974: 131–34).

The autonomy with which the Tokugawa village carried out its administrative functions is a matter of debate. One school holds that the villages were tightly controlled and "organized like prisons" (Bix 1986: xxviii, 109). I maintain, however, that although their authority was strictly circumscribed and delegated from above, as long as the villagers stayed put, paid their taxes, and neither

---

[7] In some areas village headmen were appointed by district samurai officials. There were additional local terms for all these official positions; there were also local variations and differences between domain and Tokugawa house lands in this administrative hierarchy. See Aono 1988: 66ff., 114ff.; Kelly 1985: 32–33; Chambliss 1965: 5ff.; Tozeren 1981: 91–92.

harbored criminals nor spawned insurrection, their freedom of action was considerable.[8]

Censuses and land surveys, taxes, sumptuary laws, rules for official behavior, regulations regarding status relationships, and social control were all officially in the hands of the government. Nevertheless, villages drew up their own internal codes, bought and sold property, borrowed and lent money, sued and were sued, and taxed themselves as needed. They "usurped" government roles in social control, public works, irrigation, and common land utilization, and intravillage groups established their own rules regarding morality, gambling, mutual assistance, and relationships with outsiders. Relief, while officially in the hands of the government, was in fact handled predominantly on the community level.

The village's relationship with the government in regard to the harvest was, of course, zero-sum, but by the early eighteenth century this and civil order were two of only a few areas in which the government insisted on its prerogatives and the people complied. For the rest, in the perhaps hyperbolic words of Ogyū Sorai (in Maruyama 1974: 128), "the lord of the fief and the peasants look upon each other as sworn enemies." Overall, village communities' de facto autonomy appears considerable (see, e.g., Magagna 1991; Bercé 1990: 7ff.), and even in the Meiji era it was circumscribed only slowly. The new rulers' attention was directed first to the national level, and although local authority was delegated from Tokyo, it was not until after the end of the first decade that villages actually came under the direct and unceasing scrutiny of the state (H. Smith 1981: 44; Chambliss 1965: 81).

The village headman and his colleagues were ubiquitous. There were large numbers of village officials, all commoners and many privileged and supported by allowances provided by the people, in addition to their regular taxes. (This practice was such a source of discontent that in 1713 the position of overheadman was abolished in shogunal territories [Aono 1988: 114].) They had considerable room to manipulate or evade the will of the village assembly, although extraordinary levies often required the approval of the peasant representative (Chambliss 1965: 47ff.). They enforced the laws, kept the village books, and allocated and collected taxes; it is easy to imagine their opportunities for graft, favoritism, and self-enrichment (Nakane and Oishi 1990: 53–54; Rekishi Kagaku 1974: 77ff.) and also the frequency of their confrontations with the people. They often faced the unenviable choice of leading their people and risking their lives or quelling discontent and risking disgrace or physical violence.

Thus village leaders and other commoner elites have invited varying judgments. On the negative side, some have written them off as pawns of the authorities (see, inter alia, Bix 1986), and it is unquestionable that in the course of the Tokugawa era rural elites were increasingly co-opted both politically, by

---

[8] See also Chambliss 1965: 2; Yasumaru 1975: 195; Tozeren 1981: 76ff.; Nakane and Oishi 1990: 57–58; Vlastos 1986; Bercé 1990: 7ff.

the government, and economically, by opportunities to participate on favored terms in the emerging protoindustrial and commercial economy. As incorporation into the regime and private economic gain both increased, the benefits of village office became less important and the leadership of collective action less attractive. The unsurprising consequence was the abdication by village officials of the roles the people expected them to play. Over the course of the era particular forms of contention premised on leadership of unified village communities by their formal leaders declined.[9]

On the more positive side are those who see the opening and reform—or even democratization—of village administration, the revivification of leadership in the hands of lower elements in the village, and a consequent increase in community potential for effective action (Tozeren 1981; Kaikyū Tōsō 1981: 232ff.; Aoki M. et al. 1981, 4:72ff.). But such evaluations emphasize the emergence of new leadership elements and the downward devolution of power. Traditional elites may indeed have imbibed the changing intellectual currents of the later Tokugawa era, but insofar as they *acted* politically they did so increasingly in protection of their own interests or those of the samurai (Motoyama 1962: 263).

Each of these positions has merit, contingent on local and current circumstances. In some areas village reform proceeded apace; in others administration remained in the hands of the old elite. In many cases leaders reneged on their obligations; in others they remained true to the moral imperatives of the community. In general, contention moved from west to east during the era (White 1992b: figs. 10, 11); so did protoindustrialization, but so also did village reform (Horie 1960: 86ff.). We cannot sort these things out at the macrolevel, and sweeping judgments of local officials seem risky. When leaders did not lead, it may well have been because the village was so divided that it was no longer leadable (Kelly 1985). When they did, again, it might have been not because of their virtue but because village social forces left them no choice. And even when village leaders abdicated or disintegrated, contention did not necessarily decline, for the same process of social differentiation created new issues and activist elements such as Bansuke and new forms of contention such as food riots, which were less dependent on formal leadership.

The evolution of local leadership continued beyond the endpoint of my study. Despite Meiji changes, pre-Restoration individuals and groups continued to hold office in many locales (Chambliss 1965: 72ff.; Sasaki 1973: 31; 1979: 176ff.; McClain 1988). Nor was the process of division and reintegration of village leadership, as older elements admitted or gave way to new ones, resolved in the first decade of the new era (Horie 1960: 86ff.). Thus, although structure and context changed dramatically on the macrolevel, the microlevel social context of popular contention changed much less slowly, and that, I believe, is one

---

[9] Yokoyama 1977; Kimmel 1988: chap. 8; Koschmann 1987: chap. 4; Fujitani 1982: 132–215; Rowe 1989: 349ff.

reason why we do not see significant changes in contention in the first years of Meiji.

Class and Occupational Structure

The response of communities to outside threats and their patterns of internal conflict are critically influenced by their internal cohesion; the economic and social changes typical of the Tokugawa village suggest that heterogeneity was increasing during the era. To the cleavage between commoners and samurai were added those between landlord and tenant, poor and rich, creditor and debtor, employer and employee, and producer and merchant (Fukaya 1979: 110; Sasaki 1973: 392ff.). But to leap from heterogeneity to disunion is too pat. For one thing, dimensions of differentiation can crosscut rather than cumulate; thus, a debtor could be his creditor's fellow hyakushō, and a part-tenant might also rent out a piece of his own land. Second, objective heterogeneity does not necessarily entail subjective division. And third, even deeply divided communities may, if the threat is adequate, be able to unite against outsiders (Bercé 1990: 342–43).

The three social trends most characteristic of the Tokugawa village were leveling in the seventeenth century, continuity from the seventeenth to the eighteenth centuries, and differentiation in the eighteenth and ninteenth. The first trend was initially political: masses of peasants moved upward into hyakushō status and a (lesser) mass of marginal samurai was pushed downward into the peasantry (Vlastos 1986: chap. 1), but real equalization was not immediate. Some freeholders continued to owe traditional labor services to their betters and suffered discrimination in temple and shrine affairs and access to common land and village office. It was late in the century before their struggles against such practices succeeded (T. Smith 1959: chap. 3, 49, 134; Sasaki 1974: 5ff., 170–71). Moreover, the taxes imposed on the new freeholding stratum were initially allocated equally to all households, thus burdening smaller farmers far more heavily than large ones (Sasaki 1974: 11ff.). The result was, again, a process of demands and protests which led eventually to almost universal allocations based on each family's kokudaka.

These processes put flesh on the bones of hyakushō status and led, by the early eighteenth century, to a farming stratum that resembled a class in the Marxist sense more closely than at any other time (Kaikyū Tōsō 1981: 230ff.; Burton 1978: 166), and the middle of the century witnessed a flourishing of forms of contention singularly dependent on village cohesion (Yokoyama 1977). Full homogeneity was never the case, however. Some hyakushō started off with more or better land and influence over local labor markets and common lands and were thus in a position to reclaim and develop farmland and appropriate a disproportionate share of the surplus (Hayashi 1976a: 51ff.). These surpluses became capital, which could be used either to further one's own productive efforts or to extend credit to less viable farmers (Nakane and Oishi 1990: 46). Thus, even as the freeholding stratum became internally solidified in the eighteenth century, a landless element began to drop out of it and another element began to rise and diversify.

During the latter half of the eighteenth century this differentiation became the dominant trend. Concentration of landholdings, increasing tenantry, smaller units of kinship and agricultural production, and diminished cooperative agriculture became visible everywhere (T. Smith 1959). As noted, these changes did not necessarily imply the immiserization of the landless; indeed, they were largely the result of the increased value of labor relative to land (Craig 1979: 293). But in either case, the administrative ideal—that everyone lived, cultivated, and paid taxes in the same village—disintegrated (Kelly 1985: 34, 45). By the nineteenth century, village social structure was a lengthening continuum, with a small number of prosperous landlords/creditors/merchants known as *gōnō* at the top, a number of agricultural and protoindustrial laborers and small tenants at the bottom, and a mélange of landowners, larger tenants, owner-tenants of all types, and better-off wage earners in between (Sasaki 1974: 178ff.; 1979: 133–34). The continuum was increasingly differentiated by wealth and occupation and decreasingly integrated by kinship: relationships became less and less traditionalistic, reciprocal, and ritual and more and more contractual, impersonal, and rigid. Tenants came to identify also—or even more—with their fellow tenants than with their kin (Najita and Koschmann 1982: 150ff.).

As noted, there are those who hold that these economic processes led in the latter years of the Tokugawa era to fragmentation and the polarization of the rural population between a few rich and many poor, with a shrinking middle stratum in between—as happened in protoindustrializing societies elsewhere in the world.[10] Such arguments are flawed in a variety of ways.[11] First, fragmentation can occur through tenantization, loss of land by sale or pawn, entry into part- or full-time by-employment, and in so many other ways that it becomes highly unlikely that any single social or political condition will result. Second, the evidence of polarization usually offered is the number of landless (*mutaka* or *mizunomi*) in a village or the kokudaka distribution of the households in it, but typical presentations describe as "significantly polarized" villages with landless populations running all the way from zero to 80 percent of the whole. Third, decreases in landless farmers are attributed to their exit from agriculture; that is, they do not disconfirm the argument. Fourth, village statistics are less and less accurate measures of social structure as cross-village landholding increases: a magnate in one village might own a tiny plot, and thus look poor, in another. Fifth, data that show significant rates of landlessness by the beginning of the seventeenth century—if nationally representative—suggest that any process of fragmentation was not distinctive to the Tokugawa era. Finally, landholding is an

[10] The Japanese term for the fragmentation thesis is *nōmin kaisō bunkai ron.* See, e.g., Tokyo Hyakunen Shi 1973, 1:1266–67; Sasaki 1973: 59–60; Tilly 1982; Huang 1985: 17, 106, 118.
[11] For a more detailed refutation, see White 1989; for typical expositions of the fragmentation thesis, see Ōuchi 1980 and Sasaki 1973.

imperfect measure of social position in an era when nonagricultural income was growing.

Certain facets of the thesis are quite valid, in particular the increase of the rural landless and their description as, at best, a "semiproletariat" (Sasaki 1979). Many unquestionably lost their land through pawn or bankruptcy. Such people often did not leave the village. In the later Tokugawa era there was enough economic activity that most could find local work, and many could even nurse the hope of regaining hyakushō status. They constituted a particularly volatile element in village society, for they were as vulnerable to the food supply as any urbanites; they had no ties to cooperative production groups, no pressure to conform to group norms, and presumably little love for the status quo; and they often retained a *very* strong desire for upward mobility (Sasaki 1979: 18–40; T. Smith 1959: 165). But they were not one of only two significant strata, nor were they necessarily the largest stratum in the village.

One cannot directly predict stratum- or class-based hostility from differential social position or social position from landholding alone (Kelly 1985: 9ff.; Scott 1985: 147). Nor can one confidently predict social disintegration from friction. In a freer and growing economy competition may increase manyfold; yet, if all accept the rules of the game, there can be both winners and losers and a continuing, coherent game. The nature and rate of economic growth in Tokugawa Japan suggest that intravillage contention, though it may well have increased, was based more on competition than immiserization (that is, was horizontal as well as vertical), and it was facilitated as much by new resources in the hands of previously subservient elements in the village as by the threat of loss of resources (T. Smith 1959: 172ff., chap. 12).

What one sees in the later Tokugawa village thus seems less like bifurcation or polarization than like pluralistic differentiation of a sometimes kaleidoscopic complexity.[12] Naturally, this process differed from region to region and even from community to community. It led, I have found, to greater magnitudes of overall contention and, *ceteris paribus*, to a greater relative frequency of conflict among commoners, as opposed to political confrontations with the state and its samurai agents. There was, moreover, a relative increase in village leaders as targets rather than as leaders of conflict. In either case, contending leaders and followers exhibited more socioeconomic variety.

Tokugawa cities, for their part, were richly variegated from the start. Inhabitants of the castle towns in particular ran the gamut from nobles of almost royal stature to the marginal and starving. Such towns were arenas of commerce, finance, consumption, and every form of production—protoindustrial, agricultural, architectural, cultural. They were also extensively organized under both samurai and commoner officials, as we shall see. From our perspective, the Tokugawa city had three important characteristics: a samurai population, a floating population, and a growing lower class.

---

[12] Tozeren 1981; Vlastos 1986; Kelly 1985; Chambliss 1965: 18–40; T. Smith 1959.

Unlike the countryside, the cities included a significant samurai element. The samurai population nationwide ran to almost 10 percent of the total, making it proportionately much larger than the nobility of, for example, ancien régime France, and it was concentrated in the cities. In Edo perhaps half the population was samurai and their dependents. Their presence provided more coercive resources and more direct surveillance of the commoner population—deterrents to contention—and more government agents and offices—attractors of contention.

The samurai had their work cut out for them—and their commoner minions—for the cities were also home to a great unaffiliated, unbound population. In the village almost everyone was accounted for and usually beholden to someone, but in the city masses of people came and went undocumented, and those who sold their labor casually were beholden to no one but that day's employer. This floating population had neither participatory rights, townsman (*chōnin*) status, nor allegiance to the status quo.

Also, they were predominantly poor. Servants, apprentices, peddlers, independent craftsmen, and day laborers grew in numbers during the era and, at least in Edo, grew even more deracinated as short-term work arrangements replaced long-term servitude and apprenticeships.[13] I am interested in them not because they were a festering sump of insurrectionary fever (although many of their betters so regarded them) but because they were vulnerable to reductions in the food supply and were disarticulated from structures of social control. Given the inevitable interruptions in the food supply, urban contention, mostly social, increased in the later years of the era. Politically, on the other hand, coercive presence had the opposite effect.

Social Threats and Social Controls

Country people in Tokugawa Japan lived in an essentially unpoliced, but hardly uncontrolled, society. In the city, by contrast, people were both controlled and policed. Control was exercised as part of the overall administrative structure and was, as in the village, largely in the hands of commoners, but there was also an explicit police presence.

Edo, for example, was a city of coercion: the samurai were forced to live there, and the lords were forced to reside there every other year, and both were military elites (Nishiyama 1972; Yoshihara 1980). It was also a city of violence: brawls, tumultuous festivals, extortion and intimidation, and entertainment districts whose pitch of enthusiasm was not only figuratively riotous may not have been of much concern to the state, but they created an atmosphere in which the authorities felt compelled to take a comprehensive, if normally permissive, stand (William Kelly, personal communication; Takeuchi Makoto, personal communication).

---

[13] Hayashi 1976b: 187–88; Yamada 1984: 282ff.; T. Smith 1959: chap. 8; Krieger 1967: 26ff.; Minami 1978; Aono 1988: 209; Saitō 1986; van der Woude et al. 1990: chap. 13.

Social order was imposed in principle by discipline in family and workplace, but the authorities were not kidding themselves.[14] Over the city of Edo stood three magistracies: those of Temples and Shrines, Accounts, and the City. The first had jurisdiction over all crimes committed in those precincts; the second oversaw legal affairs in Tokugawa house lands nationwide and handled all suits by commoners, even in private domains, in the region surrounding Edo; the third was a combined governor, police chief, and chief justice of Edo. There were two city magistrates in Edo, each with fire and police officials under him and firemen and policemen—the ranks of whom were commoners—under them. Separately, they presided over three commoner elders (*machidoshiyori*) who in turn administered some 250 neighborhood headmen (*machi nanushi*), whose neighborhoods were subdivided into groups of households (*goningumi*), each with a group headman (Katō 1990). These groups had surveillance and intelligence, in addition to administrative, functions, but they were nearly impossible to perform in areas with large numbers of highly mobile renters and floating laborers (Minami 1978: 241).

Each domain had extraterritorial jurisdiction in its own Edo estates and offices, but outside the samurai quarters the streets were in the hands of government patrols and fixed watchmen. The patrols were of several kinds, of which the most numerous were the three hundred or so policelike samurai *yoriki* and *dōshin* (McClain and Merriman 1990: 24). Additionally, neighborhood residents were required to establish and staff watch posts (*tsujiban* and *jishinban*), whose functions were preventive and investigative, although the jishinban also managed fire protection, relief, and resident registration. In latter-day Edo there were roughly nine hundred tsujiban and, in principle at least, one jishinban in each of Edo's seventeen hundred plus neighborhoods. Thus, although there was no unified police organization in Edo, there was a social control presence.[15] In a city of a million this presence was rather thin, especially with respect to prevention or regular patrols, but the authorities nevertheless seem to have been capable of having someone on the spot in the event of contentious incidents.

The question is, how did the government use this apparatus? In Japan, as elsewhere, there was considerable anxiety over the floating population and swift provision of relief in time of dearth, but actual rioting did not draw the immediate or sanguinary response one might expect (Mousnier 1988: chap. 7; Bohstedt 1983: 1–5). In 1787 a long run of rotten weather and corrupt, profligate, and inept government led to price hikes and rumors of hoarding in the northern city of Aomori. When a merchant was discovered sneaking rice out of the city for delivery to more profitable markets, the city blew up and ten shops were wrecked (Harada 1982: 3ff.; Aoki K. 1981: 378). The domain quickly acquiesced in the people's demands for price cuts and a ban on grain exports and distributed food

---

[14] This paragraph and the next rely heavily on Shigematsu 1986.
[15] See Shigematsu (1986: 77) and Katō (1990) for a discussion of yet other types of patrol organs and watch posts.

and money. It then brought in its forces, reneged on the demands, and arrested forty-six leaders, of whom all but one—who died in jail—were interrogated and freed.

This outcome might look dismal to some, but in the context of Tokugawa-era coercive practices it is lenient. The reasons are threefold: there was no way to catch the real leaders in most urban contention; conciliation was the best policy in time of dearth; and contention against manifestly amoral commercial practices was quasi-legitimate anyway. In fact, the Aomori episode, as we shall see, was not atypical of the official response to social conflict in the city. In the official view, as long as it did not directly threaten the state, such conflict was best handled only after it had essentially run its destructive course. The people seem to have perceived this posture and acted accordingly. The control process—and thus the whole process of contention—took altogether different forms, regardless of the magnitude of an event, in social and political confrontations.

Toward the end of the era two successive changes occurred. In the 1860s, as the shogunate neared collapse, the laws requiring samurai residence in Edo were revoked and a mass exodus resulted. Politically dissident samurai moved to Edo and, between the atmosphere of violence they created and the exodus of government personnel, the city became essentially unpoliced; the situation practically invited popular contention (Motoyama 1962: 299ff.; Totman 1980: 21–33). Then, after the Restoration, the situation was reversed. Even though a modern police organization did not exist during my period of study, there were enough elements of the new imperial army in Tokyo in particular and the cities in general to ensure civil order. Consequently, I have found a relative decline in urban contention in the first decade of Meiji.

Across regions, the most salient characteristic of Tokugawa social control was its absence from the village scene. No significant rural police was established until the 1880s, and throughout the Tokugawa era village headmen were on their own, at least when contention first broke out (Leavell 1981; Kitazawa 1982). Their primary strategy was deterrence—periodic mandatory reading to the assembled villagers of regulatory edicts, mutual surveillance and responsibility by the five-household groups and the village itself, the moral suasion of the headman, and the ultimate certainty (or so it was portrayed) of state reprisal. The resulting opportunity structure gave planners and initiators of contention great leeway but promised sanctions farther down the road.

The authorities preferred to rely on rural officials for order. They did, of course, hold their own military forces and criminal investigators in reserve, but unless directly confronted, they preferred to work flexibly—if duplicitously—first to dissuade, then to defuse or simply stand aside, and finally to punish. Everyone seems to have known how the system worked. Social conflicts could be pursued a long way with little or no government involvement and little threat of sanction, and even political protest could usually attain maximum partipation and confrontation levels before encountering direct suppression, and could result in real gains. During the event, those most in danger were the headmen and those who resisted popular demands to mobilize, but after the dust had settled the people knew that the state piper would have to be paid. How all these mechanisms actually worked is perhaps best demonstrated with an example, which suggests why people might have been deterred from contending and also the ambiguity and incompleteness of this deterrence.

My case in point is the Demma Rebellion, which blew up in the region north and west of Edo at the end of 1764 in response to an increase in the transport corvée along the highroads (Kitazawa 1982: 44–180). Initially, several thousand people gathered in response to messages posted along the roads and passed about the villages in the affected region—messages that called for every family to send one male between the ages of fifteen and sixty and threatened unresponsive villages with fire and destruction. (One reluctant village was attacked, perhaps enhancing participation.) The upshot of the meeting was the mobilization of a delegation of perhaps ten thousand, complete with food, clothing, bedding, and village banners. At first, the people acceded to the pleas of area headmen, clerics, and intendants to leave the appeal to them, and a delegation of one official and one cleric from each village went to Edo to lodge a petition for cancellation of the corvée increase.

This petition was rejected, but the Tribunal sent a representative to talk with the advancing popular host, which by now had grown to over a hundred thousand. His entreaties were in vain and the protesters continued toward the capital, enhanced in numbers by a wave of demands-cum-threats for mobilization to villages en route. Attacked by a samurai force at Kumaya, they sustained many casualties and fled in disarray. Nevertheless, the shogunate rescinded the new corvée for the moment. These two developments, one might think, would have settled the matter, but in a pattern seen in other incidents as well, the popular organization instead fragmented into multiple groups, now focused on the headmen of villages that had not participated, on the merchants who had requested the corvée increase in the first place, and on those in commerce and transport who profited from the corvée.[16]

The first week of 1765 saw bands of people scouring the countryside settling old scores, leading sometimes to confrontations with whole villages that defended the actions of their own headmen. The headmen themselves began to gather and confer and over four hundred of them reached a consensus. Recognizing that if they resisted the protesters they might be burned out but if they participated the shogunate would have their heads, they resolved to stay clear of the protest in the hope that their people would refuse to join and it would fizzle out. They also organized a goon squad, which confronted the largest body of protesters on the fifth day of the first month and killed over a hundred of them

---

[16] The typical highway corvée obliged villages along the way to provide a certain number of man-days and horse-days of transport annually, for which the merchants who used this work force paid at stipulated rates. The imposition was unpopular, for it drained resources from other work and the remuneration system invited exploitation by the merchants.

and wounded several hundred. Finally, they sent delegates to Edo asking for assistance.

What they got first was an official representative who admonished them: If a message comes to your village, trace it back to its origin; if suspicious persons come to your village, arrest them. Second, the shogunate began to send investigators into the countryside to round up officials from participating villages for interrogation. Still, the progovernment headmen were on their own, and despite their best efforts, the wave of destruction swept the region for another week or more. Finally, the authorities' strategy seems to have worked: official unity eventually starved the movement of popular replenishment, and the ominous arrival of the inquisitors reminded everyone that the state would eventually have its way.

And it did. Early in 1765, after several dozen of those rounded up had reportedly died in prison, it handed down punishments to over four hundred persons. One was executed, sixty were banished in varying degree, and the rest were fined, manacled, dismissed from office, reprimanded, or confined for a period of time. The focus of punishment was not the rioters but those responsible for letting them participate: 101 village headmen, 90 group leaders, 50 village elders, and 57 farmers' representatives were punished, along with 74 farmers and "others."

Or did the state have its way? One presumes that the state had a real interest in raising the corvée, which it relinquished. It certainly wanted to strike fear, or at least healthy respect, into the village official class, which it presumably did, but had it cowed the people? One wonders. Whoever actually led the protest and the subsequent riots largely escaped punishment. The riot leaders in particular were probably not of the official class, and it is quite possible that their evaluation of the whole affair depended heavily on the rescission of the corvée and the successful trashing of a large number of official and mercantile establishments. If fear had been struck into certain hearts, it may not have been those of the participants at all, but those of their economic and political betters. Whipsawed between people and state, forced to organize their own coercive forces of coolies, firemen, longshoremen, and petty criminals, and liable to draconian punishment if any of "their" people slipped away to join the dissidents, they cannot have been the most reliable or enthusiastic agents of social order in the countryside (Fukaya 1978: 21–22; Yashiro 1989: 86).

Indeed, the tenuous—or at best tardily effective—nature of this arrangement was remedied by the Meiji regime (Aoki M. et al. 1981, 5:94ff.). The reorganization of the rural administrative structure was to some degree intended to make it less of a lightning rod until the new state could actually send its forces of order into every nook and cranny of the countryside.

The rural social control system I have sketched—based on deterrence, exemplary punishment, low state presence, and commoner responsibility—and the sorts of contention it shaped—easy to initiate and mobilize, willing to bargain, highly organized at the outset but hard to keep that way, and inclusive in its interests and choice of targets—omits two factors. One is relief activities, which can have a strong role in social control (Scott 1985: 11, 24). The other is nonfactors—considerations of great note in other early modern societies which do not count for much in Tokugawa Japan.

Relief—loans or grants of money, seed, or food—played a variety of roles.[17] It was used to dampen price fluctuations, to silence grumbling, and to persuade rioters to go home (or, when extended by individual merchants, at least to go burn someone else out). It was most notably an urban phenomenon, although wealthy communities and individuals everywhere were adjured by the government, and acted with self-serving conscientiousness, to set aside stores for hard times and provide aid when necessary (Sasaki 1972).

Relief was also a double-edged sword. We have seen how, in the case of Aomori, a merchant trying to slip grain out of town sparked conflict. The shogunate had standing orders for rice shipments from many areas, and any astute rural merchant knew that he would get a better price in a short-supplied city. Consequently, export of grain was a frequent generator of popular contention in rural areas. In the longer run, the burden of relief on governments was staggering: Edo escaped food rioting during the famine-ridden 1830s, but masses of persons received relief in each of several years, amounting to hundreds of thousands of bushels of grain at a time (Hyakushō Ikki 1980: 334–35; Tokyo Hyakunen Shi 1973, 1:1255–63).

Relief did work. Over and over, records indicate that collective contention was brought to an end with aid; that preemptive or quick response to demands for cheap food kept peace in some areas while less flexible places blew up (Sasaki 1972: 54; Motoyama 1962: 247, 282). When government was capable, recommendations to the wealthy, community norms, neighborhood aid and welfare offices, and effective transport created a system capable of defusing most situations.[18] But when government decayed all these measures declined; when a crop failure hit eastern Japan in 1866 on top of the extraordinary food drain of the shogun's military campaign in the west, even a flood of grain (some, for the first time, imported) and money was insufficient to prevent a wave of riots in Edo (Sasaki 1972: 264–65; Tokyo Hyakunen Shi 1973, 1:1590–91).

Thus the effects of relief were primarily on interests; as a stimulus it focuses our attention on governmental sins of omission, not commission; and we find both participants and leaders in relief-relevant contention to be of the lower orders. Finally, although the government might have been ultimately responsible for food riots and the like, when contention did break out the people were

---

[17] As in other early modern societies: Bohstedt 1983: 204; Rowe 1989: 208–28.

[18] The neighborhood offices or *machi kaisho* were largely administrative but also stored grain, which they bought and sold strategically to influence prices, and money for emergencies. These offices, supported by residents' and government contributions, offered poor relief and made loans on an ongoing basis (Katō 1990).

sufficiently aware that most food and money were in private hands. Consequently, such conflict was more social than political in nature.

Japan's social structure lacked certain factors that contributed to popular contention in other early modern societies. Tokugawa Japan was singularly free of ethnic, religious, linguistic, or other communal or regional cleavages of a contentious—and, in other societies, singularly sanguinary—nature (after Rudé 1971: 268–92). Nor was Tokugawa society home to peculiarly antisystem or otherwise clandestine groups on the order of China's secret societies (Chesneaux 1972).

Religion—specifically Christianity—did surface in perhaps the most bloody episode of popular contention in Tokugawa Japan, the Shimabara Rebellion of 1637–1638. But Shimabara—which entailed "tens of thousands" of civilian deaths and over fifteen thousand government casualties—was complicated by three factors (Morris 1975: 173–75). One was the exact degree of religious relevance: in many ways the rebellion was just popular protest against government exploitation. Another was political stability: Shimabara occurred before the Tokugawa regime was fully consolidated, and it is possible that the state's no-holds-barred response had a didactic purpose. Finally, it was one of a very few instances of samurai-commoner coalition in the entire era, and the regime was merciless in dealing with class coalitions. Perhaps what was at issue was less the actual rebellion than the shogunate's perception of it as a combination of religion and subversion of the samurai which threatened the ideological and social foundations of the entire Tokugawa state.

In any case, like the suppression of religion as a political factor, the psychic, social, and physical divorce of the nobility from the people was a masterful stroke that robbed the Japanese people of a leadership resource.[19] Japan thus perhaps stands alone in the social isolation with which the people faced the state.

Sometimes elements of the nobility challenged the state.[20] But these events proceeded in grand isolation from the people, which is exactly as the warriors wanted it. There are very few unambiguous episodes of common cause between people and nobles, and the regime's response leaves no doubt how seriously it regarded them. The first was Shimabara. The second was the rebellion of Ōshio Heihachirō, a shogunal official in Ōsaka who launched an abortive revolt on behalf of the oppressed people in 1837.[21] His coalition was unprecedented since Shimabara, and the shogunate responded as if its life were in danger, executing everyone involved in the incident. But such events as Shimabara and Ōshio's Revolt were exceedingly rare.[22]

[19] Mousnier 1970: 38ff.; Brustein and Levi 1987; Kuhn 1970; Kimmel 1988: 174ff.
[20] Shigematsu 1986: 161; Dower 1975: 385; Hayashi 1976a; Huber 1981; Najita and Koschmann 1982: 109ff.; Totman 1980.
[21] Morris 1975; Hyakushō Ikki 1982; Aoki M. et al. 1981, 1:147–49; Craig and Shively 1970.
[22] And most of the events equated with them were in fact quite ambiguous. The attempted shogunal transfer of the lord of Shōnai in 1840–41 (Kelly 1985; Hyakushō Ikki 1982) was more a series of independent movements than a single collusive movement. The peasant militias (*kiheitai, shotai,* and *nōhei*) mobilized in the last years of the Tokugawa era were firmly under the control of elites and were

After the Restoration, links between the people and *dissident* samurai were just as feared as before, and not without reason. If any of the dozens of samurai risings of the early Meiji years had coalesced with some of the larger popular conflicts of the hundreds occurring in the same period, the Meiji state might have been short-lived. Thus the new regime moved unequivocally against such links (Tozeren 1981). A riot in Shinano province in 1871 had overtones of samurai leadership, and after government troops put it down additional forces were sent to arrest over 600 people, of whom several died under interrogation, 28 were executed, 124 exiled, and 477 imprisoned. Exemplary social control definitely did not end with the Tokugawa system.

Thus to understand popular contention in Tokugawa Japan we need to pay attention to those dogs that did not bark, as well as those that did. The absence in Japan of grievances, opportunities, or resources present elsewhere leads us to look for alternatives or for different patterns of contention. The absence of communal cleavages implies relatively moderate contention; that of samurai leadership, a wholly different process of catalysis, mobilization, and leadership from that employed elsewhere in the world.

Leaders, Followers, and the Social Context

The samurai, then, provided little leadership for popular contention, except in the early years of the era when samurai pressed down into the commoner class or cast adrift when their lords lost favor with the Tokugawa led a number of protests (Kokushō 1971: 8ff.). After that, leadership came primarily from preexisting roles, the natural leadership of communities. That is, social context determined leadership. In setting up village leaders and giving them considerable freedom of action, the Tokugawa took a risk on their commitment to social order. Moreover, in not providing either police or courts, the regime allowed the emergence of individuals, probably present in every village, who were both talented and trusted in the area of conflict resolution (after Fukawa 1976: 337ff.). Such individuals might keep the level of conflict low, but they were also potential leaders of popular contention.

During the later years of the Tokugawa era such individuals increased in number (Fukaya 1983: 274). The social context changed: economic growth, socioeconomic and status differentiation, and increasing levels of education broadened the horizons of more and more people, diminished their integration into the structures of the status quo, and gave them the resources to be effective social and political actors. During the first century of the era fewer than 15 percent of the counties for which data are available had schools for commoners (*terakoya*); by the late eighteenth century this figure had risen to 75 percent and

often used *against* popular contention (Sippel 1977: 309; Koschmann 1987; Rekishi Kagaku 1974: 312–13). And a series of imperial loyalist risings in 1863 were primarily aristocratic, making no real appeal to or alliance with any broad spectrum of the people (Sasaki 1979: 45–63; Huber 1981: 117ff.; Najita and Koschmann 1982: 116ff.).

by the mid-nineteenth century to 95 percent.[23] Actual enrollment figures are unavailable, but an extraordinary expansion of basic literacy occurred, and leadership accordingly became more heterogeneous. We also see more contention because, I believe, there were more people around to take the lead.

Indeed, the "mobilization potential" of the entire society grew during the era, and the ability of the fugitive Hyōsuke to support himself in his peregrinations by tutoring the children of those with whom he stayed suggests a general appetite for education. Literacy and physical and social mobility create not only more leaders but more followers as well. The entire Tokugawa system relied on "rule by document." Land and property rights, loans and pawns, commercial transactions, births and marriages and divorces and deaths, tax assessments and payments, land surveys, litigation, and a stream of government edicts—all were documented, and more and more people became enmeshed in the world of the written word, the contract, the diary, the official report, and the protest manifesto (Aoki M. et al. 1981, 4:168, 181ff.). The people were unarmed and most contention was illegal; thus they relied heavily on the legitimacy of their actions, which had to be expressed in written petitions and manifestoes (Aoki M. et al. 1981, 5:329). Mobilization required circular messages, written accusations of corrupt officials and rapacious merchants, broadsides, handbills, and written threats. Rule by document elicited protest by document, and literacy was a resource in increasing supply in the later years of the era.

Thus both fixed structures and social changes influenced the composition of leadership and participation in popular contention. The fixed structures of community and class generated types of leaders and groups of potential participants; increasing fluidity in both broadened the variety and probably increased the sum total of potential leaders and followers. The social context of contention was enriched by resources of literacy, sophistication, and risk taking. Increasingly heterogeneous leadership and participation could have resulted in more violent contention as people with less legitimate political voice and more risk-tolerant leaders ran up against the state. But in early modern Japan, the effect was the opposite: the common people were fairly perceptive and hardly suicidal; they recognized their handicap and avoided violent confrontation.

The Demographic Context

One factor of recurring interest in studies of popular contention is population. Migrant, urban, and increasingly dense populations have been linked with high levels of contention in both modern and premodern societies (Goldstone 1991; Kuhn 1970; White 1992b). In early modern Japan, we gain the most explanatory

[23] The data are from Mombushō 1980; for corroborative data, see Dore 1984; H. Smith 1981: 22. Nishikawa Shunsaku (1979: 208–11) attributes much of this growth to an increase in the supply of teachers rather than in the demands of students. However one looks at it, the expansion is extraordinary.

mileage from urbanism. It is not the rate of urbanization or the size of cities which appears to be the important aspect but rather the nature of the urban population. The size of Japan's cities was essentially set by the middle of the seventeenth century (Hall 1981: 231), and Japan's urban population remained somewhere between 14 percent and 17 percent of the total for the remainder of the era. As early modern societies go, this is a high figure, but even in 1875 almost two-thirds of Japan's 630 counties had no urban settlements with as many as three thousand inhabitants, and only 21 had more than half of their populations in such places (Rikugun 1880, 1976). In the late 1860s and early 1870s there may even have been deurbanization, as the samurai left the castle towns.[24] Overall, however, the quantitative situation in regard to urbanization was in the late 1870s still essentially what it had been during the later Tokugawa period (Kajinishi 1978: 35).

The stasis of the urban population is a problem from the perspective of urban*ization* arguments, since contention in the cities grew during the era; indeed, in the last decades of the era migration to Edo, for example, declined while contention there increased (White 1992b). But it is consistent with urban*ism* arguments, that is, that certain characteristics of the urban population are linked to contention. Specifically, urban poverty increased during the era, and few accounts of urban conflict omit mention of participation by peddlers, day laborers, vagrants, ragpickers, room renters, and so forth.[25] As the finances of domains and shogunate were strained, retainers' stipends were cut and the samurai population stagnated; many samurai families were themselves near poverty and their demand for hired help and goods and services of all kinds fell (Toyoda 1962: 260ff.; Hayami 1988b: 201). As the economies of the major cities declined, the fortunes of those at the bottom of the economic ladder suffered. In many castle towns a "casualization" of the labor force occurred, reducing the control exerted by contracts, apprenticeships, and live-in arrangements (Saitō 1986). Finally, with the relaxation in 1862 of the requirement of samurai residence in Edo, the shogunate also ordered the lords to reduce their retinues, throwing several tens of thousands of servants out of work (Tsukahira 1966: 135–36; Tokyo Hyakunen Shi 1973, 1:1557). Many such individuals must simply have left town, but one must agree with those who see urban poverty on the rise and urban social organization declining. This decline suggests another way in which the urban population figures in contention. If poverty and social disorganization were in fact elements in urban conflict, this could explain why we see relatively more social conflict—focused on merchants and not relying on

---

[24] Rozman in Jansen and Rozman 1986; Totman 1980: 440; Minami 1978: 55; Toyoda 1962: 296.
[25] A significant portion of such social elements were migrants, and therefore, some link contention to migration, rather than poverty. But the motives for migration were mixed and not necessarily linked to poverty (Hayami 1988b: 116–17, 174), and thus I focus on means, not motion. It is also important to differentiate between poverty and vulnerability, which all urbanites experienced and which I presume did not change substantially during the era.

careful planning and organization—and relatively less political protest in the cities.

The social context of Tokugawa Japan was relevant in many ways to patterns of popular contention. The macrostructure of class, and its imbrication with the political economy, helped determine interests in and opportunities and resources for contention. In a rigidly hierarchical system antipathy was inevitable; in a closed class system it would have been largely pent up; in an unpoliced society it had plenty of room to fester unchecked. But contention was also a relatively mild affair in Tokugawa Japan: the class structure militated against interclass alliances, and sociocultural homogeneity militated against communal and religious conflict, all of which achieved frightening levels in other early modern societies.

These macrostructures do not provide qualitative explanations, however. In a politicized economy, should we expect contention to be directed toward more social or more political targets? Political targets were always there, but with the decay of the polity the social aspects of the system became relatively salient. And social conflict, less likely to incur deterrent repression, suggests growing overall levels of contention later in the era.

Below the structures of the political economy, the most significant social structure was the community. The cities had certain qualities associated with contention, but so did the villages, and although one sees some association between urbanism and contention (White 1992a), one can argue that contention was highest in both urban cores and highland regional peripheries (White 1988a; Skinner 1988). I suspect, nevertheless, that the relationship is in fact between contention and vulnerability (consumer on the one hand and ecological on the other), not community structure.

Community structure does have an impact, however, through its governing and socioeconomic dimensions. Higher degrees of administrative coherence are associated with lower levels of contention (Sasaki 1972: 330ff.) By virtue of his position the village headman was the focus of much conflict, either as leader or target, and much of that conflict was social, directed at him rather than higher agents of the state. As the headman was progressively incorporated into the state's system, this governing structure stimulated more conflict, as did the social structure, which generated more varied interests. Both leaders and followers in collective action were lower in status later in the era. Related to this downward shift was a relative increase in social conflict. Official targets were farther away, and although cohesion may have been necessary for protest, the people required no unity to squabble among themselves (Huang 1985: chap. 14). Facilitating these processes, meanwhile, was the spread of education, although literacy was perhaps more essential to political protest than to social conflict: a petition has to be written; a window can just be smashed.

One reason for the lack of a strong urban-rural continuum in contention may be that, although urban interests in and resources for contention were high, control structures (including poor relief) were more firmly in place there. There was more room to plot, and especially to mobilize, in the countryside. But the presence of these structures may help us explain qualitative differences between city and village; specifically, I find social contention—easier to mobilize, requiring less planning, and far safer as long as agents of the state were avoided—relatively frequent in the city, and political protest in rural areas. This finding is underlined by the political and demographic context of the cities: less coherently and comprehensively organized and more characterized by the unintegrated poor. The increase in urban poverty during the era implies an explanation for the absolute increase in the magnitude of contention in cities and in the proportion of contention generated by issues of livelihood rather than policy or administrative behavior.

4

THE IDEOLOGICAL AND PHILOSOPHICAL CONTEXT

Did popular contention in early modern Japan derive attractiveness or support, or draw symbols, from or in contradiction to the prevailing mentality or culture of the time? The notion that deep-seated perceptions of the world and of society are relevant to contention confronts two opposing views. The first is the "mob" view: that contenders are swept along on an unthinking tide of passion and unlikely to be affected by prevailing values and norms. The second is the acultural rational-choice view: that contenders are driven by a universalistic calculus that should lead any individual, in any time or place, to react identically to identical stimuli. I hew rather to the views of such as Yves-Marie Bercé, for whom "a revolt is a cultural event before it is the possible product of economic coincidence" (1990: 334). In crisis individuals act in accord not with narrow self-interest but with "deeply entrenched 'root paradigms'" such as institutions and values, which structure their behavioral responses (Najita and Koschmann 1982: 129). Contention must be thinkable before it can be calculable.

I shall not make a case for explicit popular concepts of social contract, right of resistance, or popular sovereignty (Maruyama 1974: xxix). Many early modern societies had political and social institutions that accommodated a "rough, popular, customary, and conservative justice," of which popular contention was the "ultimate sanction," and "tended to turn a blind eye when [the people] chose to settle their affairs by popular law" (Bercé 1990: 46, 272, 337; 1980: 253). And law it may be called: a contentious "body of sanctions which amounted to nothing less than a popular or traditional code of law" for the protection of certain basic norms and values of popular culture (Bercé 1990: 45).

The Content of Popular Consciousness

The popular culture of Tokugawa Japan was a primary source of the interests that led people to contend. For our purposes, the most important characteristics of the culture of contention were its moderation and its focus on justice, that is, on the observation of customary "rights," the protection of status, and reciprocity as the obligation of elites and prosperous commoners.

Popular contention in Tokugawa Japan provides no evidence that its participants desired to destroy the political, economic, or social status quo.[1] Absence of this desire is not the reason that revolution did not occur—revolutions can well begin with modest, deferential overtures (Scott 1985: 340ff.)—but the absence of millenarian or radical ideas in popular culture powerfully shaped the incidence, magnitude, and form of popular contention.

The nonradical nature of Tokugawa contention is visible in four areas. Economically, when the people attacked manifestations of the protoindustrial process, it was not out of simple opposition but out of opposition to arbitrary, coercive, culturally unsanctioned imposition of the new (Thompson 1966: 521ff.; Tozeren 1981: 549ff.). Politically, not only did the people invoke the values of the status quo in making their case, but they consistently appealed to the duly constituted authorities. Socially, when the people fought among themselves, they sought to force others to live up to community norms. And perhaps most striking, judicially, in the aftermath of many incidents the shogunate simply summoned suspects to Edo and they went, apparently neither resisting nor delaying (Yashiro 1989: 98–99).

The common people of Tokugawa Japan did not demand equitable treatment or fairness from their rulers (Vlastos 1986), but they did demand justice, the observation of popularly felt rights to the protection of their status and livelihood and to reciprocal treatment. Rights were defined (sometimes cynically and instrumentally) in comparison with other times, places, and authorities, and they changed as people's self-perceptions changed (Ravina 1992). It was the authorities' obligation to protect principles, or *ri*, a word that connotes rightness, moral justice, or "the way things should be" (Aoki M. et al. 1981, 4:44–45). And when things were *not* the way they should be, popular remonstration indicates clearly that people felt entitled or even obliged to press for redress (see also Thompson 1966: 80ff.).

These "rights" were not individual, or to such things as freedom of expression or association, or even primarily to physical subsistence. Rather, the rights most relevant to popular contention were collective, the rights of family and village to economic viability and preservation of sociopolitical status (Vlastos 1986: intro.). A just world was one in which the position of freeholding farmer was assured, and the village was assured a level of livelihood which permitted it to pay its taxes and

---

[1] Despite the efforts of, e.g., Hayashi Motoi (1976b: 218) and Shōji Kichinosuke et al. (1981: 392).

maintain social coherence and a "decent" level of living which fulfilled, in terms of dignity, social recognition, and community membership, "what is locally defined as a fully human existence" (Scott 1985: 236–37).

The right to status and solvency was not conceived in isolation from the people's obligations to the state. Rights were part of a reciprocal relationship. I have already discussed the concept of benevolent rule, or jinsei. A change in the concept occurred during the era, an autonomous, popular universalization or nationalization, that is, the supersession in the eyes of the people of the lord by the shogun, or kōgi (Hyakushō Ikki 1982: 238; Fukaya 1979: 13). People increasingly came to speak of themselves as *kōgi no onbyakushō*—peasants of the realm, of the state, or of the shogun—and increasingly came to see the state as a court of redress for local grievances. The reasons for this change were mixed, but included domain failure to prevent misrule by local officials; the bankruptcy of domain policy vis-à-vis prices, relief, and food supplies; and increased repression and the use of firearms (Hyakushō Ikki 1982: 238–40; Fukaya 1979: 51). The overall result was the unraveling of the policy safety net guaranteeing the preservation of hyakushō status. The inference was that the lord had defaulted on his end of the jinsei bargain, and the people were entitled to withhold loyalty and to seek redress elsewhere.

One of the places they sought redress was from their fellow commoners, the most prosperous of whom grew in numbers and wealth but remained bound by principles of reciprocity, as were the elites. Extraordinary wealth incurred extraordinary obligations (at least to the less-well-off in one's own village [see Scott 1976]). Indeed, it has been argued that Japanese culture possesses such a distinctively strong element of "just desserts" or "fair share" that the customary prerogatives of subordinates may actually be greater than the formal rights of those in other cultures (Vogel 1979: 117ff.; Katsumata 1982: 25). Wealth per se was not considered bad, but if it were ill-gotten or monopolized, harmed other people or the community, manifested selfishness, or betrayed the principle of mutual obligation, then it could become a source of grievance (Najita and Koschmann 1982: 156; Bix 1986: 146; Fukaya 1979: 81). Again, neither equality nor the absence of exploitation was demanded, but reciprocity was insisted upon with a consistency that indicates a powerful, if informal, sense of right. The violation of this right by either government or commoners was an injustice. And as government declined in efficacy, the people increasingly looked to each other for the alleviation of distress, and the market replaced policy, it is no surprise that the frequency of social conflict rose relative to political protest.

The Referents of Consciousness

The people of Tokugawa Japan did not invoke these "rights" in a vacuum. They came up, with great alacrity, with referents of many kinds. Some of these referents were general and some changed over time, but they also indicate clearly that the people were not fatalistically subject to some hegemonic ideology of stasis.

One standard of comparison was administrative practice in the Tokugawa house lands. There was a general perception that the administrative hand weighed lighter there, and as the common people came to see themselves as subjects of the shogun as well as subjects of their own lords, the view that shogunal practice should be universal became a component of peasant appeals (Fukaya 1979: 26–27). This perception was much more than an abstraction: in a significant number of incidents the people of an area resisted its administrative transfer from shogunal to domain control or they demanded transfer to shogunal control.

Often the referent of an appeal was a neighboring domain. The administrative grass seems usually to have looked greener next door *unless* administrative transfer was in the offing, in which case things looked a lot better at home. The key was familiarity: ad hoc relief was nice, but what people pursued more often were clear, regular, and well-understood obligations (Fukaya 1979: 71ff.). Because understanding depended primarily on precedent, by far the most common referent of ideas about proper administrative practice was past practice. No matter how oppressive the status quo, people had usually over time worked out ways to get by—if not prosper on the sly—within it.[2]

Temporal reference points varied. Sometimes it was the day before some new dispensation was announced, a period which suddenly became "time immemorial" (Walthall 1986: 75–79; Aoki M. et al. 1981, 4:63). Often, however, the reference point was a more general golden age in which peasant status was secure, lords benevolent, harvests ample, and everyone lived up to his customary obligations. This golden age was not shrouded in the mists of time, though: it closely resembles the mid-seventeenth century, when the hyakushō class created by the Tokugawa had become firmly consolidated, when the upward mobility and economic security entailed by hyakushō status were new in the popular memory, economic change had not yet seriously compromised the political economy, and fiscal exigency had not yet prompted the government to innovative revenue enhancements (Fukaya 1979: 63ff.). The administrative structure had become in popular hands a tool for countering the evolving interests of the regime.

The Evolution of Popular Consciousness

It should be clear that popular consciousness hardly remained static. Rather, it became more aggressive, more national, and more heterogeneous.

During the eighteenth century the common people became more assertive, moving from simple opposition to tax burdens and appeals for relief to efforts to advance their own position. Their focus on guarantees of survival broadened to include the opportunity to accumulate a surplus, and they began to object not only to new obstacles to self-improvement but also to existing ones (Aoki M. et al. 1981, 4:63ff.; Walthall 1986: xi–xiii, 65ff.). Already in 1720 a group of

---

[2] Bercé 1980: 34, 1990: 90, 248ff.; Stevenson 1979: 242–43; Mousnier 1970: 341ff.

commoners in the Aizu region approached the authorities with their own alternative rate, schedule, and method of payment of the land tax and with propositions that reclaimed fields be exempted from taxation, that headmen be required to negotiate with the hyakushō on major decisions, and that the term of office of intendants be set at three years (Hayashi 1976a: 69ff.).

By the nineteenth century popular effrontery had magnified. Official accounts contain examples of disrespect, rudeness, and even abuse from the commoners vis-à-vis the samurai. In the 1840s the residence of Mizuno Tadakuni, the shogunate's top official, was stoned by a crowd, and in Morioka domain in 1853 the people, invoking their status as subjects of the state, actually called for the transfer of their own lord (Jansen 1989: 8; Fukawa 1976; Fukaya 1979: 90).

As rural society became more stratified and complex, concepts such as "village" and "farmers" became less credible referents and legitimating terms, and broader groups such as "peasants of the realm" (*kōgi no onbyakushō*), "all the people" (*banmin*) or "the people of the realm" (*tenka no min*) began to appear in the rhetoric of contention (Rekishigaku Kenkyū 1985: 103ff.; Hyakushō Ikki 1982: 216). At the same time, the failure of successive levels of leadership to attend to popular needs led to broader and increasingly national political horizons as well. Appeals to local officials were supplemented by overtures to lords, later to the shogun, and finally—in the mid-nineteenth century—to the imperial court itself (Hyakushō Ikki 1982: 234).

The most problematic aspect of this nationalization of popular consciousness was its logical terminus in shogun or emperor. Appeals to imperial authority could signify an anti-Tokugawa, antifeudal, or even revolutionary consciousness, but such appeals seem to have been the province of commoner elites, both political and economic. The currents of "nativism" or "national learning" (*kokugaku*) which swept the country in the nineteenth century and underpinned the antishogunal movement of the 1860s did penetrate the countryside but are not in evidence in most popular contention (Hyakushō Ikki 1982: 12, 216ff., 241). What is not problematic is the nationalization of the ideological resources of contention.

As the evolution of imperial consciousness implies, popular consciousness became more varied over the course of the Tokugawa era. A transformation took place during the eighteenth century with a falling away from trust in government and acceptance of the status quo on all levels (Hall 1991: 598, 630), but what replaced them varied. Village elites tended to drift toward nativism (Rekishigaku Kenkyū 1985: 68ff.). Commoners with some surplus strove for freedom of economic activity with a narrower concept of benefit; at the same time they adopted an ethos of hard work and reformism which Yasumaru Yoshio (1975: chap. 1) has attributed to a less positive source: a fear of downward mobility and loss of status amid rapid economic change, land concentration, and commodification of hitherto noneconomic goods. These two factors combined into an exceedingly sharp eye for the main chance and an equally acute sensitivity to obstacles to that pursuit or threats to achievements already made.

The orientations of the less-well-off approached class consciousness, or at least a consciousness of and unhappiness with socioeconomic hierarchy. Elites were happy to propound the values of frugality, modesty, and hard work; those at the bottom of the economic ladder, too, seized upon these values and used them to justify attacks on their better-off neighbors (Yasumaru 1975: chap. 1). These attitudes are often lumped under the rubric of "world-renewal" or *yonaoshi*, a diffuse mixture of leveling egalitarianism and hostility toward the improperly rich, commoner exploiters, and corrupt or self-serving local officials (Sasaki 1979: 10ff., 197–210; Wilson 1992). Yonaoshi ideas often took on a religious tone, with appeals to supposedly egalitarian deities (*yonaoshi daimyōjin* or *yonaoshigami*). But despite their hierarchical sensitivities yonaoshi attitudes never amounted to a denial of the Tokugawa system in particular or the idea of public authority in general. Nor were they radically millenarian.[3] Rioting against outrageous prices, yes; ransacking the stores and warehouses of moneylenders, merchants, and landlords, yes; demanding that those in favored positions live up to their obligations under the status quo, yes; but condemning that status quo? No.

The peak of yonaoshi activity came in the late 1860s, when political upheaval combined with economic chaos and perceptions of foreign threat. The world appeared to many to be turning upside down, and it is unsurprising that secular ideas were not sufficient to dominate the moment in the popular consciousness. But the moment passed relatively quickly. Levels of popular contention rose in the short run, but after the Restoration all sorts of expectations—land redistribution, tax reductions, forgiveness of debts, and so forth—were dashed (Sasaki 1979: 208–10). Moreover, the people held certain ideas that reduced the level of potential contention and faced certain dilemmas that had the same effect. Their ideas included a prior acceptance of impersonal national authority which meshed with the Meiji government's centralizing aims (White 1988c; see also Kelly 1985: chaps. 9, 11). They faced, in short order, new and far more explicit legal codes, tax regulations, and administrative procedures, and the room for honest disagreements over interpretations, inconsistencies, and interregional disparities shrank dramatically—as did the room for popular manipulation.

Finally, the common people had to reconceptualize themselves (Aoki M. et al. 1981, 2:350ff.). Where there had existed nobles and commoners, rich and middle and poor and landless farmers, and artisans and merchants, now there was a single populace of "subjects" (*heimin*). Who are we? Where do we fit? What are we entitled to? These and other questions had to be answered before the people could build a new consciousness that could help them to determine the legitimacy of authority and resistance. This development was not slow in coming: in the mid-1870s Fukuzawa Yukichi's phenomenally popular *Encouragement to Learning* set forth an argument on popular rights, political obligations, and the limits of dissent which powerfully influenced subsequent political debates and

---

[3] In my view, that is. George Wilson (1992: 71) argues the opposite.

movements.[4] But at the end of my period of study the process was still inchoate. Many of the most useful psychic resources for contention had evaporated with the structures that embodied them, and interests too were affected: people were not necessarily aware of what they were entitled to feel aggrieved about. People could always remonstrate, but without solid conceptions of self and authority, their actions lacked both internal self-confidence and external credibility. They tended to be ad hoc, parochial, incoherent, and ineffectual; unsurprisingly, even in its shaky early years the regime had little trouble putting them down.

The Style of Consciousness

It is, of course, impossible to go beyond the broadest generalities in characterizing the mentality of the Tokugawa commoners. Nevertheless, with full recognition of exceptions, I suggest that the people of Tokugawa Japan were in their thoughts about contention mythic but not mystified. Their consciousness was reasoning and calculating (if not strictly rational) to a high degree. They were mythic in that legends, myths, and tales counted for much in their evaluations of past events and leaders, in their predictions of the outcomes of contention, and in their conscious use of symbols to advance their goals (Walthall 1986, 1991; Yokoyama 1977). Many regions had tales of their own folk heroes and martyrs which generated local traditions of action against authority. Such materials transcended local relevance (Yokoyama 1977: 225), and in some instances these myths were systematically collected by those considering contention, almost like how-to manuals.

In other cases tales of contention were aimed not at the people but at the authorities themselves. Accounts of events often amounted to morality plays, showing the elites what would happen if they were derelict. Oppressive lords were dissolute, corrupt, and evil; remonstrations were by (ordinarily devotedly loyal) virtuous retainers or subjects pushed to the ends of their ropes; and in the end the evil perished and virtue triumphed, although the leaders of the movement often paid with their lives (see Rahder 1935).

Such tales were highly variable in their reflections of fact; some were overwhelmingly fictitious, and most reflected the intentions of their authors more than the events recounted. Their importance for us does not lie in their empirical accuracy. Rather, what is interesting is the function they performed for the people. As purported examples, they reassured common people that they need not remain passive in the face of injustice and that remonstration was not futile. And they were, as noted, widespread. Hundreds of Japanese villages still have local shrines to those involved in contentious events who were subsequently deified or memorialized.

---

[4] The title in Japanese is *Gakumon no Susume*. By 1876 the book was in its seventeenth printing, running to a total of over 400,000 copies, or roughly one for every hundred people in the country (Fukuzawa 1969: xi–xv).

Second, the simple fact that the people generated and perpetuated these tales demonstrates that contention was within the realm of the thinkable. To be sure, there must have been thousands and thousands of people who never entertained the slightest question as to the omnipotence and inviolability of the status quo. Fatalism was a significant part of popular life, and family records include many injunctions to frugality, submissiveness, and pride in one's station, lowly though it might be (e.g., Chambliss 1965: 8). Nevertheless, there were also, just as unquestionably, many who were not mystified by any elite world view. The Tokugawa peasantry has been credited with a "thorough, almost harshly realistic self-understanding" gained through years of difficult and oppressive conditions (Koschmann 1978: 269). They were able to see through official rhetoric and to define as immoral any actions inimical to their own, self-defined welfare (Walthall 1986: 99). Even their fatalism could become a source of strength: awareness of some transcendental social or cosmic will might well have bucked up the resolve of, say, a village headman contemplating a contentious action of decidedly fatal prospect.

Does this use of myths mean that the people were simply mystifying themselves and avoiding recognition of the madness of challenging the state? I think not. I seriously doubt that our hypothetical headman was unaware of the contradiction between his own narrow, short-term interest in staying alive and his obligations to those around him. Certainly many opted for self-interest, especially later in the era. Still, there is far too much evidence of organized, prudent, manipulative behavior (especially in the composition of protest manifestoes, which echoed ante facto the asseverations of loyalty found in the post facto accounts of folk heroes) designed to obtain popular goals at minimum risk to accept the argument that mystification clouded the calculations of the people (Walthall 1986: x; Smethurst 1986: 348; Ravina 1992). Perhaps the knowledge that one was doing the right thing brought the courage to do it. Too few popular leaders of whom we have knowledge indulged in quixotic actions or seem to have thrown their lives away for symbolic reasons for us to assume that expressionistic action was anywhere nearly so common as instrumental, rational action.

Elite and Popular Ideology

I have used the term *popular* leaders by design, for Japanese *elites* have long been inclined to quixotic protests and self-righteous self-immolation (Morris 1975). Elite and popular ideologies and mentalities did intersect in ways relevant to the understanding of popular contention. One such intersection was the popular manipulation of elite principles already discussed. Another was the development during the latter half of the era of kokugaku, "national learning" or "nativism."

Nativism, which emerged during the eighteenth century, asserted the contrived nature of all social and political orders and institutions. Sociopolitical reality was seen as the work of man, not nature, and consequently malleable by human will (Harootunian 1970: 22, 31, 65; Maruyama 1974: 189–225; Jansen

1989: chap. 3). Originally nativist thought was consistent with the Tokugawa order. Although it arose partially in response to the social consequences of governmental decline—such as popular contention—it was quite compatible with governmental reform (Maruyama 1974: 219, 231ff.). But it was easily, and perhaps intrinsically, susceptible of more questionable interpretations. On the domain level it suggested that the sociopolitical order might be remade independent of the shogunate; on the village level it implied "an autonomous and self-sufficient village, removed from the centers of power" and responsible for its own administration and well-being (Najita and Koschmann 1982: 46; Koschmann 1987: 12–13; Harootunian 1988: 32ff.).

The village-level version of nativism spread into the countryside during the nineteenth century (Harootunian 1988: chaps. 4, 5; Koschmann 1987: 5). There, far from becoming a resource base for popular contention, nativism became a tool of commoner elites in their efforts to repress the contentious tendencies of the people. The people never enjoyed the esteem of the leading nativist scholars, who saw them as amenable to benevolent rule under carefully constructed institutions (particularly the throne) but essentially crude, base, and deceitful (Harootunian 1970: 29ff.; 1988: 297). Whether or not the village official-landlord-merchant popular elites shared this contempt, it seems clear that they feared insurrectionary people more than rapacious rulers (Harootunian 1988: 404).

It is important not to lose sight of this split between commoner elites and people, a philosophical accelerator of the economic and political factors already working to divide the people from their natural leaders. The commoner elites distrusted and sought to dampen the "unruly passion" of the people by instilling the virtues of work, selflessness, and obedience to authority (Harootunian 1988: 17, 266ff.). The consequent increasing disunity of the village is equally important to bear in mind. The elites "kept their distance," living "in a different world" from the mass of the people (Fujitani 1982: 202–3), and we accordingly see more lower-stratum leadership in popular contention as the era wore on.[5] As James Scott has said, an elite ideology that does not mystify the people can still function to "secure the cohesion of the dominant classes" (1985: 320), and perhaps this is what nativism did in the Tokugawa village. That is, popular nativism, however serendipitous its emergence, seems to have been made to order for a rural elite that had already defected from the people economically and politically, yet lacked yet philosophical justification for its position and was fearful of popular contention. If nativism hadn't been available, perhaps the commoner elites would have had to invent it.

---

[5] I agree with the descriptive account of the nativist tradition contained in, e.g., the work of Harry Harootunian but disagree with his assertion that the nativist local elites sided with the people rather than with the aristocratic status quo (1988: 229). The commoner elites wanted an apolitical, self-sufficient, harmonious village free of centralized control *but under their own*. Indeed, rural nativism bears all the earmarks of a concerted effort to impose a soporific false consciousness on the people.

Religion, Consciousness, and Contention

In many lands, at many times, religion has been an element in popular contention. Religious faith can intensify, absolutize, reduce the possibility for compromise, and increase the level of violence. It does, of course, serve as a powerful resource, and in confrontations with relatively civilized states this power is, as Gandhi and Martin Luther King showed, dramatically enhanced. In early modern states, however, this moral force is reduced, and if faith leads its followers to rely on mantras or amulets rather than swords and guns, it can be counterproductive indeed.

In Europe the imbrication of religion and contention needs little recounting.[6] But what of early modern Japan, where there was after the Shimabara Rebellion of 1637–1638 almost no significant contention based on common religious *belief* (although religious *symbols* were occasionally used [Walthall 1986: 123])? Japan did see episodes of religious fervor; it was part of the same Maitreya tradition that fueled chiliastic violence in China, and it was home at times to the sorts of separatist religious communities which are likely to provoke official suspicion, hostility, and suppression. Certainly, too, it was subject to the sorts of natural and man-made catastrophes which have catalyzed religiously based contention in other societies (Cohn 1961, e.g.). Nevertheless, religious warfare has not scourged Japan since the early years of the Tokugawa era.

It was not that there was no spiritually based dissent in early modern Japan; rather, it occurred most frequently on exclusively religious terms, and what there was of a political or social nature never caught on (Staggs 1985). Nobunaga and Hideyoshi, the precursors of the Tokugawa, succeeded in obliterating religion as a political force. The Tokugawa regime itself was established as an antireligious entity, determined (despite its own reliance on neo-Confucian justifications of its rule and on Buddhist temples as agents of regulation of the people) to eliminate religious organizations and beliefs as competitors for the allegiance of the people (Aoki M. et al. 1981, 4:279ff.). Thousands were butchered at Shimabara, Christians were hunted down and persecuted without mercy, temples were disestablished, and clerics were laicized (Morris 1975; Kaikyū Tōsō 1981: 222; Collcutt 1985). Still, religion was implicated in contention in multiple ways.

Religious rituals and institutions were constructed as agents of social control and integration, and clerics were often asked by the authorities to cool down contentious groups and promote peaceable settlements (Aoki M. et al. 1981, 4:306). The people endeavored to use the same agencies. Temple and shrine grounds were frequent gathering places for contentious groups; the people asked clerics to intercede with the authorities to get leaders out of jail or otherwise mitigate punishments; pledges and petitions were made to or in the name of various deities with the hope of justifying contentious behavior and ensuring

[6] Zagorin 1982, 1:141; Goldstone 1991; Cohn 1961; Naquin 1976, 1981; Chesneaux 1972; Thompson 1966: 49ff.

success (Aoki M. et al. 1981, 4:303–15). Finally, as noted, leaders of these incidents often were themselves deified after the fact.

But the contrast with Europe and China is still stark. After the bloody denouement of Shimabara, only a few incidents had clerical leadership (Yamada Tadao, personal communication). Buddhism, Shinto, and Confucianism were all effectively co-opted by the state, and heterodox elements such as millenarian Maitreya Buddhism simply never took firm root.[7] Japanese Maitreya worship was passive, awaiting the coming of the messiah but not actively cleansing the ground for his arrival.

Yet if it was not a vehicle for contention, popular religious fervor was hardly lacking. The first major manifestation of such fervor during the Tokugawa era was the mass pilgrimage, or *okagemairi*. From time to time, two million persons or more would swell the normal ranks of pilgrims to the great Shinto shrine at Ise in central Japan.[8] These okagemairi have been variously characterized as a substitute for more politically relevant contention in the face of oppression, a reaction to enhanced economic well-being, and a form of psychological liberation from the feudal order. Objectively, they were certainly a form of liberation, being essentially months-long vacations from the daily grind, a respite from cares and customary mores for both men and women, who were free to carouse and demand alms and sustenance along the way.

But were the pilgrimages alternatives to more serious forms of contention? I doubt it. In five of the seven major pilgrimage years the magnitude of total contention nationwide did fall, but in five of these years the price of rice fell also. The pilgrimages occurred most often in good, not bad, years. Moreover, one of the years of rising prices and massive pilgrimage was also a year of rising contention. Thus the okagemairi do not seem to constitute some sort of substitute for contentious energy. They were celebrations and entertainments that skirted the edge of riot, but they did not occur either in tandem with other forms of contention or in times and places where the usual causes of contention were at a high pitch but levels of contention were anomalously low.

The second, and more problematic, form of mass religious behavior in Tokugawa Japan was the *eejanaika* movement of 1867.[9] It began amid the disintegration of the shogunate, albeit in a year when the conflict between the shogunate and its rivals was in a lull, the harvest prospects were good, and prices were falling (Sasaki 1979: 97ff.; Wilson 1992: chaps. 5–7; Totman 1980: 377–79)—that is, at a time of low sociopolitical contention sandwiched between two highly contentious years, 1866 and 1868. The movement actually began in 1866

---

[7] Yasumaru Yoshio and Yamada Tadao, personal communications; Yasumaru 1975: 94ff.; Pollack 1985: chap. 7; Miyata 1970: 243.

[8] The biggest of the pilgrimages occurred in 1650, 1705, 1771, and 1830, with smaller ones in 1718, 1723, and 1867 (Rekishi Kagaku 1974: 256; Takagi 1983; Fujitani 1982). The following discussion draws also on Aoki M. et al. 1981, 4:331; Sasaki 1974: 64, 283; and Wilson 1992.

[9] The term is a saying repeated by the participants, translatable as "That's all right" or "Isn't that good?" or perhaps "Anything goes" or "Do your thing."

with the mysterious falling from the sky—most frequently upon the homes of prosperous commoners—of both Shinto and Buddhist amulets, which augured miracles and other beneficent things (Takagi 1983: 12ff.). Those thus blessed (?) moved to put up religious decorations and to offer food, drink, and sometimes money to neighbors, kin, friends, and increasingly, strangers, who came transported by religious—and subsequently alcoholic and, some argue, political—ecstasy to share in the miraculous happenings and carry the news to other households, which apparently felt well advised to provide amply for the celebrants also.[10]

The movement began along the central Pacific coast and spread rapidly during 1867, moving along the highways toward both Edo and Ōsaka. The atmosphere seems to have been predominantly good-humored, although this festive mood also seems to have been a thin veneer over rather bald extractions by the poor from the rich, accompanied by hints of divine punishment for those who did not provide food and money. As this behavior suggests, the movement was far more oriented to this-worldly benefit than to millenarian salvation. Its zealotry is also open to question. When local authorities looked suspiciously into the falling of amulets and took a firm stand against unbridled celebration, the movement tended to fade quickly (Takagi 1983: 96, 171, 179). In late 1867 the movement dissipated as it spread in an ever-widening circle from its region of origin.

The timing of the eejanaika movement, and its pointedly socioeconomic targeting, has moved some observers to classify it with other, more secular forms of popular contention. Some have characterized the movement as "violent, political, and antibakufu" (Bix 1986: 171), and the complicity of anti-Tokugawa elements in stirring it up has been charged, but a more common interpretation is that the movement was not part and parcel of contemporaneous political contention but served, in fact, to defuse popular energies that might otherwise have pushed Japan in a more revolutionary direction.[11] It seems to have been a sublimation of popular attitudes, not their realization.

But the eejanaika movement is historically complex, given its contemporaneity with "world-leveling" or "world-renewing" (yonaoshi) contention, another form of religiously tinged collective behavior. The yonaoshi, a lower-stratal form of outburst aimed at commoner elites, were heavily laden with the religious symbolism employed to indicate divine sanction of the egalitarian distribution of wealth and power and the restitution to the dispossessed of land and goods. The yonaoshi were as ambiguous as the eejanaika, albeit in the opposite direction: the eejanaika were primarily religious and only debatably political; the yonaoshi were clearly social but problematically religious. Some historians have expanded the yonaoshi into a separate genre of contention. I have not, because events with

---

[10] This account draws primarily from Minami 1978: 308ff.; Fujitani 1982; Takagi 1983; Sasaki 1979: 97–143; Najita and Koschmann 1982: 160; Rekishi Kagaku 1974: 324ff.

[11] Rekishi Kagaku 1974: 324ff.; Fujitani 1982: 126ff. George Wilson (1992: 113) labels it "evidently apolitical."

yonaoshi banners, rhetoric, and so forth took multiple forms and pursued a wide variety of goals. At the same time, contention by the poor aimed at the rich sometimes took on yonaoshi characteristics and sometimes did not, in no systematic fashion. Yonaoshi elements cut across contentious phenomena, and even at their height the yonaoshi never produced a coherent, systemic solution to the problems whose concrete, local manifestations they attacked (Yasumaru 1975: 142ff.).

Therefore I tend to see the last years of the shogunate as a time of great ferment in the popular consciousness—medieval notions of loan and tax forgiveness (*tokuseirei*) revived; new Western political ideas introduced; and stresses on economy, society, polity, and psyche leading many to supernatural explanations and remedies. Religious imagery alone does not necessarily make social contention religious, and aggressive behavior does not necessarily make a religious celebration a political movement. In any case, the yonaoshi faded quickly after the Restoration, and religion provided little more basis for popular contention during the Meiji era than before. Shinto became part of the state structure; Buddhism was attacked and caved in; and the spate of new religious groups that appeared in the decades around the end of the Tokugawa era were either quietistic, apolitically this-worldly, or co-opted as "extensions of state authority" (Hardacre 1985: 56; Staggs 1985). Such developments postdate my study.

The centrality of conceptions of justice to the consciousness of Tokugawa commoners had important implications for popular contention. In the first place, injustices of various kinds were major sources of grievance, both in the long term (as interests, in the present terminology) and in the short-term, or catalytic, form. Indeed, many of the manifestoes presented by contentious popular groups recited long litanies of unjust public and private behavior, topped off by some violation of the social compact which—perhaps because it came in conjunction with a natural disaster or poor harvest—was just too much to bear. This focus on justice entered into the calculations of potential leaders and followers. A feeling that one's cause is just is, of course, a resource as well, but the knowledge that elites to some extent recognize this justice also may contribute to expectations that success will be more likely and punishment less likely than otherwise.

The pursuit of justice also influenced the process of contention. Other things being equal, the natural leaders and protectors of the community—those responsible for justice on the local level—loomed large among the leaders of contentious action. Finally, I suggest that justice as the core of consciousness, depending on state response, led to less radical, more moderate and deferential contention than might otherwise have been the case. After all, the people were pursuing only what was rightfully theirs and what the state should provide; it was not as if they were demanding major policy or structural—much less systemic—change. This characteristic faded somewhat during the era, as the people came increasingly to contend against obstacles to their achievement of new advantages and against basic policies the legitimacy of which a debilitated government could no longer credibly propound. Still, the overall quality of contention throughout the era—again, contingent on state response—was a moderate reflection of a moderate mentality.

The basic reference points of this mentality—administrative practice in specific other times and places—also influenced contention. The variety of domain administrative practices and the general laxity of shogunal administration gave dissatisfied or affronted people many resources, and policy divergences either from the past or from neighboring domains were frequent catalysts of contention. Indeed, "preemptive referencing" was common: localities slated for administrative transfer often protested in advance, comparing their present situation with that anticipated under their prospective lord.

Temporal referencing also increased the frequency of contention over time, since the political and social implications of economic change diverged from the practices of the good old days. Impecunious domains could not stick with failed policies indefinitely, but change invited resistance, and protoindustrialization, by creating a wealthy commoner stratum, also led popular elites astray from their immemorial obligations, prompting popular attempts to keep their feet to the communitarian fire.

Qualitatively, too, referencing shaped contention. For one thing, administrative transfers often stimulated contention in favor of community divorce from present administrators or in opposition to integration into other jurisdictions. The spatial and temporal immediacy of the points of reference chosen meant, moreover, that contention was likely to be relatively moderate, rather than directed at some millenarian golden age.

During the Tokugawa era popular consciousness evolved in a more proactive and more universal or national direction. It also diversified into at least three currents: that of the wealthy commoner elites, that of the middling, freeholding hyakushō, and that of the poorer or landless elements that approached proletarian status. Such differentiation had several marked effects on contention. First, we find more heterogeneous motivation behind contention later in the era: the interests of different strata diverged, as did the focus on targets of both grievance and redress all across the political hierarchy. Moreover, interests in the achieve- ·ment of new goals and new statuses—as opposed to the simple protection of prior positions—appeared in the constellation of causes of contention.

Second, national symbols provided the people with a new resource. A domain might be utterly opposed to popular petitions to the shogun, but it was powerless to deny them. De facto obstruction was possible, of course—domains exerted great efforts to keep insubordinate commoners away from Edo—but not de jure. The jurisdiction of the shogunate extended wherever its pleasure led. The resource picture was mixed, nevertheless, for the differentiation of consciousness made a unified peasantry a thing of the past (Kelly 1985). Mobilization was less likely to comprehend whole villages; intravillage opposition to contention was more likely; local elites might actively attempt to suppress it; and the government could more easily label contenders as deviant minorities. Yet as this differentiation might divide communities, it also created the possibility of broader regional coalitions of groups in the same popular stratum. We do not find anything approaching a class-, or even a stratum-for-itself attitude, but we do find more contention that swept up many communities and crossed political boundaries.

Which is to say, contention qualitatively increased in scale, not in intensity but in numbers of participants and geographical scope. There was also more conflict among the common people relative to political protest, which, I hypothesize, required more popular unity given the greater prospect of its bloody suppression. Social conflict proportionately increased, therefore, and the contentious repertoire diversified, with forms of behavior requiring less organization becoming more common. For example, we find more riots and fewer elaborately planned political protests later in the era. And as repertorial differentiation increased, so did leadership. As natural community leaders were alienated from the popular consciousness, contention came to be led by individuals from a variety of backgrounds.

The style of the popular mentality of Tokugawa Japan—mythic, perceptive, and calculating—provided the people with two resources. In the first place, they were obviously capable of imagining substantial violations of elite prerogatives, of perpetuating them in myth and legend, and of acting them out. On one level Tokugawa political principles were of course hegemonic: there was almost never even a whisper of antisystemic popular feeling. But on another level the system was open to constant questioning and contentious renegotiation, made possible by the people's ability to see through elite rhetoric and practice and to mobilize their own counterrhetoric of martyrdom and remonstration.

A calculating style of contention makes rational-choice conceptualizations of both leadership of and participation in contentious actions attractive. We see more contention that might be viewed as nonrational later in the era—not less rational, perhaps, but less calculated and more spontaneous. Throughout the era we see less behavior of an explosive and anomic type than we would otherwise, because, on the one hand, contention did not require some apocalyptic leap through the psychological barriers of mystification, and on the other, it was the result of a reasoned balancing—to put it crudely—of costs and benefits.

Such calculations changed, of course, during the era, most strikingly across strata within the commoner class. What benefited each stratum changed, and thus the interests of upper and lower commoners diverged. This divergence—because many saw it as improper—itself became the source of contention, leading (I assert) to a relative increase in conflict among the people over time. Even as the elite-popular value cleavage increased contentious interests, however, it also reduced the resources for contention. Nativism, in particular, drove a wedge between commoner elites and the people.

Contradictorily, however, the elite values of benevolence, reciprocity, and community welfare provided the people throughout the era with a resource to use against their plebeian and samurai betters. Popular manifestoes make it clear that the manipulation of elite values was an important part of the calculus of contention. Whether it led to more or to less contention I cannot say. Differentiation of values among the people may have generated more contention, but it is also possible that there was less contention by a now-disunified populace. Qualitatively, it is clear, diversity became the trend.

Finally, we have a nonfactor: religion. The low salience of religion robbed the people of what served as a major resource for contention in other societies and thus may have diminished the total frequency—and also the intensity—of contention in Tokugawa Japan. At the same time it is highly likely that if religion had been a major component of the culture of contention, far more people would have died both at the hands of religiously dissident fellow commoners and at those of the state. Would outcomes have been different? That is, would the people have gained more with religion in their arsenal, even at a greater cost in lives? I cannot say, but my most powerful suspicion is not that contention would have been more frequent in a more religiously inspired context, or more "successful," but that it would have been far more violent and more violently suppressed. The bloody eradication of politicized religion in the sixteenth century provides the counterfactual case for believing that Tokugawa Japan was lucky to be so secular.

PART II

THE TEXTURE AND CONTENT OF CONTENTION

5

FREQUENCY AND MAGNITUDE

Popular contention in Japan did not begin during the Tokugawa era, but a new political economy and a new social structure—working on the perceptions, preferences, and ideas of millions of individuals—wrought such extensive changes in the forms and frequencies of contention that it is legitimate to see 1600 as a watershed. Before the Tokugawa era the most common form of popular remonstration against intolerable authority was collective flight, coming after petition proved fruitless (Keirstead 1990). This highly scripted form of negotiation represented defiance, not desperation. The goal of it was return, to an improved situation. But the best-known form of contention was not flight but *ikki*. Originally the ikki was not a form of contention at all but a spontaneous, special-purpose organization created contractually among (or between) either elites or people designed for the pursuit of goals impossible to achieve through ordinary channels or by individual striving (Aoki M. et al. 1981, 1:25ff., 45; Katsumata 1982: 2–3). Ikki were organized on the basis of locality, kinship, or social or organizational (including religious) ties, through explicit compacts and oaths based on relatively egalitarian and majoritarian principles (Davis 1974: 221ff.).

Unsurprisingly, in the sixteenth-century context of civil disorder followed by state expansion, the purposes of ikki were often political and contentious. Some were for self-defense, some (especially those based on the Ikkō sect of Buddhism) were attempts to carve out independent political jurisdictions, and some aimed simply to win relief or concessions from the local overlord or estate proprietor (Hall 1966: 274–75; 1981: 211). They evolved, however, into a fairly consistent form of resistance against the unifiers in the last years of the century.

As noted, many ikki involved both warriors and commoners. In those days the borderline between the two was fuzzy, and commoners were often as well armed as samurai. Nevertheless, they were more intra- than interclass, and the major distinction was between the predominantly samurai "provincial" ikki and the predominantly popular "landed" ikki.[1] The provincial ikki tended to be temporary alliances of small lords. Found as far back as the fourteenth century, they were directed both at domineering local imperial officials and obstreperous peasants. Kaga province was in fact ruled by an ikki between 1488 and 1580 (Murakami 1984: 321ff.; Davis 1974: 233ff.). Later, these ikki contended against the encroaching power of the lords.

In fact, there was a fairly smooth elision from the pre-Tokugawa provincial ikki to the early Tokugawa *dogō* ikki. The dogō were minor samurai overlords whom the new regime wanted to strip of their lands, retinues, political powers, and extractive rights vis-à-vis the people, and to push down into the new commoner class (Fukaya 1979: 153 n. 14; Burton 1978: 144ff.). Their ikki were directed against policies, such as land surveys, designed to reduce the status of the dogō. Although they originated in the upper stratum their opposition to radical change often drew popular participants, but all of them lost, and with them went elite participation in contention for almost the rest of the era.

The landed ikki were organized by commoners against their political betters and pursued concessions within the status quo—debt cancellations, elimination of toll barriers, rent moratoriums, and tax rescissions (Davis 1974: 228ff.)—given in the form of "edicts of benevolence" (or *tokuseirei*). This form of contention can be seen as late as 1721, when a shogunal decree forbidding alienation of land through pawn was interpreted as a *tokuseirei* by people in two different localities, who demanded return of pawned land but were spurned by a shogunate attuned more to social order than to benevolence (Katsumata 1982: 181ff.).

The earlier landed ikki involved an armed populace often linked to aristocratic elements and able to battle it out with the political elites on roughly equal terms. Provincial ikki, too, were often multiclass coalitions. In this sense the Eurocentric term "peasant war" is more applicable to the pre-Tokugawa era,[2] although the sorts of massive, highly organized, and often ideologically motivated peasant armies found in Europe are nowhere to be seen in Japanese history.

Tokugawa Contention—Querulous or Quiescent?

Compared to other societies, Japan may appear relatively quiescent. In fact, there was a great deal of contention, and it is very hard to say that there was more or less than elsewhere. Contention in Tokugawa society has been described as an "almost daily" occurrence (Yasumaru 1975: 151), much as in other early modern societies, where people "protested *all* the time," where contention was "institutionalized" and "habitual," a veritable "occupational hazard" for the govern-

---

[1] The provincial (*kuni*) ikki included also the *kokujin, ichizoku*, and *tō* ikki; the landed (*tsuchi*) ikki were also called *tokusei* ikki, or ikki aimed at special dispensation from debts or at tax forgiveness or moratorium. See Aoki M. et al. 1981, 1:2ff.; Hall 1991: 13, 96.

[2] Yasumaru Yoshio, personal communication; Norman 1965: 8; Hayashi 1976a: 344; Zagorin 1982; Blickle 1981; Cohn 1961.

ment.[3] Aoki Kōji (1981: 639–73) has recorded 321 incidents of collective contention during the period 1400–1589, and that figure seems rather low. During the Tokugawa era he records 7,664. I have here eliminated 333 of these events, which seem to have been wholly within-channels petitioning or litigation,[4] but that still leaves us with 7,331 events spread over 288 years, or roughly 25 episodes annually—one every other week in a country roughly the size of California. But of course they did not occur regularly, as Figure 5 shows; rather, they varied from zero in 1647 to 187 in 1866, which is more like one outburst every other day.

There is yet another way to compare, and that is in terms of time *and* space. Tokugawa Japan had 631 counties; the 288 years of my study thus generate 181,728 county-years, in only 7,331 of which (or 4 percent) did an event occur. Japan appears quiescent again, but only until one adduces a comparison and a reminder. The comparison is with Ming China, which, according to James Tong's (1991) calculations, witnessed episodes of collective violence in only 630 of 303,869 county-years. Even if one narrows the Japanese data to the 1,258 openly aggressive events or the 811 violent ones, Japan now appears to be much more contentious than China (even more so if one per-capitizes the data, since Japan's population was probably only about one-fifth of Ming China's). The reminder is that many Japanese counties were only a few square miles in area; a contentious event in the next county was, in terms of communication and political implications, right next door.

Quantitative data are also available on:

- over 1,000 incidents in the English Swing Riots of 1830–1832 (Stevenson 1979: 237);
- 1,800 episodes of "peasant violence" in Russia in 1772–1861 (Bercé 1980: 219);
- 35 "uprisings" in Upper Austria in the sixteenth and seventeenth centuries (Rebel 1983: xv);
- 8,088 "contentious gatherings" in southeast England during thirteen years between 1758 and 1820 and in Britain as a whole between 1828 and 1834 (Charles Tilly, personal communication, August 1993);
- 1574 "indictable riots" in England and Wales in 1857–1870 (Stevenson 1979: 295);
- 740 riots in England in 1790–1810 (Stevenson 1979: 306);
- 2,261 manorial protests in Russia in 1796–1855 (Magagna 1991: 193);
- an annual average of 411 crimes against "public order" in England in 1834–1892 (Stevenson 1979: 309); and

---

[3] Dunbabin 1974: 27; Zagorin 1982 1:227; Bercé 1990: 237, 166.
[4] I am indebted to William Kelly, who convinced me that these events were much too dubiously "contentious" as defined here.

Figure 5. Frequency and magnitude of popular contention in early modern Japan

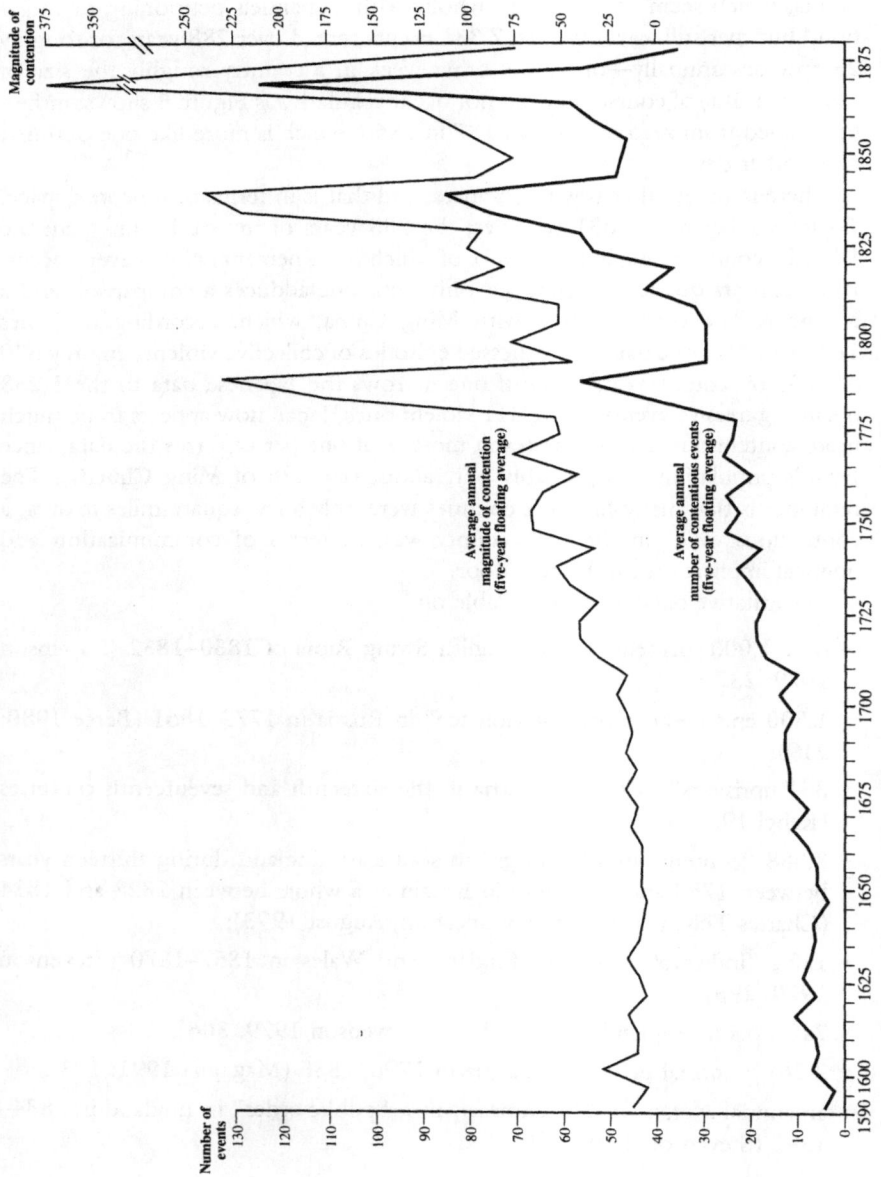

• between 450 and 500 popular revolts in southwestern France between 1590 and 1715 (Bercé 1990: 327).

Problems of definition, data source, per capitization, periodization, and classification frustrate any direct comparison of data on early modern Japan with any of these data, but Japan does, if anything, seem less contentious. I have already noted the relative absence of large-scale civil warfare during the Tokugawa era; one is tempted to think of Japan as less contentious at lower magnitudes of conflict also. An emphatic rejection of any innate impulse toward harmony among the Japanese is in order here, although a healthy respect for the coercive system established by the shogunate, and perhaps for the rationality of the people, are in order also.

Contention across Time and Space

The pattern of contention shown in Figure 5 has four aspects deserving of note. First is the relatively low level during the seventeenth century. The farther back one goes, the greater the danger of underreporting, but the consistency of the pattern all the way from 1590–1595 to 1705–1710 suggests that this is more than missing data. Second is the step-level change in contention occurring between 1710 and 1725. This jump around the time of the Kyōhō era—a time of fiscal retrenchment and crop failure—appears modest, but it amounts to a near doubling of the annual number of incidents and more than a doubling of the total magnitude of contention nationwide. It looks like a point of no return, a takeoff point for subsequent trends in contention. Yasumaru Yoshio (1973: 94–95) has held that it was also a time of qualitative change and of increasingly epidemiological spread of contention.

The subsequent trend is my third point. From the first quarter of the eighteenth century to the end of the Tokugawa era contention gradually increased in frequency and magnitude. This trend was broken three times—my fourth emphasis—during the 1780s, 1830s, and late 1860s when, as in the Kyōhō period, natural disaster and political upheaval and reform combined (albeit in different sequences). Exactly why these peaks, or cycles, of contention began is unclear thus far, as is why they ended so abruptly. The magnitude, if not the frequency, of contention in the period immediately following each peak was almost always *below* that immediately preceding. The return of good harvests and the efficacy of both political reform and repression have been mentioned (Hayashi 1976a: 12; Bix 1986: chap. 11), and all appear to have played a role in one or more cases.

Finally, Figure 5 must be considered demographically. We cannot calculate per capita contention for Tokugawa Japan.[5] Nevertheless, during the seventeenth

---

[5] We can, however, approximate per-capitization using the kokudaka of geographical units. The correlations between kokudaka and population in a variety of provinces, counties, and domains run

century, Japan's population rose from about 12 million to about 31 million, or nearly 150 percent, while the magnitude of conflict rose only about 15 percent (comparing the first quarter of the century with the last quarter), which means that the rate of contention in fact declined markedly. During the eighteenth century (again comparing its first and last quarters) the magnitude of contention rose by either 288 percent for all years or 135 percent if we exclude the extraordinarily contentious years 1783, 1786, and 1787. Population, meanwhile remained stable at 31 million. In other words, per capita contention rose dramatically. And in the nineteenth century (comparing the periods 1801–1825 and 1853–1877) an increase in the magnitude of conflict of either 134 percent or 48 percent (excluding 1823, 1858, and 1866–1871), along with a gradually growing population, suggests a rise in the rate of contention, but of far less moment than that of the previous century.

Thus the temporal pattern of popular contention underscores my focus on the political, ecological, and economic context. It also recommends close scrutiny of the eighteenth century, which seems to be a major transformative phase. Exactly what sort of a transformation it was we cannot yet say, but it followed more than a half century of popular learning, during which the Tokugawa system created new social strata and collectivities and political and economic institutions and norms, and the people in these structures became increasingly familiar with them, and with the possibilities for betterment within them (Aoki M. et al. 1981, 2:168ff.; Kaikyū Tōsō 1981: 219).

It has been argued that repression worked in Tokugawa Japan, and that very few villages saw more than one significant contentious event (Walthall 1986: 38). The spatial patterns of contention, however, exhibit a more complicated picture. Villages were close together and counties so small that contention must have been felt countywide. What is more significant is the clustering of contention in certain counties (Kokushō 1971: 31ff.; see also Bercé 1980: chap. 5). Sixty-eight of Japan's 631 counties had no recorded incidents at all; 5 had over a hundred, and another 32 had between forty and a hundred. Four pairs of adjacent counties recorded 88 and 2, 95 and 4, 55 and 4, and 98 and 5 events respectively. Amakusa county, scene of the Shimabara Rebellion, saw at least 62 events, most of which occurred after the rebellion (Hyakushō Ikki 1982: 138ff., 177). Certain constellations of structural factors did cluster in certain areas, but we must also pursue the notion of local "cultures of contention."

Figures 6 and 7 present the spatial distribution of popular contention in early modern Japan, on the provincial level.[6] In Figure 6, four areas are prominent. The first is the mountainous central core of the main island of Honshū centered

---

substantially over $r = 0.80$. Therefore, except where noted, magnitudes of contention in geographical units will always be related to the kokudaka. Of the variety of kokudaka figures available, I have used the more accurate "internal" kokudaka (*uchidaka*, *kusadaka*, or *jitsudaka*) data in my calculations. See Iinuma 1991: 102, 107.

[6] Recall that these data are corrected for provincial size, using the kokudaka surrogate for population.

Figure 6. Total magnitude of contention, 1590–1877

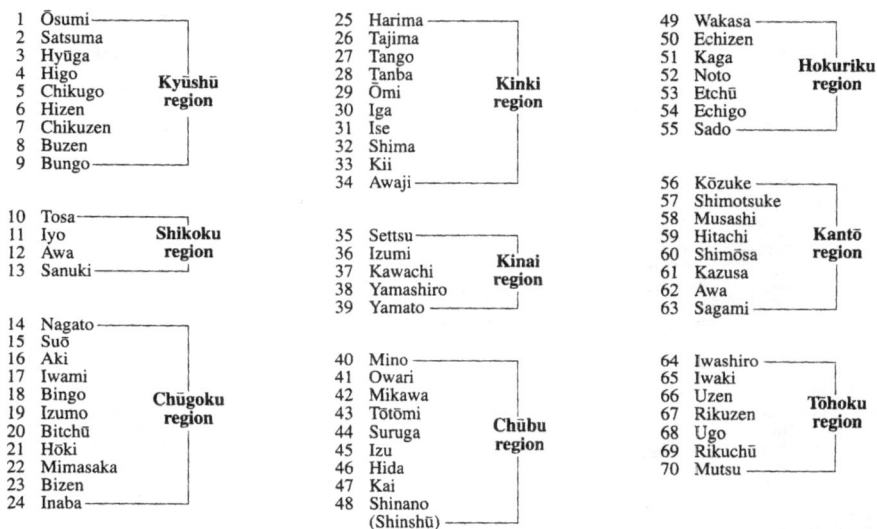

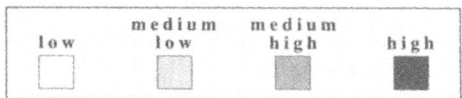

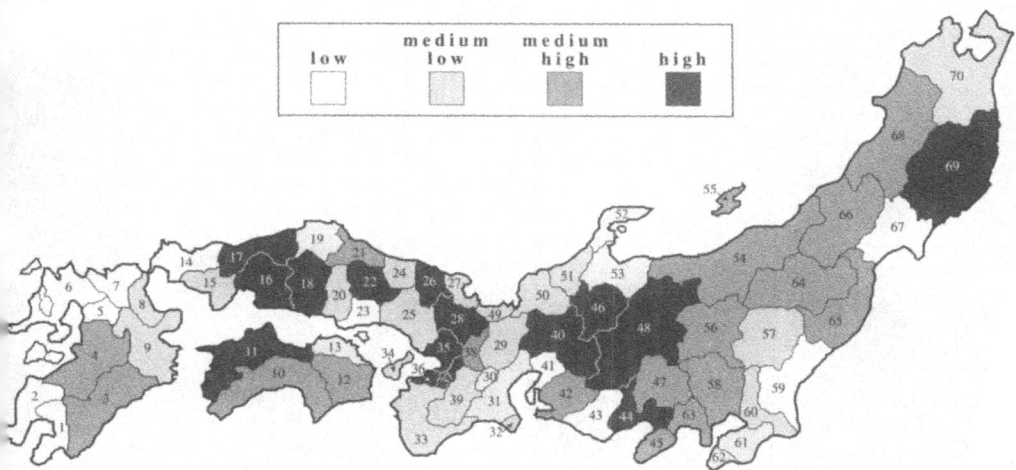

1	Ōsumi		25	Harima		49	Wakasa	
2	Satsuma		26	Tajima		50	Echizen	
3	Hyūga		27	Tango		51	Kaga	
4	Higo	**Kyūshū**	28	Tanba	**Kinki**	52	Noto	**Hokuriku**
5	Chikugo	**region**	29	Ōmi	**region**	53	Etchū	**region**
6	Hizen		30	Iga		54	Echigo	
7	Chikuzen		31	Ise		55	Sado	
8	Buzen		32	Shima				
9	Bungo		33	Kii				
			34	Awaji		56	Kōzuke	
10	Tosa					57	Shimotsuke	
11	Iyo	**Shikoku**	35	Settsu		58	Musashi	
12	Awa	**region**	36	Izumi		59	Hitachi	**Kantō**
13	Sanuki		37	Kawachi	**Kinai**	60	Shimōsa	**region**
			38	Yamashiro	**region**	61	Kazusa	
14	Nagato		39	Yamato		62	Awa	
15	Suō					63	Sagami	
16	Aki		40	Mino				
17	Iwami		41	Owari		64	Iwashiro	
18	Bingo	**Chūgoku**	42	Mikawa		65	Iwaki	
19	Izumo	**region**	43	Tōtōmi		66	Uzen	**Tōhoku**
20	Bitchū		44	Suruga	**Chūbu**	67	Rikuzen	**region**
21	Hōki		45	Izu	**region**	68	Ugo	
22	Mimasaka		46	Hida		69	Rikuchū	
23	Bizen		47	Kai		70	Mutsu	
24	Inaba		48	Shinano				
				(Shinshū)				

upon Shinano, Mino, Hida, and Suruga. The second is the Kinai region, around Ōsaka, and its hinterland: Settsu, Kawachi, and Izumi provinces, plus Tajima and Tamba from the Kinki region. Third is a sort of "western core" including Hōki, Mimasaka, Aki, Iwami, and Bingo on Honshū and Iyo on Shikoku. And fourth is a lesser concentration of contention in the east, led by Rikuchū and extending down the west coast and inland all the way to Edo.

Figure 7. Increase in magnitude of total contention, 1590–1749 vs. 1750–1877

1 Ōsumi		25 Harima		49 Wakasa	
2 Satsuma		26 Tajima		50 Echizen	
3 Hyūga		27 Tango		51 Kaga	
4 Higo		28 Tanba	**Kinki**	52 Noto	**Hokuriku region**
5 Chikugo	**Kyūshū region**	29 Ōmi	**region**	53 Etchū	
6 Hizen		30 Iga		54 Echigo	
7 Chikuzen		31 Ise		55 Sado	
8 Buzen		32 Shima			
9 Bungo		33 Kii			
		34 Awaji		56 Kōzuke	
				57 Shimotsuke	
10 Tosa				58 Musashi	
11 Iyo	**Shikoku region**	35 Settsu		59 Hitachi	**Kantō region**
12 Awa		36 Izumi	**Kinai**	60 Shimōsa	
13 Sanuki		37 Kawachi	**region**	61 Kazusa	
		38 Yamashiro		62 Awa	
		39 Yamato		63 Sagami	
14 Nagato					
15 Suō		40 Mino		64 Iwashiro	
16 Aki		41 Owari		65 Iwaki	
17 Iwami		42 Mikawa		66 Uzen	
18 Bingo	**Chūgoku region**	43 Tōtōmi	**Chūbu region**	67 Rikuzen	**Tōhoku region**
19 Izumo		44 Suruga		68 Ugo	
20 Bitchū		45 Izu		69 Rikuchū	
21 Hōki		46 Hida		70 Mutsu	
22 Mimasaka		47 Kai			
23 Bizen		48 Shinano			
24 Inaba		(Shinshū)			

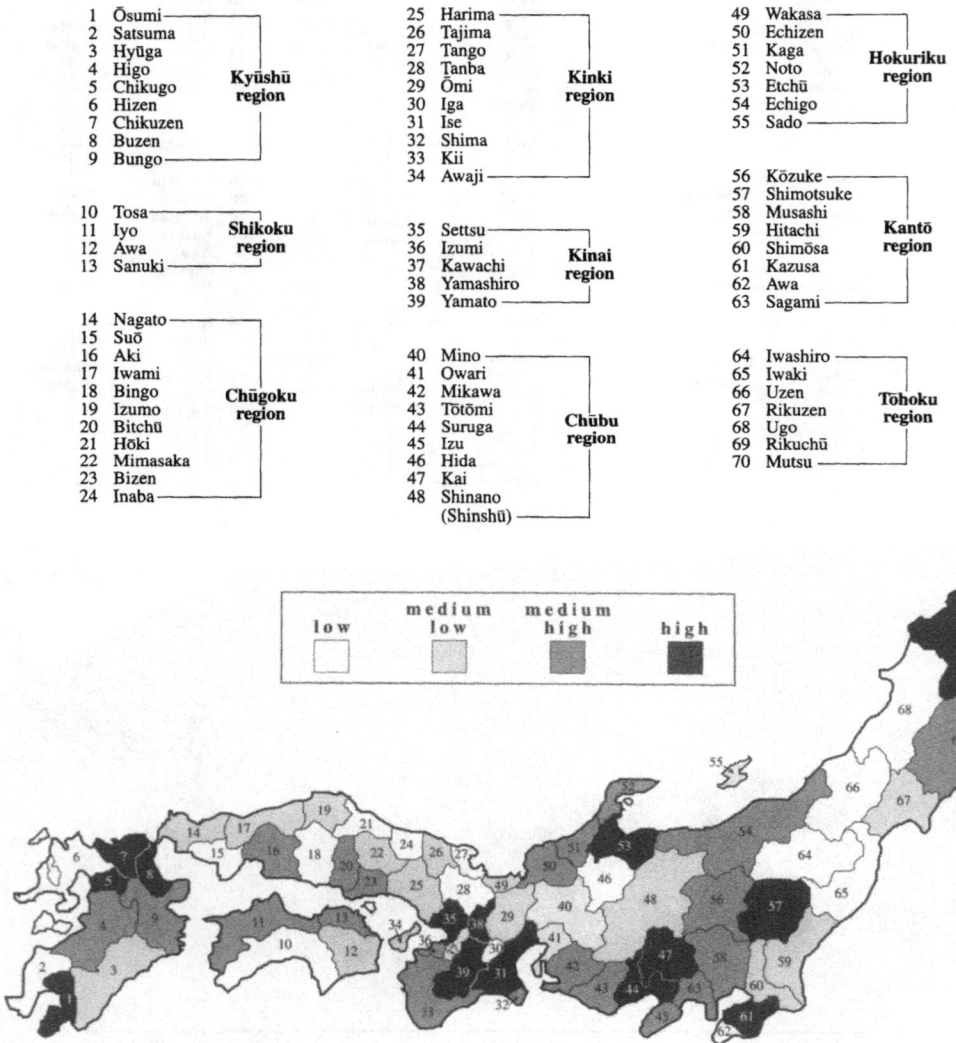

A partially contrasting picture is presented in Figure 7, which shows rates of increase in contention. From these data is it clear that eastern Japan and the central core were contentious throughout the era, showing little change from one half of the era to the next. The regions that saw the most dramatic increases in contention were the Kantō region centered upon Edo, the Kinai and its eastern hinterland, and northern Kyūshū Island. That two of these regions included Japan's two metropolitan areas is suggestive; why Kyūshū should have joined this list is less clear, but Figure 6 suggests that what we see is simply a radical proportionate increase from a very low level of contention to a merely moderate one.

The patterns indicated in these two figures cast light on a number of spatial hypotheses regarding contention. The first concerns center and periphery. Contrary to data from other societies,[7] it does not appear that Japan's most distant periphery was its most contentious zone. Western Honshū and the northeast were hardly at the vibrant center, but the Kinai and the Edo regions were, and Shinano, though mountainous, was a center of economic growth (Yokoyama 1986). Looking at change during the era, it is true that the two most peripheral provinces of all—Mutsu and Ōsumi—stand out, as does northern Kyūshū, but our attention is drawn also to Edo and the Kinai.

Perhaps a national perspective is too gross. It is clear that the peripheries of the metropolitan areas were highly contentious; indeed, in regard to rates of change it is possible that these hinterlands were more contentious than their metropolitan cores (Jansen 1989: 73, 75). In the northeast—now Fukushima prefecture—Stephen Vlastos (1986) found a clear distinction between the relatively constant frequency of contention over time in the mountainous, isolated Aizu district and the rapid rise in contention over time in the central and economically developed Shindatsu district. And an intensive study of the central Nōbi region, surrounding the city of Nagoya, concludes that intraregional contention does indeed vary along a core-periphery continuum, although this continuum is most fruitfully thought of as being multidimensional: a composite of administrative fragmentation (which increases toward the edges of the region) and physical terrain (which becomes more rugged at the edges). William Skinner's ecological index of core and periphery is the most powerful predictor of contention, which does indeed increase as one moves outward from the regional center.[8]

A second spatial model thrown into doubt by these two figures is that of an east-west (or Tōhoku-Kinai) dichotomy. The model is basically an ecological-economic one: the east, colder and more rugged, hence poorer, was said to be more contentious. But the dichotomy seems exaggerated on the ecological and economic dimensions (Hanley and Yamamura 1977), and neither Figure 6 nor Figure 7 supports the model. Moreover, comparison of total magnitudes of contention in eastern and western Japan reveals no significant correlations whatsoever between region and conflict.

A final spatial description of my data involves city and countryside. Urban counties had slightly more contention than rural counties, and the contention was of a greater magnitude. Both Musashi and Settsu provinces (home of Edo

---

[7] Brustein and Levi 1987; Wolf 1969; Skinner 1979; Bercé 1980: 184ff.; Mousnier 1970; Kuhn 1970.
[8] See White 1988a. The city of Nagoya is located in Owari province; the Nōbi region (as defined in this study) included also Ise, Shima, Mikawa, Mino, and parts of Tōtōmi, Shinano, and Hida provinces.

Table 1. Magnitudes of contention in different types of domains, 1600–1868

	total national kokudaka in	*all contentious events in*	*total magnitude of contention in*	*total magnitude of contention, 1600–1749, in*	*total magnitude of contention, 1750–1868, in*
			Percentage of		
Tokugawa lands	15%	31%	26%	20%	28%
Hatamoto domains	10	10	7	7	7
Hereditary lords' domains	38	33	33	37	32
Outer lords' domains	37	25	34	36	33
	100%	99%	100%	100%	100%

Sources: Contention data: Aoki data set (see Appendix 1); kokudaka data: Totman 1967: 33; Craig 1961: 15; Murakami 1965; Kitazawa 1982: 36–37.

and Ōsaka respectively) were relatively high in contention and in its rate of increase, but it is also clear—as has been found elsewhere (Tilly 1989b; Bercé 1980; Rowe 1989: 1, 49)—that the metropolitan hinterlands are a large part of this picture. These hinterlands were highly commercialized and poorly garrisoned, and metropolitan opportunities for litigation were conveniently near (Jansen 1989: 73, 75). Within the metropolitan areas my data do show (White 1992a) that it is not the core metropolitan counties but those immediately outside them which saw the most contention. Whether the outlying counties or provinces had all the characteristics of the metropolis except its close social controls, or whether urbanization overall even plays a role, we cannot yet say (indeed, there are some quite rural provinces high in contention in Figure 6). But the spatial distribution of population and that of contention do appear linked.

The units we have looked at thus far are no respecters of politics. Some political phenomena did vary systematically over time, and one could attribute both the secular increase and the three cycles of contention to political factors. Moreover, many of counties and several provinces were governed by single administrative units, but these are not sufficiently numerous to enable national-level generalizations. For that, we must turn to a comparison of levels of contention in different types of political units.

The units I compare—Tokugawa house lands and the domains of the hatamoto, the hereditary lords, and the outer lords—are clearly characterized by different levels of conflict.[9] Table 1 shows the relative levels of contention, and we can see that the shogunate's own territories, while accounting for only 15 percent

---

[9] The Tokugawa family's three branch houses (*go-sanke*) and its related houses (*kamon*) are included among the hereditary lords.

of Japan's economic productivity, experienced over a quarter of the total magnitude of contention and almost a third of all events. Moreover, the turbulence of these lands became more disproportionate over time (Aoki K. 1966: 26–27). The hatamoto domains, contrary to my expectations, were proportionately contentious, but the lords' domains, as expected, were less contentious than their size would suggest and became relatively less contentious over time.

Moreover, these figures understate the difference between shogunal and lordly territories, for over the years the shogunate gave some of its lands to its vassals. In addition, although these kokudaka figures are the most accurate available, it is possible that those from the outer domains are underestimates and, therefore, that the level of contention was even lower than this table indicates. My data also indicate that, overall, lordly lands were *less* favored ecologically than shogunal lands and that this ecological vulnerability was positively linked to contention— and yet, there was *more* conflict on the shogun's lands.

The Magnitude and Violence of Contention

Despite the unfortunate tendency to translate *ikki* as "revolt" or "rebellion," popular contention in early modern Japan was overwhelmingly nonviolent (Sasaki 1979: 307; see also Tilly 1982). The common people were vastly outmatched by the coercive capabilities of the regime, and a deferential invocation of officially accepted norms, along with a show of numbers (an overt indicator of the magnitude of the problem and a tacit predictor of the scope of any violence that might ensue), was in most instances the most effective strategy (DeNardo 1985; Kelly 1985; Sasaki 1979: 317). Certainly there were exceptions, such as the Shimabara Rebellion. And to say that contention was nonviolent is not to say that it was nondestructive. During some urban riots hundreds of shops, warehouses, and houses were destroyed, and commoner groups sometimes burst right into administrative offices or castle towns despite the resistance of warrior guards (Harada 1982). Nevertheless, the majority of contentious events were rather small in scale and mild in behavior.

There are a variety of ways to measure the magnitude of contention. One of the simplest is to count a single indicator such as numbers of participants or deaths in collective violence. Other techniques involve combining measures of size, duration, and lethality (Gurr 1980; Sugimoto 1978; Tilly 1978a: chap. 3). I opt for the latter, combining (see Appendix 2) three measures of size (number of participants, number of villages involved, and duration) and three of intensity (the presence or absence of threatening, aggressive, or destructive activity). But an accurate picture of the magnitude of popular contention requires some disaggregation.

First, with regard to overall magnitude, of the 7,331 incidents of contention, 64 percent scored only 1, the lowest possible score on my 10-point scale. They were small, brief, and nonthreatening to persons, property, state, or society. Seven percent of the events received a 2, 17 percent scored 5, and 12 percent scored 10, falling into the most intense category· of all. Only 1,258 events involved aggressive behavior of one kind or another, of which 736 involved some destruction of property, documents, or buildings and 51 involved physical violence against persons. In another 348 cases threats were made, but not all were carried out. In terms of size, only 637 events involved more than one community, 342 carried beyond the borders of one county, and 87 beyond the borders of one domain; only 339 lasted more than one day, and only 950 involved more than fifty participants. Ikki may be a legitimate term for popular contention, but rebellion it was not.

Figure 5 presented data on the average annual magnitude of total contention nationwide during the era. Its correspondence with the curve of number of events is close, although during most of the periods of exceptional contention it appears that magnitude rose more precipitately than the frequency. Indeed, over the entire era the magnitude of the average incident increased also. On my 4-step scale of magnitude, the average for all events was 2.8. Events occurring between 1590 and 1699 averaged 1.9; those occurring between 1700 and 1799 averaged 3.1; those between 1800 and 1867, 2.7; and those between 1868 and 1877, 4.4. Two things about this trend stand out: first, the eighteenth century again appears to be *more* contentious than a cursory look at Figure 5 would suggest but *less* an onward march of ever-growing contention. Second, the magnitude of a given incident seems to have risen dramatically after the Restoration, whether because of violence or size we shall see.

Figure 8 presents data on the magnitude of the average contentious event through time. The beginning and end of the era were periods of relatively intense conflict, as was the Temmei period and, less so, the mid-eighteenth century and the Tempō period. Clearly, the major cycles of contention brought not only more incidents but more intense ones. Size and aggressiveness had different effects on intensity, however. The two upper curves in Figure 8 show relatively big, and relatively aggressive, incidents as a proportion of all events. (Relatively big means above the median in number of villages, counties, domains, participants, or days involved [n = 2,081]; relatively aggressive means characterized by aggressive, destructive, or violent behavior [n = 1,291].) Only rarely was more than one-quarter of the average year's contention aggressive. It was relatively so at the beginning and end of the era; the seventeenth century gives way to an aggressive trend in the first quarter of the eighteenth, and thenceforth 10 percent or more of all events were aggressive, destructive, or violent. The Temmei period saw a big jump, as did the Tempō and Keiō periods, but there was a clear dropoff after the Restoration.

Size shows a contrasting pattern. Large size was markedly more common than aggressiveness—although, here too, large-scale events were infrequently more than one-third of the total—and it was much more consistent than aggressiveness throughout the era. Between 1700 and 1750 the proportion of large-scale contention increased, but between 1750 and 1850 it appears to have *decreased*, from 30 percent or more of all incidents to little more than 20 percent. Nor was

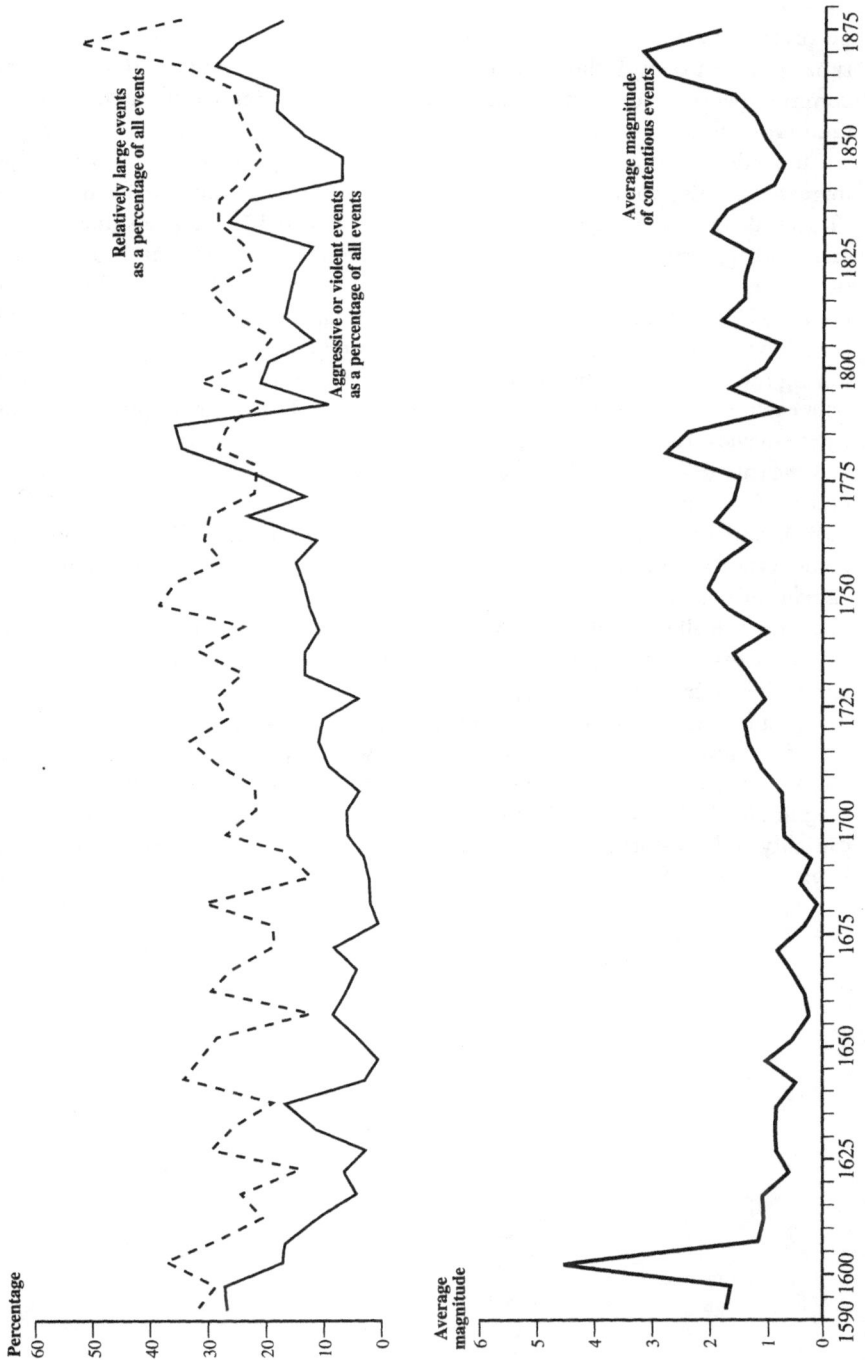

Figure 8. Average magnitudes of contentious events, 1590–1877, quinquennial averages

there much increase in size during the Temmei and Tempō peaks. There was, however, a dramatic jump in large-scale events after the Restoration, at the same time as violent ones declined. This pattern is consistent with the notion that the common people, faced with a more coercive regime after 1868, made a tactical (and rational) switch from aggressiveness to numbers.

In tandem, these two curves suggest that the aggressiveness of contention increased relative to its scale in early modern Japan. The increase in the overall magnitude of the average incident between 1700 and 1775 appears due to both scale and aggressiveness, but the jumps in Temmei and Tempō can be attributed predominantly to increased aggressiveness, and that of the post-Restoration period to increased size. The most interesting impression derived from Figure 8 overall is that, while the total magnitude of contention nationwide was increasing during the later part of the Tokugawa era, the magnitude of the average event (if one excludes the three peaks) was diminishing. Both size (after 1750) and aggressiveness (after 1770) appear to have declined.

One can, of course, object that the peaks cannot be excluded, that it is during cycles of contention that the characteristics of an era are epitomized (Tarrow 1989), and that the successively higher peaks of Temmei, Tempō, and Keiō demonstrate a rising tide of contention. One can also maintain that the national climate of contention is more important than the characteristics of the average incident: overall social disruption may be of more consequence than the disruptiveness of the average event. Yet the image of an increasing tide of contention, driven by increasing frequency, should not obscure the image of moderating magnitude. The curve of total magnitude presented in Figure 5 could be produced by fewer events of greater magnitude or by the opposite; the gradual convergence of the two curves in that figure suggests more events of smaller magnitude. And this is not simply a descriptive anecdote. I maintain that both the causality and the consequences are different for many small events than for a few large ones.

6

REPERTOIRES

Thus far we have looked at popular contention as an undifferentiated phenomenon, although it is in fact nothing of the sort. Repertoires of contentious behavior vary widely, constrained by context, by groups' interests and perceptions of resources and opportunities, and by their pasts and the pasts of those known to them (Tilly 1978: 156; 1989a: 147ff.). But people choose, and they choose on the basis of what is familiar and sensible. That is, contention grows out of everyday life. I do not mean that radical contextual change—such as the overthrow of a regime or an extraordinary wave of contention which sweeps a society—cannot bring brief moments of repertorial innovation or radical behavior change. But repertorial change is in most instances quite slow, reflective of the pace of institutional and cultural change in most times and places.

Thus a look at the people's repertoire of contentious behavior helps to explain the causes and consequences of conflict. In reverse, moreover, change in contention may alert us to ongoing contextual change. Inasmuch as contentious behavior is heavily symbolic, its forms also tell us much about the meaning such behavior has for the lives of those involved.

My descriptive strategy here is to let the record tell us what the popular repertoire was. I exclude elitist, as opposed to popular, contention, because elite and popular orders were sharply differentiated both socially and physically and because there was a relatively clean break between elite and popular repertoires of contention in Japanese culture.[1]

Types of Contention

I use the term *ikki* sparingly. The *hyakushō* ikki of the Tokugawa era had a core of meaning—unarmed, secular petitions by commoners, mostly freeholders mobilized on the basis of villages, directed at (but presupposing the fundamental

---

[1] Granting that there has probably never been a social movement in which all participants were identically motivated, there is in Japan a relatively clear distinction between moderate, realistic,

139

legitimacy of) the officials or agents of the Tokugawa state, and illegal by virtue of their premeditated organization and extra-institutional channels.[2] So restricted, the term is quite close to the definition of political protest. As William Kelly has observed, however, the term has been thrown around so indiscriminantly that it now "homogenize[s] a vast range of non-violent petitions and violent confrontations, isolated incidents and organized resistance. . . . The very act of pigeonholing what are usually incidents of multiple motivations and composite strategies has trivialized the variegated expressions of popular discontent" (1985: chap. 11, n. 1).

Accordingly, I use the term "popular contention," and I subdivide the general phenomenon three ways: by magnitude, at which we have looked already; into social and political conflict and political protest; and into a behavioral typology to be explained. Each method gets at the popular repertoire of contention in a different way. Magnitude is, of course, a constrained choice: people choose with less than complete freedom to act modestly or go all-out, and they choose to emphasize aggressiveness and numbers in differing ways. Social and political conflict and protest are defined in terms of actors and targets. And the typology I shall introduce elaborates specific forms of behavior—petitions, squabbles with neighbors, flight, insurrection, and so forth.

Mine is of course not the only possible typology. Aoki Kōji himself (1966, 1981) differentiated among ikki, commoners' disputes (*murakata sōdō*), and urban riots (*toshi sōjō*). More detailed typologies have been generated by many students of the topic, and my own significantly overlaps some of them.[3] I have elected not to copy any of them because I have disagreements with each. In the first place (see Appendix 2), many typologies rely solely on Tokugawa legal terminology. I prefer to add the legal-illegal, deferential-challenging, and vertical-horizontal dimensions, and aggressiveness and size in combination. Second, many are too gross, dividing the topic into only three or four forms and thus merging different forms of behavior.

---

instrumental, and pragmatic forms of contention and radical, Manichaean, expressive, and self-destructive ones. Ivan Morris (1975: 345) has distinguished between "sincere" and "realistic" contention; Tetsuo Najita (1974: 2) between "bureaucratic" and "idealistic" political action; Richardson and Ueda (1981: 179ff.) between "ideological" and "institutionalized" protest. Other authors have focused on one or the other current—Margaret McKean (1981), Stephen Vlastos (1986), and Yokoyama Toshio (1977) on the popular; Ellis Krauss (1974), Patricia Steinhoff (1978, 1981), Robert Lifton (1979), and Victor Koschmann (1978) on the elitist. As I have argued (White 1993b), the difference between the two currents is not so much a matter of conservative/rightist versus progressive/leftist political orientation as of social status. The progressive/leftist approach characterizes those higher (or, like students, anticipatorily higher) in the political and social hierarchies. There is also a repertorial difference: elitist contention is far more lethal, suicidal, and symbolic, not necessarily less rational but certainly more "value-rational" than "instrumentally rational," to use Max Weber's (1977: 53–55) terms, or perhaps more heroically rational, à la Georges Sorel (1961; Roth 1980).

[2] Sasaki 1974: 26; Kokushō 1971: 27ff.; Fukaya 1979: 24–36, 99–118; Yasumaru 1984: 408.

[3] Some of the more ambitious typologies include those of Yokoyama Toshio (1977: 34ff.), Stephen Vlastos (1986), Aoki Kōji (1966: 33–34; 1981), Yoshio Sugimoto (1978: 2), Horie Eiichi (1960: 90ff.), Kokushō Iwao (1971: 47–48), and Ōno Takeo (in Aoki M. et al. 1981, 1:253).

Many are too broad, including forms of petition and litigation which were so wholly within the bounds of legitimacy and legality that I have excluded them from consideration altogether.[4] All-inclusiveness would have forced me to rely on fragmentary data, blurred my focus, and quite possibly overwhelmed me: the Edo city magistrate, for example, accepted 35,790 petitions (out of 47,731 received) in 1718 alone (Shigematsu 1986: 54). A fourth, also excessively broad, approach includes surreptitious behavior such as "demoralized grumbling, social avoidance, and character assassination" (Scott 1985: 133). Such behavior is inaccessible from the sorts of data at our disposal. I look at "grumbling" of an overt, behavioral sort—perhaps better described as disorderly or contentious gatherings or, as the authorities called them, "disquiets" (*fuon*). For example, in September 1866 thousands of poor people camped in temple and shrine grounds in Edo and extorted food and money from local merchants (recording "receipts" on the walls of shops and storehouses). They were dispersed after about ten days by promises of relief, shelter, and price reductions (Tokyo Hyakunen Shi 1973, 1:1584ff.). This sort of thing was no doubt disquieting to the better orders, but it differs in quality from the covert behavior analyzed by Scott.

Fifth, and again too broadly, some treatments of contention include (usually violent) forms of contention with an elite component too great to permit them to be categorized as *popular* contention. Sixth and finally, other typologies of popular contention in early modern Japan are usually at the same time too narrow, focusing on ikki *or* on village disputes *or* on urban riots *or* on the yonaoshi, overlooking the fact that many ikki were not rebellious, many village disputes turned into political protest, many riots were rural, and the yonaoshi are arguably better categorized under other headings. My typology is—I think—the first to incorporate systematically all the incidents in the Aoki compendium.

As noted, one dimension of the repertoire of popular contention involves its magnitude; the other two, its social or political composition (defined in Appendix 2) and its behavioral forms. As shown in Table 2, the social/political dimension disaggregates the totality of contention broadly but informatively. It reveals one of the problems already noted: any analysis of popular contention in early modern Japan which focuses only on the political misses the greater part of the phenomenon. Also, because my typology is actor-based, it gives us a first glimpse of the social composition of contention. But first I must define the behavioral/tactical repertoire, before we can see how it too helps to map contention.

Review of the Aoki data set and extensive reading in the field produced the behavioral repertoire presented in Table A of Appendix 2; subsequently, I reduced this typology to a smaller one, with nine categories, also shown in Table

---

[4] This exclusion includes the *kokuso* or *kuniso*—literally, provincial appeals—merchants' pleas to government for commercial respite (from official regulation) or advantage (through official favoritism and versus other commercial groups [see Appendix 2, Table A, no. 21]). Aoki records 97 such events, all occurring in the Kinai region around Ōsaka, most of which were launched by rural merchants against the privileged urban merchants and guilds. They could be extremely large, involving coalitions of thousands of villages. But they were within the legal framework and I have excluded them.

Table 2. Composition and repertoire of contentious behavior

Type of contention	Percentage of all events
Sociopolitical Composition	(n = 6,933)
Social conflict	53%
Political conflict	14
Political protest	33
	100%
Behavioral Repertoire	(n = 6,755)
Disorderly or contentious gathering	9%
Conflict among commoners	42
Intercommunity conflict	1
Litigation, petition, appeal	9
Flight	4
End-run appeals	11
Coercive appeals	13
Riots	10
"Rebellion"	1
	100%

2. The first category of the behavioral repertoire—which accounts for almost one event in ten—is the "grumbling" or "disquiet" I have spoken of, which includes a wide variety of contentious and disorderly but inconclusive gatherings not beyond the concern of the authorities, but undeserving of repression (though not necessarily punishment).[5] The vast majority of disquiets were mild affairs; the key, however, is that despite a possibly rebellious mood no appeal was lodged, no concrete action taken, and no one—commoner or elite—targeted.

The second type of behavior—by far the most common during the whole era—covered a wide miscellany of conflicts among the common people, rural and urban. The generic term for such contention is *murakata sōdō*, or village dispute, but much occurred in urban areas too; together, such behavior probably occupied more of the time people spent contending than all their political activities combined. Social ostracism, demands, meetings and plots, unneighborly squabbles of all sorts, tenant disputes, accusations leveled at community officials, arguments about shrine membership and religious prerogative and privilege, conflicts over social and political status, disagreements over village elections—all pitted some members of the community against others, in contravention of the ideal of community solidarity.[6] The most frequent target of such conflict was the

---

[5] The category includes the *fuon* (no. 25 in Table A, Appendix 2), the *tonshū*, and the *shōshū*.
[6] Nos. 1, 2, 8–18, 35, 36, and 45 (of Table A, Appendix 2) are included here, but events in categories 1, 10, 11, 12, 35, 36, and 45 are included only if they are secondary descriptors of events primarily categorized as 13 (village disputes) or 36 (urban disputes). See also Fukaya 1979: 45–46; T. Smith 1959: chap. 12.

village officialdom, with its powers, perquisites, opportunities for graft and favoritism, and compromising links to the authorities above.

The third category of contention is similar: it too is conflict among the common people, but between communities, involving contention over village boundaries, water or fishing rights, fields, common land utilization, and so forth.[7] Unlike the previous category, this one does not denote the decay of community solidarity; indeed, it presupposes the opposite. It was a minor current of contention—we have fewer than a hundred cases on record, although this must be an underestimate—but a potentially destructive and violent one, since physical facilities and physical incursions were most often its focus, and the demands of ongoing social life did not impose restraints.

The fourth category comprehends petitions, appeals, and litigation of a magnitude, disputatiousness, or moment sufficient to move it into the class of popular contention. It accounted for approximately 9 percent of the events (although for a complete picture one could add to this the 333 instances of noncontentious petition and litigation I have excluded from this analysis). Orderly petitions, petitions submitted to official petition boxes, and generic pleas and petitions on whatever issue—overwhelmingly low-key affairs—fall into this category.[8] Such behavior could be collective, but it could also be representative of only a small part of a community, and directed at another. The next category, however—flight—was almost exclusively collective and involved the abscondence of whole villages.[9] This minor but significant form of protest usually took its participants beyond the borders of their domain; it was not a passive escape from hardship but an active form of petition the behavioral text of which the lord could read: "Our present treatment is intolerable; give us what we want and we shall return." Their domain of refuge could read: "We have been intolerably treated in our home domain; please intercede with our lord so that we may obtain that treatment which is rightfully ours." Over time such flight grew in scale and in the explicitness of its demands; it could be quite successful (a domain without people was not economically viable), but it was seen, and treated, as what it was. An abscondence by some seven hundred persons from Tosa domain in the 1780s (to escape, and demand the elimination of, the domain paper monopoly) resulted in the freeing of the paper trade—and the execution of three of the leaders of the movement (Yashiro 1989: 35ff.).

The sixth category of contention was a prominent one—the "end-run" appeal, in all its forms, in which groups of commoners took their appeals beyond unresponsive immediate superiors to higher levels of the political system. Quite

---

[7] Nos. 3–7 of Table A are included here, as are incidents termed *irikumi* (having to do also with borders) and *mizu sōdō* or water disputes.

[8] Nos. 19, 20, 22, 23, and 24 of Table A are included, as well as such generic terms for petition and litigation as *chinjō*, *shusso*, and *jōso*.

[9] Nos. 28 and 29 of Table A are included here, as are such other terms for flight as *tōbō*, *dassō*, and *ekkyō*. See also Kokushō 1971: 5; Aoki M. et al. 1981, 2:172ff.; Rekishi Kagaku 1974: 37; Hayashi 1976a: 33.

often inevitable because the local authorities were the cause of the appeal, end runs were explicitly illegal (although customarily quite deferential) and highly risky. They took the form of written demands posted on building walls, scattered in the streets, thrust into the palanquins of passing officials, presented at the gates of an office, or carried (often precipitately) right into the office uninvited.[10] Such protests required planning, commitment, organization, and leadership; they produced most of the popular martyrs of the era and won many concessions from the elite, despite the official principle of rejection regardless of their merits (Yokoyama 1977: 85). They often reflected strong persistence, inasmuch as they followed upon unsuccessful appeals to the officials of first instance, and in many cases communities and groups of communities lodged appeals at successively higher levels of the system until a final resolution emerged. In Sakurada domain in 1671 a new, more stringent land survey coupled with a bad harvest prompted appeals to the domain and then to the lord's residence in Edo; a domain elder, two intendants, and six commoner officials were punished and the survey was rescinded. In Tanimura domain in 1681, by contrast, the representatives of nineteen villages appealed their general distress first to the domain and then to the lord in Edo; he ordered them home and jailed their leaders. Other representatives lodged a further appeal with the Edo city magistrate; seven of them were executed and their appeal was rejected (Yashiro 1989: 135–36, 17ff.).

A slightly more frequent, and considerably more contentious, version of the end run was the coercive appeal, in which (usually lower-stratum, more numerous, and more aggressive) commoners directly confronted officials with their appeals or demands.[11] Confrontation sometimes included not only presentation of demands but also efforts to realize them on the spot, for example, by burning tax records. Such appeals were largely a legal category, although the term reflected a marked absence of deference. In substance they also signified community stratification and the decay of community leadership, since end runs under the control of community leaders tended to be assiduously deferential.

Despite the greater size and aggressiveness of the coercive appeals (see Appendix 2, Table C), they were in most cases hardly insurrectionary. In 1866 in a hatamoto domain in the Gifu region, some one thousand persons gathered to protest the tardiness of a response from Edo to a petition requesting a 60 percent tax cut; some village headmen rushed to intercept them and negotiated a 30 percent cut, but over a dozen people were later arrested and exiled (Yashiro 1989: 22ff.). In 1866 Kawagoe domain established a rural popular militia and assessed every village in the domain for conscripts and supplies. The people gathered and chose representatives to remonstrate; the domain took four of these hostage but offered to free them and rescind the supply exaction if the villages would take their conscripts only from their own upper strata. The villagers, seeing through this attempt to divide them, gathered and set off for Edo, but were met

---

[10] They include nos. 30, 31, and 38–42 of Table A.
[11] Or *gōso*—no. 46 in Table A.

by domain officials who persuaded them to disband. Eighteen were subsequently arrested, but all were later released and the people's demands accepted (Yashiro 1989: 107). At the other end of the continuum of coercion, in 1768 insurgents protesting the high, price and unavailability of food actually took over the town of Niigata for twenty days (Aoki M. et al. 1981, 2:241).

Rioting,[12] which accounts for about one in ten of the events, often accompanied coercive appeals. Where they occurred in tandem, however, the rioting was often a tactical aspect of the appeal, with demonstrators tearing up shops and offices on the way to and from lodging an appeal, rather than vice versa (Yasumaru 1984: 411; Borton 1938: 16–17; Fukaya 1979: 11). I have accordingly categorized such riots as appeals, hence political conflict or protest, rather than social conflict. In most cases they occurred alone, as popular sanctions of immoral behavior by the rich, merchants, moneylenders, or landlords, without any appeal or threat to the authorities. They might involve the destruction of tenancy or pawn agreements, forced sale of food (or seizure and sale by the rioters themselves) at low prices, the sheer destruction of property, or the ransacking of warehouses and shops with the poor invited to take what they needed (Shōji et al. 1981: 406, 415; Sasaki 1974: 297ff.; Minami 1978: 211ff.). The rioters themselves often explicitly refrained from taking anything, preserving their "judicial" dignity and keeping their role as selfless protectors of the community unclouded. Aggressiveness was more marked in this than any other part of the contentious repertoire: anywhere from one to hundreds of shops might be destroyed, although violence against persons was very rare.

Indeed riots were actually more aggressive than what I have here described as uprisings or rebellions, the last element in my repertorial typology.[13] This last type of contention was, as seen in Table 2, rare; incidents were often massive, however, some involving over a hundred thousand participants. But even such outbreaks should not be equated with the "peasant armies" of European history: the figures were to a certain extent hyperbolic, and although the participants were organized in the sense that those from specific villages stuck together and shared aims, they were more likely to consist of numerous bands than a single host (Sippel 1977; Yashiro 1989: 215ff.). Still, they frightened the authorities immensely, especially in the later years of the era when the regime's coercive resources were at a low ebb. Their very occurrence demonstrated the incapacity of the regime both immediately—there was no deterrence left—and broadly— any regime whose rule produced such popular discontent was of questionable legitimacy. When armed encounters did occur, these "revolts," like many of their more violent counterparts in early modern Europe, tended to evaporate in a *sauve qui peut*. Nevertheless, they portended major systemic instability.

For the most part my behavioral and sociopolitical repertoires correspond closely. We can interrelate them in three ways: behavior and sociopolitical

---

[12] Nos. 47 and 33 in Table A.
[13] This category includes nos. 48–52 of Table A.

composition, behavior and magnitude, and composition and magnitude. In the first instance, contentious gatherings, for example, were part of a political conflict 20 percent of the time and part of a protest, 78 percent. Conflict among the people was 99 percent social, and the other 1 percent escalated into political conflict; conflict between communities stayed in that social context 92 percent of the time and escalated into political conflict in 8 percent of the cases. Litigation and petition appear to have been overwhelmingly the *result* of social conflict to which the contenders sought official resolution: 96 percent of it was political conflict, although 3 percent of it was sufficiently insubordinate to constitute political protest. Flight was overwhelmingly a political phenomenon, as noted: 93 percent was protest, although 7 percent was political conflict, representing attempts by the absconders to get the government to do something not about their home lord but about the economic situation back home.

Appeals to the government, both end run and coercive, were almost exclusively political. End runs were purely political protest 81 percent of the time and the by-product of social conflict 19 percent; 97 percent of the coercive appeals were protest from the very beginning, and only 3 percent constituted political attempts to obtain government resolution or to attack the government for its treatment of a social problem. "Uprisings" and "rebellions" were similarly political: 95 percent of them were protests, and 4 percent were political conflicts. Riots, on the other hand, were almost totally social, in origin if not conclusion: 92 percent pitted commoners against commoners, and 6 percent escalated into political conflicts. In only 1 percent of the cases recorded was a riot used as a political protest.

The second repertorial combination involves behavior and magnitude. Conflict among the people, litigation and petition, flight, and end runs scored magnitudes of 1 over 90 percent of the time; in the case of end runs in particular—one of the quintessential uses of the term *ikki*—it is clear that "peasant rebellion" is a poor translation. Contentious and disorderly gatherings were actually of a higher magnitude: 93 percent scored 2, in light of their politically disturbing nature; 89 percent of the contention between communities and 98 percent of the coercive appeals scored 5. This intensity is symptomatic of the sort of grass-roots violence that characterized such communal conflict in early modern Europe as well (Tilly et al. 1975). And riots and "rebellions" were the biggest and most aggressive forms of contention: over 95 percent of each type scored 10 on my scale of magnitude.

The final interrelationship I wish to examine involves the composition and magnitude of contention. Here we find an interesting pattern: social conflict is concentrated at the poles, in terms of magnitude, while political protest is a middling phenomenon: 75 percent of the social conflicts scored 1, whereas only 37 percent of the protests did; 18 percent of the social conflicts scored 10, compared to 6 percent of the protests. On the other hand, only 7 percent of the social conflicts scored 2 or 5, whereas 57 percent of the protests did. Political conflict was, by a slight margin, the most modest form of contention. It appears—unsurprisingly—that when the people went to the government for resolution of a social conflict they went humbly indeed. Overall, it looks as if popular contention in early modern Japan had a threefold composition: there was a massive current of low-key social conflict; there were occasional outbursts (predominantly social) potentially of great size and aggressiveness; in addition, there was a less frequent and generally deferential current of political protest, supplemented by other political overtures of a supplicatory nature.

I do not by any means claim that my typologies and definitions are impeccable. I have used as my units of observation and analysis "events"—single outbursts of behavior. Many of the phenomena, however, are in fact sequences of actions. End runs, for example, were hardly ever the initial step in a contentious process. The events on which I have focused do in some cases connect; in the great majority of cases, however, they are the *acme* of a sequence. By classifying the most salient types of behavior involved in the contentious process, I am able to measure the maximum magnitude of a conflict, but I lose the richness of detailed case studies of sequences and interactions, and I underestimate the undercurrent of low-key activity leading up to the documented events. I use cases to throw light on otherwise cold numbers, but we must recognize that there is more to the fabric of contention than numbers can really express.

For example, in Shinano province in 1686 Matsumoto domain found itself in a fiscal crisis and imposed a land survey and a tax increase. Widespread grumbling—often at the tax offices—ensued, and in the tenth month one tax agent was stoned. A group of headmen met and a former village headman, Tada Kasuke, and seven others organized an appeal against the measures. The organizers went to the castle of the domain and filed five demands, including a revision of the rice-coin exchange rate in the farmers' favor. The domain rejected this end run, but the next day a less deferential mob of perhaps ten thousand commoners rioted in the streets of the castle town, wrecking the homes and shops of the wealthy, especially those merchants linked to the domain government. The authorities reconsidered the petition, but the people refused to disperse until they promised to accept Kasuke's demands, whereupon both the appellants and rioters dispersed. The next day the leaders and their families were arrested; twenty-nine of them were executed for the crime of coercive appeal, and the domain's promises were revoked (Yokoyama 1986: 123ff.; Yashiro 1989: 93ff.).

We have here a variety of interwoven actions by both commoners and regime—dearth, deprivation, policy making, plotting, desultory complaining, assault, calculated and perhaps altruistic action, deferential petition, widespread destruction and popular judgment of the rich, apparent victory, betrayal, and death—all summed up as *gōso*, political protest, magnitude 5. When this case is added to the other 874 coercive appeals, I hope that emerging patterns in the data will give us a richer understanding of the origins and processes of contention involving such people as Kasuke, but we must always keep in mind that units of quantitative analysis mask sequences and combinations of actions. The most common combination is that of roughly simultaneous appeals and riots, of which

I have spoken. In most cases they operated together, although we shall see cases in which they operated at cross-purposes, with rioters accusing appellants of selling out and appellants fearing that rioting would harden the authorities (see, e.g., Hyakushō Ikki 1980: 181).

At the other extreme from events that involve more than meets the eye are those involving less: village disputes. Some Japanese scholars see such disputes as political struggle (Shōji 1970: 94ff.; Sasaki 1973), and indeed, many of them inolve confrontations between the people and village leaders. My own view is that some of these observers have a vested interest in seeing class conflict everywhere; that many such disputes were as driven by personal rivalries and social enmity as by political considerations; that even though village leaders were part of the political apparatus, they were commoners and part of that class widely divided from the warriors who controlled the upper reaches of the system; and that the classifications used here do enable us to catch those village disputes that escalated into direct contact with the upper echelons of government. Contention among commoners of all sorts, I maintain, was significantly different from contention that involved the samurai class and its institutions and powers in any way.

Composition and Repertoire across Time and Space

Figure 9 shows the changing sociopolitical composition of popular contention across the era of my study. The period begins on an overwhelmingly political note: 90 percent or more of the total magnitude of all sorts of contention was accounted for by political protest during the first fifteen years. The rest of the seventeenth century saw considerable fluctuation, because of the low volume of contention, but the trend is clear: declining political and increasing social contention. This trend continued through the eighteenth and nineteenth centuries, reversing only with the Restoration. Of the four key points emerging thus far from the data, the first (in the first quarter of the eighteenth century) was a time of dramatically renewed political protest; all the other three—albeit to diminishing degrees—saw declines in the proportion of protest and increases in social conflict.

The clarity of the pattern is impressive, and dovetails with observations already made. The Tokugawa era was one of glacial economic development, social stratification, and political decay (albeit broken by periods of reform)—all of which are consistent with more social and less political contention. As time wore on those without land (and thus untaxed) increased in numbers; their enemies were not the government but landlords, moneylenders, hoarders, sake and soy sauce brewers and other entrepreneurs/employers, and the village officials beneath whose status they fell farther and farther (Shōji et al. 1981: 405; Kokushō 1971: 145). Even for the better-off, the government itself made few claims upon the autonomy and solidarity of the village once the system was established; this factor agrees both with the dominant role of social conflict throughout the era (see Table 2) and with the trend seen here (Magagna 1991). During the early

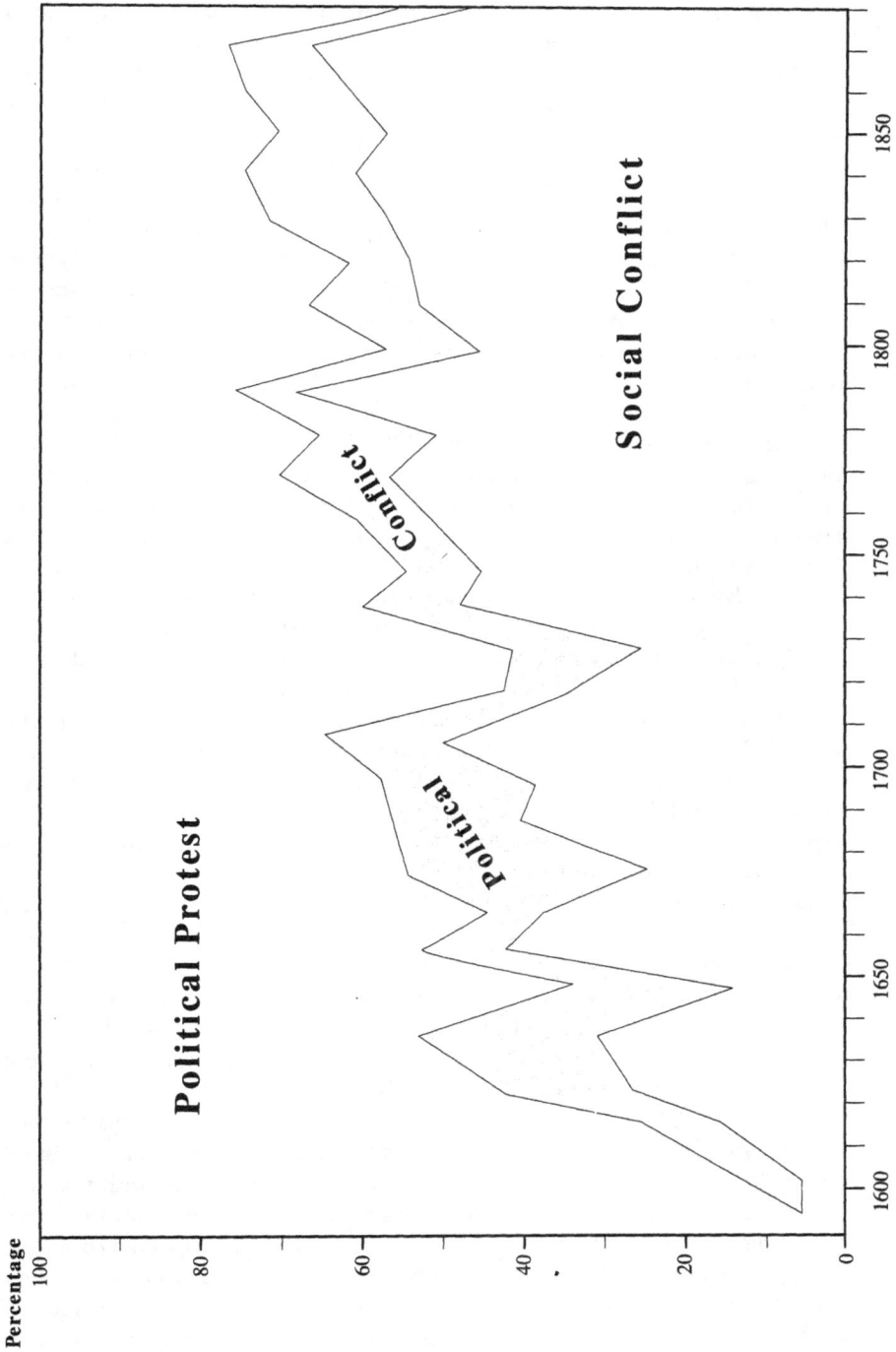

Figure 9. Composition of contention in Japan, 1590–1877

eighteenth century a period of vigorous reform may be responsible for the rise in protest; by the next period of reform, in the 1780s, the government had become less able to enact far-reaching (and contentious) measures, and economic development may have eclipsed the salience of the polity in the lives (and interests) of the people.

With the Meiji Restoration the context and the composition of contention changed radically. In early modern Europe the consolidation of states was followed by a relative diminution of political protest (Manning 1988: chap. 12; Bercé 1990); the same thing happened in the early seventeenth century in Japan. But in 1868 the situation was reversed, and the climate was once again highly politicized: old and new regimes vied for loyalties; tradition competed with innovation; and many groups tried to make political hay in the brief, unstable moment while the political sun shone brightly. I suspect that political protest declined relatively after the first decade of the new era.

Figures 10 through 13 further clarify my view. Figures 10 and 11 show the total magnitude of social conflict and political protest across the country on the provincial level, corrected for kokudaka. Social conflict is most highly concentrated right where one might expect: in the areas of protoindustrial economic development in the central core and Kantō, and in the Kinai (Saitō 1985). There is a secondary concentration in north-central Japan, where, especially in Echigo and Uzen, rich rice productivity spurred commercialization in the same way that sericulture did in the central core. Political protest, by contrast, is spread much more evenly across the country, but especially in the west.

The lordly domains were also disproportionately in the west. I have already noted their more aggressive attitudes and overreaching policies, which I expected to stimulate political contention. Additionally, popular contenders in the domains might well be more inclined to choose political techniques and targets, regardless of issue, as a way to draw the (frequently punitive) attention of the shogunate to domain misrule. This strategy was unavailable to those in the shogun's own lands; there, if a village or local official were the focus of grievances, people might as well go straight after him (Jack Goldstone, personal communication). There was, to be sure, much protest in the central core and, again, in remote and rugged Rikuchū (ruled by the notoriously harsh Nambu family), but overall, it seems that social conflict was characteristic of the more developed, more often bakufu-controlled core, and protest, of the less developed and more often daimyo-ruled periphery (White 1992b).

But these maps give a static picture. Figures 12 and 13 add a dynamic one, showing the percentage increase in total magnitude of social conflict and political protest in each province in the second half of the era, compared with the first. One can see that the central core was a highly contentious area from the very beginning of the era, as were the Japan Sea coast and the metropolitan cores; the metropolitan hinterlands (a ring around Edo from Kazusa to Hitachi and around Ōsaka from Kii to Yamashiro), the far north, and the far southwest also showed marked proportional increases in conflict, albeit from a relatively low base.

Figure 10. Total magnitude of social conflict, 1590–1877

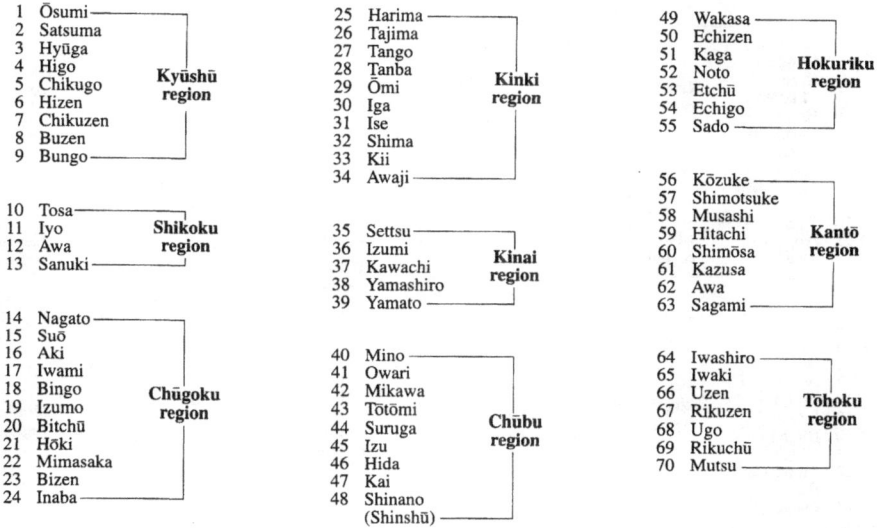

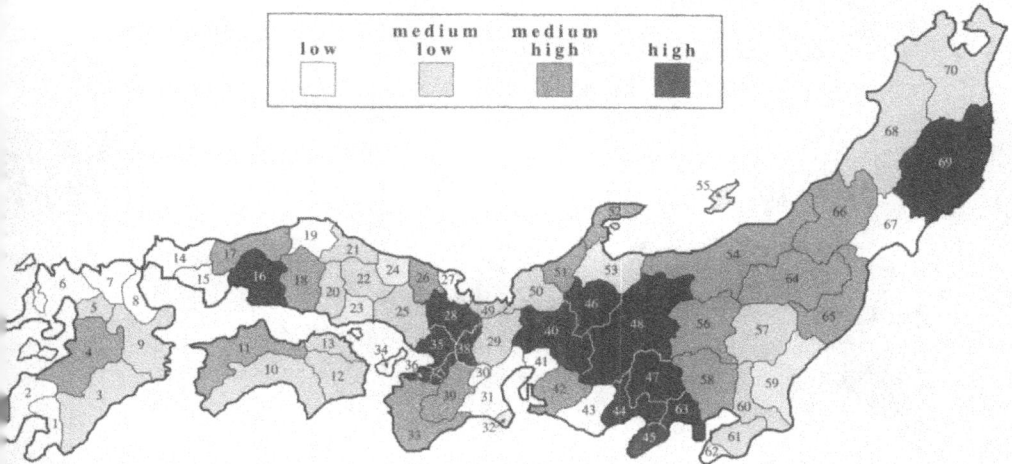

1 Ōsumi	25 Harima	49 Wakasa
2 Satsuma	26 Tajima	50 Echizen
3 Hyūga	27 Tango	51 Kaga
4 Higo **Kyūshū**	28 Tanba **Kinki**	52 Noto **Hokuriku**
5 Chikugo **region**	29 Ōmi **region**	53 Etchū **region**
6 Hizen	30 Iga	54 Echigo
7 Chikuzen	31 Ise	55 Sado
8 Buzen	32 Shima	
9 Bungo	33 Kii	
	34 Awaji	56 Kōzuke
		57 Shimotsuke
10 Tosa		58 Musashi
11 Iyo **Shikoku**	35 Settsu	59 Hitachi **Kantō**
12 Awa **region**	36 Izumi	60 Shimōsa **region**
13 Sanuki	37 Kawachi **Kinai**	61 Kazusa
	38 Yamashiro **region**	62 Awa
	39 Yamato	63 Sagami
14 Nagato		
15 Suō		
16 Aki	40 Mino	64 Iwashiro
17 Iwami	41 Owari	65 Iwaki
18 Bingo **Chūgoku**	42 Mikawa	66 Uzen **Tōhoku**
19 Izumo **region**	43 Tōtōmi **Chūbu**	67 Rikuzen **region**
20 Bitchū	44 Suruga **region**	68 Ugo
21 Hōki	45 Izu	69 Rikuchū
22 Mimasaka	46 Hida	70 Mutsu
23 Bizen	47 Kai	
24 Inaba	48 Shinano	
	(Shinshū)	

Overall, as the increasing national magnitude of contention has suggested, few provinces showed neither high magnitudes of social conflict nor significant increases during the era.

Political protest is a different thing altogether. The areas of high era-long magnitude and those of marked increase are quite different, with increases

Figure 11. Total magnitude of political protest, 1590–1877

1 Ōsumi	25 Harima	49 Wakasa
2 Satsuma	26 Tajima	50 Echizen
3 Hyūga	27 Tango	51 Kaga
4 Higo	28 Tanba	52 Noto **Hokuriku**
5 Chikugo **Kyūshū**	29 Ōmi **Kinki**	53 Etchū **region**
6 Hizen **region**	30 Iga **region**	54 Echigo
7 Chikuzen	31 Ise	55 Sado
8 Buzen	32 Shima	
9 Bungo	33 Kii	
	34 Awaji	56 Kōzuke
10 Tosa		57 Shimotsuke
11 Iyo **Shikoku**		58 Musashi
12 Awa **region**	35 Settsu	59 Hitachi **Kantō**
13 Sanuki	36 Izumi	60 Shimōsa **region**
	37 Kawachi **Kinai**	61 Kazusa
14 Nagato	38 Yamashiro **region**	62 Awa
15 Suō	39 Yamato	63 Sagami
16 Aki		
17 Iwami		64 Iwashiro
18 Bingo **Chūgoku**	40 Mino	65 Iwaki
19 Izumo **region**	41 Owari	66 Uzen
20 Bitchū	42 Mikawa	67 Rikuzen **Tōhoku**
21 Hōki	43 Tōtōmi	68 Ugo **region**
22 Mimasaka	44 Suruga **Chūbu**	69 Rikuchū
23 Bizen	45 Izu **region**	70 Mutsu
24 Inaba	46 Hida	
	47 Kai	
	48 Shinano	
	(Shinshū)	

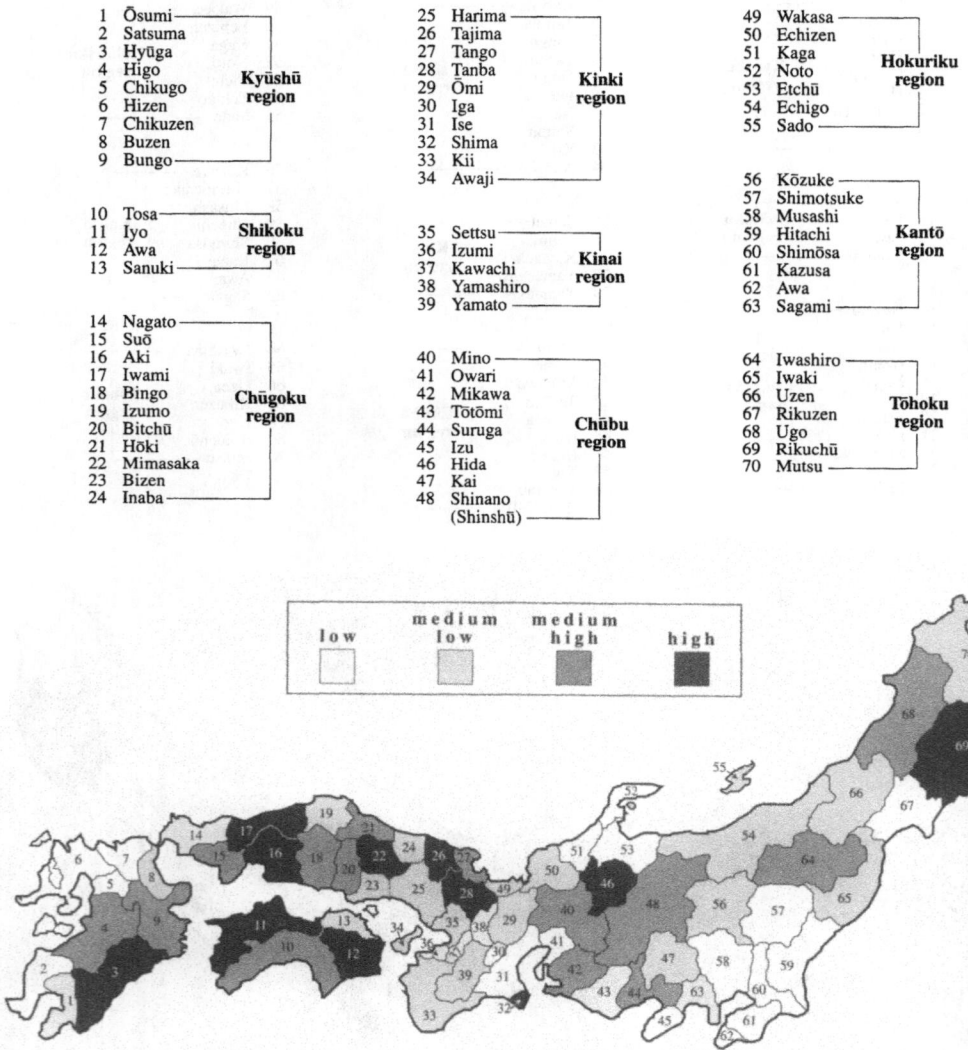

concentrated in a core region running from Shimōsa to Settsu and Awaji (with the exceptions of Mutsu in the north and Ōsumi and Higo in the south). Again, the most protest-racked regions overall were so from early in the era, and those that increased the most still did not reach the levels of the really contentious provinces. As social conflict dispersed during the era, protest centralized.

Figure 12. Increase in magnitude of social conflict, 1590–1749 vs. 1750–1877

1	Ōsumi		25	Harima		49	Wakasa
2	Satsuma		26	Tajima		50	Echizen
3	Hyūga		27	Tango		51	Kaga
4	Higo	**Kyūshū**	28	Tanba	**Kinki**	52	Noto
5	Chikugo	**region**	29	Ōmi	**region**	53	Etchū
6	Hizen		30	Iga		54	Echigo
7	Chikuzen		31	Ise		55	Sado
8	Buzen		32	Shima			
9	Bungo		33	Kii			
			34	Awaji		56	Kōzuke
						57	Shimotsuke
10	Tosa					58	Musashi
11	Iyo	**Shikoku**	35	Settsu		59	Hitachi
12	Awa	**region**	36	Izumi		60	Shimōsa
13	Sanuki		37	Kawachi	**Kinai**	61	Kazusa
			38	Yamashiro	**region**	62	Awa
14	Nagato		39	Yamato		63	Sagami
15	Suō						
16	Aki		40	Mino		64	Iwashiro
17	Iwami		41	Owari		65	Iwaki
18	Bingo	**Chūgoku**	42	Mikawa		66	Uzen
19	Izumo	**region**	43	Tōtōmi		67	Rikuzen
20	Bitchū		44	Suruga	**Chūbu**	68	Ugo
21	Hōki		45	Izu	**region**	69	Rikuchū
22	Mimasaka		46	Hida		70	Mutsu
23	Bizen		47	Kai			
24	Inaba		48	Shinano			
				(Shinshū)			

Regions at right: Hokuriku region (49–55), Kantō region (56–63), Tōhoku region (64–70)

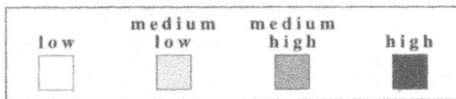

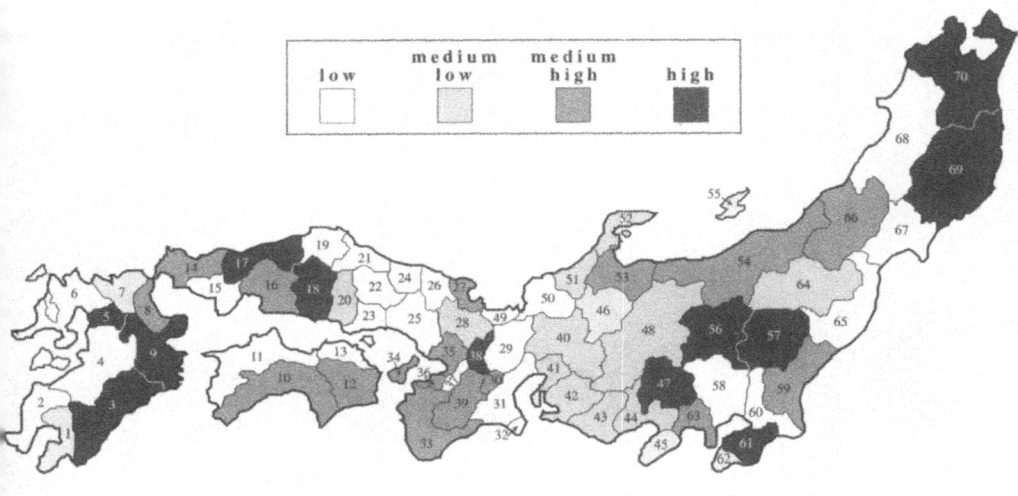

But did it urbanize? And did it concentrate in the lordly domains? To answer these questions we must look at contention across social and political space, not simply geographical. The answer to the first question appears to be negative: my data show no variation in composition from the least to the most urban counties although, as we would expect, the proportion of all contention accounted for by

Figure 13. Increase in magnitude of political protest, 1590–1749 vs. 1750–1877

1 Ōsumi 2 Satsuma 3 Hyūga 4 Higo 5 Chikugo **Kyūshū region** 6 Hizen 7 Chikuzen 8 Buzen 9 Bungo	25 Harima 26 Tajima 27 Tango 28 Tanba 29 Ōmi **Kinki region** 30 Iga 31 Ise 32 Shima 33 Kii 34 Awaji	49 Wakasa 50 Echizen 51 Kaga 52 Noto **Hokuriku region** 53 Etchū 54 Echigo 55 Sado
10 Tosa 11 Iyo **Shikoku region** 12 Awa 13 Sanuki	35 Settsu 36 Izumi 37 Kawachi **Kinai region** 38 Yamashiro 39 Yamato	56 Kōzuke 57 Shimotsuke 58 Musashi 59 Hitachi **Kantō region** 60 Shimōsa 61 Kazusa 62 Awa 63 Sagami
14 Nagato 15 Suō 16 Aki 17 Iwami 18 Bingo **Chūgoku region** 19 Izumo 20 Bitchū 21 Hōki 22 Mimasaka 23 Bizen 24 Inaba	40 Mino 41 Owari 42 Mikawa 43 Tōtōmi 44 Suruga **Chūbu region** 45 Izu 46 Hida 47 Kai 48 Shinano (Shinshū)	64 Iwashiro 65 Iwaki 66 Uzen 67 Rikuzen **Tōhoku region** 68 Ugo 69 Rikuchū 70 Mutsu

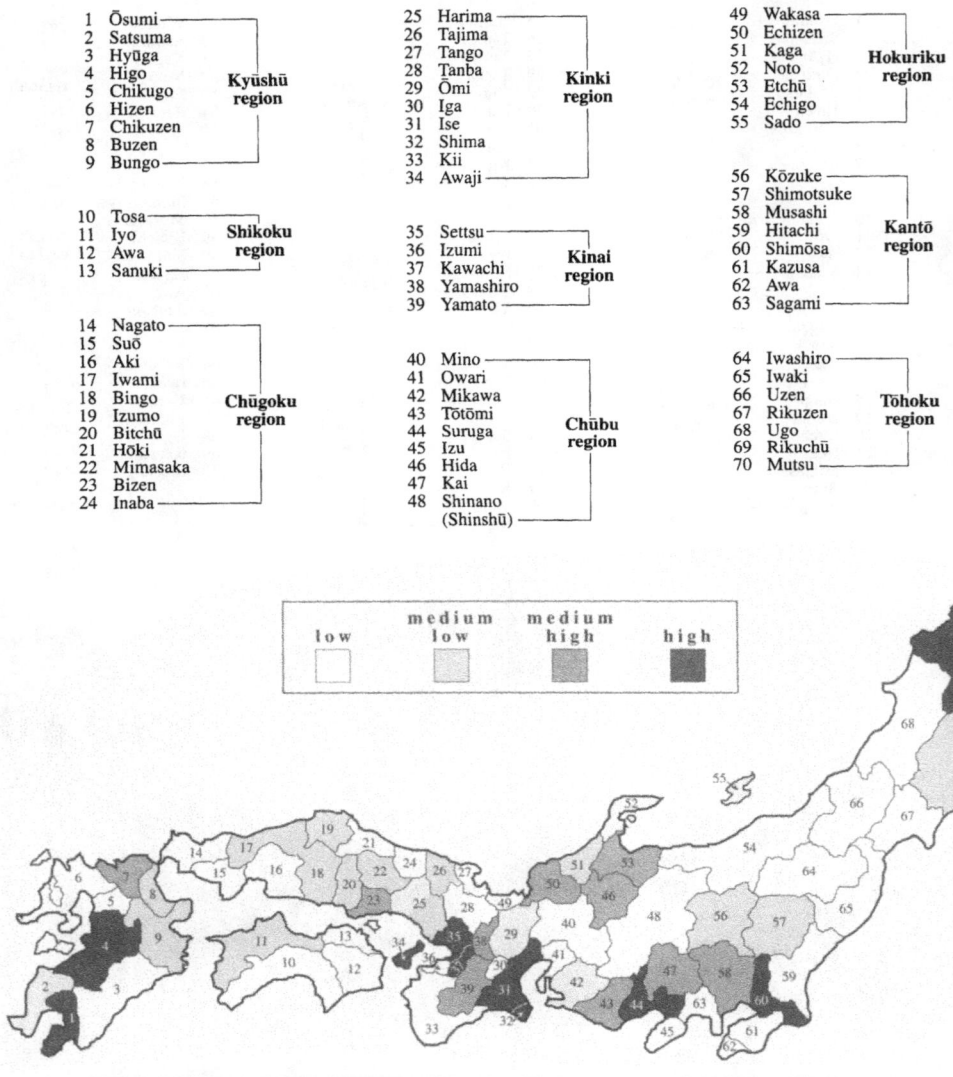

social conflict was higher in Ōsaka, the quintessential mercantile city, than in Edo, the quintessential political city.[14] But the apparent influence of political

[14] The data on levels of county urbanism are from Rikugun 1976; level of urbanism is measured as the proportion of county population living in urbanized communities with four thousand or more inhabitants.

Table 3. Composition of contention in different political jurisdictions

	Tokugawa lands	*Hatamoto domains*	*Hereditary lords' domains*	*Outer lords' domains*
Social conflict	62%	64%	54%	38%
Political conflict	18	13	12	11
Political Protest	20	24	34	51
	100%	101%	100%	100%

Note: n = 6,357.

context on composition is impressive, as shown in Table 3: in the Tokugawa house lands and the hatamoto domains over 60 percent of all contention was social, whereas political protest accounted for only 20–25 percent. In the outside domains this situation was reversed: half of the contention was political protest, and less than 40 percent was social conflict. The hereditary lords ruled domains somewhere in between, seeing more social conflict and less protest than the outer domains, and less social conflict and more protest than the shogunally ruled lands.

As the maps suggest, the complexion of contention changed markedly during the course of the Tokugawa era. This change can be looked at in two ways: in the absolute frequency of different types of behavior and in the relative proportions of the totality of contention accounted for by each type. Table 4 presents the absolutes, and Figure 14 the relative proportions. Unsurprisingly, given the gradual rise in popular contention throughout the era, almost all forms of contentious behavior were more frequent at the end than at the beginning of the period, many showing monotonic increases. The one exception is flight, which faded continuously during the era as the authorities came to look on it with less and less sympathy. But two other major transitions are also visible.

The first occurred in the eighteenth century, especially in its first half. Roughly speaking, during this half century the average number of disorderly gatherings per year tripled, the frequency of popular conflicts doubled, that of intercommunity contention tripled, the number of coercive appeals quintupled, uprisings reappeared after a fifty-year absence, and the number of riots increased more than twenty-five times. Additionally, in the second half of the century "disquiets" quadrupled, coercive appeals and popular conflicts almost doubled, and riots increased almost eightfold.

The other transition occurred with the Meiji Restoration. Two types of contention—social conflict among commoners and relatively deferential end runs—peaked in the last years of the Tokugawa era, while the number of coercive appeals and uprisings rose sharply. I have already suggested that the decrease of social conflict was the consequence of the politicization of the general atmosphere in the 1860s; end runs also relied heavily on—though they calculatedly sidestepped—an explicit hierarchy of adjudicators, which disintegrated in the 1860s. Coercive appeals could be lodged with any nearby official; not only did grass-roots authority not disintegrate during the Restoration, but the new regime

Table 4. Evolution of the repertoire of popular contention (average annual number of events)

	1590–1649	1650–1699	1700–1749	1750–1799	1800–1849	1850–1867	1868–1877
Disorderly gatherings	0.13	0.24	0.66	2.26	4.04	6.33	9.30
Contention among commoners	0.80	2.86	5.82	9.82	21.32	27.89	13.40
Intercommunity contention	0.17	0.10	0.32	0.18	0.46	0.50	1.60
Litigation and petition	0.83	1.20	1.70	1.66	3.82	3.78	4.40
Flight	1.22	0.98	0.90	0.68	0.90	0.33	0.10
End-run appeals	0.73	1.82	2.40	2.72	4.06	4.67	1.20
Coercive appeals	0.32	0.52	2.72	4.28	4.74	5.83	10.30
Riots	0.00	0.02	0.56	4.08	4.24	7.00	10.60
Uprisings	0.45	0.00	0.18	0.32	0.32	0.22	2.00

Note: n = 6,471.

in many ways reauthorized existing local authorities, thus keeping them available as targets of contention. And uprisings were focused specifically on the new regime and its dramatic and sweeping measures of national renovation.

As noted, calculating absolute numbers of events of each type gives an incomplete picture, because the total number of events varied from year to year. Accordingly, I present Figure 14, which shows how the common people invested their time and energies in the different types of contentious behavior. The greater relative frequency of a certain type does not necessarily mean that it was the most-*liked* form of contention. It may have been chosen for reasons having little to do with abstract likes and dislikes and everything to do with contextual constraints and calculations of relative efficacy. Still, this figure does give us, in two ways, some insights into possible contextual and microlevel factors.

First, let us look across Figure 14. Disorderly gatherings show a steady increase, with a jump in the Meiji, era when, one may speculate, people faced with a transformative and coercive state turned from more moderate forms of contention toward either inaction or violence. Contention among the people was the single most common type during almost the entire era; reflecting Table 4, it occupied the largest share of the totality of contention during the last decades of the Tokugawa era, when the impression is of wholesale popular conflict until one recalls that the magnitude of most of these events was quite low. And of course, given this low magnitude, the retreat of social conflict of this sort after the Restoration is striking.

Litigation and petition and flight became decreasingly popular during the era. The eclipse of flight is the more dramatic: from over one-quarter of all events to less than 1 percent of the total. More active forms of contention, especially their

Figure 14. Evolution of the repertoire of contentious behavior, 1590–1877

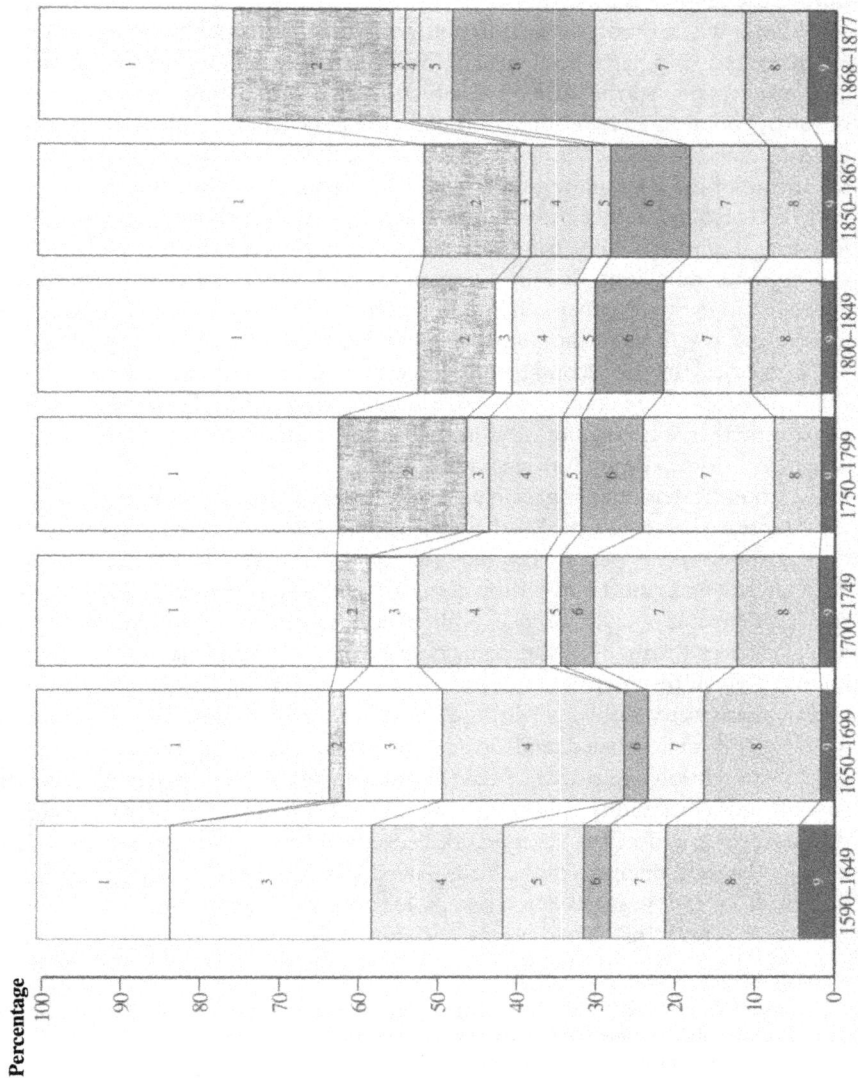

Percentage of the total magnitude of popular contention accounted for by:

1. contention among the commoners
2. riots
3. flight
4. end run appeals
5. uprisings
6. disorderly gatherings
7. coercive appeals
8. litigation and petition
9. intercommunity contention

more aggressive forms, grew. We have seen that both end-run and coercive appeals increased in number (at least until the Restoration), but proportionately, end runs began to fall during the eighteenth century, as social stratification made representation more and more difficult, while coercive appeals began to grow during the same period, peaking after the Restoration. Riots showed a similar pattern to coercive appeals, joining the popular repertoire in the eighteenth century (only one riot is recorded before that), swiftly becoming a well-used tool, and also peaking after the Restoration. Most systemically sensitive of all were uprisings, which occurred in the unstable early years of the Tokugawa and again during the first decade of Meiji.

Second, we can look at the different periods of the era. The early years were characterized by polarization, typified by litigation and flight, on the one hand, and insurrection, on the other (Hayashi 1976a: 351ff.). Attainders and transfers of lords, abolition and consolidation of fiefs—all generated contention, typically led by retainers of the lord or ex-lord. In other instances commoners took advantage of the wars among their betters to pursue their own ends (Aoki M. et al. 1981, 2:162ff.). Once the shogunate established its authority, such rebellions lost their usefulness. Shimabara was a transition: some claim that it was the last of the regional rebellions, led by remnants of the pre-Tokugawa warrior elite, against the new state; others, that it was a new type of contention, a farmers' ikki against the exactions of the domain government (Fukaya 1979: chap. 2).

In any case, the the second half of the seventeenth century was far quieter than the first. People were coming to understand the new political economy; the new social structure was creating meaningful groups with common interests, at least within individual communities; and the rules of the new game were increasingly understood. Deferential litigation and end runs set the tone; flight declined, and the "representative end run" led by village officials epitomized the contention of the time.[15] The people learned quickly: by the late seventeenth century domainwide end runs launched by dozens of villages in concert, with dozens of specific demands, gave evidence both of standarization of administrative and fiscal practices throughout the domain and of the domainwide commonality of interests which resulted.[16]

But there were problems with the end-run strategy. Those who employed it were easily double-crossed, and the few leaders were easily apprehended; it was a type of contention easily decapitated (Hayashi 1976a: 3ff.). At the same time, the sort of tight community coherence that the end run presupposed had begun to decline by the end of the seventeenth century. Additionally, by the turn of the century the fiscal dilemma of the lords—fixed revenues and increasing expenses—was pushing them to heavier levels of extraction (Vlastos 1986). The consequences of both of these factors included the initial signs of unmediated

[15] Hayashi 1976a: 3, 351ff.; Vlastos 1986: chap. 2. "Representative end run" is *daihyō osso* in Japanese; other terms for flight include *hashiri*, *ketsuraku*, and *taiten*.
[16] Domainwide end runs are *zempan osso* or *zempan ikki*. Aoki M. et al. 1981, 2:181ff.

lower-stratal participation and direct action, both open confrontations with the authorities and rioting as an expression of popular resolve (Aoki M. et al. 1981, 2:215ff.). Early examples of this transformation include Tada Kasuke's protest in Matsumoto domain in 1686, but historians tend to see the first quarter of the eighteenth century as the real transition, with the efflorescence of the coercive appeal, the most notable subtype of which was the mass protest, or *sō-byakushō ikki*.[17] The biggest examples of the mass protest occurred in midcentury, with more than 150,000 participants in one in Kyūshū's Kurume domain in 1754, and well over 100,000 in the Demma Rebellion in Musashi province in 1764 (Yokoyama 1977: 106).

The transitional eighteenth century showed the richest and most variegated repertoire of all the periods. No one type dominated relatively, although the coercive appeal emerged, the more popular forms of the previous century continue to decline, and other types began to climb. Everything is in evidence contentiously, as was also the case politically, socially, and economically. Protoindustrialization continued, as did alienation of land, social stratification, and the authorities' extractive response: the taxation of nonagricultural pursuits and establishment of official monopolies and monopsonies (Aoki M. et al. 1981, 1:143–46; Fukaya 1979: 120–22). I have already noted the remarkable increase in magnitude and frequency of contention; qualitatively, also, the period is characterized by the full integration of rioting into the popular repertoire (Rekishigaku Kenkyū 1985: 79ff.; Burton 1978: 142ff.).

The Temmei cycle of contention casts light on certain trends in popular contention. First, it was the first really nationwide wave of conflict. During the 1730s a crop failure in western Japan caused little stir in the total magnitude of contention nationwide; in the 1780s integration of markets and communications, the national implications of shogunal policy under Tanuma Okitsugu, and the nationwide decline in lordly coercive capabilities have been cited as the links between widespread crop failures in eastern Japan and the dramatic national upswing in popular contention.[18] Second, Yokoyama Toshio (1977: 129–35) dates from approximately this time a trend noted earlier: more, but smaller, events. This pattern he attributes to social differentiation, and he sees the occasional larger regional conflicts as designed to minimize the sorts of reprisals that were gradually contributing to the eclipse of the representative end run.

Indeed, social differentiation is a plausible explanation for the trend seen subsequently. The mixed eighteenth-century repertoire gave way, between 1800 and 1867, to a predominance of popular conflict, including riot. Rioting was a less-preferred instrument than in the late eighteenth century, but the social

---

[17] Also called *zempan sō-byakushō ikki*. Hayashi 1976a: 351ff., 1976b: 117–19; Aoki K. 1966: 74; Yokoyama 1986: 151ff.

[18] Aoki M. et al. 1981, 2:245ff. In Hosaka Satoru's words (in Aoki M. et al. 1981, 2:235ff.), it was a time not only of nationwide contention but of extraordinarily large "regional struggles" (*kōiki tōsō*) such as the Demma Rebellion of 1764.

harmony of the community appears to have reached a low point. Rural elites were increasingly incorporated into the ruling structure, leaving the rest of the people on their own. And economic growth did not eliminate economic vulnerability. When the Tempō crisis hit in the 1830s there were rural conflicts between authorities and merchants who wanted to ship rice to the cities and residents who wanted to keep it at home, and in the cities there were food riots (Aoki M. et al. 1981, 2:267ff.). Compared to the Temmei cycle, consumer-driven contention seems to have outweighed producer-driven, and there was relatively little protest against taxation or regulation of commerce (Hyakushō Ikki 1980: 378).

But in 1868, relatively at least, people's minds seem to have been taken off contending among themselves by the overwhelming changes of the Restoration, to which they responded—as they had 250 years before—with a bipolar pattern of contention: grumbling and murmuring on the one hand, rioting and rebelling on the other. We get to this state by different routes: insurrection is the only type of contention that actually peaked in both periods, but two relatively passive and deferential types of behavior—flight and litigation—gave way to another—disquiet—such that bipolarity was created by two different repertoires. The social basis of the repertoire—well-advanced differentiation—seems to have continued (Kelly 1985: 285ff.), but my view is that the predominance of forms of contention presupposing limited social organization is more the reflection of the changing context, truly a moving target, than the changing constituency of contention.

Such, then, is the picture of the repertoire of contention across time. It remains for us to look at it also across space—geographical, social, and political. Table 5 begins this exercise by presenting regional variations in the repertoire of popular contention, and it reinforces impressions already gained. Basically, the west appears to have been the locus of a more political, more aggressive type of contention than the east. Uprisings, coercive appeals, and flight were characteristic of the west (with the exception of coercive appeals in the northeast Tōhoku); the east, by contrast, saw far more conflict among the people, with an additional concentration of rioting in Kantō and an exceptional scarcity of such contention in Tōhoku. Social conflict thus seems rather to be a core phenomenon—like, one cannot refrain from noting, economic development—whereas coercive appeals and perhaps uprisings are typical of the periphery. Disorderly gatherings vary considerably across regions, but without discernible pattern; litigation, conflict between communities, end-run appeals, and riots are spread relatively evenly across the country. Riots, however, show a counterintuitive pattern. They are usually thought of as an urban, if not metropolitan, phenomenon, but in fact they were concentrated in Hokuriku, Kyūshū, and Tōhoku; Edo's Kantō region falls below, and Ōsaka's Kinki region only at, the national mean of 10 percent.

We can look more directly at this element by comparing regions (counties, in this case) at differing levels of urbanization. What we find is that riots are, in fact, a disproportionately but not exclusively urban phenomenon: 15 percent of all the contention in the most urban counties took the form of riots, as did 8 percent of

Table 5. Variation in contentious repertoires across regions

	Tōhoku	Kantō	Hokuriku	Tōzan	Tōkai	Kinki	Sanin	Sanyō	Shikoku	Kyūshū
Disorderly gathering	5%	6%	16%	5%	11%	8%	16%	13%	9%	16%
Conflict among people	30	55	35	61	44	49	20	22	19	14
Intercommunity conflict	1	1	1	1	1	2	1	3	3	2
Litigation	12	10	5	11	6	10	5	7	6	2
Flight	5	1	3	2	1	1	1	2	16	20
End run	11	12	9	9	14	9	13	17	9	12
Coercive appeal	21	7	13	6	13	10	28	23	25	16
Riot	13	8	17	5	8	10	12	10	10	16
Uprising	2	1	1	1	2	1	4	3	3	3
Total	100%	101%	100%	101%	100%	100%	100%	100%	100%	101%

Notes: n = 5,649. For provincial composition of regions see Figure 10.

the contention in the least urban counties. And none of the other elements of the contentious repertoire varied significantly along the dimension of urbanism. But in contrast to urbanism, or social space, political space does appear to be a significant differentiating factor in determining the contentious repertoire, though not in all cases. Disorderly gatherings, intercommunity conflict, end runs, riots, and uprisings are more or less evenly distributed across political jurisdictions of various types, but disorderly gatherings, flight, and litigation and petition, on the one hand, and coercive appeals, on the other, are strongly associated with political system.

Specifically, the inhabitants of shogunal and hatamoto territories had a marked predilection for fighting among themselves: 52 percent of the contention in shogunal lands and 61 percent of that in the hatamoto lands was among the people, as opposed to 44 percent in the hereditary domains and only 23 percent in the outer. Additionally, 11 percent and 9 percent, respectively, of the contention in the shogunal and hatamoto jurisdictions was litigation and petition, compared to 8 percent in the hereditary domains and only 6 percent in the outer. On the other hand, in the outer domains 8 percent of the contention took the form of flight; this proportion was 4 percent in the hereditary domains and only 1 percent in shogunal and hatamoto lands. Finally, 23 percent of all contention in the outer domains was coercive appeals; the figure for the hereditary domains was 14 percent, and 5 percent and 6 percent, respectively, for Tokugawa and hatamoto territories.

Thus the lordly domains—especially the outer—saw more, and more aggressive, political contention and less social. Why should this have been so? I have already noted that the domains were more coercive. Why, then, did the people not incline toward safer social conflict? At this point the most attractive hypothesis concerns policy: the domains were more coercive but also more provocative and thus more salient in the lives of the people. And the reverse—Why did the people not directly attack the more vulnerable shogunal and hatamoto adminis-trations?—leads to a complementary hypothesis: the ineptitude of the shogunate meant less coercion but also less relevance—both as cause and cure—to the grievances that mobilized the people.

Thus interests might take causal precedence over opportunities in the etiology of contention. Other aspects of the distribution nevertheless suggest that political opportunities count and that economic development—a constellation of inter-ests, opportunities, and resources—is significant too. Clearly, a multivariate ap-proach to contention will be essential. For the time being, we shall move on from the outward appearance of contention to its internal process and structure.

7

PROCESS AND CYCLE

The previous chapter set forth the most general patterns of popular contention, but we need a more holistic, dynamic, and qualitative picture. I want first to look at specific cases and then to summarize the typical process: the run-up of past grievances and incidents, murmuring, and planning; the mobilization of contenders; the interaction between the contenders; the decay of the movement; and its end. We can also look at process in aggregate terms, that is, at the massive cycles of contention occurring at separate points in the Tokugawa era as single processes with characteristics of their own, apart from the events they comprised.

In 1708 Mito domain was racked by contention when several thousand of its people made a coercive appeal.[1] The domain, north of Edo, was ruled by a branch of the Tokugawa family. Like many other domains, Mito was by then in a fiscal crisis to which its rulers responded in a variety of ways: the land tax was raised by 20–30 percent, domain currency was issued, private woodlands were confiscated and reclaimed for agriculture or converted to commons, and the stipends of the domain's retainers were cut. What set the people off, however, was a plan for a canal designed to facilitate commerce—which the domain could tax—between northern Japan and Edo.

The canal actually concerned only the people of southern Mito, whose land would be taken and who would be dragooned into labor service to build it, and they began to discuss remonstration as soon as they got wind of it. Their intent solidified when the project got under way; the corvée laborers decided not only that their pay was set too low but that the administrators of the project were welshing on even that wage agreement. At first, individual villages appealed to the authorities; after several of these appeals proved unsuccessful, a representative group burst into the offices of the county intendant to demand a halt to the

---

[1] This account is based primarily on Shōji et al. 1981; and Nagasu 1986.

project, and subsequently another group lodged a protest with the domain authorities at the castle town.

The southerners were not alone. People in the northern part of the domain, angered at the tax increase at a time of poor harvest, were appealing to the intendants for a survey of the crop to verify their claims of dearth; if refused, they intended to go to the county magistrate. These appeals were legal, since they were lodged by separate villages' officials without prior concert. Their focus on the application of tax policy also differentiated them from the southerners, who wanted domain policy changed and those responsible for it fired. Nevertheless, the northerners too were rebuffed on the domain level, and in the twelfth month of 1708 some thirty to fifty of them went to Edo to present their petition at the mansion where the lord of the domain was in residence. This petition was rejected, and the petitioners sent word back to Mito, calling for reinforcements.

More people—perhaps three thousand—came to Edo from throughout Mito. Once in the capital, they drafted a petition that combined the respective demands of north and south and presented this to the domain. The domain accepted some of its elements, rejected others, and ordered the petitioners home. Some of them (mostly northerners) did return. On the way, however, they encountered another band of southerners headed for Edo, and many turned around and went back to Edo too. Others of the southern band had never left Edo, hiding at inns in the city in violation of the domain's command. Soon the two groups got together, chose a man named Tōemon as their representative, and agreed on a set of twenty-eight demands that amounted to a direct rejection of domain authority over taxes, public works, and personnel.

With this dangerous document in hand, the petitioners attempted in the first month of 1709 to approach the lord's palanquin as he returned to his mansion from Edo Castle. His retainers rerouted him and kept the three hundred plus farmers at bay, although the image of a lord—a Tokugawa at that—being chased around the shogun's own capital by rabble of his own domain must have been hugely embarrassing. The next day another thousand or more people arrived from Mito, and another overture was planned; Tōemon and two others approached the mansion of Moriyama domain (a branch domain of Mito). At first they were turned away, but the second time they tried they were admitted, Moriyama passed the word to Mito, and Tōemon and his group, along with some Moriyama officials, went to the Mito mansion.

The Mito officials were partially conciliatory, conceding on tax relief and maladministration but insisting that domain policies themselves were nonnegotiable. Tōemon, who may have smelled weakness or may have known that he could have been clapped in irons at any time, was back the next day, still pressing his demands. The day after that the domain informed him that the canal program was canceled and the responsible officials dismissed, and told him and his confederates to go home. Which they did.

Mito's cave-in to popular pressure (albeit pressure applied in the bright light of the shogun's front yard) is not, perhaps, earthshaking. Mito had no particular

reputation as a hard-nosed domain and little experience in dealing with protesters. Nambu domain was another story. Located in the far north, the Nambu
family had a well-deserved reputation for oppression and heavy taxation. In 1853,
however, they too were the target of a lengthy, involved end run by disgruntled
commoners.[2]

The long-term grievance of the people was the rice purchase system, through
which the domain forcibly bought rice from the people at a low price, sold it in
Edo at a high price, and pocketed the difference. During the calamitous and
famine-racked 1830s, the domain had continued its exactions, ignoring crop
failures, enforcing the purchase system more strictly, and extracting specie from
the populace with forced "loans" and domain paper currency. The people responded with more than seventy separate protests during the period: riots in the
castle town of Morioka in 1833 led the domain to try to divert rice stocks there,
but this attempt elicited screams from the countryside, culminating in a coercive
appeal in 1836 by several thousand people from all over the domain. The domain
responded with some concessions on taxes, loans, and currency policy; reshuffled
some officials; and attempted to persuade the people to lodge their appeals
through legal channels—complaint boxes and special domain emissaries. The
people were undeterred and presented repeated demands to the authorities. In
1837 over two thousand subjects absconded to neighboring Sendai domain to
ask for intervention; they returned with few concessions but with a promise of
amnesty, which Nambu promptly broke by executing four participants.

Thus the omens were hardly bright in 1853, when once again, after years of
exploitation, inept rule, and broken promises, the people were saddled with a
forced loan. The loan was imposed in late 1852, and planning took until the
following spring, when leaders began to circulate through the domain mobilizing
support for an appeal. This process took some two weeks, and the inaction of the
domain meanwhile, though it must at least have suspected something, may have
brightened the omens a bit. The leaders gathered more than eight thousand
people under banners representing their respective villages, and they set off for
Sendai in orderly but armed (even with a few firearms) procession.

Once across the domain border they lodged their petition with Sendai, and a
radical note it was. They wanted either to have the lord of Nambu replaced by his
predecessor or to be placed under Sendai or shogunal rule. In addition, they
made sixteen demands for administrative reforms (mostly for a reduction in the
number of expensive rural officials); ten for reform of the media, payment
schedule, and level of taxes; and twenty-three for deregulation and tax exemption
of commerce and industry—plus, once again, amnesty. No response was immediately forthcoming, and after ten days the demonstrators left for home, leaving
forty-five representatives in Sendai to press the case. Sendai vacillated, at one
point threatening to remand the protesters to Edo, but eventually it began to

---

[2] This account is based primarily on Hyakushō Ikki 1980; Shōji et al. 1981; Fukaya 1983; and
Nishikawa 1979: chap. 6.

make noises about taking over the Sanhei district (the focus of the administrative transfer demand) and passed the petition along to the shogunal Council of Elders in Edo. At this point—the tenth month of 1853—Nambu also acted, with alacrity: officials were fired, policy was reformed, and thirty-nine of the forty-nine substantive demands were accepted, in addition to a blanket amnesty, whereupon the forty-five returned home.

This may have been the end of the story; then again, maybe it wasn't. The domain carried through on its promises, but the following year one of the leaders of the protest, Miura Meisuke, was accused of (some say framed for) complicity in a small protest; he fled the domain but returned in 1857. Upon his return he was arrested, and he died in 1864 in prison. One is mildly disinclined to see the domain as sufficiently vengeful and sophisticated to go through so much to get back at Meisuke, but we cannot be sure. Or perhaps our suspicion is due precisely to their customary view of punishment, which was exemplary, didactic, and deterrent. None of these objectives was well served by punishing Meisuke for unrelated behavior.

In these two stories, and in those of Hachiemon, Hyōsuke, and Bansuke, we can see many of the precursors of contention: long-standing policy grievances, past episodes of conflict, short-term policy changes, natural calamities *without* policy change, and extensive advance planning and repeated legal appeals. Rather rarely, there was a direct link: 102 incidents were the overflow of events occurring nearby, and 204 were the continuation of immediately preceding events in the same locale. But overall, my impression is that precedent was a larger factor in the approach of contention than immediately proximate contention.

Many of the more active precursor steps could hardly have escaped the attention of at least local officials (Aoki M. et al. 1981, 5:346), although some— for example, prior conflicts—might have been seen quite differently by elites and people. A 1698 protest in Tsuyama domain, for example, was followed by four executions and the strengthening of the rural control system, which the regime might well have thought would subdue the people. In fact (Bix 1986: chaps. 1, 2), the protest seems to have set a precedent for insubordination. When the lord of Tsuyama died in 1726 (the domain not having mended its exploitative ways), the people took advantage of the resultant administrative chaos to seize rice stocks, oust local officials, and riot. The domain crushed the movement, exacting a toll of fifty lives this time (Bix 1986: chap. 3) and reestablishing firm control. But even this crackdown did not suffice, as the subsequent record of Tsuyama domain—twenty events in the years following 1727, including four political conflicts and eight protest actions—makes clear.

Precedent frequently combined with catalyst to produce an extensive planning process. One popular protest was six years in the making; another took four (Aoki M. et al. 1981, 3:66); many took several months (Bix 1986: chap. 6). Plans included initial legal appeals, the geographical scope and numerical magnitude of mobilization, contingency plans, methods of communication and organization (all the way from the village banners used in Nambu to how much food participants should bring), and rules of conduct for participants, which usually warned against theft, drinking, and the danger of fire (Aoki M. et al. 1981, 3:81–94). Sometimes the planners even publicized their intent: contentious events in the cities were often preceded by posters and handbills accusing and warning miscreant merchants and officials, as well as by petitions (Harada 1982: 359). It is, of course, impossible to know in most cases whether such threats and demands were a step in a plan or were themselves a hoped-for corrective for policy or personal behavior, but sometimes major riots were preceded by such publicity, and those whose shops were destroyed were in fact among those who had been targeted rhetorically. Plan or suggestion? One cannot say, but even urban riots had a higher degree of organization than has sometimes been assumed (Aoki M. et al. 1981, 3:95).

This organization became clear when people actually began to mobilize for conflict. Circular messages of various kinds preceded mobilization, following the same routes and procedures as official messages (Aoki M. et al. 1981, 3:77). These messages might, for example, call for each village to provide one male participant aged between fifteen and sixty for every ten families, armed with a farm tool, and carrying three days' worth of rice. Contentious groups larger than a single village were organized into village groups, and there was considerable coordination among them. In Bansuke's operation in Nanzan there was a sort of "coordinating committee" of fifteen, each with multiple functions such as publicity, fund raising, lodging different petitions, and so forth (Nomiya 1992: 176ff.).

Participation and nonparticipation were both collective. Calls for participation were to villages in toto, and threats to punish nonparticipation—usually with the torch—were likewise directed at whole villages (see also Bercé 1990: chap. 2). Such threats probably increased participation out of both fear and rational calculation: collective participation assured large (and accordingly anonymous) numbers, and coerced participation reduced any sense of personal guilt and offered an exculpatory argument if one did end up in the hands of the law (Yasumaru 1975: 221; Aoki M. et al. 1981, 3:87–90). In other words, did "coerced" participation constitute the sort of selective sanction that, some have theorized, can overcome the "free rider" problem, or was it rather a licence to do what one found desirable or obligatory for entirely other reasons? One suspects the latter, especially later in the era, because such threats were in practice directed at village leaders, not the villagers as a whole (Shōji et al. 1981: 396). Nonparticipation was also collective: villages subject to calls for participation tended to decide collectively whether all or none should participate (Sasaki 1974: 254ff.).

If the word was "go," actual mobilization was sometimes simply the overflow of a peaceable meeting, a rising pitch of conflict originating on a festival or market day, or the rebuff of a specific demand. Such cases occurred in the context of a preexisting crowd. Sometimes it was launched by dramatic design, with signal fires, drums and bells, and the blowing of conch horns across the countryside to generate a crowd. Yet although such techniques lend themselves to chronicling, they were far less common than the sort of written or word-of-mouth communication characteristic of everyday life in the village.

The reason communication was that of ordinary village life has already been given: by far the greatest number of contentious events involved a single village. I have noted that many incidents were the culmination of a long process, but the actual events themselves tended to be small (almost 80 percent involved only a single village, and 96 percent a single county, and the median number of participants was roughly 160) and short-lived (85 percent of the actions lasted only one day).

But small scale does not imply simplicity. Contentious actions tended to be disciplined and focused, tactically flexible, and careful to minimize danger.[3] Regulatory measures included rioters' injunctions to take nothing for one's own use; selling or distributing loot to the crowd was acceptable, but often the property and goods of offending parties were simply destroyed. Participants were to injure no one, avoid fires, and not bring military weapons. Grievances and demands were clarified, targets were often given the opportunity to acquiesce, and nonprofiteering merchants and nonexploitative landowners were often explicitly spared (Vlastos 1986; Yamada 1984: 250ff.; Sippel 1977: 293ff.).

Actual tactics, as we have seen, often involved simultaneous actions: petitions to multiple targets; peaceful meetings, negotiations, appeals, and riots; private and public appeals; and both aggressive and deferential behavior (Kelly 1985: 287; Nagasu 1986: 11). Sometimes a clear continuum or sequence was visible; at other times overt action began with both appeals and riots; and sometimes the expected sequence was reversed. Sometimes urbanites went straight from grumbling to a riot, and then, the intensity of their views made manifest, they would lodge appeals (Harada 1982). Sometimes, after a popular demand had been accepted by an administration, the contenders would tear up the property of their adversaries on the way home (Yamada 1984: 175).

These actions were often designed to split the elite. In the 1840–1841 attempt of the shogunate to transfer the lord of Shōnai the people of the domain explicitly attempted to pit the lords and shogunate against each other, sending petitions to several other domains, which in turn sent "queries" to the shogunate regarding the reasons for the transfer (Hyakushō Ikki 1982: 113ff.). They also openly criticized the shogunate's decision, although open contradiction of the shogun's will was not part of Shōnai's official position (Hyakushō Ikki 1982: 120). Moreover, despite my earlier assertion that the people acted alone, it has also been proposed that the domain authorities were surreptitiously in collusion with commoner elites, who were, for whatever reason, punished only pro forma (Sasaki 1972: 45ff.).

Throughout this process, the people were conscious of the dangers they ran. Consequently, they began with legal actions, compiled long lists of legitimating grievances, couched their appeals in official jargon, invoked official values and

---

[3] See also Rudé 1964: 253; Blickle 1981: xxi; Stevenson 1979: 240ff., 312–13; Bohstedt 1983: 3.

ideology, protested their loyalty (and intention never to do this sort of thing again if their needs were satisfied), and kept themselves as anonymous as possible, with the exception of village officials who, as representatives, sometimes had to stand forth, and the Robin Hood types of the later era, for whom the zest of contention itself appears to have assuaged whatever fears they might have embraced. In one episode in Fukui domain in 1768 rural leaders mobilized some twenty thousand to thirty thousand people from over 250 villages; organizing them into five groups, they sent them against different targets, making sure to send each group away from its own locality to minimize the danger of being recognized (Hayashi 1976a: 81).

Supravillage mobilizations tended to be agglomerative or epidemiological (there is a third, or contextual, type visible in the cycles of contention which I shall look at hereafter). Agglomerative mobilizations were like that of Fukui: each of many villages provided a number of participants upon a prearranged signal, and a massive group seemingly coalesced out of nowhere (see also Bercé 1990: chap. 3). Epidemiological mobilizations moved more like waves: the eejanaika movement of religious ecstasy began in central Japan and swept along the highways, never amounting to huge numbers of people at any one time but, as a movement, involving thousands upon thousands before it ran out of steam. The massive Bushū Uprising of 1866 in Musashi province was also made up of mobilizations in successive villages (Sippel 1977: 302) and was itself part of a wave of contention which began in the Ōsaka area earlier in the spring of that year (Sasaki 1972: 247ff.). Such mobilizations gave the process a motion and flexibility difficult to respond to politically. Militarily, however, when the authorities were able to confront specific bands of protesters, they were able to put them down with little difficulty.

Given the brevity of most of the incidents under consideration, their trajectories—inception, mobilization, culmination, and termination—were compact and allowed for little dissipation of energy and effect. Where incidents were prolonged, however—and particularly if they included a riotous component—a process of decay was often visible. It does not appear related solely to size but to a combination of size with time and interaction with the elite. Size, in fact, may well have resulted from decay rather than the other way around. By the time a protest had been lodged, the risk attaching to further participation had substantially vanished; opportunities for looting, however, had grown as social order declined. The result was that thieves, beggars, those initially coerced into participation, and the urban poor came to the fore, earlier organization and discipline fell apart, and drunkenness and theft ran rampant (Shōji et al. 1981: 402ff.).

Hyōsuke's "uprising" in 1836 began as a grain seizure. Once the contenders moved beyond the borders of their region, however, the movement was swamped by outsiders and "outlaws." Most of those from Gunnai dropped out and returned home, but the new elements—whose numbers rose to over thirty thousand—laid waste to some five hundred shops in dozens of towns and villages before dispersing (Takekawa 1961: 33ff.). In 1866–1867 many events in the wave of contention began as appeals (usually coercive), but as the appellants moved into the castle towns to lodge their petitions the movements drifted into the hands of the poor and unorganized and turned into unruly riots (Sasaki 1979: 80ff.; see also Vlastos 1986; Bercé 1990: 44–45).

Such riots usually blew themselves out in fairly short order. What is more surprising is that even the best organized, focused, and disciplined contentious actions seem to have collapsed quickly when threatened by armed force, fobbed off by the authorities, or thrown a concessionary bone. Over and over, well-planned and extensively mobilized movements made their case to the authorities and then immediately disbanded. In the Demma Rebellion of 1764 groups of some dozens of hired thugs repeatedly dispersed bands of thousands of protesters (Kitazawa 1982). Since contenders did not question the system, perhaps they felt that once they had made their appeal, there was nothing left to do (Yasumaru 1975: 229). Perhaps they simply had no alternative; they had no protective structure like China's secret societies or sanctuary like Europe's free cities, and few Tokugawa farmers had the option of fleeing as Hyōsuke did. On the other hand, perhaps it was success (at least expected success) that explains this collapse: protest was often initially met with at least the promise of consideration, if not concession; further contention was discouraged and repression promised; and amnesty could be expected for most participants (see also Mousnier 1970: 67ff, chaps. 3, 4; Bercé 1990: 103). Given such options, it was perhaps unsurprising that contentious events blew up and blew out so quickly.

That is not to say that they were resolved quickly. Only about 30 percent of the incidents were resolved—by some decision, positive or negative, and by some dispensation for participants and officials involved—on the day they occurred. Another 20 percent were resolved within another month and 11 percent more before six months had elapsed. Often the authorities moved deliberately: 13 percent of the events took between six months and a year to resolve, and 26 percent dragged on for over a year. The single most common type of resolution included at least symbolic (and, as time went on, substantive) concessions and punishment for leaders of the action and, less frequently, punishment also for selected officials or merchants and commoner leaders (Harada 1982).

As noted, inconsistency was the norm through the period and throughout the country. Nevertheless, certain patterns can be seen. In the Kamo region of Mikawa province in 1836 over 240 villages rose against both merchants and authorities to demand lower food prices and reduced exactions (Fukawa 1976: 98ff.). Most of the local lords were hatamoto, whose authority was fragmented and impotent. They called for help from lordly domains in the region, but these held their forces back. The hatamoto, with little choice, gave in to almost all the people's demands and cooled the situation, whereupon the domains sent in troops to mop up. They chased some people, shot a few, caught significant numbers, took their names, and sent them home into their respective lords' custody (a not uncommon procedure). Only then, when the dust had settled, did investigators sweep through the countryside—although "investigation" or "examination," the usual terms for the process that followed, hardly convey the brutality of the methods of interrogation used. In any case, most of the participants in the event escaped unscathed—physically, at least. Four persons died in custody; two were executed; and four were exiled. Then the authorities reneged on almost all their promises.

A similar process unfolded over a longer period of time in the town of Niigata in 1768 (Hayashi 1976b: 268ff.; Harada 1982: 30ff.). The town had fallen on hard times in preceding decades. Nevertheless, Nagaoka domain tried to remedy its fiscal crisis with a forced loan from the townspeople in 1767. The townspeople, led by a merchant named Tōshirō, responded with appeals for a delay in payment of the loan and a cut in the price of rice; these petitions grew to include the election of town officials and the allocation of town taxes by townsmen's representatives. The town magistrate, hearing of the appeals, arrested Tōshirō and arrested or reprimanded his confederates. The townspeople organized and, at the signal of a nighttime bell, some fifteen hundred of them freed Tōshirō and moved against the offices of the magistrate and his commoner officials, of whom several were beaten or driven from the town. A gathering of the town's leading merchants then decided to run the town themselves and fired all the remaining officials.

For two months the townspeople ruled Niigata. They cut prices and the interest rate on pawned goods and gave relief to the poor. Meanwhile, the domain sent warriors to Niigata but decided to negotiate rather than attack. Talks began, during which the domain sent rice to the town and summoned officials and merchants targeted in the contention to the castle for questioning. Public resolve began to weaken, and the domain was able to lure some two hundred of the movement's leaders to the castle, where it promptly arrested them. With its leadership gone, the movement soon collapsed, and the domain reasserted control. The next summer the domain resolved the issue at its leisure, with two executions (one was Tōshirō's) and a few imprisonments, banishments, and fines. In light of the enormity of the event—not exactly the Paris Commune, but a far cry from docile commoners—the punishments appear light.

These were isolated incidents, but as we have seen already, such incidents tended to cluster at certain times in such numbers as to suggest a wave, or cycle, of popular contention.

The concept of contentious "cycles" has been most extensively treated in the work of Sidney Tarrow (1989, 1990), who accords to such cycles the following features:

1. an increasing and then decreasing magnitude of disruptive direct action;
2. an increasingly and then decreasingly broad spectrum of social sectors involved in disruptive direct action;
3. increasing geographical diffusion of contention;
4. increasing involvement of organizations designed specifically for contentious action as the cycle nears its peak;

5. broadening of grievances and demands from concrete, direct popular interests toward the reconstruction of society's overall concept of popular contention; and

6. repertorial evolution from more institutional and patterned behavior to more confrontational and tactically versatile activities, and back.

Moreover, such cycles putatively leave behind political residues, particularly policy reform and more variegated opportunities for contention, and popular change, particularly enhanced popular receptivity to contentious avenues of behavior in the future.

Some of these characteristics appear to apply intuitively even to early modern societies, but one must keep in mind that they were all derived from the experiences of advanced industrial democracies. Even presuming that similar-appearing waves of contention also characterize early modern Japan, there are reasons to expect this model to fit uncomfortably in light of that society's much lower (and agrarian) level of economic development, the rudimentary nature of its communications networks, and the far lower level of politicization of the populace. Nevertheless, we can still examine the model for its suggestive and descriptive possibilities.

The first step involves seeing if the pattern of popular contention in early modern Japan reveals anything resembling waves; we have seen already that it does in the early eighteenth century, the 1780s, 1830s, and late 1860s. I have extracted these four periods and presented them in Figures 15–18. For illustrative purposes, three other data have been added to these figures:[4] the four-city mean annual rice price (Iwahashi 1981), wages in building trades in the city of Kyoto (excepting the Kyōhō period; Umemura 1961), and the total number of provinces affected by all forms of natural disasters in each year plus the previous four years (Arakawa 1964). The heavy line demarcates the period of political reform accompanying the cycle. All these curves are logarithmic. The left-margin scale is to be used for the contention and disaster curves, which are absolute magnitudes. The right-margin scale is to be used for the wage and price curves, which are index values, varying positively and negatively from 100 (1840–1844 in the case of rice prices, 1801–1810 for wages).

Examination of these four periods generates several impressions. The Kyōhō period seems to be less a cycle than a step-level change in contention, after which the low levels of the seventeenth century were never to be seen again. The reforms of the period included a widespread program of land reclamation and the imposition of a less flexible standardized tax system. They look as if they were quite successful in bringing down the price of rice, although in an agrarian society the coincidental decline in disasters probably also contributed. Unfortunately, the reforms brought the price of rice so low that government revenues (denomi-

---

[4] See, inter alia, Aoki M. et al. 1981. English sources include Bix 1986; Kelly 1985; Vlastos 1986; Walthall 1986.

Figure 15. Kyōhō, 1715–1735

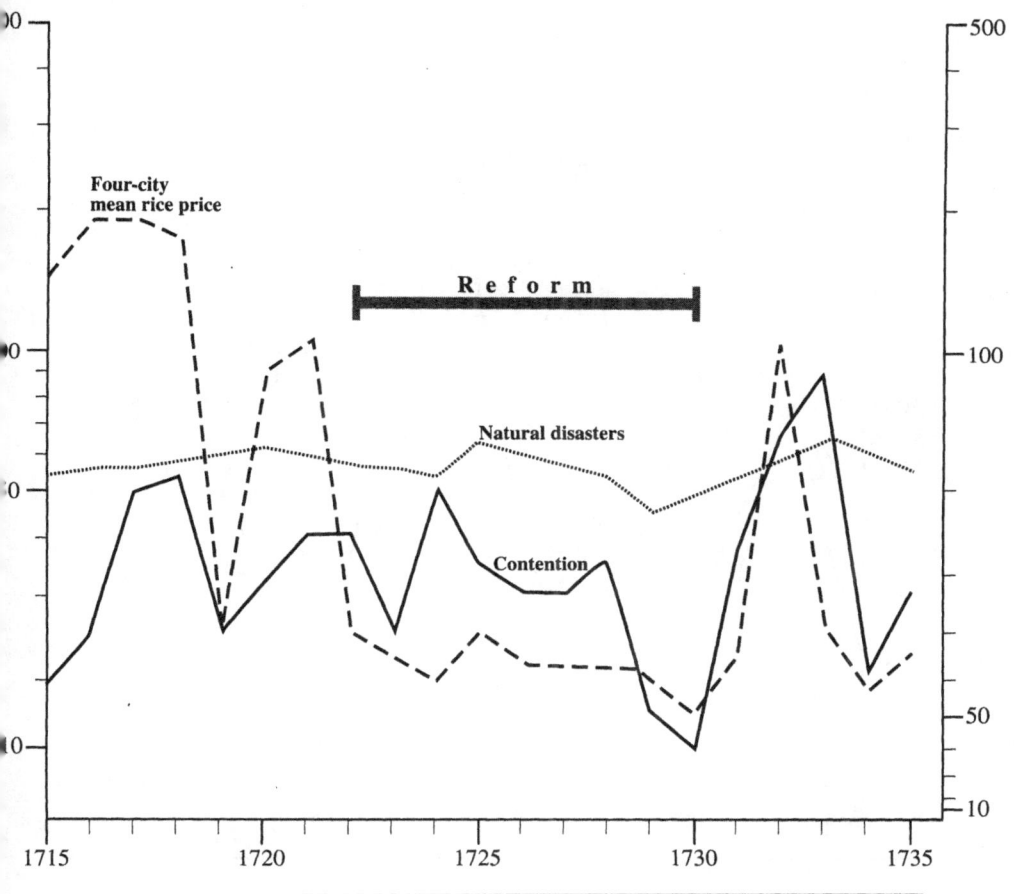

nated in rice) were threatened; a new price support program took hold just in time for a plague of locusts in western Japan. Together they drove rice prices up in 1732–1733, and contention followed. Thus the contentious dimension in this period seems to have followed reform, not preceded it (Yamada 1984: 204ff.).

The Temmei period perhaps exemplifies the contentious cycle: government profligacy in the 1770s combined with natural disaster in the 1780s, resulting in a great wave of conflict, wholesale personnel changes and policy reforms, and a fall in prices and contention which lasted for some decades (Yamada 1984: 237ff.). The Tempō period was characterized more by disaster than by governmental factors, but the ensuing wave of conflict similarly led to reform; the reforms themselves, however, and their effects, were much more short-lived this time (Aoki et al. 1981, 5:51ff.). The Keiō period was a time of extreme economic

Figure 16. Temmei, 1775–1795

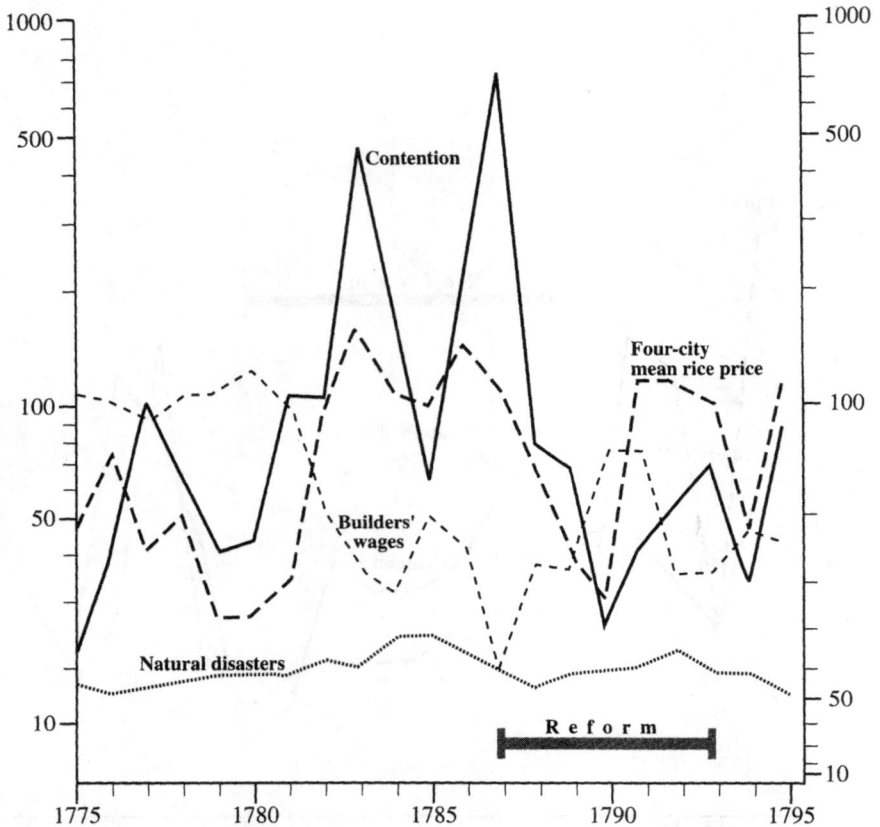

fluctuation and sharp inflation, exacerbated by the full opening of Japan to
foreign trade and by a poor harvest in 1866. But this period is complicated by the
snowballing disintegration of the Tokugawa state, the growth of domestic elite-
level challengers (to which the reforms were mainly responding), and the collapse
of the regime in 1868.

These four periods suggest that political variables may well play a role. The
interval between cycles went from 120 years (1600–1720) to 60 to 50 to 20
years as the system decayed (and the opportunity structure for contention expanded). The cycles themselves became more compressed, and within each cycle
conflict intensified, as successive peaks grew higher. Still, the ambiguous role of
reform and the clear parallels among prices, wages, disasters, and contention also
suggest that in preindustrial society economic factors play a larger role than they
do in modern societies. Moreover, the geographical diffusion proposed by
Tarrow does not accurately describe these phenomena: whereas the 74 years

Figure 17. Tempō, 1825–1845

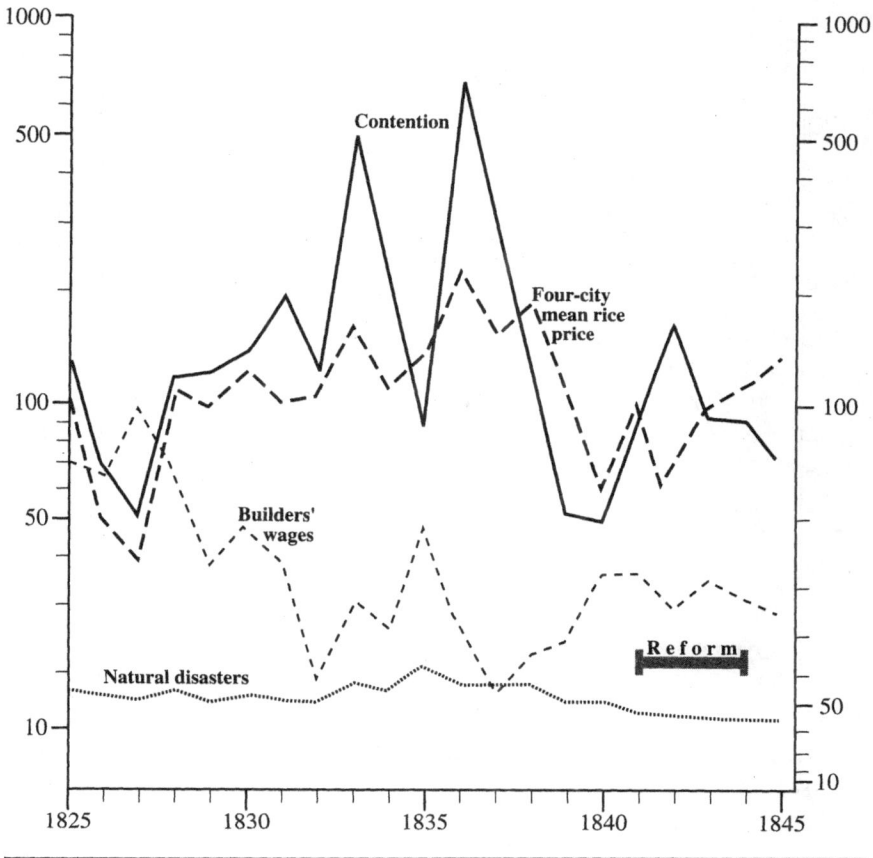

Contention

Four-city
mean rice
price

Builders'
wages

Natural disasters

Reform

within these four cycles and the 214 noncycle years (see below for periodization) saw almost equal numbers of contentious events (47 percent in the cycles, 53 percent in the noncycles), the events occurring in cycle years took place in only 397 of Japan's 631 counties, whereas contention in the noncycle years was spread over 521 counties. One suspects that cyclical conflict was concentrated where economic conditions were most severe *and* political responses—always highly variant in different units of the Tokugawa system—least flexible. For example, the peak of contention during the Temmei period actually came after the famine began to lift: it was the government's response that was too little and too late (Yamada 1984: 237ff.). Thus, although except in the Kyōhō case these waves of contention look on the surface much like Tarrow's cycles, it is quite possible that they are very different indeed.

For example, the peak of conflict in 1732–1733 possibly resulted from simple bad luck, since the reforms stemmed the falling rice price without driving

Figure 18. Keiō-Meiji, 1862–1872

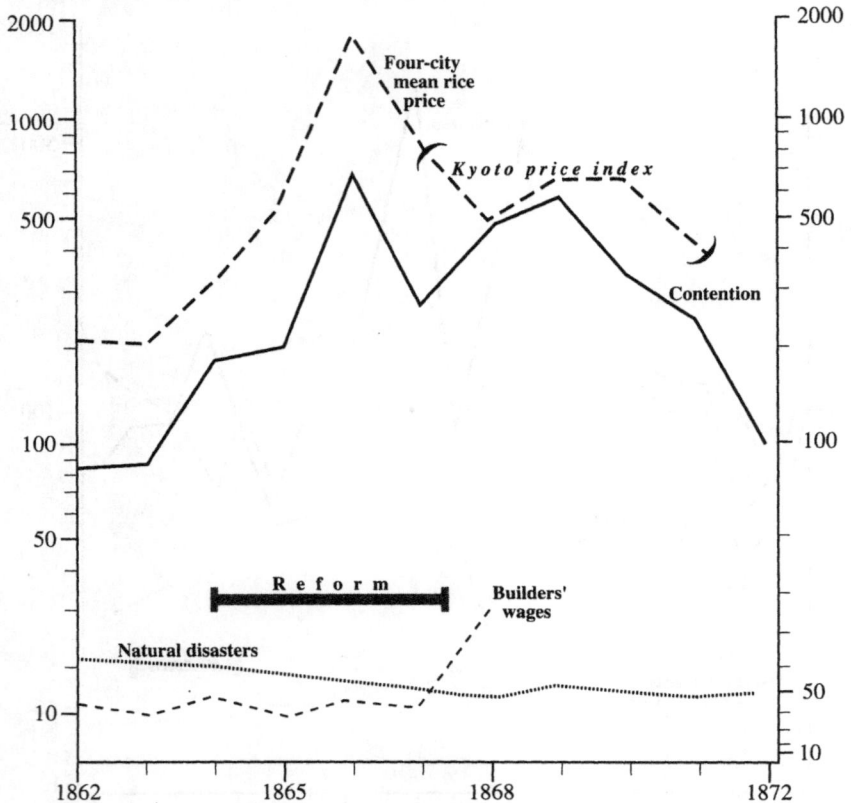

contention above familiar levels. And contention faded quite quickly after prices fell in 1733–1734, unaccompanied by any policy response. In the Temmei and Tempō periods conflict again seems to have been economically driven; in both cases reform got into gear only after the peak of conflict; the reforms themselves stimulated some conflict (especially in Tempō, when prices fell and conflict nonetheless rose in 1842), but they were generally followed by (if not the cause of) the desired effect. In the 1860s political instability was accompanied by economic turmoil, and it is impossible to disentangle the two. After the Restoration as well the new regime both stabilized the economy and controlled contention far more effectively.

Still, these periods also have distinctive properties in common. The four cycles, as presented in the figures, were periodized into 21, 21, 21, and 11 years, respectively, generating a total of 74 cycle years; the remaining 214 years of my data were then compared in the aggregate with the cycles. What I found is that the cycle years saw *more* incidents (in 74 years, or 26 percent of the entire era, 47 percent of all the events occurred—42 incidents annually, as compared to 16 per noncycle year) and *bigger* incidents (the cycle years contained 55 percent of the total magnitude of contention, and the average magnitude of events during cycle years was 3.27, as opposed to 2.43 in noncycle years).

Looking at the cycles separately, the Kyōhō period remains slightly anomalous. The average magnitude of events in that cycle was 2.33 (*less* than that of the average noncycle year), whereas that of Temmei events was 3.68; of Tempō, 2.90; and of Keiō, 3.85. But one must recall that the Kyōhō period ended a relative honeymoon for the state: in contrast to the fifty years previous to 1715, in which an average of 9 events occurred annually, 16 per year occurred in 1715–1735.

Thus the four periods do appear exceptional, and not solely in their magnitude. In their composition too these periods were different from the norm (see Table 6). In the first place—and reinforcing my earlier suspicions about economic factors—the increased magnitude of conflict during cycle years seems disproportionately due to an increase in social conflict, not political protest. This composition becomes increasingly clear when one disaggregates cycle years. In the Temmei and Keiō periods social conflict accounts for almost two-thirds of the total, and this huge predominance is particularly striking in light of the extreme *political* ferment of the Keiō period. Even the Kyōhō period represents a distinct

Table 6. The composition of conflict

	Cycle and noncycle years				
	Social conflict	Political conflict	Political protest		Total contention
214 noncycle years	48%	12	41	=	101%
74 cycle years	59%	12	29	=	100%
Kyōhō period	35%	12	54	=	101%
Temmei period	64%	9	26	=	99%
Tempō period	57%	16	27	=	100%
Keiō/Meiji period	63%	11	26	=	100%

	Cycle and precycle years	
	Social conflict	Political protest
1590–1714	24%	61%
Kyōhō period	35	54
1736–1774	48	41
Temmei period	64	26
1796–1824	54	35
Tempō period	57	27
1846–1861	60	28
Keiō/Meiji period	63	26
1873–1877	40	43

depoliticization of contention compared to the previous century, as seen in the comparison of cycle and precycle years (Table 6).

But do the cycles represent eruptions of something new, or are we simply looking at the glacial trends of the era, highlighted by peaks? The second part of Table 6 (simplified by excluding the relatively invariant political conflict) suggests novelty. During the seventeenth century, state consolidation, and consequently a high volume of political protest, took place; in the Kyōhō period and every subsequent cycle, the proportion of total contention accounted for by political protest declined, and that of social conflict rose. Even during the Keiō-Meiji period it was only after the Restoration in 1868 that the proportion of protest rose, to 27 percent in 1869, 43 percent in 1870, and 53 percent in the 1870s, as, again, a new state was created and imposed in many instances over the opposition of the people. Thus, waves of popular contention in Tokugawa Japan not only coincided with distinctive patterns of economic fluctuation; they also represented distinctive repertorial patterns in contrast to noncycle years in general and to the periods between cycles in each particular case: economic causes brought social results. But perspective is crucial. On the basis of Figure 9 (see Chapter 6) one might well incline to the view that cycles are less important than glacial trends. They are high points, to be sure, but really just points on an era-long, consistently rising curve of social contention.

Before moving to Tarrow's last question—Do these cycles witness repertorial innovation and creativity?—I should address again his assertion that cycles of contention come primarily in response to changes in the political opportunity structure. My expectation was that in relatively unpoliticized and repressive agrarian states this hypothesis would not hold. The supplementary data presented in Figures 15–18 contribute impressionistically but clearly: economic factors, while not necessarily *more* powerful than political factors, certainly *appear* powerful in their own right. Across the board the price of rice varies closely with contention, followed (inversely) by wage levels. One cannot assess the relative weight of political and nonpolitical factors on the basis of these data, but we certainly see enough to recommend a more detailed statistical analysis later. It is probable that political opportunities play a smaller role, and *conjoncture* a larger, than in Tarrow's analysis. Granted, in the Kyōhō case the jump in rice prices resulted in large part from government price supports, and in Keiō-Meiji prices rose partly because of inflation, apart from poor harvests, and the government was blamed accordingly.

In addition to the composition of contention, I am interested in its magnitude, and a comparison of cycle-of-contention years with noncycle years (see Table 7) implies both a relationship and a distinctive quality in contention during the cycles.[5] The overall pattern is first, and strikingly, extraordinarily deferential

---

[5] Aggressive behavior, in this table, includes theft, seizure (of land or property), or coercive "borrowing"; obstruction of or resistance against someone else's actions; forcible entry into or occupation of buildings; and rioting; inter alia. Destruction includes, inter alia, that of shops, offices, houses, or buildings; of records of debt or land titles; or of dikes, fields, crops, or irrigation facilities.

Table 7. Proportions of intense contention

Proportion of events with no reported aggressive, destructive, or violent behavior	
Cycle and noncycle years	
214 noncycle years	87%
74 cycle years	78
Cycle and precycle years	
1590–1714	93%
Kyōhō period	91
1736–1774	85
Temmei period	71
1796–1824	83
Tempō period	81
1846–1861	86
Keiō/Meiji period	73
1873–1877	82

popular behavior: during noncycle years for only 13 percent of all events was aggressive, destructive, or violent action reported; even during the cycles only 22 percent of the events included such behavior. When one compares the different cycles, again, the Kyōhō period seems to be less a massive eruption—aggressive behavior was slightly more common than in the prior 125 years—than a period of transition to a more contentious age. It was a sea change more than a rising and receding wave, as the data for 1736–1774 show. The other three cycles, however, present sharp contrast to the years on either side, especially Temmei and Keiō, when almost 30 percent of the incidents included aggressive action. Moreover, these three cycles all represented increases in intensity over prior years and were followed by a falloff in intensity thereafter.

Two steps remain in the present exercise. The first is to examine behavioral repertoires—in this case, a simplified typology emphasizing differing degrees of social cohesion and different physical loci of contention (and therefore levels of socioeconomic change) and different degrees of popular receptivity to violent contention. The second is to pursue the question of whether cycles are simply extraordinary waves of conflict which advance and then recede or whether they leave polity and culture durably changed. Some of the data thus far direct our steps: the increased salience of social conflict during cycles suggests social disorganization and friction, and Table 7 suggests a gradually rising level of repertorial intensity during the Tokugawa era.

I focus on six types of behavior here. The first two (combined for this analysis) are end runs and absconding, both of which imply considerable community cohesion and deferential attitudes. The third type is the coercive appeal, which was much more confrontational; moreover, its leadership tended to come from sub-elite elements among the commoners, and such appeals imply both the inability of officials to represent the whole community and a decline in popular awe of government and its objectively decaying coercive powers. The fourth type of action was the riot; the fifth the uprising; and the sixth the intravillage dispute, which could take any number of levels of intensity but is significant here because it is a barometer of conflict within the peasantry.

Table 8 shows the basic comparison between cycle and noncycle years in respect to these five action types—which together account for roughly three-fourths of all contention during the era—and cycle years appear to be considerably more urban, more plebeian, and more aggressive. The proportion of end runs falls by half during cycles, signifying a diminished role for local elites. Coercive appeals increase slightly, representing a similar popular autonomy and also a less deferential outlook. And the relative frequency of riots more than doubles. Village disputes decline slightly, but the data on riots, end runs, and coercive appeals nevertheless indicate considerable social turbulence during the cycles.

As decisive events in the evolution of a national culture of contention, however, the cycles do not appear so dramatic. Table 9 shows data on the five components of the contentious repertoire, and the long-term, glacial trends in Tokugawa society and policy seem to count for as much as the transformative impact of cycles of contention. In some instances cycles have consistent effects on conflict: all four cycles represent drops in end runs and abscondings from the previous period, and increases in riots. On the other hand, coercive appeals increase twice and decrease twice as precycle periods give way to cycles, and both uprisings and intravillage disputes seem to be responding to glacial trends: high during both polar periods of regime transition for uprisings, and high during the mid-era years of relative depoliticization for intravillage conflict.[6] Even the data on end runs could be interpreted as an almost monotonic trend irrespective of cycles. Did the cycles drive this trend? We cannot yet tell.

Looking at the different cycles, those of Kyōhō and Keiō-Meiji appear most influential. Kyōhō saw a drop in end runs and insurrection and a rise in coercive appeals and riots; Keiō-Meiji, a drop in end runs and increases in coercive appeals, riots, and insurrections. The Temmei cycle, like the Kyōhō, saw a drop in end runs and an increase in riots; the Tempō period, for all its turbulence, does not seem to matter very much in the repertorial evolution of contention. Taken together, the influence of the cycles is consistent with the view that they contributed to a lasting change in the social coherence, homogeneity, and aggressiveness of contention.

---

[6] The low proportion of total contention accounted for by these five behavioral types is also related to era-long trends, I think. The proportion of total conflict accounted for by diffuse grumbling and unrest (*fuon*) and pacific, quite often legal appeals (*shūso*) was 19 percent in the seventeenth century, fell to 10–13 percent during the mid-eighteenth and early nineteenth centuries, and rose to 41 percent in 1873–77. Insurrection described a similar parabola, smooth and almost unaffected by cycles. These data suggest that for the most part the people tended to restrain themselves rather than get their heads beaten in during periods of repression.

Table 8. Repertoires of contention in cycle and noncycle years

	Noncycle years (n = 214)	Cycle years (n = 74)
End run and flight	15%	7%
Coercive appeals	11	13
Riots	6	14
Uprisings	1	1
Intravillage disputes	48	44
Percentage of total contention	75%	77%

Table 9. Cycles and precycles in the repertoire of contention

	End run, flight	Coercive appeal	Riot	Uprising	Intravillage disputes		Total
1590–1714	30%	7	0	3	38	=	78%
Kyōhō period	18%	18	2	1	43	=	82%
1736–1774	15%	16	8	2	39	=	80%
Temmei period	7%	15	18	1	38	=	79%
1796–1824	9%	11	8	1	56	=	85%
Tempō period	7%	10	11	1	52	=	81%
1846–1861	8%	8	6	0	63	=	85%
Keiō/Meiji period	3%	13	20	2	37	=	75%
1873–1877	0	21	9	5	22	=	57%

This exploration enables me to make some observations regarding Tarrow's generalizations about cycles and repertoires of popular contention, and also implies the etiology of popular contention. First, where the economy has not yet been industrialized, society has not been fully politicized, and politics has not been nationalized, cycles of popular contention respond more to economic/conjunctural than to political factors, and reflect sudden changes in levels of popular grievances rather than in the political opportunity structure. In a sense the causation of conflict cycles in preindustrial societies is more "external" to the world of contention, whereas Tarrow found that causation was largely "internal," involving competition between movement organizations and interaction of contentious groups with a popular audience and with the mass media.

Second, conflict cycles in Tokugawa Japan differ in some ways from those in contemporary society. The cycles seen here do consist of increasing and then decreasing magnitudes of disruptive action and do seem to involve a wider spectrum of social elements (particularly lower strata) than does contention at other times. Yet contention does not appear to diffuse geographically. On the contrary, localized causes appear key, and there is probably much less spreading because the communications media that facilitate such a spread were absent.

In terms of the organization of contention, cycles—inasmuch as relatively less contention is generated by established groups such as cohesive, coherently led communities—do imply a more fluid and socially heterogeneous organizational basis for action. As organization seems to change, so does repertoire, becoming more plebeian, more violent, and more urban. At the same time, the distinctive contribution of cycles to these changes is difficult to assess. Patterns of change in the salience of social conflict, as opposed to political protest, and in the relative frequency of insurrection and intravillage disputes, all suggest that cycles are simply "more of the same," distinctive points along glacial curves. One can also see the overall trend as one of decreasing and then increasing tactical variety across the entire era, regardless of cycles.

It is difficult to assess the residue of conflict cycles. Three of the four Tokugawa-era cycles were immediately followed by periods of reform, but by far the most important political residue was a major, if tacit, transformation of state policy. By the late eighteenth century the government was unwilling to court widespread popular unrest by further raising the basic rice tax. This failure of will, which became apparent after the Kyōhō period, had three consequences: first, it resulted in stagnant government revenues, which eventuated in decaying state capabilities; second, it led to a search for new revenue sources; and third, by leaving more wealth in the hands of the people, it contributed to economic development and to the contentious social consequences thereof. Some of the new revenue sources were politically "safe," such as forced loans from merchants and cuts in the stipends of the lords' retainers. But others, such as taxing newly developing protoindustrial activities, were counterproductive because they too generated popular grievances and raised society's potential for contention.

8

PROTAGONISTS AND ANTAGONISTS

I have looked at the size, shape, and process of popular contention in attempting to infer its causes. In refining my inferences before testing them, I now turn to the dramatis personae. Leaders I leave for later, since I think of them as part of the catalysis of contention. For the moment I concentrate on the spear carriers and their targets.

Research on popular contention in early modern societies has dispelled earlier notions of those involved as the dregs of society, moved by misery and desperation. The marginals were there, and they did form a permanent potential constituency for contention, especially for urban riots. The most salient elements in premodern contention, however, were people with some possessions, prerogatives, and privileges to protect and extend: landowning farmers, artisans and apprentices, shopkeepers and clerks, the protoindustrial working class, peddlers, porters, and wage earners of myriad kinds.[1]

Data from early modern Japan corroborate this picture. For example, of those punished in the aftermath of Hyōsuke's Gunnai upheaval in 1836 (Takekawa 1961: 41; Tezuka 1962: 2), marginal (landless or homeless) individuals amounted to approximately one-fifth of the total; small landowning farmers accounted for between 60 percent and 90 percent, and village leaders for another 5 percent to 15 percent. It was the volatile marginal farmers who frightened the authorities the most. In 1866, amid a civil war, several domains pulled their forces out of the shogunal army in order to go home and confront a series of contentious groups of primarily lesser status (Aoki M. et al. 1981, 2:295) but from whom it appears they had less to fear than from the mainstream of their

---

[1] Calhoun 1983: 887; Blickle 1981: 114–15; Zimmermann 1983: 386–87; Hobsbawm 1959: chap. 7; Rowe 1989: chap. 9.

people. In a riot in Ōsaka in 1768 61 percent of those arrested were presumably lower-class house renters; 9 percent were homeless; and 15 percent were home-owners (Harada 1982: 138).[2] A more impressionistic analysis of participants in a massive riot in Edo in 1786 in which over eight thousand shops were destroyed suggests that the core were needy lower-class workers—peddlers, artisans, and day laborers—usually married and with families, supplemented by a "secondary" element of onlookers, revelers, and looters (Harada 1982: 108ff.). In the country-side, too, movements of farmers to enhance their status and political power often included not only the poor but those who had prospered and who now sought privilege commensurate with their economic position (Sasaki 1973: 225–53).

My own data confirm this pattern, as seen in Table 10. Landed farmers—most, granted, small ones—were the major participants in fully half of the events, and one may count householders in this mainstream social stratum. After this came groups at both ends of the social ladder: 13 percent of the events were primarily the work of landless farmers, and almost as many—12 percent—were that of community officials of various types. Occupational groups—again, hardly affluent but hardly marginal either—were the vehicle in 6 percent of the events. The lower orders—subordinate and marginal groups—were most salient in 8 percent of the incidents, but even if one adds the landless farmers to this category, it appears that only about one in five events occurred outside the social mainstream.

Some of the implications of these data are clear. The interests involved in popular contention revolved around the protection and expansion of established positions more than around desperate need. The resources brought to the fray included relatively high degrees of sophistication, literacy, and organization, especially when marginal elements were supplemented by mainstream elements (Harada 1982: 204). We may infer that measured calculation outweighed com-pulsive leaps into action. It is also likely that popular contention, because carried forward by social elements that had much to lose, was moderate in tone.

But such sweeping inferences need refinement; accordingly, I have looked at the social composition of contention across four dimensions: sociopolitical com-position, magnitude, repertoire, and evolution. Taking the first three dimensions, we find our social groups in six clusters. The first is occupied by the marginals: they figure disproportionately in political protest and high-magnitude conten-tion, primarily in the form of rioting (Aoki M. et al. 1981, 5:87ff.; Tokyo Hyakunen Shi 1973, 2:1279). Second are those low on the ladder but with at least a foot on the bottom rung: subordinate groups, the landless, and small farmers. All three were primarily engaged in social conflict, presumably against their betters, as tenants endeavored to shuck off traditional obligations and resist intracommunity discrimination (Rekishi Kagaku 1974: 27ff.), the landless tried to recover their lost status, and small farmers tried to stay above water economi-

[2] In Tokugawa cities, home renters were predominantly lower-class: Minami 1978; Saitō 1987.

Table 10. The social composition of contention

Social group	Proportion of events in which group was the first or second type of participants recorded
Marginals: the poor, gamblers, thieves, beggars, the homeless, outcasts, day laborers, renters, etc.	4%
Subordinate groups: servants, younger sons and young men, persons not members of community organizations, etc.	4
Landless farmers[1]	13
Small landowning farmers[2]	27
Medium and large landowning farmers[3]	23
Community residents, householders, members of community organizations,[4] etc.	8
Occupational groups: laborers, miners, fishermen, boatmen, woodsmen, salt workers, livestock owners, merchants, etc.	6
Local officials[5]	12
Members of the warrior class[6]	2
Total (n = 1,346)	99%

1. Terms for landless farmers and tenants include *hikan, kosaku, mizunomi, mutaka, nago,* and *shimobyakushō.*
2. Terms for small farmers include *komae, kobyakushō, wakibyakushō,* and *kodaka-byakushō.*
3. Medium and large farmers include landlords.
4. Community organizations were commonly open only to householders (in the towns) and landowners (in the country).
5. Local officials included *shōya, nanushi, ōjōya,* and *hyakushōdai.*
6. Samurai elements included both masterless (*rōnin*) and vassal (*kerai*) warriors, generic warriors (*bushi*), and aristocratic officials such as intendants.

cally. All three groups were very deferential, engaging in quite low-magnitude forms of contention which seldom went beyond low-level social grumbling and quarreling and seldom became political.

The third group is the secure farmers, of different sizes of holdings. They were relatively prone to political protest but not particularly aggressive. Indeed, in magnitude and repertoire the landed farmers parallel the overall pattern of contention. Residents' and occupational groups, on the other hand, although, like farmers, typically ending up in the political system, moved in that direction only as the expansion of social conflicts. Political conflict was the type of behavior relatively common among them, and it was political conflict of a relatively high magnitude. On the one hand, these two groups tried to settle their grievances through litigation and petition; on the other, they were also the most likely of all groups to launch coercive appeals. Clearly they were less risk-averse than the farmers.

And they were much less risk-averse than local officials, who were the most modest of all in the magnitude of the contention in which they appeared. They had no particular inclination toward political or social contention, but they were

Table 11. The evolution of participation, 1590–1877

	1590–1649	1650–1699	1700–1749	1750–1799	1800–1849	1850–1867	1868–1877
Marginals	0%	0%	3%	4%	4%	4%	13%
Subordinate groups	3	5	6	4	4	3	0
Landless farmers	1	16	8	8	19	11	21
Small landowning farmers	6	18	23	14	31	40	41
Medium and large farmers	48	30	24	34	17	15	10
Householders and organization members	10	7	10	12	8	5	5
Occupational groups	2	3	7	9	5	8	3
Local officials	7	21	16	13	11	14	6
Samurai class	22	0	3	1	1	0	0
Total (n = 1,299)	99%	100%	100%	99%	100%	100%	99%

Notes: Figures represent the proportion of all events in the period in which a group was recorded as the major actor. Zeros represent frequencies amounting to less than 0.5% of all events during the period.

very deferential: litigation and petition and end runs were their typical strategies. Those with the most to gain realistically—subordinate groups and landless and small farmers—and those with the most to lose—in the case of village headmen, their headships and perhaps also their heads—pursued the most low-key forms of contention, while those in between—landed farmers, householders, and occupational groups—could afford to be more aggressive, and those with little to gain *or* lose could afford to attack the system head-on.

Also apparently willing to challenge the system directly were the warriors. In those few cases where they figured prominently political protest was their habit, aggressive action their preference more than any other group, and rebellion the core of their repertoire. Thus the social extremes were most aggressive; elements just above the bottom and below the top were least so, and those in the middle of the ladder were also middling in the magnitude of their contentious behavior. It is also interesting that the groups at the extremes were the most political.

A more dynamic portrayal of the data (see Table 11) suggests the reasons behind these patterns. The most vivid image conveyed here is the downward movement of the social locus of contention during the era (Rekishigaku Kenkyū 1985: 79ff.; Hayashi 1976b: 181ff.). The number of events in which marginals and landless and small farmers were most salient increased, from 7 percent of the total in 1590–1649 to over half in the nineteenth century and fully three-quarters in the immediate post-Restoration years. These figures do not simply mean that these three groups were separately more contentious. Farmers from surrounding areas often played a major role in contention in the towns and cities (Rekishi Kagaku 1974: 215ff.; Harada 1982: 82). This trend masks another, minor, trend—the push for upward mobility among the landless and subordinate groups during the later seventeenth century (Aoki M. et al. 1981, 1:111ff.)—but whereas the landless emerged again in the nineteenth century, the subordinate groups (having to some degree succeeded?) appear to have faded from a major role in popular contention.

The reverse of this picture is the exit of society's more established elements from their earlier central role in contention. The samurai all but disappeared after the consolidation of the Tokugawa state. Medium and large landowners, house-holders, and other solid members of the community also faded, but more gradually. These two groups together constituted the major participant groups in 58 percent of all events early in the era; by the nineteenth century they were down to 20–25 percent, and after the Restoration they were in the fore in only 15 percent of the incidents. One explanation for the rise of social conflict during the era is that these established groups tended toward political conflict and protest, whereas the lesser orders inclined toward social conflict. In turn, the eclipse of the mainstream suggests both the decay of the state and the growth of the economy. Those in the best position to gain from economic growth would have less interest in at least certain forms of contention, and the diminishing relevance of the state would eliminate the primary target of their contention.

Finally, Table 11 illuminates the role of commoner elites and contentious repertoires. Local officials played a salient role in popular contention between 1650 and 1750—the heyday of the end run—after which they faded from the scene. Because they came from the established strata of society they might well be expected to fade (whether they faded also from their *leadership* role we shall see), but we should also recall the socioeconomic differentiation of communities, and the increasing state co-optation of local leadess for purposes of social control.

Overall, Table 11 suggests that interests, particularly socioeconomic griev-ances, may have increased their causal role in contention relative to opportunities and resources over the course of the Tokugawa era. The groups that came to participate more and more were those one might expect to have more such grievances than those above them. The pattern is also consistent with the cycles of contention, in which major peaks of conflict were intertwined with poor harvests and famines and characterized by increases in social conflict, not protest, despite the periods of political reform. It is also consistent with the increasing average magnitude of contentious incidents during the era. As the highly defer-ential established commoner elements were superseded by less established ones, the more aggressive forms of behavior preferred by the latter became more common. The qualitative changes in contention become clearer also: the lower orders were less familiar with the sorts of sophisticated overtures made by their betters, less literate, and more inclined to use a meat-ax approach to contention—a riot instead of a multipronged appeal, perhaps. They were not necessarily any less effective, but their means were different.

The groups against which popular contenders took action can be categorized first into three types: those within the community, those outside, and other communities. The last type of contention was primarily social collectivity against

Table 12. The targets of popular contention, 1590–1877

	Intracommunity targets	Extracommunity targets	Total
Other community members	3%	N.A.	1%
Community organizations or their leaders[1]	5	N.A.	3
Local commoner elites[2]	11	4%	8
Merchants[3]	23	11	17
Local commoner officials and leaders[4]	51	5	29
Lower samurai officials[5]		17	
Medium-ranked officials[6]	7	10	42
High-level officials[7]		53	
Total (n = 1,714)	100%	100%	100%

1. Community organizations include temples, shrines, *miyaza*, *kō*, etc.

2. Local elites include persons with surnames, landlords, leaders of occupational groups, rich families or farmers, *osabyakushō*, etc.

3. Merchants include shippers, moneylenders, hoarders, pawnshop owners, privileged merchants, etc.

4. Local officials include village headmen or elders, village or town *yakunin*, *kumigashira*, *warimotojōya*, *kashirabyakushō*, etc.

5. Samurai officials, when intracommunity targets, include local samurai, *tedai*, magistrates, and local enfeoffed warriors and lords. Among the lower officials who were extracommunity targets were intendants, local samurai, guard stations, tax offices, jails, government rice storehouses, or offices (*jin'ya*).

6. Middle officials who were extracommunity targets include *gundai*, domain and shogunal officials and retainers, *metsuke*, *junkenshi*, *jitō*, etc.

7. High officials who were extracommunity targets include magistrates, domain governments or elders (including *tairō*, *rōjū*, and *yōnin*), castles and lords' Edo residences, lords, the city of Edo and its offices (including the Hyōjōsho and Kanjō Bugyō), and the Kyoto Shoshidai.

collectivity: 70 percent of the events in which intercommunity targets were specified took the form of attacks on the buildings, fields, forests, or irrigation facilities of other towns or villages. In only 21 percent of the cases were another community's leaders a target, and their residents were targets in only 8 percent. This last type of conflict arose exclusively in situations in which the ownership of land in one village by residents of another became a bone of contention.

The targets of contention within and outside the community are shown in Table 12. Intracommunity targets were overwhelmingly local officials and merchants; higher officials who happened to be located in the community were seldom the focus of action, and other community organizations and members were rarely involved. Local commoner elites—who overlapped significantly with the official and commercial elements—were frequently embroiled in contention, but contention appears most often to have been functionally focused.

Commoner elites outside the community were also occasionally attacked, and outside merchants also, with greater frequency. But going outside the community appears to have been a decisive step: when contenders made this move, they were not aiming simply at minor functionaries but, in fully half of the cases, at officials and offices at the very highest levels of the political system. It is as if they reckoned, If you're going to go outside, go all the way. My data represent the high points of contentious action: it is quite possible that an overture to the domain government was preceded by approaches to several lower echelons of the system. In any case the fact that fully 42 percent of these cases involved contact—however deferential—with samurai officialdom belies the image of the supine Tokugawa peasant.[3]

An examination of my data on targets in relation to types, magnitudes, and repertoires of contention offers further insights. Intercommunity targets are the simplest to summarize. Contention against other communities' residents is social; that against their facilities is somewhat disproportionately political protest. Contention against the leaders of other communities was most aggressive, whereas contention against individual residents was quite mild. This pattern is corroborated repertorially: contention directed against residents of other communities was predominantly low-level, involving miscellaneous social quarrels and confrontations, whereas contention against the leaders of other communities was strikingly likely to involve rioting. My suspicion is that what we see is a pattern in which people from one community went to another for the express purpose of trashing either the headman's home or—less likely—some other government office located there.

Targets within the community were so overwhelmingly the focus of social conflict that—with the exception of political protest against higher officials who happened to be located in the community—few other patterns in the composition of contention are apparent. In regard to magnitude, however, there were sharp differences. Contention against local officials, leaders, and organizations was exceptionally mild and deferential, taking the repertorial form of low-level disputatiousness. Contention against higher officials located in the community, however, was more aggressive, inasmuch as they were most often the targets of end runs and coercive appeals. Against merchants and other individual members of the community (who were most often, one may suspect, among the privileged) the people pulled out the stops: contention of the highest magnitude was typical, with riot the weapon of choice.

Against extracommunity targets, again, the class membership of the targets correlated with the composition of contention. Again, contention directed against political targets was milder than that directed against social: contention against commoner officials was relatively aggressive, but that against higher officials was much more deferential and became increasingly so as contention

---

[3] One should not interpret these figures (71 percent of all targets were local, domain, or state officials or agencies) as contradicting my earlier observation that most contention in early modern Japan was social, not political. Contention between a village headman and his people is categorized here as social (i.e., within the commoner class), not political, conflict if it remained on that level.

moved up the governmental ladder. The aggressiveness of contention against commoner officials was due to a repertorial mixture of grumbling and dissent, miscellaneous squabbling, and rioting. Against the lowest samurai officials the people used both litigation/petition and coercive appeals; litigation/petition was also used against middle-ranking officials, but coercive appeals gave way to more deferential end runs. Against the highest officials, end runs were the distinctive form of action, with flight also relatively common, usually to seek refuge in another domain and appeal to that domain to intercede with the absconders' own lord.

When dealing with other commoners, however, deference to authority seems to have given way to indignation over the violation of social norms. Contention against extracommunity merchants was the most aggressive of all, primarily because rioting was the preferred type of action. Overall, this pattern reinforces what I already suspect: that political contention was more instrumental and opportunity-driven, where as social was more grievance-driven and perhaps passionate. Aggressive action was more likely to be taken against largely unprotected social adversaries; those disposing of coercive resources were treated with far greater care. In a word, calculation appears to typify popular contention.

When one looks at the same data across time, one can see systemic change operating on contentious behavior through its implications for individual interests and opportunities. Across the seven periods into which I have divided the era, the distribution of intracommunity targets shows an almost monotonic decrease in contention directed against local officials and higher officials located in the community. Merchants and other members of the local social elite, by contrast, became more and more common foci of contention. Contention against targets outside the community became more and more frequently directed against commoner elites and, even more strikingly, merchants. Contention directed against lower-level samurai officials also increased, but that against middle-ranking and higher officials faded. From being the most common target of all in the seventeenth century, they diminished progressively, almost to zero after the Restoration, when the new regime seems to have choked off popular access to higher officialdom.

The state, even under the Tokugawa, seems to have lost its relevance, presuming that the people were able to perceive, in contention, where satisfaction of their interests was most likely to be found. Contention seems to have come closer and closer to home, both structurally and spatially. Higher levels of the system were less and less often the target, people in one's own class more and more often. Targets outside the community drew less and less contention. Up until 1750, extracommunity targets accounted for over half of those recorded; by the first half of the nineteenth century they accounted for only about one-third, and in the years after the Restoration, only 22 percent. The post-Restoration upsurge in political protest appears to have been directed almost exclusively at the lowest-level agents of the new government. If one mark of state building is the ability to insulate higher levels of government from direct popular challenge, then the Meiji regime appears to have gone about its job with remarkable speed.

My last task here is to look briefly at the two elements of the *dramatis personae* together and see which actors tended to choose which targets. During the era as a whole, few dramatically specialized foci are apparent. Marginal and occupational groups tended to target merchants; small farmers and local commoner officials tended to target other commoner officials, and landless farmers and local officials tended to target officials of the samurai class. More interesting is the pattern of change during the era. In the years before 1750 contention by socially lesser groups (marginals, subordinates, the landless, small farmers, and occupational groups) against their betters within the commoner class accounted for 26 percent of the events in which we know both actors and targets; in the years after 1750 this proportion rose to 43 percent. By contrast, the proportion of contention accounted for by action by upper commoner elements (householders, officials, and middle and large farmers) directed against agents and offices of the domains and state went from 35 percent of the whole to only 14 percent. And although the actions of lesser commoners were throughout the era predominantly directed against their social betters, even these betters changed the focus of their contention away from the state. In the first part of the era 56 percent of the events in which they were the main actors were directed at higher levels and agents of the system; in the latter part of the era this proportion fell to 31 percent. The decline of political protest during the era was not simply due to declining contentiousness in the elite strata of the commoner class later in the era. These strata, following the lead of the lower ranking, turned their attention away from the polity and toward social contention as a way of achieving their goals.

This last point should remind us how complex is the causation of popular contention. The decline in targeting of political actors might be seen as contradicting my earlier assertions that the polity was in decline, since I have also hypothesized that opportunities were key elements in the causation of contention. I also argue for the importance of interests, however. Even a tottering government may remain free from attack if no one thinks it worth knocking over. What we shall see is what happened when weak regimes did give people reason to kick back, that is, when they overreached their capabilities with aggressive or ambitious policy. All I can say at this point is that the relationships between actors and targets over time imply the depoliticization of popular contention, for whatever reason.

9

TWILIGHT OF THE IKKI

The Meiji era (1868–1912) was an ambiguous time, with the old fading and the new as yet inchoate, but at least in its first decade, it is a significant part of my data. Moreover, given the dramatic changes of the Restoration, it casts light on some of the generalizations made about the early modern period. Additionally, it tests my generalizations concerning the continuity of contention.

The Restoration led in the short run to sharply increased numbers and varieties of fears, insults and grievances and to broadened opportunities to challenge an unstable system (Najita and Koschmann 1982:166ff.; Aoki M. et al. 1981, 2:303ff.; Sasaki 1972: 57ff.). The people were encouraged to anticipate beneficence, and moved nationwide to demand the cancellation of Tokugawa taxes, the return of pawned land, the redistribution of land and wealth, and the elimination of corrupt or oppressive community headmen, their privileges, and the autocratic method of selecting many of them. The traditional political economy and its social superstructure were under wholesale grass-roots attack.

At first the new government seemed responsive, but shortly three things happened: credible armed threats to the regime disappeared; the regime began to impose the policy reforms it deemed necessary for modernization in all spheres; and it became apparent that contention per se was a destabilizing factor. The result was a transformation in contention and its official treatment: The people moved increasingly into confrontation with the state, and the state pulled off its kid gloves. Unprecedented policies were imposed by imperial officials who were strangers in their new jurisdictions and under great presure to get things done, and who consequently brooked no disagreement. Perhaps, contrary to my earlier observation, antisystemic sentiment was *not* infrequent. Perhaps contention focused on local officials because they alone were available, not because of popular parochialism (Yasumaru 1975: 273ff.).

But Restoration did not bring any new resources. I presume that grievances kept pace with the rate of policy change and innovation, but learning how to take advantage of the system and acquiring appropriate resources took more time than my ten-year focus spans. Thus, I am unsurprised to see either the peak of contention around the time of the Restoration or its rapid drop in the 1870s. Additionally, contention began to pluralize during this period. Popular contention declined, at least temporarily, but suggestions of new forms—tenant disputes and labor unrest—were in the air; at the same time, nascent commoner appeals for broader rights of political participation were heard (Bowen 1980; Akita 1967; Ike 1950), and elite-level contention grew beyond what had characterized the early modern period (Jansen and Rozman 1986: chap. 2; Beasley 1972: 341; Sugimoto 1978). This current culminated in 1877 in the Satsuma Rebellion, a threat to the regime which, when put down by the new conscript army, marked the end of systemic threats on any level and thus—along with the termination of the Aoki data set—brings a convenient end to this book.

The period also comes to a natural end because the early modern context of contention had by the late 1870s given way to something quite new. The elimination of the Tokugawa class system; the replacement of the decentralized and relatively nonpenetrating shogunate by a centralized, modernizing state; the replacement of the domains by prefectures and other units under strict central control; the development of wholly new coercive, judicial, and grievance-resolution structures; the creation of a land tenure system based on individual private ownership; the imposition of taxes on individuals, unmediated by the village; the initiation of modern economic growth based on markets and private enterprise—all these contextual developments induced a sea change as well in the actors, targets, issues, and eventually the repertoires of contention.

Exactly when the change took place, and what (if any) continuity it evinced, are matters of debate. The last of the Tokugawa-style ikki has been variously sighted in 1871, the mid-1870s, 1876, roughly 1877, 1880, and as late as 1887.[1] In any case, my end point of 1877 does not seem to do injustice to reality. Additionally, some observers have suggested that the ikki lived on, at least derivatively, in the attacks on the new government and on into the Freedom and Popular Rights movement of the 1880s, which pushed for broadened political rights for the people. Those who posit for discontinuity (Yasumaru 1973: 95; 1975: 150), however, have a better case.

As we have seen, the total magnitude of popular contention peaked in 1865–1870, dropping sharply thereafter. Moreover, the average magnitude of events also declined after the Restoration, in both size and aggressiveness. This is not to say that large conflicts disappeared. For example, an 1873 protest in Fukuoka against the emancipation of the outcasts (a variety of other policies were at issue also) involved well over a hundred thousand people, who took over the prefectural capitol, killed twelve officials, and destroyed some forty-five hundred buildings. It was, rather, more likely that the official response to the Fukuoka uprising

---

[1] In Yokoyama 1977: 50–51; Haga 1973: 21; Fukaya 1979: 125; Yasumaru 1973, 1975; Aoki M. et al. 1981, 1:160; and Aoki K. 1968a, 1968b.

was instructive: 70 people killed or wounded, 3 executed, 110 sentenced to prison, and 64,000 others—fully 15 percent of the prefectural population—punished in some way or other (Hayashi 1976b: 240; Uesugi and Ishitaki 1988). It has been suggested that the new regime's standard use of troops to suppress contention provoked escalating violence (Sasaki 1979: 182), but most of the violence was visited upon the people.

In fact, the early Meiji era may represent a low point in popular contention during the last three centuries of Japanese history. Qualitative changes in contention and dramatic changes in record keeping and legal definition make continuous estimation impossible, but observers have noted the relative calm—in both frequency and scale of conflict—following the state's demonstration of its willingness to crack down (Hayashi 1976b: 229–44; Aoki K. 1968a, 1968b; Tsuchiya and Ōno 1931: 653–65), and others have analyzed later levels of contention, which rose in the early twentieth century to an average of over a thousand events annually (Smethurst 1986: 316 and passim; Garon 1987). If this suspicion is well founded, then an explanation of contention in terms of opportunities (which were reduced) and resources (which had not yet been built up) relative to interests (which must have been high at this time) gains ground.

During the first years of the Meiji era popular contention became far more political, with riots, coercive appeals, and uprisings increasing in relative frequency and flight, conflict solely among the people, and end-run appeals—the quintessential form of ikki, in the view of many—fading from view. Defensive contention, in opposition to new policies, was not in itself new, but the "proactive" contention in pursuit of new rights and advantages seen among up-and-coming entrepreneurs during the Tokugawa era spread dramatically on the village level in opposition to residual feudal prerogatives, procedures, and dues (Dower 1975; Tozeren 1981: 365). The two were often intermingled, as when old, autocratically selected headmen became agents of state penetration and control, but overall, one can see a trend—the reverse of the standard expectation—from proactive, "antifeudal" contention to defensive resistance to modernization: conscription, land reform, the Western calendar, taxes, compulsory education, the liberation of the Tokugawa-era outcast class, and so on and so on (Vlastos 1981: 1; Uesugi and Ishitaki 1988; Aoki M. et al. 1981, 2:283–364).

One can also see in the late 1870s the beginnings of the tenant-based modern farm movement, the labor movement, and the movement for political liberties (for the upper class, at least) and representative government which blossomed in the 1880s (Vlastos 1981: 1). Labor unrest as a proportion of total contention began to rise, from under 5 percent before 1880 to 20 percent or more in the mid-1880s, and tenant disputes also rose from under 20 percent of all agrarian unrest to 20–50 percent after 1880 (Aoki 1968a, 1968b). But these had more humble social constituencies, and perhaps more continuity with early modern contention, than the rights movement, which may explain why they both evince more spatial continuity with Edo-era contention than does the rights movement.

Specifically, some historians perceive continuity from the early modern period to grass-roots contention both urban and rural (Kokushō 1971: 131ff.), and others see continuity in the popular rights movement (for a summary of the debate see Fukaya 1979: 284ff., 357ff.). I examined the relationships on the county level between popular contention of different types during the Tokugawa era alone and during 1590–1877, on the one hand, and two measures each of Freedom and Popular Rights movement salience and general popular contention on the other.[2]

The results were consistent and clear-cut. Movement-related unrest bore no relationship of any significance to any dimension of early modern contention. Liberal Party membership, by contrast, was modestly related to both social and political conflict (but not political protest): measures of association (r) ranged from 0.17 to 0.22. Popular contention in 1878–1894 was correlated with all three dimensions of contention in earlier periods at magnitudes of between 0.19 and 0.39, and contention in 1895–1911 correlated at magnitudes of between 0.26 and 0.35. Thus, there is a clear spatial connection, at least, between popular contention of all types before and after the Meiji Restoration, and I believe that quantitative and qualitative links are also more likely to be found here than between early modern contention and the elitist (Jansen 1989: 405ff.) rights movement.

Overall, however, qualitative analogies between early modern contention and later Meiji or modern contention are forced, except on an empirically unhelpful level of generality. Analogies have been drawn between Tokugawa contention and a variety of more recent conflicts,[3] even that of the students of Waseda University, who in 1989 festooned their campus with signs calling for a "student ikki" against administration oppression. To the extent that context matters, it seems unhelpful to attempt to go far beyond the boundaries of early modern society.

Thus, for anyone familiar with contention during the early modern period, the first decade of Meiji holds few surprises. In 1869 the government of Shinagawa prefecture announced the creation of a disaster reserve of rice and money, for which villages would be assessed according to their kokudaka (Sasaki 1972: 114ff.). The people, quite aside from their natural aversion to such levies, were doubly loath to comply because the new reserve was to be held in the prefectural capital (not the villages themselves, as had been the Tokugawa custom) under prefectural control. Their suspicion that the government might not release it as needed was in fact not misplaced, for the reserve was to be a money-maker for the prefecture, which intended to lend it out at interest.

---

[2] The measures were occurrence in the county of movement-related unrest, and county membership in the Liberal party as of October 1884 (source: Nihon Rekishi Daijiten 1979); and the number of popular disturbances, urban and rural, in the county in 1878–94 and 1895–1911 (source: Aoki K. 1967, 1968a, 1968b).

[3] Upham 1976: 611; Lewis 1990; Kano 1973: 280; see McKean 1978 for a discussion.

In any case, the people opposed the reserve, and many petitions to that effect were transmitted, even though two village representatives died under interrogation about their activities. Ultimately, the government partially relented, exempting poor farmers from the assessment, but the people were unmollified and continued their agitation. More leaders were arrested, and the government made attempts to co-opt or buy off others. The people, now largely on their own, argued that a response to the government would take time and the arrested leaders were freed, but mobilization had not ceased, and in January 1870 a group went to the capitol.

Upon their arrival they were invited in, but they refused, aware that under Tokugawa law their appeal would, upon their entry into the capitol, become a coercive appeal. Their worries were mooted, however, when the gates burst open and troops poured out, wounding many, arresting fifty-one, and putting the rest to flight. Those arrested were interrogated—in traditional style—and in February punishments were announced (but only for the leaders, who were charged with stirring up the otherwise blameless people). Fifteen persons—all village headmen—received sentences from prison to flogging, although four had already died in custody. Then the government gave in on the assessments.

The script followed by both challengers and authorities in this episode harks back to the Tokugawa period. In the government's overall posture, however, it stands somewhere between earlier and subsequent events. In early 1869, for example, the new and singularly heavy-handed governor of Takayama prefecture canceled prior tax reductions and traditional exemptions, strengthened trade controls, and established a corvée for land reclamation and a conscription system for the local militia (Yashiro 1989: 54ff.). Petitions poured in, but the governor arrested their presenters and executed one. On February 29 a crowd that had gathered at a fire in the prefectural capital of Hida rioted, wrecking thirty-six buildings belonging to the governor's supporters; in subsequent days the rioting spread throughout Hida, until the participants were confronted on March 10 by the governor and his men. The people, however, were also armed and in the ensuing gunfight the governor was wounded and fled the scene. On March 14 he was dismissed and arrested, and his successor revoked his policies and dealt out a few pro forma punishments.

In marked contrast is the case of Yamanashi prefecture in 1872. In June the central government decreed the end of a distinctive local Tokugawa-era tax system; the new dispensation meant a real increase in the tax burden.[4] The month of August saw almost daily demonstrations, gatherings, and petitions involving from a few to a few thousand persons, and from single villages to groups of several dozen. There was much inconclusive toing and froing between officials and people, and on August 23 several thousand petitioners entered the prefectural capital of Kōfu. At this point the prefecture called for troops, but before they arrived the house of Wakao Ippei, the prefecture's richest merchant and a close

[4] Yamanashi-ken 1978; Kajinishi 1978: 92–120; Smethurst 1986: 138.

associate of the government, was destroyed by a mob. By the end of the month, however, troops had restored order, and in the next few days officials met with now-submissive village representatives. The tax revision went through, and for their part in resisting it 3 persons were executed and 4 others sentenced to prison, among almost 4,000 persons punished: 75 village headmen, 325 subheadmen, 244 farmers' representatives, and 3,128 farmers.

These three incidents are more representative than epochal, and in some ways—for example, the central government's willingness to hold local officials to account for their actions—they reveal consistent practices of the new state (Kelly 1985: chaps. 5–9). But that state grew less conciliatory as its self-confidence grew (Beasley 1972: 404; Aoki M. et al. 1981, 2:343). In popular behavior we can see initial belligerence give way to, at most, older and safer riotous practices; we can also see a residual leadership role by pre-Restoration village elites, at least in the petitioning and end-run stages of contention. Overall, the frequency and magnitude of contention declined quickly after the Restoration, although uprisings, riots, and coercive appeals became relatively more salient; disaggregating the Meiji years, we see that aggressive contention was concentrated in the first five years of the era.

There is also a correspondence between my data on process and repertoire, magnitude and frequency, and participation. Village leaders continued to play a role, and as the data on those punished suggest, solid elements of society continued to be important.[5] But what got the state's reluctant attention were the mass actions that accompanied the petitions—actions largely supported by marginal groups (who tripled in salience after the Restoration [Sasaki 1979: 72–80]) and landless farmers (who doubled). Local leaders were the leading elements in a diminishing number of cases, because, one suspects, they were more available for punishment and consequently much quicker to learn the new state's view of popular dissent. The mass of the people were still, in the 1870s, resisting an unknown adversary on a terrain with few guideposts, and it was some years before a new social contract was hammered out (Aoki M. et al. 1981, 2:343–59). And "hammered" is an apt image; those who erred on either side—from the governor of Takayama (who died in jail in 1870) to the sixty-four thousand found guilty of rebellion in Fukuoka—suffered egregiously as the two sides gradually worked out what was acceptable.

This process of working out proceeded on many levels. Wealthy farmers and merchants like Wakao Ippei remained a focus of grievances, as did moneylenders and landlords (Tozeren 1981: 146; Sasaki 1979: 169; 1972: 236ff.). Village headmen, still in their Janus-like role, were often the only authority to be found during the interregnum between effective domainal rule and the imposition of Meiji state control, and when the new regime did move in, it often co-opted such

---

[5] A massive riot in Nakano prefecture in 1871 shows the same pattern: all those punished were taxpaying farmers, mostly smaller ones, and most had families (Tozeren 1981: 532).

leaders. Unsurprisingly, both situations kept village leaders in their historical position as both actors and targets of contention (Sasaki 1973: 82, 98).

But the people also apparently learned fairly quickly to target the new government in their contention. Along with wealthy farmers and merchants, prefectural and local officials (primarily the *ku kochō*, or district administrator) soon became common extracommunity objects of contention (Sasaki 1973: 64ff.). Overtures to higher officials, however, declined sharply from pre-Restoration levels. The Meiji state appears to have temporized at first vis-à-vis contention, then thrown up walls, and finally, only toward the end of my period of study, worked out a series of mediated access points in the walls through which the people could pursue remedial action (Kelly 1985: chaps. 7–9). This access was determined by the state, however, on its own terms, in sharp contrast to the situation that developed under the shogunate, when the system of access evolved largely in response to popular action. Granted, the Japanese people have in the modern era shown extraordinary ingenuity in contending effectively within a series of unresponsive systems. Nevertheless, the process of state building is illuminated as clearly in the light of declining popular contention after the Restoration as it was by rising contention during earlier centuries.

PART III

THE CORRELATES AND CAUSES OF CONTENTION

10

CORRELATION AND CAUSATION

Thus far I have described the context, content, and characteristics of popular contention in early modern Japan. I have also tried to infer the etiology of conflict from an examination of what it was—in Part II—and when and where it happened—in Part I. This interpolation has been guided by the theoretical insights and fruits of earlier research recounted in the Introduction. Now, I want to bridge the inferential gap more systematically.

In this chapter I look quantitatively at economic, political, and social correlates of contention, on the assumption that the first best indicates the interests that lead people toward contention; the second, the opportunity structure they face; and the third, the resources at their disposal. This correspondence is hardly perfect. Obviously, there are economic resources, political grievances, and social opportunities, to name but a few, and I take note of such exceptions. Most of the data available for this sort of analysis are structural. Moreover, many of the data used here are, taken singly, of limited reliability. What I seek are consistent, corroborative findings using data on multiple levels from multiple sources which bear on contention in multiple contexts.

After looking separately at economic, political, and social correlates of contention across time and space, I combine them in Chapter 11 in order to assess the relative importance of interests, opportunities, and resources. Interests, and economic causation in general, appear to play relatively larger roles than is the case in modern societies (see, e.g., Tarrow 1989; Muller and Opp 1986). The correlations among the trends of contention, prices, and wages in early modern Japan, as we have seen, are close and grew closer over time. Interests are also relatively closely connected with social conflict, and opportunities with political protest. I would be surprised if any one of these three explanatory factors contributes nothing at all to the quantitative analysis of conflict to follow; even if I so find, I am disinclined to ignore the qualitative evidence of tripartite causation. Quantitative analysis is essential but not by itself definitive.

I cannot claim either simplicity or complete clarity for the analysis to follow. First, the phenomena measured are contingent (Ragin 1987). Increasing food supply per capita might imply a rising standard of living, fewer grievances, and less contention, but it might also mean more resources in the hands of the people and, other things being equal, more contention. Or if accompanied by commercialization of agriculture, it might imply fragmentation of the farming class and both more grievances *and* less social cohesion—an important resource. Second, the quantitative data at my disposal are skewed toward economic indicators. I do not have quantitative indicators of all the factors of interest to us. Third, my data are complex. Ideally, each indicator should represent one and only one variable; some of mine represent more than one. For example, oppression implies grievances against the state, but it also implies reduced opportunities for contention. Fortunately, in many such instances, equally intuitive implications are incompatible and only one can hold true. Finally, this analysis does not include any of the sorts of attitude-related variables that alone can directly address the question of behavioral decision making. I move in that direction in Chapter 12, but here I face a major inferential chasm.

Some observers resist such inference and generalization.[1] My own view is that explanation is so important that it demands addressing with the best data available and in the most judicious manner possible, even if our procedures are less than ideal and our conclusions less than ironclad. I shall show how each of my measures suggests interests, opportunities, or resources and how, separately and together, they are associated with different magnitudes and types of contention. What I look for is cumulation: similar causal inferences flowing from mutually independent data. If such cumulative findings are consistent with both my theoretical expectations and my qualitative data, then I can feel more confident that I am not simply speculating.

Economics and Interests

I have proposed five ways in which economic factors shape interests and grievances as they bear upon popular contention. First, positive levels of well-being and positive changes in it per se reduce incentives to contend. Improvement may also put more resources in the hands of the people, but my hypothesis here focuses rather on the interests that derive from material deprivation or prosperity. Second, unstable and vulnerable levels of living conduce toward contention. Third, economic development, and protoindustrialization in particular, diversifies socioeconomic strata and economic interests and increases the potential for conflict between them. Fourth, natural disasters bring economic reversals beyond the immediate abilities of the system to cope and are thus linked to grievances and thence to contention. Finally, upward fluctuations in prices and taxes, and downward fluctuations in wages, stimulate grievances and lead, *ceteris paribus*, to contention.

---

[1] See, e.g., Bix 1986: xxiii; Naquin 1976: 38, 1981: 45.

Table 13. Economic well-being and popular contention

	Social conflict	Political conflict	Political protest
County-level measures			
Assessed agricultural productivity per capita	−0.18	−0.15	−0.18
Food supply in calories per capita per day	−0.11	−0.14	−0.12
Provincial-level measures			
Assessed agricultural productivity per square kilometer	−0.23	(−0.18)	−0.53
Domain-level measures			
Assessed agricultural productivity per capita	−0.15	−0.14	−0.18

Note: In Tables 13–19 all measures of association are zero-order Pearson correlation coefficients, or r's. Coefficients in parentheses are not significant at the 0.05 level, although one should note that the numbers of cases involved (for counties, usually over 600; for domains, usually over 250; for years, usually over 250; for provinces, usually over 60) may render province-level relationships artificially insignificant.

The measures included in Table 13 are real county kokudaka in 1875 (Kodama 1967) divided by county population in 1875 (Rikugun 1976); available food supply (Fujiwara 1964) in calories (Pennington and Church 1980) in the early 1870s divided by county population in 1875 divided by 365; real provincial kokudaka in the 1830s (Nakamura 1968: appendix 2) divided by provincial area in square kilometers (Ōtomo 1979: 24–26); and real domain kokudaka in early Meiji period divided by domain population in early Meiji (both from Nihon Tōkei Kyōkai 1982 as revised by Nishikawa Shunsaku). Additionally, a measure of land quality (a county-level, multiplicative combination of hectares of arable land per capita [both from Rikugun 1976] times assessed agricultural production per hectare of arable land [Kodama 1967; Rikugun 1976]) was tried, and it too correlated inversely with contention, but it was multicollinear with productivity per capita; so only per capita productivity was kept. All independent and dependent variables have been reduced to quintiles to compensate for error in the original data.

As noted, popular contention has historically been associated with absolute material deprivation, although the relationship is seldom exclusive and often modest.[2] In preindustrial societies such deprivation can be measured in terms of food supply per capita. My own analyses of pressure on the food supply in early modern Japan (White 1992b) suggest that such pressures may independently count for little, but as Table 13 shows, there are bivariate relationships, which offer more support for an interest- or deprivation-based explanation of contention than a resource-based one. Food supply per capita, whether measured in terms of calories or total assessed food productivity, is inversely related to all types of contention. And it is gross production that counts: when one uses after-tax food supply, the relationships weaken, which does not surprise me, inasmuch as the living standard of which people in a region can conceive includes, in the last analysis, food they can withhold from the authorities.

---

[2] The positive evidence includes Esherick 1987: 14–15; Huang 1985: chap. 3; Miller 1985; Gurr 1980; Barnes, Kaase, et al. 1979: 100; Choucri 1974: chap. 11, 1984: chap. 1; Zimmermann 1983: 99; Gurr and Weil 1973. Caveats are presented by Aoki M. et al. 1981, 1: 7–8; Bercé 1990: 334; Stevenson 1979: 302; Fukaya 1979: 38–39.

Table 14. Vulnerability and popular contention

	Social conflict	Political conflict	Political protest
County-level measures			
Urbanization	0.22	0.23	0.09
Vulnerability of the agrarian economy	0.13	0.19	0.25
Province-level measures			
Vulnerability of the agrarian economy	0.33	0.32	0.35

Note: The variables in this table include multiplicative indicators of agricultural vulnerability based on county/provincial number of frost-free days per year times mean county/province altitude, with high-altitude, cold regions presumably the most vulnerable (International Society 1974), and an additive county-level measure of urbanism which combines the proportion of county population in 1875 living in urbanized communities of four thousand persons or more and whether during the Tokugawa era the county included no, one, or more than one significant towns or cities (Rikugun 1976; Fujimoto 1976: 13–28).

Even decent levels of living may be precarious, however, especially for those who do not produce their own food. Involvement in markets I consider under the rubric of development; here my attention is directed to climatic instability and urbanism. Neither is an ideal indicator. In both cases we have to make two inferential leaps—first from climate and place of residence to social and economic conditions and then from these conditions to attitudes—before we get to contention. But I have already ascertained an overarching association between economic vulnerability and contention.[3]

As Table 14 shows, both of the forms of vulnerability of interest here are positively related to all forms of popular contention, with, if anything, agricultural vulnerability more strongly related to political protest and urbanization to social conflict. Neither is solely an indicator of potential interests. Agricultural vulnerability is greatest in marginal upland regions where commercial, nonfood crops were popular and monetization of the economy advanced; as we shall see, such regions had distinctive social structures also. Urban populations, too, had distinctive social structures and were, moreover, more directly under the eye of the authorities. To the extent that endemic economic insecurity typified these two types of regions, one can easily envision the sorts of anxieties engendered by sudden failings of market, crops, and food supplies.

Part of the vulnerability of social groups was due to economic development. There is general agreement among Japanese historians that development contributed to contention. The question lies in the mechanism. A resource-based approach suggests that simple economic improvement, in a context of more or less endemic oppression and economic fluctuation, would lead to more contention, and my own work (1992b) has suggested that absolute increases in per

---

[3] See also Scott 1976: chaps. 2, 7; Lee 1977: 280ff.; Anderson 1980: 67ff.; Skinner 1987; White 1988a; Tozeren 1981; Vlastos 1986.

Table 15. Economic development and popular contention

	Social conflict	Political conflict	Political protest
County-level measures			
Proportion of commercial crops in county agricultural production	0.10	0.13	0.12
High commercialization and low tenancy	0.09	0.11	0.17
Province-level measures			
Increase in agricultural productivity, 1720–1880	0.31	0.17.	(0.11)
Degree of commercialization of agriculture	(0.17)	(0.16)	(−0.01)
Nongrain products as proportion of total agricultural production	0.45	0.38	0.30
Region-level measures			
Level of protoindustrialization	0.77	0.61	(−0.09)

Note: The variables in this table include the value of overwhelmingly commercially oriented "special-use agricultural products" (*tokuyū nōsambutsu*) as a proportion of total county production in the 1870s (Fujiwara 1964); the combination of a high proportion of such products with low rates of tenancy (taken from all prefectural yearbooks in the early years of the Meiji era); the combined provincial increase in the productivity of agricultural land and labor between 1720 and the late 1770s (Nakamura 1968: 183); the commercialized proportion of the provincial agricultural sector in 1877 (Nakamura 1968: 156); and nongrain products as a proportion of the value of provincial agricultural production in 1877 (Nakamura 1968: 125). The regional-level measure is Saitō Osamu's (1985: 211) measure of protoindustrialization in sixteen regions. Given the small number of units, the coefficients presented here are Spearman rank-order correlation coefficients.

capita food supply *from an initially low base* are indeed associated with increased contention, especially social conflict.

Nevertheless, the inverse relationship between well-being and contention also offers support for the most consensually agreed-upon interpretation of development, which is that agricultural commercialization and protoindustrialization, which were intimately linked, stimulated contentious interests of myriad kinds. They did so not through fragmentation and polarization of the peasantry, but through the increased vulnerability of those now out of food production or in the market and through the simple differentiation of social strata and economic interests.[4] Again, a resource-based explanation implies less contention because of diminished social cohesion, and I shall investigate these intermediate mechanisms; for the moment, however, let us look at the macrolevel relationship.

This relationship, presented in Table 15, indicates a consistently positive relationship between agricultural commercialization and protoindustrialization and popular contention, particularly social conflict. Since protoindustrialization

[4] Sugimoto 1978; Yokoyama 1977: 167–246; 1986; Nishikawa 1985: 140. For similar conclusions reached by research in other societies, see Anderson 1980; Goldstone 1991; and Hibbs 1973: 28–42, who found a curvilinear relationship in a set of developing and advanced societies. In a wholly premodern society, however, one would expect all counties to be on the rising side of the curve and thus would expect to find a linear relationship.

was to a large extent based on the processing of agricultural products, data on commercial crops and nongrain products represent the process as well as do more explicit measures of protoindustrial activity per se. And the combination of high commercialization of the agricultural sector and low tenancy represents development of a particularly relevant type, that is, the production of sericultural cash crops such as silkworms and eggs, cocoons, mulberry, and silk in the highly contentious central highlands, which, First, enabled marginal or submarginal freeholders to stay on the land and, second, provided employment for those deciding to shift entirely out of agriculture. It is a measure, thus, of both developmental type and social organization; I return to it in the social context. It has also been considered in another pattern—high commercialization and high tenancy—as an indicator of polarization of the peasantry and immiserization of the landless, and thus an indicator of interests. I found, however, that this pattern bore no association with contention, confirming my earlier argument that the polarization/immiserization thesis is a weak one.

Another complex factor is tenancy, which has often been cited as an indicator of development and social fragmentation and as a direct cause of grievances and contention. Specifically, it has been cited as a cause of more social conflict and less political protest. Here, however, tenancy by itself proved to be insignificantly related to any form of contention. My view is that development increases the potential for contention but does not all by itself generate new masses of aggrieved people.

One of the things that could realize such a potential, of course, is sudden economic reversal, either naturally caused or man-made. The first type of reversal, natural disaster, is, we have seen, linked with the major cycles of contention in early modern Japanese history. These cycles, however, also possessed man-made components (Fukaya 1983: 66), which I look at later. The figures presented earlier indicate that natural disaster was endemic in early modern Japan; all in all, it comes as little surprise that disasters by themselves, across the whole sweep of the era, bear only a modest relationship to popular contention. Provinces with large numbers of disasters were slightly more prone to social conflict ($r = 0.18$, not significant) and political conflict ($r = 0.28$) than others, but no more likely to witness political protest.[5] Temporally, the years *following* years with widespread natural calamities were somewhat more contentious in all three respects ($r = 0.20, 0.20, 0.18$, respectively), supporting a grievance-based interpretation of contention, but again, human agency was probably a factor in the conversion of natural disorder to social.

Such human agencies might include governmental extraction and the movement of prices and wages. Taxes and other forms of governmental economic extraction could have two sets of implications. On the one hand, they enhance state capabilities and reduce the opportunities for contention; on the other, they generate grievances and stimulate contention. Systemically, they appear to accord

---

[5] The data on natural disasters are from Arakawa 1964.

Table 16. Economic reversals and incursions and popular contention

	Social conflict	Political conflict	Political protest
Domain-level measures			
Domain tax rate	0.16	0.17	(0.10)
Rate of extraction	0.13	(0.07)	0.11
Degree of penetration	0.21	(0.18)	0.26
Extraordinary revenues as percentage of total	(0.13)	(0.14)	0.18
Temporal measures			
Kyoto consumer price index	0.56	0.51	0.57
Builders' wages in Kyoto	−0.39	−0.36	(−0.22)
Four-city rice price index (three-year lag)	0.44	0.47	0.57
High rice prices and cumulative natural disasters	0.40	0.41	0.48

Note: Measures of domain extraction include the tax rate (Kodama 1979: 425ff.); a measure of extractive potential (real agricultural productivity as a proportion of officially assessed productivity [Nihon Tōkei Kyōkai 1982, as revised by Nishikawa Shunsaku]); the rate of revenue penetration (the product of tax rate times extraordinary revenues as a proportion of total revenue [Beasley 1960]); and extraordinary revenues (levies on commerce and industry, which were particularly likely to incur popular wrath) as a proportion of total revenue (Beasley 1960). I also attempted to test the proposition that domain monopolies (Yoshinaga 1973) stimulated contention, but so few domains did not have monopolies of any kind that the test could not be done.

Measures of fluctuation include the Kyoto retail price index and real wages in the building trades in Kyoto (Umemura 1961: 175); the three-year lagged annual mean rice price index in the four cities of western Hiroshima, the economic core of Ōsaka, the eastern capital of Edo, and northeastern Aizu (Iwahashi 1981: 460–65); and the product of the mean rice price and the total number of natural disasters (Arakawa 1964) in the year under consideration plus the previous four years. I also initially included measures of agricultural wages in the Ōsaka region (Saitō 1973: 185); the Ōsaka wholesale rice price index (Shimbo 1978: 30ff.); and the Ōsaka wholesale price index (a composite of multiple commodities [Saitō 1975: 772]). These all showed the same relationship to contention, thus strengthening my confidence, but were so highly intercorrelated with the data presented in this table that their presentation added nothing.

with the capability-enhancement, opportunity-reduction model: on the county and province levels, year by year, tax rates are inversely related to contention; thus, I examine them in the context of opportunities. Among the domains alone, however, extractions were positively related to contention.

Prices and wages are more straightforward, being primarily indicators of interest. Their relationships to disaster and to official attempts to ameliorate economic conditions make the exact association—and its timing—complex,[6] but the overall pattern is clear, as seen in Table 16. Across the board the more extractive domains are slightly more contentious; it may well be that the cost in

---

[6] See, e.g., Stevenson 1979: 112; Thompson 1966: 63; Goldstone 1991; Bohstedt 1983: 11–22; Tilly 1986: 183ff.

contention outweighed the benefit in revenue, as the wholesale reluctance of the domains to raise taxes in the latter years of the era suggests. Apart from conscious government incursions, however, economic fluctuations appear to have had a distinct positive effect on contention of all sorts. The relationship may be difficult to disentangle, for several reasons. First, although behavior seems to respond to prices and wages immediately, the four-city mean rice price has its strongest effect on contention only three years after its peaks. Second, some of these phenomena have a cumulative impact: the contention in any given year appears to vary positively with the price of rice in that year in combination with the total number of natural disasters nationwide during that and the previous four years. Third, prices seem to affect behavior more than do wages. Fourth, political reform, nature, and economics are intertwined: prices, wages, and disasters show somewhat stronger relationships to contention in the cycle years than in the other years of the era (White 1993a). Given the driving force of social conflict in the cycles, it is possible that these factors influence such conflict more than other forms of contention, but the analysis thus far permits only this suspicion. Overall, my analysis suggests a highly meaningful effect from at least economically based interests on all forms of contention,[7] which vary across multiple dimensions of time and space with arguably interest-laden phenomena such as poverty, vulnerability, protoindustrial development, natural calamity, political extraction, and sudden economic deprivation.

Politics and Opportunities

Many opportunities for popular contention can be addressed only through qualitative data, but others can be found among quantitative data. Three specific propositions and one composite can be examined here. The first is that governmental fragmentation contributes to contention by reducing the effectiveness of social controls. The second is that political institutionalization and control deter contention when high and invite it when low. The third is that popular contention varies inversely with governmental extractions, which build strong institutions and reflect official intentions to regulate and penetrate society. And the fourth is that governmental "overreach" is a singular problem in early modern states, and those political units trying to regulate more with less were particularly susceptible to contention.

A variety of observers (Nomiya 1992; Hyakushō Ikki 1982: 75) have cited administrative fragmentation as a cause of specific social and political conflicts. The Kamo Uprising of 1836 occurred in a county with twenty-five different domains—clerical, hatamoto, and Tokugawa—of which nine ruled only a single village and only six ruled more than ten (of the county total of 222 villages

---

[7] It is crudely instructive to see that the 23 correlations cited in this analysis average $r = 0.26$ for social conflict, 0.25 for political conflict, and 0.23 for political protest. Thus, I hesitate to assert that economic factors overall possess greater explanatory power vis-à-vis any one form of contention than another.

[Fukawa 1976: 236]. Fragmentation, moreover, often typified single villages. One in Kōzuke province had an assessed productivity of 1,010 koku, of which Lord A took 39 percent; Lord B, 22 percent; Lords C and D, 10 percent apiece; and Lords E and F, 9 percent apiece (Hyakushō Ikki 1980: 356ff.). No one lord had preponderant control of such a village, and none of these lords relied on this particular village for more than 30 percent of his revenue. A disinclination to take responsibility for public order can easily be imagined, as can popular awareness of this fragmentation.

My own data indicate that thirty provinces with no hatamoto domains (41 percent of the provinces) saw 18 percent of all contentious events, and those thirteen provinces with fifty or more hatamoto domains (18 percent of the total) saw 30 percent. Thirty-three provinces (45 percent of the total) containing three or fewer lordly domains saw 20 percent of all events, and eleven provinces (15 percent of the total) with fifteen or more domains saw 35 percent. More systematically, I created a measure of administrative fragmentation, which scores as high in fragmentation those counties with large numbers of small domains plus a large (and, one will recall, fragmented among intendants) shogunal presence.[8] This measure was significantly associated with all three types of contention, although much more strongly with social ($r = 0.27$) and political ($r = 0.25$) conflict than with political protest ($r = 0.08$).

Putting aside for a moment the (paradoxical?) relative weakness of the tie between political cause and political effect, I look next more directly at the notion of control, for which fragmentation is a surrogate. In fact, the two are closely intertwined. The number of different domain types was most closely tied to contention when weighted for administrative coherence; moreover, a county-level measure of control—that is, the simple relative administrative presence of (laxer) shogunate and (tighter) domains—was so highly interrelated with my measure of fragmentation that I considered them not essentially different.

In any case, many observers have attributed the overrepresentation of shogunal territories in popular contention to a weaker administrative hand, which, although not calculated to provoke the people, gave them relative freedom to contend over whatever issues may have interested them. I have also noted the relative frequency of contention in the rugged regional periphery. Thus we see administrative units with presumably higher levels of institutionalization and control less plagued by contention. Nonshogunal units, stabler units, longer-lived units, larger units, fiscally viable units—all these should have experienced less conflict (Kokushō 1971: 102).

---

[8] The exact construction of this measure is as follows. First, the shogunal share in each county's kokudaka was calculated. Second, kokudaka per nonshogunal administrative unit was calculated as 100% of the county kokudaka, minus the shogunal share, divided by the sum of (a) the number of lordly domains and (b) twice the number of less administratively coherent hatamoto and clerical domains (all from Kimura 1954). Third, counties with a high shogunal presence and many small domains were scored high; those with no shogunal presence and a single domain were scored low; and intermediate counties scored in between.

Table 17. Contention and control

	Social conflict	Political conflict	Political protest
Province-level measures			
Proportion of villages under Shogunal jurisdiction	0.55	0.55	0.23
Domain-level measures			
Hereditary or outer domain	−0.13	(−0.08)	(−0.08)
Domain population	0.33	0.29	0.31
Lifetime of domain in years	0.33	0.33	0.32
Average number of years per ruling family in domain	0.12	(0.10)	0.12
Temporal measures			
Shogunal finances, lagged three years	−0.25	−0.24	−0.25

Note: The measures in this table include proportion of provincial villages under shogunal jurisdiction (Murakami 1983: 20–21); whether the domain was an inner or outer domain (Kodama 1979); and shogunal finances (Shimbo 1978), lagged three years previous to the year in which contention was measured. Two other measures of shogunal presence (proportions of provincial and county kokudaka subject to shogunal extraction [Kimura 1954]) were also used, but they were so highly correlated with village jurisdiction that I set them aside. Moreover, original measures of domain institutionalization included size (Kodama 1979) and real assessed productivity and total revenue (Nihon Tōkei Kyōkai 1982, revised by Nishikawa Shunsaku), but all were collinear with size as indicated by population, which was kept. Additionally, average years of rule by each lord during the lifetime of a domain (Kodama 1979) were originally used because they, like years per family, indicated the absence of interregna, succession disputes, regencies, and various other sorts of instability. This measure, however, was collinear with years per family and was set aside.

My indicators of governmental control are presented in Table 17, and they suggest a substantial but partially problematic relationship between control and contention. On the provincial level shogunal control is indeed strongly related to high levels of contention, and *not* because shogunal lands were more agriculturally vulnerable or otherwise ecologically disadvantaged. The shogunate's fortunes also mattered; although the Tokugawa family ruled only about a third of the country itself, its own fiscal deficits affected contention nationwide three years after they occurred. Within the Tokugawa lands the correlations were in the range of $r = -0.40$, but it appears that the shogunate's fiscal crises reflected public finances—and, by implication and after a delay, governmental effectiveness—nationwide. That the financial picture was of independent significance, and not, for example, simply reflective of climatic or economic problems, is suggested by the total noncorrelation of shogunal finances with natural disasters or with prices. Finally, the more tightly ruled outer domains appear to have been slightly more quiescent than the hereditary domains.

Certain of my expectations were confounded, however. For one thing, the proportion of samurai in domain population (Nihon Tōkei Kyōkai 1982) seems to have had no effect on levels of contention. More significant, domain size and lifetime and familial stability were all associated with more, rather than less,

Table 18. Extraction and contention

	Social conflict	Political conflict	Political protest
County-level measure			
County tax rate	−0.17	−0.15	(−0.06)
Province-level measure			
Provincial tax rate	−0.34	(−0.17)	(−0.06)
Temporal measure			
Estimated tax rate in shogunal territories	−0.39	−0.48	−0.50

Note: Measures included in this table include county and provincial tax rates as of 1872 (Nakamura 1968: 196). The original data for this measure are provincial; county tax rates are a crude estimate, with each county assigned the tax rate of the province in which it is found. Estimated tax rates for shogunal territories are from Hara n.d.

contention. We have already seen that the more extractive lordly domains were more contentious; these were also the bigger, older, and stabler domains. Perhaps I was in error to see this group as more administratively able. Certainly the biggest of all, Kaga domain, was unable to avoid chronic insolvency (McClain 1988). Perhaps the biggest domains were not massively institutionalized and effective administrative edifices but rather dinosaurs whose efforts to penetrate and regulate their domains overreached their capabilities and gave rise to, rather than quelled, contention.

On the national level, however—which includes the less penetrant shogunal, clerical, and hatamoto administrations—it appears that revenues were an indicator of opportunity rather than interest. In the domains alone, with administrative characteristics held relatively constant, taxation appears to have enhanced contentiousness. On the macrolevel, however, the effect may be just the opposite, as Table 18 suggests. These measures are not the best—the county and provincial data are from the same source, and the shogunal tax rate is only an estimate—but they corroborate my earlier surmise that low tax rates may indeed have mollified the people on one level, while on another they both reflected and led to weak institutions and weakened the will to extract from a recalcitrant populace (Nakamura 1964a: 149). Moreover, they are consistent with the imposition of tax increases after the contentious cycles of the Tempō and Temmei periods had peaked, and the tax increases of the earlier Kyōhō period amid a rising curve of contention, which they did not perceptibly influence (Hara Akira, personal communication).

Thus interests appear of less import here than opportunities. How the two sets of factors compare we do not yet know; for the moment it suffices to note that, insofar as my quantitative data are any help, they suggest that, indeed, administrative fragmentation, fiscal solvency, shogunal and hereditary lord jurisdiction, and low rates of taxation—from all of which I infer greater opportunities for contention—were all associated with higher levels of contention and, if anything, more strongly related to social and political conflict than to political protest. But so were the presumably more institutionalized—that is, larger, older, and more familially stable—domains, a puzzle to which I shall return.

Resources: Social Structures and Mobilization

I am least happy with this part of my quantitative picture of the correlates of contention. The sorts of resources which research has suggested are relevant, such as social cohesion and organization, dense habitation and good communication links, and awareness of the world all about and its past, are not the stuff for which firm quantitative indicators often survive.

Nevertheless, there are some bits and pieces that will suffice for at least this preliminary analysis. The first is demographic structure, specifically population density and distribution. The second is social structure, particularly that entailed by the commercial and protoindustrial development of the countryside, with all it implies for social solidarity. Third is the fuzzy heading of "social mobilization," the availability of people for mobilization by contentious movements of various kinds.

I have considered population in the context of food supply, as a possible source of hardship and, by inference, grievances. As a resource for contention, density is significant mostly as a facilitator of communication, organization, and mobilization. Earlier, I found density to be positively associated with some forms of contention in some regions, but there is no general relationship (see also Gurr and Weil 1973). Density of a particular type, however—urbanization—is another story, albeit a complicated one. Cities are concentrations of the vulnerable, and therefore possibly prone to a heightened interest in contention. They are also better connected to the seat of government than are remote villages, thus possibly providing urbanites with more opportunities for contention. On the other hand, they are relatively closely under the eye—and fist—of government, which may strip them of opportunities. Also in the category of resources, cities are typically considered the vanguards of social mobilization, and their inhabitants relatively ready for innovative behaviors, including contentious ones, of various kinds.

Keeping the messiness of both the real world and the city in mind, I have thus far seen cities as socially conducive to contention. They were dense and densely communicative and intimately linked by myriad social and economic relationships. They were internally organized but more fluid than villages and thus much harder for the authorities to monitor. The vulnerability of their populations to food shortages goes without question, and I realize the artificiality of categorizing cities as resource- rather than interest-generating contexts. Later I shall consider them with the sensitivity they deserve, but for the moment they are demographic concentrations that facilitate contentious actions contemplated for other reasons.

As such, they are linked to contention. We cannot get at *rates* of urbanization in early modern Japan, but we can compare *degrees* of urbanism across space. My measure is a composite of the proportion of county population living in urban-ized communities with four thousand or more inhabitants and whether or not there were zero, one, or two or more significant towns or cities in the county during the Tokugawa era (Rikugun 1976; Fujimoto 1976: 13–28). The measure is modestly but significantly associated with all three forms of contention, at $r = 0.22, 0.23$, and 0.09 respectively, supporting my overall expectations and my hypothesis that political protest was least responsive to variations in urbanization. Actually, there is quite a clear tie: as a proportion of total contention, political protest increases as one goes from the most to the least urban counties (White 1992a). But there is also a puzzle: I have found contention frequent also in regions characterized by ecological vulnerability, which tend to be relatively remote and rural.

The puzzle becomes more tractable in light of social structure. I have already noted that the more ecologically vulnerable regions were more precarious but not necessarily poorer (Yokoyama 1986). This is so, at least in part, because such regions had in large degree converted from food to cash crop production, becoming integrated into markets and witnessing the differentiation of socioeco-nomic strata and interests. But although commercialization of agriculture suggests a decline in the social solidarity that could serve as the vehicle for political contention, it might have enhanced the potential for social conflict. And some types of commercialization might not have had a depressant effect on contention at all.

Indeed, the primary measure of commercialization, differentiation, polariza-tion, and poverty used by Japanese historians has been tenancy (Ōuchi 1980), which we have seen is unrelated to contention (Miyamoto and Yamamura 1981: 390ff.). Moreover, some forms of economic development entailed little tenancy. For example, counties in which the primary cash crop was silk, tobacco, hemp, or paper—upland crops, tended with little dependence on tenants, which might keep marginal farm families viable (Vlastos 1986; Saitō in Jansen and Rozman 1986)—were significantly more socially and politically contentious ($r = 0.08$ and 0.12) and protesting ($r = 0.16$) than counties in which the primary cash crop was cotton, rapeseed, wax, or sugar, which were dependent on extensive lowland holdings and tenant labor (Fujiwara 1964; see also Sugimoto 1978; Sasaki 1974: 194ff.). Unsurprisingly, the socioeconomic combination of highly commercial-ized agriculture and low tenancy is also positively related to all three forms of contention ($r = 0.09, 0.11$, and 0.17). These relationships are modest, but keep in mind that political protest—the form of contention I suspect is most reliant on the resource of social organization—is most strongly influenced by that type of development most consonant with continued village social cohesion. We have seen already that development, from which I have inferred interests, can also imply resources; at the least, I can say that certain forms of development need not be incompatible with the sorts of social resources often deemed important to contention, and whose loss would otherwise influence behavior in a way contrary to the influence of interests.

Another reason that commercialization and protoindustrialization may contribute to contention despite a putatively deleterious effect on social solidarity is that they are associated with the creation of new resources through the agency of social mobilization. A mobilized population—usually measured in terms of education—is an extremely important resource for building a movement (Lerner 1958; Barnes and Kaase 1979), and we should expect in early Japan also that popular awareness, consciousness, breadth of knowledge, and ability to conceive of alternatives to the status quo should be positively related, other things being equal, to contentious behavior.

In the case of both Japan and other early modern societies three factors have frequently been cited as suggestive of social mobilization: education or literacy, urbanization and communication, and past levels of contentious behavior, which provide an intellectual legacy. Additionally, in the case of Japan parallels have been noted between religious movements and the phenomena of popular contention (Aoki M. et al. 1981, 4:347–48; Tozeren 1981: 24; Takagi 1983), and we should see if regions characterized by high levels of one also saw frequent occurrence of the other.

My initial quantitative exploration indicates that, indeed, social mobilization is positively associated with popular contention, albeit not dramatically. First, I have already found urbanization to be linked with social and political conflict. Additionally, the presence of roads in a county contributes to the magnitude of contentious behavior found there.[9] The association is not uniform—for social conflict $r = 0.17$, for political conflict $r = 0.18$, and for political protest $r = 0.04$—but it is as expected.

Education is exceedingly difficult to measure in early modern Japan. The data I have used refer to numbers of *terakoya*, or temple schools for commoners, and the numbers of students attending them. The data are rough and the associations they imply modest, but again they are consistent with expectations: county by county, the numbers of schools and students per capita are positively related to political protest ($r = 0.06, 0.07$), and students per capita are also related to social ($r = 0.10$) and political conflict ($r = 0.09$).[10] And the hypothetical mental broadening of the world of the possible is also suggested by data on contention

---

[9] This discovery follows the finding (Weber 1976; Markoff 1986) that communications links, particularly roads, are major arteries of flow for ideas with stimulating potential. My communication links indicator is a scale running from zero (no seaports or major roads in a county) to five (one of the five major roads, or *kaidō*, runs through the county). Nihon Rekishi Daijiten 1979: plate 34; Kobayashi 1978: 212–15.

[10] The data on numbers of schools and students in each county during the Tokugawa era (Mombushō 1980) were gathered in early Meiji and are not renowned for their reliability. They consisted of prefectural submissions in response to a central government directive, and there was great variation in the diligence with which prefectures gathered the data. Some submitted nothing at all. Prefectural comparisons, therefore, are a better measure of administrative efficiency than of education. What I did was to calculate whether the number of schools and students per capita in each county was above or below the mean *for that prefecture*. Thus each county scored either 0 or 1 according to its relationship to its own prefectural mean.

in time past. As is usual with time-series data, levels of contention in any given year are highly correlated with levels in the previous year. Additionally, when we sum magnitudes of contention in a number of previous years, a positive association remains. The more years such a sum includes, however, the more we lean toward a suspicion of learning, of the accumulation, if you will, of intellectual resources. In the case of early modern Japan, indeed, there appears to be such an accumulation, which reaches maximum influence over a span of five years. In other words, the relationship between contention in year T and the sum of contention in years T -1 and T -2 is stronger than that between year T and the previous year (T -1) alone. The relationship with the sum of years T -1, T -2, and T -3 is yet stronger, and that between year T and the sum of the five preceding years is strongest of all (correlations with the three forms of contention are 0.52, 0.54, and 0.57, respectively). When more and more years are added, however, the relationship weakens.

Such a finding is consistent with a learning, or mobilization, interpretation of contentious behavior. It is also consistent with long-term continuity of causes of grievances and of opportunities and with an interpretation of contention as a cyclical phenomenon. We have seen how some episodes of contention reflect decades-long accumulations of injustice, hostility, and calculation. Usually, I suspect, neither interests nor opportunities are so durable, but contention per se, whether successful or not, becomes a resource upon which later people can draw.

Religious activity, by contrast, does not so appear. I have already noted my skepticism about the connection between popular contention and religious ecstasies and mass pilgrimages. What I have done here is see whether the provinces most involved in the mass pilgrimages of 1770 and 1830 and the counties most involved in the eejanaika movement of 1867 also had high levels of contention; and whether the years of pilgrimages were also years of frequent contention.[11] In almost every case no relationship whatsoever was found. Two hypotheses have been offered regarding the relationship between religion and contention: some have seen them as covariant, others view them as alternative responses to similar causes, with one substituting for the other. My investigation suggests that neither view is correct, but for the rest, my feeling is that social mobilization in particular and social or intellectual resources in general did indeed contribute to the potential for popular contention.

Interests, Opportunities, Resources, and Composition

We have thus far seen some consistent relationships between various contextual, structural characteristics of early modern Japan and magnitudes of popular contention. All forms of contention appear to have varied with levels of poverty and

---

[11] The data source for pilgrimages is Fujitani 1982: 83, 35–36; Takagi 1983: 215; and *Rekishi Kagaku* 1974: 256; for eejanaika it is Takagi 1983.

want, both agrarian and urban vulnerability, protoindustrialization and agricultural commercialization, natural disasters, and prices and taxes (at least within the domains); and to have varied inversely with wage levels. Politically, contention was most frequent where government was either fragmented or in the hands of the shogunate, although this relation was markedly weaker in the case of political protest than in that of social or political conflict. Contention was also relatively frequent when and where the shogunate's finances were shaky and taxes—and, by inference, administrative capabilities—were low. Controlling for regime type, we have seen that the biggest, oldest, and most stable domains also had relatively high magnitudes of contention. Finally, all forms of contention were associated with social factors such as education and past levels of contention. Moreover, urbanism and communications links seem to conduce to social and political conflict, and sericulture and the combination of commercialized and freehold agriculture seem to conduce to political protest.

Popular contention in early modern Japan thus appears to have had a multiplicity of causes—or at least of correlates—and I shall disentangle some of them later. But before that, I can look at my data from another perspective in order to suggest some of the differences between social and political contention. Specifically, I want to examine the same contextual factors in relation to the proportions of the total magnitude of contention accounted for by social conflict and political protest, the polar types of contention in my typology. The results are shown in Table 19.

Table 19 shows that, in terms of the inferability of grievances, social conflict is associated with prosperity and economic development, tenancy, and economic reverses—high prices, low wages, and many natural disasters. Protest, by contrast, was relatively common in chronically undeveloped, deprived, and rural regions but does not appear to have been a response to economic reversals. Social conflict—the less dangerous and demanding form of contention—appears to have been relatively common where political opportunities were greatest: in fragmented and shogunally run regions, where taxes were low and regulatory capacities and proclivities—as suggested by hereditary domain location and the number of samurai as a proportion of domain population—were lowest. Protest, curiously, characterized the outer and more heavily warrior-populated domains (Hall 1991: 190) and regions with unified, nonshogunal rule and relatively high taxes.

Protest appears to have been salient in regions of presumptively low social mobilization, and social conflict common where mobilization was arguably high. Thus we face at this point a partial paradox. It is no surprise that social conflict, which I have surmised results largely from individual responses to the vagaries of fortune amid large-scale social and economic change, is relatively frequent in more developed and mobilized, and dramatically reversible, times and places. That political protest should be relatively frequent in those times and places in which opportunities are minimal is puzzling, however.

Part of the answer is that the proportion of total contention accounted for by protest varies inversely with total magnitude of contention. That is, protest is

Table 19. Correlates of the composition of contention: A multivariate analysis

	Economic (interest) factors		Political (opportunity) factors		Social (resource) factors	
	Social conflict	Political protest	Social conflict	Political protest	Social conflict	Political protest
County measures						
Urbanization	n.s.	−0.10			n.s.	−0.10
Tenancy	0.10	−0.12			0.10	−0.12
Administrative fragmentation			0.19	−0.19		
County tax rate			−0.10	0.12		
Sericulture					−0.7	0.08
Communications links					0.10	−0.10
Provincial measures						
Agricultural productivity per sq. km.	0.32	−0.32				
Increased agricultural productivity	0.17	−0.14				
Commercialization of agriculture	0.21	−0.21			0.21	−0.21
Nongrain products	0.17	−0.13			0.17	−0.13
Disasters	0.20	−0.25				
Villages under shogunate			0.18	−0.21		
Provincial tax rate			0.22	−0.12		
Domain measures						
Hereditary or outer domain			−0.10	0.10		
Samurai percentage of population			−0.11	0.11		
Temporal measures						
Kyoto price index	0.23	−0.21				
Builders' wages	−0.37	0.40				
Mean rice price index, 3-yr. lag	0.14	−0.11				
Disasters and rice prices, 2-yr. lag	0.29	−0.21				
Bakufu tax rate			−0.30	0.23		

relatively common where contention is relatively rare. And this is where the sorts of interests and resources conducive to contention are least in evidence, as are opportunities. (With two exceptions: the social obverse of economic development is community cohesion, a tremendously important resource, and where development did occur, if it did so in a context of low tenancy and on a basis of sericulture—which also imply cohesion—this suspicion grows even stronger.) But perhaps political protest occurs relatively frequently where the conditions for contention in general are adverse, and social conflict is relatively frequent in contexts of least resistance.

11

A MULTIVARIATE ANALYSIS

I have found three constellations of factors which are related to popular contention. At this point I wish to integrate them further, to see if they contribute to both magnitude and composition of contention differently when used together than when related to contention one by one. To do so, I shall adopt a different approach to the data, two different methodologies, and a different interpretation.

So far, my approach has been to go descriptively across dimensions of context and contention, one constellation at a time; looking first at interests vis-à-vis each type of contention, then at opportunities vis-à-vis each type, and so on. In this chapter I focus on types of contention, comparing the relative contribution of each constellation to each type of contention on each spatial and temporal level. To do so I use a statistical method called multiple regression, which enables me to measure interests, opportunities, and resources and estimate the unique influence of each, *independent of all the others*, on each type of contention.[1] Thus, if political opportunities are the most powerful causes of contention, the independent effects of economic and social factors will fade in a regression analysis. Moreover, by combining all the causal factors, regression also tells us what proportion of the total variation in each type of contention is accounted for by all explanatory constellations together. Thus the technique allows me to estimate the total explanatory power of all my measures and the contribution made by each one to the magnitude and composition of popular contention.

The second methodological shift follows. I categorize counties, provinces, domains, and years according to whether they score "high" or "low" on those

---

[1] Multiple regression provides reasonable estimates of the contributions of a set of predictor variables to some dependent variable insofar as (a) the relationships in question are linear and (b) whatever errors may exist in the predictor variables are unrelated to each other. The relationships I shall test were vetted for linearity, and the data on the independent variables selected from a wide variety of independent sources, as can be seen, in order to minimize the chance of correlated errors.

measures of interests, opportunities, and resources which are related to contention. If all three constellations operate as expected, times and places "high" on all three constellations should evince higher levels of contention than those "low" on all three. This method, like regression, also allows us to see which of the three is exercising the greatest influence on contention. Finally, I combine my temporal and spatial data sets and categorize the resulting units—county-years, province-years, and domain-years—in terms of indicators of contextual proclivity to contend. Again, units "scoring" high or low—that is, either presumptively contentious or quiescent in terms of both characteristics of each place in each year—should be subject to differing levels and compositions of contention.

Finally, my interpretive stance changes. Thus far I have proceeded descriptively, seeking simple associations. Now, however, the independent effects on contention of the measures of my constellations begin to justify some assertions that these measures are in fact indicators not simply of correlates but rather of causes of contention. Whether my assertions are justified is for the reader to decide.

Social Conflict

Table 20 presents data from four regression analyses of social conflict.[2] In interpreting it one should keep in mind, first, that the coefficients of correlation, or betas, normally vary between 1 and -1, with bigger coefficients representing stronger effects. Second, these coefficients represent the direct, independent effect of each explanatory variable on magnitude of social conflict. There are many interrelationships among the explanatory variables; for example, on the county level administrative fragmentation has, in addition to its direct effect on social conflict, an association of -0.41 with the tax rate. Thus the total effect of fragmentation on social conflict includes both a direct effect of 0.28 *and* an indirect "path," or effect, through the tax rate. This latter equals the product of the "paths" from fragmentation to taxes (-0.41) and taxes to conflict (-0.12), that is, 0.05. Thus the sum total of direct and indirect effects of fragmentation on social conflict is 0.33, not 0.28. In the great majority of cases these indirect effects make almost no difference in the substantive effect of the explanatory variable. Where indirect paths lead through statistically significant variables, however, or where indirect paths through other statistically significant variables add up to what would be statistically significant total effects—for example, in the case of provincial agricultural vulnerability, which (through its effect on productivity, economic growth, and commercialization) has a negligible direct

---

[2] In these exercises all independent variables have been vetted for multicollinearity. A wide variety of interaction effects—for example, between urbanization and agricultural vulnerability—were investigated, but all generated multicollinearity problems and none contributed more to levels or composition of contention than their original components; so none were used here.

Table 20. Correlates of social conflict: A multivariate analysis

	Interests (economic)	Opportunities (political)	Resources (social)
County level (R^2 = 19%)			
Agricultural product per capita	−0.12*		
Food supply per capita	−0.05		
Urbanization	0.05		0.05
Agricultural vulnerability	0.19*		
Commercialization of agriculture	−0.08		−0.08
High commercialization/low tenancy	0.05		0.05
Administrative fragmentation		0.28* (0.33)	
Tax rate		−0.12	
Communications links			0.07
Provincial level (R^2 = 49%)			
Agricultural product per sq. kilometer	−0.26*		
Agricultural vulnerability	−0.04 (0.17)		
Increasing agricultural productivity	0.06		
Nongrain agricultural product	0.37*		0.37*
Natural disasters	0.16		
Villages under the shogunate		0.40*	
Tax rate		0.02	
Agricultural population			−0.02
Domain level (R^2 = 17%)			
Resources	−0.19* (−0.24)		
Tax rate	0.01		
Extraction	−0.05		
Extraordinary revenue	0.11		
Hereditary or outer domain		0.13	
Domain population	0.29* (0.28)		
Domain lifetime	−0.19*		
Average years per ruling family		−0.07	
Samurai as percentage of domain population		−0.18*	
Temporal correlates (R^2 = 32%)			
Disasters in previous year	0.23*		
Kyoto price index	0.61*		
Rice price index 3 years previous	0.02 (0.42)		
Shogunal tax rate		−0.13	
Cumulative shogunal deficits		−0.08	
Cumulative protest, previous 5 years			−0.25*

Note: All coefficients are standardized regression coefficients (betas). Starred coefficients are significant at $p < 0.10$. Figures in parentheses represent the total of both direct and indirect effects from statistically significant independent variables through other statistically significant variables to the dependent variable.

effect and a substantial, positive indirect effect—I have included the total effects parenthetically.[3]

The first two things that stand out from Table 20 are that, taken together, my contextual surrogate measures of interests, opportunities, and resources explain somewhere on the order of 20–50 percent of the magnitude of social conflict and that each constellation of putatively causal factors fulfills some of my expectations.[4] The least prepossessing constellation is that of resources; my measures of schools and students contributed nothing independently, nor did the configurational economic-social variable of sericulture. Excluding the measure of cumulative conflict (about which more hereafter) the six remaining measures had an average effect of only 0.11, most of that contributed by the configurational variable of nongrain agricultural production. Nevertheless, effects are as predicted. I have been unhappy from the beginning with my quantitative measures of resources, but this result suggests that resources, to the extent that they were analytically important, were a relative constant in early modern Japan. The other two constellations, however, appear relevant and similarly so. Twenty economic indicators (the eighteen included here, plus the inconsequential sericulture and provincial commercialization of agriculture measures) have an average total effect of 0.16, and the eleven political indicators average 0.18.

Looking across levels of analysis, we find convergence. Deprivation, whether measured in county agricultural productivity per capita or food production, provincial productivity per square kilometer, domain resources, natural disasters, extraordinary domain exactions, or high prices, is associated with social conflict. The effect of county agricultural productivity is enhanced by its effect on actual food production; domain resources are indirectly influential in that richer domains levied lower taxes, used fewer extraordinary taxes, and possessed more samurai; and earlier high rice prices eventuated in rises in the Kyoto price index, an extraordinarily powerful predictor of conflict.

Both agricultural vulnerability and the market vulnerability resulting from commercialization of agriculture, protoindustrialization, and urbanization also contribute to social conflict. The independent effect of agricultural vulnerability on the provincial level is puzzlingly (albeit insignificantly) negative, but its strong association with nongrain production, low agricultural productivity, and natural

---

[3] This data presentation is, as those conversant with multiple regression will suspect, based on a series of path analyses (four in the case of Table 20). I have not presented these results in toto, because there are twelve of them behind the tables in this chapter, and each includes roughly ten independent variables. The data presented in these tables accurately reflect the role that indirect effects play in the data.

[4] Fully recognizing the limitations of the data and the strictures of technique, I base my interpretations on both the statistically significant relationships *and*, because almost without exception they point in the hypothesized directions, the other relationships as well. No single finding counts for much, but I think the overall pattern justifies my conclusions.

disasters generate an indirect effect on social conflict of 0.21, for a total effect of 0.17.

My indicators of political opportunity perform relatively well vis-à-vis social conflict. Fragmentation per se, direct shogunal rule, and reduced taxes (and, by extension, capabilities) all lead to conflict.[5] The provincial tax rate and shogunal deficit contribute little, however. The effect of fragmentation is enhanced, as noted, by the low tax rates in fragmented counties. On the domain level, it appears that big,[6] *un*stable (because either short-lived or familially fluid), and underpoliced domains—the "dinosaurs" of which I spoke—saw the most conflict, although the effect of size is reduced by its association with greater domain life and familial stability. It also appears that outer domain status (which appears to enhance conflict) is really of little import, since it is also associated with conflict-dampening familial stability and larger samurai populations. Finally, domain extraction (although not simple taxation) appears to fall into the pattern observed in counties, provinces, and years, varying inversely with conflict and thus possibly representing governmental resources rather than a source of grievance. Extraordinary revenues, on the other hand, behave as expected, seemingly a source of popular dissent. So a picture reemerges of higher levels of social conflict in big, unstable, underregulated, underfunded, and overreaching domains.

One last word on the magnitude of social conflict regards the measure of cumulative contention in years past.[7] When previously correlated simply with current conflict, both measures of past contention were related positively, suggesting that some sort of social learning was going on. Here, however, the measure used (and every other measure of past conflict, either annual or aggregated) is negatively related to conflict. The reason, I surmise, is the cyclical nature of contention: peaks in the price and disaster curves came more than five or ten years apart, and so, consequently, did contentious years. Since one may expect the interest constellation to fluctuate more than the opportunity constellation,

---

[5] My notion that taxes are in fact an indicator of regime resources, and therefore of opportunities, is enhanced by the association, at least for the shogunate, of tax rates and budget surpluses at $r = 0.58$.

[6] One should keep in mind that domain population is a surrogate measure for size in terms of assessed agricultural productivity and a number of other criteria, with which it is correlated at over $r = 0.90$.

[7] Those familiar with time-series analysis will recognize the danger of serial autocorrelation in Table 20. Indeed, the magnitudes of social and political conflict and political protest in any given year are highly correlated with the sum of each type of contention in the previous five years. To control for autocorrelation, I ran all the analyses in this chapter with and without the cumulative magnitude of contention over the previous five years. The exclusion of the cumulative measure reduced R^2's by 2–4 percentage points. With all the other variables included, however, only in the case of social conflict (see Table 20) was the beta between current and cumulative past contention significant. As Tables 20–22 show, even with past contention controlled for, the impact of the independent variables is substantial.

Table 21. Correlates of political conflict: A multivariate analysis

	Interests (economic)	Opportunities (political)	Resources (social)
County level (R² = 21%)			
Agricultural product per capita	−0.06 (−0.16)		
Food supply per capita	−0.11		
Urbanization	0.17*		0.17*
Agricultural vulnerability	0.23*		
Commercialization of agriculture	−0.01		−0.01
High commercialization/low tenancy	0.05		0.05
Administrative fragmentation		0.17*	
Tax rate		−0.05	
Communications links			0.14*
Provincial level (R² = 49%)			
Agricultural product per sq. kilometer	−0.14		
Agricultural vulnerability	−0.01 (0.20)		
Increasing agricultural productivity	0.05		
Nongrain agricultural product	0.29*		0.29*
Natural disasters	0.28*		
Villages under the shogunate		0.52* (0.43)	
Tax rate		0.21*	
Agricultural population			−0.03
Domain level (R² = 11%)			
Resources	−0.07		
Tax rate	0.06		
Extraction	−0.19*		
Extraordinary revenue	0.12		
Hereditary or outer domain		0.04	
Domain population		0.24* (0.17)	
Domain lifetime		0.02	
Average years per ruling family		−0.04	
Samurai as percentage of domain population		−0.04	
Temporal correlates (R² = 46%)			
Disasters in previous year	0.17*		
Kyoto price index	0.72*		
Rice price index 3 years previous	−0.16* (0.27)		
Shogunal tax rate		−0.27*	
Cumulative shogunal deficits		−0.03	
Cumulative protest, previous 5 years			−0.09

Note: All coefficients are standardized regression coefficients (betas). Starred coefficients are significant at p < 0.10. Figures in parentheses represent the total of both direct and indirect effects from statistically significant variables through other statistically significant variables to the dependent variable.

this finding adds to my esteem for the interest cluster as a cause of the magnitude of at least social contention.

Political Conflict

Table 21 presents the results of my analysis of political conflict. On two counts they parallel my previous findings: the explanatory power of these structural features vis-à-vis political conflict (R^2) ranges between 11 percent and 49 percent, and both the economic and political constellations play substantial roles (with average total effects of 0.16 and 0.13, respectively). The resource constellation again contributes only modestly, and primarily through the configurational variables it shares with interests; nevertheless, the average total effect in this constellation is 0.12.

Once again, contention appears to be generated by a hardscrabble existence in general and both cumulative and sudden reverses in particular, especially past levels of disasters and rice prices and the current level of prices in Kyoto. The impact of county agricultural productivity is enhanced by its influence on urbanization and on food supply, and provincial agricultural vulnerability again comes out of nowhere through its indirect influence on contention, via its links to agricultural product and disasters and to increased agricultural production in general and nongrain production in particular. Vulnerability seems to have pushed affected regions toward commercial and protoindustrial development. And although the price of rice three years previously had a negative direct effect on conflict—within three years its cyclical variations in price may have subsided—when its indirect effects through the current price index and tax levels are calculated it becomes a powerful contributory factor to conflict.

Heavy domain reliance on extraordinary revenues is also linked to contention, although efficient domain extraction has a dampening effect. Perhaps such capability is a better indicator of regime resources than of popular interests. Nevertheless, attempts to remedy precarious finances through economic development are also associated with conflict, albeit modestly.

On the political dimension, once again, fragmentation and shogunal rule appear to provide opportunities to contend. The role of taxation—with the exception of efficient extraction and extraordinary revenue—is ambiguous, and I reserve further comment until I see what role it plays vis-à-vis protest. But domains that were bigger, less familially stable, and less populated by samurai again seem to have been prone to contention, regardless of whether they were ruled by inner or outer lords.

Social resources, as noted, matter more with respect to political conflict than to social. Urbanization, communication links, and agricultural commercialization (especially in a context of low tenancy and thus inferentially high community cohesion) are all tied to conflict. Perhaps political conflict—the pursuit into the political realm of originally social conflicts—is more dependent upon some sort of sophistication which is being tapped by these measures.

Political Protest

Political conflict, as one might expect of a phenomenon that begins as social conflict, has similar causal patterns. Of political protest we have come to expect different things, and Table 22 does not disappoint us. In the first place, the overall explanatory power of the structural/contextual factors adduced here is slightly less, with a maximum R^2 of 42 percent. Second, the relative influence of the three constellations of factors is anomalously skewed. The average total effect among the indicators of interests is 0.18, but that for opportunities is only 0.10, and for social resources, 0.07. One might expect political contention to have distinctively political roots, but these data certainly do not support such an expectation.

What *does* seem to drive political protest is chronic deprivation. Including its indirect effects, through food supply and urbanization, county agricultural capacity affects protest more strongly than it does either social or political conflict; agricultural vulnerability on both county and provincial levels does the same, although provincial vulnerability once more exercises most of its influence indirectly, through agricultural commercialization and growth and through capacity. Provincial agricultural capacity and domain resource level are also far more closely related to protest than to other forms of contention. Yet imposed deprivation in the form of taxes has no consistent impact on protest: county, shogunal, and domain tax and extraction rates matter little, if at all, and only extraordinary revenues suggest the sort of relationship I expected.

Chronic deprivation appears more significant than short-term reverses. Last year's natural disasters count, as do past rice prices (which, again, act also through taxes and the price index) and the current Kyoto price index, but in comparison with both social and political conflict and the relative strength of endemic factors, these fluctuations appear less important here.

Chronic dearth also appears to outweigh the effects of economic development. Vulnerable regions did tend to develop more than others, showing positive relationships to commercialization on both county and provincial levels and to nongrain production and growth in agricultural productivity. But the influence of developmental variables is slightly less with respect to protest than to the other forms of contention. Agricultural productivity does grow prominently, but commercialized agriculture does not, and one suspects that in these chronically poor, high-protest regions this growth took place disproportionately in (perhaps even subsistence-level) food production.

Of all my political indicators, only domain size and shogunal deficits appear to influence protest. The pattern is fully consistent with expectations—administrative fragmentation and shogunal rule may contribute, as may administrative instability and samurai presence—but the coefficients are insignificant. Bigger and poorer (they tended to be the same) and innovatively extractive domains were perhaps more likely to see protest than either social or political conflict, but the overall strength of these relationships, again, fades beside the economic factors.

Table 22. Correlates of political protest: A multivariate analysis

	Interests (economic)	Opportunities (political)	Resources (social)
County level (R^2 = 15%)			
Agricultural product per capita	−0.22*		
Food supply per capita	−0.04		
Urbanization	0.03		0.03
Agricultural vulnerability	0.30*		
Commercialization of agriculture	−0.02		−0.02
High commercialization/low tenancy	0.04		0.04
Administrative fragmentation		0.07	
Tax rate		0.02	
Communications links			0.01
Provincial level (R^2 = 42%)			
Agricultural product per sq. kilometer	−0.54*		
Agricultural vulnerability	0.06 (0.31)		
Increasing agricultural productivity	0.14		
Nongrain agricultural product	0.22*		0.22*
Natural disasters	−0.19*		
Villages under the shogunate		0.14	
Tax rate		0.12	
Agricultural population			−0.09
Domain level (R^2 = 19%)			
Resources	−0.25*		
Tax rate	0.03		
Extraction	−0.01		
Extraordinary revenue	0.13		
Hereditary or outer domain		0.07	
Domain population		0.24* (0.32)	
Domain lifetime		−0.06	
Average years per ruling family	−0.03		
Samurai as percentage of domain population		−0.02	
Temporal correlates (R^2 = 28%)			
Disasters in previous year	0.29*		
Kyoto price index	0.49*		
Rice price index 3 years previous	−0.17* (0.42)		
Shogunal tax rate		0.12	
Cumulative shogunal deficits		0.19*	
Cumulative protest, previous 5 years			−0.15

Note: All coefficients are standardized regression coefficients (betas). Starred coefficients are significant at $p < 0.10$. Figures in parentheses represent the total of both direct and indirect effects from statistically significant independent variables through other statistically significant variables to the dependent variable.

So do social resources. Across the board, the lagged magnitude of protest appears to be an indicator of cyclical economic factors, and the relatively strong impact of nongrain production is in fact less than it is on social and political conflict, and it is also partly an indicator of economics, not social dynamics. Among the rest, little explanatory power can be discerned. Indeed, one conclusion to be drawn from this analysis is that social resources, as quantitatively measured here, are of limited help in explaining anything but political conflict.

A second conclusion is that taxation is an ambiguous factor. Shogunal tax rates are for the most part inversely related to contention, as are county tax rates (except vis-à-vis protest); provincial tax rates seem to be directly related. On the domain level the simple tax rate—and, more strongly, the role of extraordinary revenues—appears to be directly related to contention, whereas the efficiency of extraction is more probably inversely related. At this level a pattern emerges: better-endowed domains taxed less, levied fewer extraordinary taxes, and enjoyed quiescence. Also, domains with more stability and more samurai extracted resources from their jurisdictions more effectively and thus may have been able to afford more effective governance and more social control. At any rate, they too had relatively low levels of contention. In contrast, we have the "dinosaurs" or "overreachers"—bigger, poorer, less stable, less policed domains unable to extract resources with great efficiency and yet inclined to impose precisely those sorts of new taxes most likely to incite the people to dissent.

Taxes overall remain a puzzle. In all likelihood they were, as I feared, a double-edged sword: the key to greater regime resources, but a dangerous stimulus to contention. Their role may have been contingent on other factors, and it deserves attention as we proceed.

Finally, quantitative analysis has pushed me toward a qualitative interpretation of contention. Specifically, social and political conflict appear to be the product less of dearth than of development, short-term reverses, relatively open opportunities for contention, and political and social factors in general. Political protest, however, seems to be produced by dearth, by chronic conditions, and by economic factors. One can see this pattern in the sorts of interests to which each is a response. I have conflated in my analysis factors that are intuitively generative of three different types of interests: hardship-related, development-related, and reversal-related.[8] If we take only those that are significantly related to contention, we find that the average total effect of the hardship-related interest indicators is

---

[8] Indicators of chronic hardship include county agricultural productivity per capita, food supply, and agricultural vulnerability; provincial productivity per kilometer and vulnerability; and domain resources. Developmental indicators include county urbanization, commercialization of agriculture, and commercialization plus low tenancy; and provincial agricultural increase and nongrain production. Short-term reversals are indicated by provincial disaster frequency; domain taxes, extraction, and extraordinary revenues; and past disasters and rice prices and current retail prices. I have excluded wage levels from this analysis because they are multicollinear with prices.

0.20 vis-à-vis social conflict, 0.22 vis-à-vis political conflict, and 0.32 vis-à-vis protest. For development-derived interests the relative impacts are 0.37, 0.23, and 0.22; for reversal-related interests they are 0.42, 0.33, and 0.35.

There is a similar difference in the response of different types of contention to political structures and performance. In terms of average total effects of significant explanatory factors, there is little difference, but whereas six of these factors have a significant effect on social conflict and five on political conflict, only two are significantly related to protest. Thus, although related, the forms of contention appear distinctive, and a more sharply focused look at these distinctions is in order.

The Composition of Contention

I want to focus on the two most clearly differentiated forms of contention: social conflict and political protest. Whereas political conflict occupied a more or less consistent share of the totality of contention, social conflict and protest tended to vary inversely as proportions of the total. It is well to bear in mind that all my types of contention covaried, and thus we should not expect to find great proportions of their differential variances explained by the sorts of structural factors adduced thus far. Even so, the differences in strength and direction of relationships might be enlightening.

Specifically, I expected on the basis of the temporal trends in these proportions (see Figure 9) to find protest responding more to political factors and social conflict to economic ones. My regression analyses suggest the contrary. Data from other early modern societies (Kimmel 1988) also suggest that social conflict grows relative to economic growth; the corollary—that protest should be more common in less-developed areas—is suggested by the chronic indicators of economic dearth already presented, by a separate analysis of economic development and contention (White 1989), and by a more intensive analysis of one region in Japan (White 1988a). Resources I suspect to be of little relevance, since they were fungible—equally applicable to either form of contention. Thus I eliminate political conflict from consideration here, and resources also. Additionally, I present here only those factors whose associations with contention were statistically significant.[9]

Table 23 presents the results of several regression analyses of the proportions of total contention accounted for by social conflict and political protest. Initially, I included all the explanatory factors used previously; this table includes only the significant ones, but the pattern is clear. Social conflict is associated on the county level with low regulative and administrative capacities; on the provincial level with relative prosperity and reversals thereof; on the domain level with big, unstable, underregulated regimes; and over time with high prices, another form of economic reverse inferentially a source of grievances. Political protest, by contrast, is

---

[9] As before, I am considering significant any beta for which $p < 0.10$.

Table 23. Composition of popular contention: A multivariate analysis

	Proportion of total contention accounted for by	
	Social conflict	Political protest
County level: R^2 =	10%	7%
Agricultural vulnerability	—	0.21
Administrative fragmentation	0.22	−0.11
Tax rate	−0.12	—
Provincial level: R^2 =	19%	20%
Agricultural productivity per square kilometer	0.32	−0.30
Disasters	0.23	−0.28
Tax rate	−0.22	—
Villages under shogunal rule	—	−0.18
Domain level: R^2 =	9%	15%
Domain population	0.28	0.25
Lifetime of domain	−0.18	—
Samurai as percentage of population	−0.19	—
Temporal level: R^2 =	11%	19%
Kyoto price index	0.29	−0.16
Rice price index 3 years previous	—	0.21
Tax rate in shogunal territories	—	0.22

associated on the county level with unified administration and precarious existence; on the provincial level with tighter (that is, domainal) rule and endemic hardship; on the domain level with larger size; and through time with administrative penetration and past but not current economic reverses. Social conflict appears to result from *both* political opportunities and economic interests, whereas protest appears to stem more from interests. Protest appears relatively common where life is tough and so is the government (Hall 1991: 190); social conflict is common where life is relatively good but fluctuating, and the authorities are weaker and less obtrusive. Perhaps fluctuations are likely to stimulate contention where people have already achieved some modicum of prosperity, but stimulate only a scramble for survival where life is close to the bone.

Again we see that people seem to protest in precisely the least promising circumstances. An answer to this puzzle may lie in the constellation of interests as reflective of governmental *salience*. It seems to me that tight and obtrusive government generates grievances sufficient to overcome a paucity of opportunities. The tendency to social conflict in administratively weaker regions implies opportunities, but perhaps in such regions the polity was simply not as salient, as key to the fulfillment of the interests that drove contention. If this assessment is accurate, then the contradiction between the regression analysis and Figure 9 dissolves. Perhaps people simply scratched whatever itched the most, and if government itched more than the market or one's fellow commoners then that is where and when people scratched, no matter what the price.

Interests and Opportunities across Time and Space

To complete the picture, interests and opportunities must be combined. This exercise, fruitfully used by James Tong (1991) in his analysis of popular contention in Ming China, enables us to examine the fundamental rationality of people in early modern society. Tong gave spatiotemporal units (county-years) scores on two dimensions: economic dearth and tightness of political rule. The first implies individuals' calculations of their ability to survive hardship; the latter, their calculations of survival as outlaws. Where the first is high (i.e., in comfortable conditions) and the latter low (i.e., where government is effective), rational individuals should rarely opt for contention; in opposite situations contention should peak. If interests (that is, survivability of dearth) count for more than opportunities (i.e., survival through contention), then units with high hardship scores will be more contentious regardless of opportunities; if a purely utilitarian calculus is operating, then hardship will be irrelevant and opportunities alone will determine levels of contention. Tong (1991: 92) found a powerful relationship between the cumulative effects of *both* interests and opportunities and the contentiousness of different times and places.

I want to address the same question: Does the behavior of the common people appear consistent with the rational calculation that the stronger the interest in contention and the greater the opportunities, then the more contention there shall be?[10] But I disaggregate my answer a bit more than did Tong, who looked at a single dimension of interest on a single level, that of the county-year. I look separately at my three intuitively attractive types of interests (those deriving from chronic dearth, economic development, and reverses) on three spatial levels (counties, provinces, and domains) and then on three spatiotemporal levels (county-, province- and domain-years).

Initially, I created a single composite measure of all three types of interests on the basis of the significant relationships revealed in Tables 20–22.[11] Opportunities were measured by fragmentation on the county level, proportion of villages

---

[10] I do not include resources in this analysis, inasmuch as my regression does not indicate that enough of our measures thereof are related to contention strongly and independently enough.

[11] On the county level I included urbanization (at face value), vulnerability (weighted by a factor of 2.5), and productivity per capita (weighted by 2). On the provincial level I used productivity per square kilometer (at face value for social and political conflict and weighted by 2 for protest), vulnerability (at face value), and nongrain production (at face value for protest and weighted by 2 for social and political conflict); on the domain level I used extraction (at face value), extraordinary revenue (weighted by 2), and resources (weighted by 3). The measures were additive, with weights arrived at simply by eyeballing the relative magnitudes of the different explanatory factors' effects on contention. Factor analysis did not indicate any completely clean dimensions, and it takes me farther from my data than I feel comfortable going.

Table 24. Interests, opportunities, and popular contention: Counties, provinces, domains

Interests	Social conflict			Political conflict			Political protest		
	Low	Med.	High	Low	Med.	High	Low	Med.	High
County level									
Opportunities									
Low	38	44	62	28	36	44	40	48	68
Medium	48	56	64	34	46	54	48	60	68
High	58	66	76	40	56	70	50	58	70
Provincial level									
Opportunities									
Low	35	38	65	33	33	45	50	55	83
Medium	45	60	83	33	53	65	50	65	83
High	50	70	88	75	63	83	60	75	63
Domain level									
Opportunities									
Low	35	58	75	30	50	50	40	48	70
Medium	68	58	78	43	48	50	58	63	68
High	68	65	80	53	43	58	60	65	75

under shogunal control on the provincial level, and a combination of domain status, size, duration, familial stability, and samurai population on the domain level.[12] Interests and opportunities were reduced to three-point scales (low, medium, high), producing the three-by-three tables presented in Table 24. The figures in the tables are the mean magnitudes of each type of contention of the units in each cell, converted to a hundred-point scale.

My expectation was that as one goes from the upper left cell to the lower right cell of each table—that is, as interests in and opportunities for contention grow—the magnitude of contention would increase. And what we see is an extraordinary consistency between popular behavior and the assumption of popular rationality. In eight of the nine tables there is a clear linear progression diagonally from one corner to the other. In four tables the magnitude of contention increases between two and three times; in another four it roughly doubles, and in only one (protest on the provincial level) is it not perfectly linear. Moreover, as one goes from cell to cell along either the rows or columns of each table (that is, as *either* opportunities or interests increase), over 90 percent of the steps result in increases in contention. On the average, contention doubles along the diagonal in the nine tables.

Thus both interests and opportunities appear to be at work. Interests may have a slightly greater influence: in seven of the nine tables, the increases in mean

---

[12] The weighting of this scale was: lifetime, familial stability, and samurai population at face value, domain status weighted by a factor of 2, and size weighted by 3.

magnitudes of contention along the rows are greater than those down the columns. The differences are noteworthy in six of the seven tables. This is the same pattern—modest but clear—that Tong found (1991: 92; Little 1991: 171), and I am inclined, with him, to emphasize the apparently rational response by the people to *both* opportunities and interests.

It may be variably rational, however. For example, the increase in magnitude of both social and political conflict along the diagonal is 2.3 times; for political protest, in contrast, it is only 63 percent. Moreover, interests overshadow opportunities most strikingly in regard to protest. Is protest, then, a less rational form of behavior than social or political conflict? I think not, but it may well result more from calculation of the economic future of one's family or village than from calculation of one's personal survival.

I have maintained that interests are not unidimensional. Indeed, protest seemed to be a systematic response more to chronic dearth than to economic development or short-term economic reverses. So I created separate measures of these three speculative types of interests. There were not enough measures of each type of interest on every level to be comprehensive, but I was able to create such measures for dearth and development on the county and provincial levels and for dearth and reverses on the domain level. Thus I was able to observe six different combinations of interests and opportunities vis-à-vis each of the three types of contention. I have not presented all eighteen of the resulting tables, but they further support the previous discussion. Seventeen of the eighteen tables show linear increases in contention from one corner diagonally to the other. The role of opportunities and interests is more or less equal: opportunities appear to exert greater influence in nine tables, and interests in seven. As was the case in Table 24, the cumulative effect of interests and opportunities was greater on social and political conflict than on protest: protesters may have been less rational than social contenders, or they may simply have been influenced less by structure and more by leadership or will. But disaggregation of types of interests does not improve our understanding a great deal. Factor analysis suggested that there was no clear differentiation between dimensions of interest. My eighteen tables suggest that vis-à-vis social conflict, hardship and development have more or less equivalent effects, which are greater than those of reverses. Vis-à-vis political conflict, all three types of interest had roughly similar effects. Vis-à-vis protest, dearth was more influential than development and reverses.

But thus far I have not been able to incorporate reverses fully in my analysis, for I have not yet incorporated time. Thus I move on to the final stage of this analysis, the examination of spatiotemporal units.

I generated three types of such units: 21,312 province-years, 102,816 domain-years, and 181,728 county-years (based on 288 years, 74 provinces, 357 domains, and 631 counties). The number of units in which contention occurred is so small (4 percent of the county-years, 6 percent of the domain-years, and 26 percent of the province-years) that the skewness of the data distribution makes me reluctant to use regression. Moreover, given the limited number of measures,[13] I do not attempt to disentangle temporally short-term from spatially chronic interests and opportunities. Finally, with occurrences of all types of contention so rare, there is little point in disaggregating contention either by magnitude or by type. Therefore, I look here only at the frequency of occurrence of contention of all types in units categorized simultaneously by long- and short-term causal factors.

In my selection of measures of interests and opportunities I have proceeded conservatively and impressionistically. I have not created any sophisticated composite measures that take me far from my data. What I have done, rather, is select and weight measures on the basis of impressionistic observation of Tables 20–22.[14] What I end up with are categories that capture *both* chronic conditions such as tight rule and hardscrabble existence *and* economic reverses and governmental lapses (Hyakushō Ikki 1980: 254ff.). I have then calculated for each combination of interests and opportunities the proportion of all units in which contention occurred. The results are presented in Table 25.

At each level of analysis, from units in which presumed popular grievances are minimal and the opportunities for contention limited to those in which people are presumably both aggrieved and able to contend relatively freely, the proportion of units in which contention occurred rises dramatically. The proportion of those county-years most likely to see contention (the lower right-hand cell) which actually did so was 7.5 times larger than the proportion of county-years (in the upper left-hand cell) in which I expected to see little contention. In the case of domain-years the increase was 15 times, and for province-years it was slightly over 7 times (versus the fourteenfold increase found by Tong [1991: 92]). Clearly, my attempts to measure opportunities and interests have captured something that in combination is powerfully related to the occurrence of popular contention.

As before, I focus more on the combination than on the relative strength of opportunities and interests. Still, examination of the magnitude of increase in contention horizontally across opportunities, and then vertically across interests, reveals a linear increase in almost every instance, and suggests that opportunities

---

[13] In the sense of having statistically significant or substantively meaningful relationships with contention.

[14] For county-years I have selected as measures of interest disasters, Kyoto prices, the rice price index, rice production, and agricultural vulnerability; the magnitudes of these measures' correlations with contention recommended an additive index of interests weighted thus: (disasters × 2) + (Kyoto prices × 3) + (rice price × 2) + productivity + (vulnerability × 2). My additive, weighted measure of opportunities was, similarly, bakufu tax rate + (administrative fragmentation × 2) + county tax rate. Each measure was trichotomized into low, medium, and high.

For domain-years the index of interests was (rice price index × 2) + (Kyoto prices × 3) + (disasters × 2) + domain resources. The index of opportunities was bakufu tax rate + type of domain + (domain population × 2).

For province-years the index of interests was disasters + (Kyoto prices × 2) + rice price index + agricultural productivity + agricultural vulnerability + nongrain production. The index of opportunities was bakufu tax rate + (proportion of villages under bakufu jurisdiction × 2).

Table 25. Interests, opportunities, and popular contention

Interest in contention	Opportunities for contention		
Percentage of county-years (n = 181,728) in which contentious events occurred			
	Few	Medium	Many
Low	2%	3%	4%
Medium	2	4	7
High	6	7	15
Percentage of domain-years (n = 102,816) in which contentious events occurred			
Low	1%	4%	10%
Medium	1	4	10
High	3	4	15
Percentage of province-years (n = 21,312) in which contentious events occurred			
Low	7%	16%	27%
Medium	12	24	34
High	15	35	50

slightly outweigh interests at the county-year level, although this situation is reversed in domain- and province-years. I have a gratifyingly close parallel to Tong's findings for Ming China, but I follow his example in not attempting to disaggregate it further.

I begin my summary of this chapter with its final analyses, which, in concert with Tong's, suggest that a structural combinaton of opportunities for and incentives to contention, measured as properties of temporal and spatial entities but acting through the grievances, indignation, and pragmatic calculations of individuals, leads to popular contention of all types in early modern societies. Interests may have the stronger influence, especially on political protest, not, I maintain, because protesters are less rational but because protest is relatively more agent-driven and less structure-driven than social conflict. Among interests, both chronic conditions and short-term reverses play a role, but neither narrowly based deprivation nor opportunity models of contention provide us with a full explanation.

My regression analyses add detail to this picture. The actual amount of variance in magnitudes of contention explained by all the factors adduced approaches 50 percent in some instances, with interests, opportunities, and resources all influencing contention as predicted. Some of my variables—such as urbanization and nongrain production—are configurational, once more pushing us toward an overarching, integrated conclusion rather than precise estimates of the relative effects of interests, opportunities, and resources, or of hardship, development, and reversal. Nonetheless, the tripartite model is persuasive.

Among the different forms of contention, social and political conflict appear to be more likely in the context of long-term economic development and prosperity and short-term reverses where the political opportunity structure is relatively open. Political protest, on the other hand, seems to develop from chronic hardship and dearth, relatively independent of the rigor of the opportunity structure. Indeed, protest appears positively related to the tightness of rule, especially in the "dinosaur" domains characterized by large size, relative poverty, administrative instability, and a tendency to overreach themselves.

When we turn from the absolute magnitude of contention to the proportion of all contention accounted for by its different types, the picture is further clarified. The *relative* magnitude of political protest is better explained by structural factors—in particular, dearth and tight regulation—than is social conflict. The relative salience of social conflict, as before, depends on prosperity and development, with fluctuations and reverses, and on a relatively weak administrative context. Initially the examination of the composition of contention raised a contradiction. Figure 9 suggests that political protest responded to a politicized context, whereas my regressions suggest that social conflict was in fact more responsive to an open political opportunity structure. But my look at composition in this chapter resolves the puzzle. The aspect of government which matters is *salience*: when the context is relatively politicized, so is contention. A relatively open political opportunity structure, by contrast, bespeaks a distant government, which is perceived as neither cause nor cure of popular grievances. It contributes to overall higher levels of contention and to frequencies of social contention relatively higher than those of protest. A tighter political context, even if more repressive, leads disproportionately to political protest simply by virtue of its propinquity to the people. As we shall see, government did repress protest more assiduously than social conflict. It was thus a far more parlous activity than sacking a merchant's store. Therefore we cannot remain simply on the macro, structural level in attempting to explain contention. We must turn to its inception and to its leaders.

12

THE INCEPTION OF CONFLICT

Social, economic, and political context exerted a substantial influence on the quality and quantity of popular contention in early modern Japan, but the etiological picture is incomplete. For one thing, the contextual factors I have adduced do not and cannot fully explain contention. Interestingly, statisticians refer to the unexplained variance in phenomena they wish to explain as "error." To me it seems rather a matter for celebration: people are not simple automatons, responding involuntarily to contextual stimuli. Structure is not destiny; agency counts.

The second reason we must dig deeper concerns the aggregate level of my analysis thus far. To get from structures to contention I have inferred individual reactions to context. We need to get closer to the individual level in order to evaluate these inferences, to assess the causal potential of the correlates already found, and to spell out the mechanisms by which context influences behavior. To some extent we can use the words of the contenders themselves in this effort, but we can also use quantified lower-level data on contentious events themselves. Both are necessary.

I organize this exploration under three topics. First, I want to know *what* people contended about. What were the grievances or opportunities that set them off and the demands they made in response? Second, I ask *who* took the lead. What was the composition of the leadership and how did it evolve? The focus here is on resources, of which community cohesion and (intimately linked to it) leadership were perhaps the two most important.[1] Finally, I ask *how* contention was mobilized, how the everyday interaction of rulers and ruled,

---

[1] The importance of leadership is, I suspect, one reason why resources performed so poorly in the quantitative analysis in Chapters 10 and 11.

exploiters and exploited was transformed from subservience to insubordination, from "deference to defiance" (Waddington et al. 1989: 21ff., 158ff.; Kelly 1985). The focus here is on opportunities and interactions. We have seen that political protest was common where it seemed unpromising; thus opportunity encompasses not only chinks in the state's armor but also the position of the state in society. If the state is the source of grievances or the perceived source of resolution, then that is where contention will focus, perhaps regardless of the prospect of success.

Grievances and Demands

The immediate issues that stimulated contention in early modern Japan were most generally of four types: social and communal, economic, fiscal, and political and administrative.[2] Exactly which was most important or most common we cannot tell, since the record is fragmentary at best; nevertheless, in two-thirds of the events compiled by Aoki Kōji there is some cause imputed to the incident, and in roughly 40 percent, some demands made by those involved have been set down. The two are not identical: reasons were often inferred by observers, sometimes long after the fact. Although this retrospection suggests greater reliability for demands, demands were often rationalizations intended to mobilize participants, justify dubiously legitimate behavior, and persuade antagonists, not simply explanations of why people were *actually* on the warpath (Ravina 1992).

Moreover, I am as interested here in how people presented themselves as I am in the context that conduced to contention. Therefore I look at both demands and imputed reasons; in fact, there are parallel patterns in both. I shall consider each type of reason and demand later; the most general pattern is presented in Table 26.

In this table I have divided social and communal reasons and demands into five types. The first three are more or less "horizontal." Among the most common social reasons were quarrels among groups of commoners (both within and between families) over violations of village laws and status rules that governed, among other things, clothing, festival participation, and house construction. Religious reasons were more social than doctrinal—and relatively rare at that. Rivalries among groups over ritual participation, disagreements about the upkeep and construction of temples and shrines, and accusations of clerical dishonesty set the tone. Collective reasons were intervillage disputes, primarily over use and rights with regard to water, timber, and common lands. Intracommunity reasons and demands—the commonest category here—and tenancy-related reasons and demands, on the other hand, were more "vertical" in nature. Intracommunity disputes most often involved village officials' dishonesty

---

[2] This summary is supported by, inter alia, Aoki M. et al. 1981, 3:98ff.; Harada 1982: 365ff.; Borton 1938: 23–30; Kokushō 1971: 14; Tozeren 1981: 43ff.: See also Stevenson 1979: chap. 2; Bercé 1990: chap. 4; Tilly 1986; Tilly et al. 1975.

Table 26. Reasons for and demands made during contentious events

	Number of events in which at least one such reason or demand is recorded	Percentage of all events (n = 6,933) in which such reasons or demands are recorded
Social and communal		
Social reasons	264	4%
Religious reasons	77	1
Collective reasons	345	5
Intracommunity reasons	1,838	27
Intracommunity demands	375	5
Tenancy-related reasons	152	2
Tenancy-related demands	106	2
Economic		
Economic reasons	1,271	18
Economic demands	491	7
Fiscal		
Fiscal reasons	671	10
Fiscal demands	929	13
Political and administrative		
Administrative reasons	639	9
Administrative demands	409	6

and the processes by which leaders were selected, taxes assessed, and village monies dispersed. Accordingly, intracommunity demands most often called for the opening of village books, for "transparent" decision processes, and for the resignation or dismissal of officials. Tenancy disagreements most often involved terms of tenancy and title and the rate and payment schedule of rent; related demands were almost exclusively for rent reductions.

Economic reasons and demands were straightforward: bad harvests, increasing food prices, famine, and drought led to contention, and the people demanded food aid, lower prices, and an end to hoarding. Fiscal reasons included excessive or new and special taxes and dishonest means and media of taxation, and they most often brought demands for tax reductions or cancellations. The interesting thing about the fiscal category is that in this area alone demands are recorded more commonly than reasons, largely, I believe, because fiscal demands were in many instances a response to economic causes. Finally, the administrative reasons for contention focused on unjust, unlawful, or unresponsive behavior by district, domain, or shogunal officials; resultant demands included cancellation of land surveys, dismissal of individual officials or abolition of administrative positions, and revocation of official actions of various kinds.

One must approach these figures with caution. Although substantial proportions of all cases entail one or more reasons or demands, the frequency of each specific type of reason and demand is relatively low and without doubt an underestimate. Social and communal reasons in particular were far more common than this table suggests. Whether or not these figures are comprehensive, however, is less important than whether or not this *sample* of reasons and demands is biased. I have no reason to think so, except that social contention is undersampled.

Another reason for caution is the complex causality of contention. The historical record indicates that few conflicts resulted from a single cause (Rekishi Kagaku 1974: 112–15; Yamada 1984: 267ff.). Moreover, since demands had an important legitimating function, there was a tendency for the people to throw everthing but the kitchen sink into their manifestoes. Such litanies of grievance often grew during the course of a contentious event, with almost an "Oh yes, while we're at it, we *also* think the intendant is a crook" tone about the process. Moreover, the scope of contention grew during the era, embracing larger numbers of villages, each of which brought distinctive demands into play (Aoki M. et al. 1981, 2:190ff.). Thus, with the two caveats that my data are a sample only, and a sample of major causes and demands at that, I want to explore their relationships to the other factors of interest here.

The first such factor is magnitude of contention and, as Table 27 shows, different reasons led to very different magnitudes. Social and communal reasons and demands commingled in mild and low-key conflict, with the exception— found in other early modern societies—that "collective" quarrels between communities had relatively high levels of aggressive behavior. Fiscally and administratively generated contention reached middling magnitudes, although one should note that in the administrative category 80 percent and 78 percent of all events—mostly political protest—evidenced no aggressive behavior at all, their magnitude being due rather to their larger size and longer duration. Economic contention, by contrast, was markedly higher in magnitude, although this magnitude was higher for reasons than for causes. Many economic causes led to fiscal or political demands, which were expressed much more deferentially than unmediated or socially targeted economic demands. Consequently, one sees the converse, that contention involving fiscal and political demands was more intense than that with fiscal and political reasons. Finally, the magnitude of contention varies directly with the number of both reasons and demands, although I have not included these figures in the table, because I am not sure whether they reflect reality or the more complete documentation available for larger-scale events.

Table 27 also reveals the composition of contentious events deriving from different reasons and generating different demands. With the exception of intercommunity, "collective" contention, social and communal reasons are overwhelmingly associated with social contention, and although the state became embroiled in a substantial number of cases, such overtures were rarely initiated as political protest. The same pattern is visible in conflicts eventuating in demands focused on intracommunity matters. At the other extreme is contention with fiscal and political reasons and demands. In only one-quarter to one-third of these cases did the people contend among themselves. Moreover, although it

Table 27. Magnitude and composition of contentious events by types of reasons and demands

	Average magnitude (10-point scale)	Proportion of events with aggressive actions*	Proportion of total contention accounted for by				
			Social conflict	Political conflict	Political protest		Total
Reasons							
Social	1.5	9%	90%	6	4	=	100%
Religious	2.7	19	71%	12	17	=	100%
Collective	2.9	21	56%	14	30	=	100%
Intracommunity	1.3	4	76%	17	7	=	100%
Tenancy related	1.3	8	84%	15	2	=	101%
Economic	5.2	48	42%	14	44	=	100%
Fiscal	3.4	25	28%	10	62	=	100%
Administrative/ political	3.1	20	25%	9	66	=	100%
Demands							
Intracommunity	1.3	3	83%	12	5	=	100%
Tenancy related	1.8	13	68%	15	17	=	100%
Economic	4.5	41	41%	18	41	=	100%
Fiscal	3.8	26	20%	14	66	=	100%
Administrative/ political	3.7	22	36%	12	52	=	100%

* The occurrence of aggressive action includes one or more of the following: threats of violence; aggressive actions vis-à-vis individuals; destruction of individual, community, or state property; or violence against individuals.

might seem strange that protest would not *always* accompany fiscal or administrative demands, in fact fiscal and administrative reasons and demands often began and ended on a level at which officialdom was composed of commoners, not samurai.

Only economic reasons and demands do not clearly point toward either social conflict or political protest, although collective social reasons are also anomalous within the social/communal category. Economic and collective reasons were also, as seen, associated with relatively intense contention. Therefore, I disaggregated both, looking at the magnitudes of those events with economic and collective reasons which took the form of either social conflict or political protest. What appeared in each instance was that social conflict stemming from such reasons was significantly larger in scale and more aggressive than political protest stemming from the same reasons. The average magnitude of collectively caused social conflicts was 3.1, and 25 percent of such events included aggressive actions. When economic reasons led to social conflict, their average magnitude was 7.7, and 73 percent of them eventuated in aggressive actions. When political protest stemmed from collective reasons, though, the average magnitude was only 2.8, and only 18 percent included aggressive actions, and when protests followed from economic reasons their average magnitude was 3.6, and 30 percent of them eventuated in aggressive actions. Finally, political conflicts resulting from these types of reasons were even more low-key than protest. When the people took disagreements of any kind to the government, they were much less aggressive than when they worked them out among themselves. And it appears that economically related and (within the social/communal category) collective contention was so intense because much of it was social conflict rather than political conflict or protest.

The last general aspect of reasons and demands I want to discuss is their evolution over time. I have already suggested that political reasons and demands were relatively frequent at the beginning and end of the era (Kokushō 1971: 22ff.) and that the number of demands, if not of reasons, increased over time (Aoki M. et al. 1981, 3:97–98). We can do little with the absolute numbers of reasons and demands recorded, since their numbers will surely reflect changes in the number of events; moreover, there is a chance that Aoki Kōji attempted some sort of even coverage, perhaps accounting for the rough constancy of the proportion of events for which some reason was recorded—at 30–35 percent—throughout the era. Events for which multiple reasons were recorded diminished slightly (from 10 percent to 6 percent of the total), but this reduction could be due to the increasing number of events Aoki had to include in later years.

In any case, the proportion of all recorded reasons and demands which is accounted for by each type seems to be a more valid focus here. First, social and communal reasons overall, social reasons, and intracommunity demands all describe a curve, peaking in the middle of the era along with social contention.[3] This pattern, however, masks linear increases in tenancy-related reasons and demands and (until the Restoration) intracommunity reasons, both of which reflect the economic and political differentiation of the village community. It also overlays an inverse curve in *inter*community reasons, which, like the curves for political reasons and demands, is higher at the beginning and end of the era than in the middle. The curvilinear quality of the political is fully expected; that of intercommunity reasons is due, as already noted, to the relatively large number of intercommunity-related contentious events which took a political form. Perhaps (with the exception of the highly politicized early Tokugawa and early Meiji years), the state was unlikely to be seen either as something to protest against or as someplace to seek redress.

Economic reasons and demands rise from early in the era to the later eighteenth century—the time of the Temmei famine—and remain at a high level thenceforth: they do not fade, but neither do these data suggest that economic hardship increased later in the era. Fiscal reasons decline from 1590 to 1700 and

---

[3] With the exception of the latter half of the eighteenth century, when the upsurge of economic reasons noted hereafter temporarily depressed the proportions accounted for by all others.

remain constant thereafter, and fiscal demands peak in 1650–1750 and decline gently thereafter, perhaps reflecting the resignation of the state in the face of popular resistance to taxation: no rise in impositions, no rise in grievances. Thus the overall pattern that emerges is one of relatively frequent political and fiscal (which are also, after all, political in origin) reasons and demands early in the era, giving way to economic and social/communal reasons and demands in the middle of the era. Thereafter, fiscal and economic factors maintain their salience, while social/communal factors decline and the political rises in the latter years under examination.

But this overview masks the variety of reasons. Tables 28–31 remedy this shortcoming, revealing both the variety and tendencies among the motivations. As we see in Table 28, when the common people contended among themselves on more or less equal and neither political nor economic terms, the major nexus of conflict was social status. Extensive sumptuary laws regulated the social hierarchy in Tokugawa Japan, and the progressing socioeconomic differentiation during the era led, as I have noted, to increasing challenges to everything from village authority in general to the restricted overhang of the eaves on the house of a family of lesser status. Other social reasons for contention were more consistent, including squabbles between associations of young men (*wakamonogumi*) and shrine parishioners (*miyaza*) and mutual aid societies (*kō*), and routine violations of village law. Inter- and intrafamilial contention was certainly not as rare as shown here. One must keep in mind that we are looking here not at family friction in general, but only at that which generated public contention on a significant scale.

Shrine groups frequently quarreled; but such quarrels were more often matters of social status than of faith. As Table 28 indicates, religious faith was a minor factor in popular contention in early modern Japan. Of far greater moment were popular objections to clerical profligacy and temple construction and the impositions they necessitated, and the abuse by temples and shrines of their taxation prerogatives. Next in frequency—and also more social than spiritual in tone—came contention between the various community groups involved in the wide variety of festivals and rituals which marked the village year. Who got to enter the sacred precincts first, whose float led the parade, who contributed what to the harvest festival—all such matters were imbued with status significance, and the relegation or exclusion of one group or another could easily spark conflict.

All of which is not to say that religion had no significance but the social. Both contention between religious sects and popular resistance to restrictions on the exercise of religous belief did generate contention. Inter-sectarian disputes, one must admit, were sometimes simply power struggles. Religious resistance, however, was in reaction to the severe early Tokugawa enforcement of anti-Christian edicts and to the Meiji state's later oppression of the same faith and, in between, to administrative transfers of community shrines and appearance in the community of the ritually unclean.

Table 28. Reasons for popular contention and demands made during contentious events

Social reasons	
Disputes between community organizations	17%
Status conflicts over clothing, building, etc.	62
Violations of village law	19
Disputes within or between families	5
Other	3
	106%
Religious reasons	
Temple/shrine administration corrupt, impositions too heavy; quarrels over clerical behavior and rights	40%
Conflicts over festivals: events, who participates, who stages, etc.	26
Conflicts within and between sects	19
Matters of faith: antireligious laws, incursions into sacred forests, entry of the unclean, temple transfer	17
Other	3
	105%
Intercommunity reasons	
Conflicts over disputed space and the resources in or on it: fodder, grass, timber, fishing and hunting rights, etc.	59%
Disputed village borders	27
Water rights and allocation	19
Disputes over flood-control and dredging obligations	6
Other	3
	114%
Intracommunity vertical reasons	
Village leaders dishonest, negligent, unfair	48%
Disputed village policies: tax, land, and corvée allocation; leadership selection and village accounting procedures, etc.	37
Disputes between village groups: small vs. large farmers, farmers vs. leaders, etc.	23
Use of and rights to common land	2
Other	4
	114%
Tenancy-related reasons	
Objection or refusal to pay rent	50%
Terms of tenancy and rights of tenant	15
Disputes over land title, eviction, foreclosure and return of pawned land	13
Landlord dishonesty	5
Other	21
	104%

continued

Table 28. *continuing*

Intracommunity demands	
Demand resignation of village leader	43%
Object to decision or action of leader	22
Object to selection of leader	6
Demand change in or reform of village policy or procedure: accounting and tax recording, repeal of village tax, intravillage administrative subdivisions	11
Demand participation in or exemption from village affairs or organizations	9
One village group demands restrictions on another	6
Other	3
	100%
Tenancy-related demands	
Demand rent reduction	100%

Note: Totals may exceed 100% because of multiple reasons and demands.

Still, on a more or less "horizontal" level we find contention between communities. Japan was in the early modern period already a densely settled society, with maximum exploitation of available resources. Consequently, the prerogatives to gather grass for hay, reeds for roofing, forest litter for fertilizer, and wood for building and fuel from fallow lands and woods; and to hunt and fish were incessant cause for contention. Such prerogatives were largely determined by the location of village borders, another extremely touchy subject. And in a society largely based on paddy rice, the allocation of water rights was certainly worth fighting over. Too much water was just as bad as too little and, in the same way that up- and downstream communities had to divvy up a river among themselves, the responsibilities for maintaining channels, dikes, and water gates were a collectively shared task and a constant temptation to cheat.

Admittedly, many of these factors included a large element of vertical contention within the elaborately graduated social hierarchy of early modern Japan. But even more unequivocally vertical are the reasons that involved politically differentiated groups within the community and landlords and their tenants (see Table 28). As I have noted, village office entailed myriad opportunities to skim, play favorites, and impose unauthorized burdens on the people. And although villagers constantly contended to improve their relative positions and diminish their obligations under the status quo, the most frequent recorded reason for intracommunity political conflict was the mis-, mal-, or nonfeasance of duty by officials. They allegedly cooked the village books, concealed personal gain, withheld state aid intended for the people, connived with merchants, and misused village funds; and sometimes they simply didn't do the job at all. And if they did their job, they could be attacked by those who objected to the status quo. Appointment, election, and succession of leaders were contentious processes, and the relationship of parts of the community to the whole was a matter for repeated renegotiation.

So were relationships between parts of the community. A host of social and political rights varied with landownership and economic position; the adjustment of these rights, as Thomas Smith (1959) has noted, did not keep pace with objective changes in the economic positions that rationalized them, and popular contention resulted. The most frequent single manifestation of such contention, at least later in the era, was that between landless and landed, and specifically between landlords and tenants. As we can see from Table 28, radical attacks on the institution of tenancy were rare; in the overwhelming majority of instances the reasons given for contention were simply that the rent was too high or due too soon. The system itself was problematic. What made foreclosure into tenancy or eviction of a tenant legitimate, what opportunities a tenant deserved to redeem his land, and how usufruct rights were to be divided—all fueled contention. Far more common, however, was more particularistic conflict over the honesty and demands of the landlord.

All these reasons are aggregated in Table 28 in the sections outlining demands, and here we can see how village leaders became the lightning rod for a wide variety of complaints. Almost three-quarters of the demands recorded by Aoki Kōji focused on village leaders; in a significant number of cases all that was demanded was a different decision, but more often the dismissal of the leaders themselves was sought. And sometimes the reorganization of the village, with new subunits and leaders acceptable to these subunits, was the goal of contention. Sometimes village groups wanted in, wanted fully participatory community rights; sometimes they wanted out, wanted to set up shrine or mutual aid or political organizations of their own. Sometimes they sought equality with other groups or even special privileges, and sometimes they wanted the traditional status or economic prerogatives of other groups cut down to size. But more often than not it was the headman who was the target of contention.

There is considerable interrelationship among the economic factors presented in Table 29. The demands flow directly from the reasons, and many of the types of reasons given here are in fact different aspects of single phenomena (e.g., natural disasters) or results of each other: high prices might follow from hoarding caused by a poor harvest. None of these reasons—with the possible exception of volcanic eruption—will be novel to those familiar with contentious behavior in other early modern societies, including *kaimai*, the shipping of rice out of producing areas to the cities and central markets (Wong 1982; Tilly 1986; Bercé 1980). One distinctive reason, included in merchant behavior, was the sale of rice to sake producers at times when the people wanted it as grain; in Matsumoto domain in 1825 such sales prompted a riot that grew to over two thousand participants who overwhelmed a force of some three hundred hired heavies and smashed eighty-seven shops and residences before being suppressed by domain warriors (Yashiro 1989: 14ff.).

Table 29. Economic reasons for popular contention and demands made during contentious events

Reasons	
Poor harvest	38%
Increased consumer prices	36
Poverty and famine, food shortages, inability to pay taxes, insufficient relief, bankruptcy	21
Natural disaster: volcano, frost, drought, rain, typhoon or wind, insects, fire, hail, etc.	12
Merchants' behavior: hoarding, price gouging, interest rate hikes, rice exports from community (*kaimai*), etc.	10
Other	4
	121%
Demands	
Food or money aid from government	26%
Food or money loan from government	13
Food or money aid from merchants	4
Food or money loan from merchants	2
Price reductions	10
Regulation of sales, prices, commerce: government sale of food, ban hoarding, etc.	17
Ban on rice exports from community	8
Free, unmonopolized commerce	1
Debt, rent reductions, return of pawned land and property	17
Higher wages and producer prices	9
Other	2
	109%

As reasons concatenated, so did demands. In the Kamo Uprising of 1836 the people demanded reductions in interest rates and the price of rice, sake, and other consumer goods; a ban on hoarding and kaimai; and elimination of commercial monopolies (Hyakushō Ikki 1980: 186–187). What is interesting about these demands is their moderation. Requests for outright grants of food, money, or seed and for forgiveness of debt (the return of pawned land) were common, but so were those simply for loans and for reductions in prices and rents: the people may have been asking for half a loaf because they figured that that was all they could hope for, but it is also likely that they accepted the system and were requesting only a relaxation, not an elimination, of their obligations under it.

The other interesting thing about the imbrication of economics and contention is its seasonality. Many have pointed out that contention tended to peak at the end of the year when the crops were harvested and taxes paid, and during the summer when food was short in the cities (Kokushō 1971: 29; Fukaya 1983: 90); my data confirm this observation. The frequency of contentious events averaged 479 per month in October and November, the season of harvest and taxpaying.

It then moderated to 423 per month during the winter and bottomed out at 331 during the spring planting season, before rising to 365 per month as food became short during the summer and early fall. The average magnitude of events, by contrast, peaked when contention was least frequent: on my 10–point scale the average event scored only 3.3 from August to December and 2.8 in January–March, and peaked at 3.9 in the summer. And it was aggressive or violent behavior that drove magnitude: a third of the events involved aggression during the summer, as opposed to only 21–27 percent during the rest of the year.

These figures are explained nicely by other data in my set. Social conflict, typically larger in scale and more aggressive, is relatively frequent in March, April, June, and July, whereas the more deferential political protest (against, e.g., taxes) is most frequent between September and December, when the frequency of contention reached its peak. Month-by-month examination of reasons, demands, and repertoires rounds out the picture: tenancy-related reasons and demands peaked during September–November, as did economic reasons and fiscal demands, and administrative reasons also peaked in August and October. Finally, riots and urban disturbances of all kinds were at their peak during the summer, whereas coercive (and political) appeals were most frequent in October and November, with a secondary concentration in September and December; full-blown uprisings were most common in September, and tenant disputes tended to occur in August through November. Thus the cycle of the agricultural year, especially its implications for the food supply and for government revenues, is clearly reflected in the pattern of popular contention.

The fiscal concomitants of contention (see also Kokushō 1971: 13ff.) reveal this reflection quite clearly also, as seen in Table 30. Assessments (often made late in the summer) prefigured the tax burden; from then on, one could expect contention. There were other governmental fiscal practices that threatened the viability of the farm economy. Monetary policy was a basic revenue-enhancement tool: domains issued paper currency or debased coin and forced the people to accept it in exchange for more valuable media. The exchange rate of rice for money was also commonly manipulated either by the state itself or by merchants acting as its agents. Moreover, both shogunal and domain governments attempted to capture the fruits of protoindustry by chartering merchants who paid handsomely for the privilege of monopolizing certain commodities, or by decreeing that certain commodities had to be sold to state monopsonies (Aoki K. 1966: 119).

As before, the multiplicity of reasons reflects reality. The protest in Mito domain in 1708, already discussed, resulted from a series of fiscal reforms initiated from 1704 on: increased taxes, new taxes, land reclamation that required investment capital and corvée laborers, control of commerce in some agricultural goods, and issue of domain notes culminated in the grandiose canal construction project for which massive numbers of laborers were dragooned and fields were expropriated (Nagasu 1986). Some events were sparked by specific measures: an 1814 ban on farmers' travel out of Kai province (for the purpose of selling their

Table 30. Fiscal reasons for popular contention and demands made during contentious events

Reasons	
Taxes or assessment too heavy or raised	52%
Tax burden or allocation unjust	12
New tax policy, procedure, structure	6
New tax imposed	14
Monetary policy: cash-rice exchange rate, currency debasement, new currency imposed or old currency invalidated	9
Government regulation of commerce: guilds, monopolies or monopsonies, controls established	7
Other	6
	106%
Demands	
Tax reduction, rebate	50%
Corvée reduced, eliminated	5
Delay in tax payment	5
Established tax repealed	10
New tax or tax increase rescinded	17
New method/medium of tax payment	10
Government repay tax overpayment or loan	3
Free trade, regulation or elimination of guilds or monopolies	8
Abolition of new or reintroduction of old currency	3
Other	1
	115%

paper mulberry), the 1764 expansion of the corvée on the Nakasendō Road, and the exactions prompted by the shogunate's military expedition against rebellious Chōshū domain in the 1860s all stimulated popular contention (Takekawa n.d.: 40–41; Yamada 1984: 154–55; Fukaya 1979: 260ff.). We must look further to see the extent to which these measures were complete causes or simply catalytic forces.

We can see once more the essential moderation of the people in their demands. In the case of new or increased taxes, in the case of official monopolies, and in a few instances of established taxes they did call for repeal; far more commonly, however, they called only for a reduction, a partial rebate, a procedural change, or a delay in fulfilling their normal obligations. As we saw in the story of Hachiemon, the elimination of a tax discount was acceptable, and so was a tax increase—but not all at once, and not during a poor crop year (Fukaya 1978: 87).

Again, about 90 percent of the recorded demands involved taxes. Free trade and economic stability were also matters of intense interest among some, but it was most often direct state exactions from the people which formed the center of contention over fiscal policy and practice.

Table 31. Political and administrative reasons for popular contention and demands made during contentious events

Reasons	
Administrative malfeasance: dishonest land surveys, tax assessments or recording, official corruption, common lands dishonestly delimited	43%
Administration, law enforcement, extractions arbitrary, oppressive, unfair	29
Administrators inept, incompetent, quarrelsome, unfairly chosen, unresponsive to people	16
Domain-level policy: transfer, imposition of lord, division of domain, village boundaries or structural position changed, too many officials	12
Other	8
	108%
Demands	
Oppose local official or his action(s)	18%
Demand transfer, dismissal, punishment of local official	16
Demand transfer, dismissal, punishment of extralocal official	6
Oppose transfer of official	6
Demand abolition of office	8
Oppose new land survey	13
Oppose jurisdictional transfer of village	5
Demand jurisdictional transfer of village	12
Want tax burdens readjusted	4
Demand village adminstrative reform: officials elected, accounts opened, etc.	6
Servile cultivators (*nago*) want farmer status	3
Other	11
	108%

When one turns to the closely related topic of politicoadministrative reasons behind and demands made during contentious activities, no such concentration is apparent. As Table 31 shows, there was a primary focus—local officials—but they were involved in no more than about half of all reasons recorded, and a smaller proportion of all recorded demands. The opportunities for graft and favoritism open to village officials are reflected here: embezzlement, tax manipulation, padding of expenses (paid for by village levies), and nepotism always threatened (Vlastos 1986). As the era wore on and the village leadership stratum became largely coterminous with the landlord-moneylender-merchant stratum, the line between administration and private benefit became increasingly blurred (albeit not to the people). In one episode in Kōzuke province, for example, some village leaders actually sold the villagers' mountain rights to wood and forage to merchant interests (Yashiro 1989: 85).

Even if corruption was not charged, the absence of restraints on arbitrary administrative practice is also apparent here. Of course, what constituted oppression is hard to say. In many cases there was truly rapacious taxation and draconian law enforcement. Nevertheless, one suspects that in many instances "oppression" described the thwarting of popular desires to accomplish some political or economic goal.

To a lesser extent, leaders who ignored popular needs or who fought among themselves were a source of grievance, as were domain or shogunal policies under which villages had their territories or administrative overlords changed or had new officials imposed upon them—usually at their own expense. The transfer of lords was always a delicate time: it created an authority vacuum, a tide of anxiety about the extractive inclinations of the new lord, and fears that the domain would have its agricultural productivity reassessed and its tax obligations increased (Kokushō 1971: 8–20). Thus the tendency, seen in Table 31, to oppose officials' transfers and administrative reorganizations does not necessarily bespeak a fondness for the status quo; sometimes it did involve a respected, if not revered, lordly family's departure, but as often as not it probably reflected a simple preference for the devil people knew.

It also reflects the tendency of popular contention to be personalized, to focus on specific evildoers or protectors. But one must not overemphasize this tendency. Demands revolving about burdensome official positions, land survey plans, changes in tax policy and village jurisdictional position, local political reform, and (early in the era) collective social mobility also occurred with significant frequency. Accusing individuals was safer. One could attack a village headman and simultaneously protest one's undying loyalty to the system. But the tendency to personalize contention and the frequent assertions of obedience (contingent, of course, on benevolent rule) did not, as one can see here, hide a willingness to take up cudgels against, at least by implication, the state itself.

This willingness was enhanced by the instability and indecisiveness of government in the first years after the Meiji Restoration. As we have already seen, popular contention during these years was relatively political. It was also intense: the average magnitude of post-Restoration events was 4.4 (versus 2.8 for all events occurring during 1590–1877), and aggressive behavior occurred in 38 percent (versus 22 percent) of the incidents. When the policies of the new regime were the reason for contention, average magnitude was 4.7 and 42 percent of the events were aggressive; when they were the object of demands, magnitude rose to 5.7 and aggressive behavior characterized fully 53 percent of them. Thus, as the frequency of popular contention dropped off after the Restoration, its intensity rose.

But perhaps the single most frequently posed question regarding the early Meiji era concerns continuity. Was popular contention in those years simply more of the same, or did it demonstrate significant new tendencies and characteristics? I have maintained thus far that it was mostly more of the same. Repertorially, the Restoration does not constitute a sharp breaking point. Nor was there any abrupt change in reasons and demands. In regard to reasons, there were slight upturns in intercommunity and tenancy-related contention and a slight downturn in intracommunity "vertical" contention, but otherwise, pre-Restoration trends carried through. In regard to demands, only an upturn in fiscal demands distinguishes the period.

More specifically, among post-Restoration contentious events, reasons specifying policies of the new regime were recorded in only twenty-nine cases. Additionally, over 60 percent of these reasons involved taxes. Granted, the two taxes most often cited were the new land tax imposed after the Meiji land reform, and the *mimpi*, a new local tax. The mimpi, however, was often allocated by techniques used under the Tokugawa and one suspects that in the eyes of the people, a tax was a tax was a tax. By contrast,

- tenancy-related reasons were recorded for 25 cases;
- religious reasons for 6;
- intercommunity reasons (primarily about water and forest rights) for 29;
- fiscal reasons (mainly regarding excessive taxes and currency reform) for 35;
- administrative reasons (mostly official dishonesty or unresponsivness) for 41;
- intracommunity reasons (involving headmen's dishonest or unjust dealings, intergroup conflict, or leadership selection processes) for 88; and
- economic reasons (as before, poor harvests and high prices) for 98.

When one turns to demands, a focus on Meiji government policies is more visible. Such demands were made in 78 cases; by contrast, there were

- demands for rent reductions in 14 cases;
- intracommunity demands (mainly calls for leaders to resign or for different selection procedures) in 26 cases;
- administrative demands (mostly for the dismissal of officials, abolition of offices, or opening of administrative records) in 50;
- economic demands (for price reductions and government relief) in 66; and
- fiscal demands (for reduction or cancellation of tax payments or rescission of new taxes) in 107.

Disaggregation of demands focused on the new regime's policies also reveals novelty. For one-third of the relevant events the demands recorded involved opposition to the new conscription system, and one demand in five involved opposition to the land reform. Another one in five involved religion: opposition to the new government's anti-Christian policies or to shrine consolidation or the cutting of sacred forests or calls for protection of Buddhism in general or for the observation of Buddhist strictures against slaughter of cattle for food. Also in this category came contention against the liberation of the outcasts, whose status was due to their ritual impurity. Nevertheless, here, as before, what one sees is a concomitance of traditional causes—the massive antioutcast riots of 1873 in Fukuoka occurred also in a bad crop year (Uesugi and Ishitaki 1988)—and less of a communal bloodletting among the people over their religious differences than the desire of the Meiji state—like the Tokugawa—to impose religious orthodoxy on society.

Additional demands included opposition to both the land tax and the mimpi and to government expropriation of land for factories, schools, military bases, and other uses. It was not simply the weight of taxes which people objected to: tax payments went from kind to cash; assessments went from variable and crop based to fixed and land value based; and the free sale of land commodified what had previously possessed a major significance for family identity, status, and continuity (Irokawa 1966: 38). The purposes for which land was expropriated were also cause for contention. The new education system of 1873 was suspect for its Western curriculum, for its compulsoriness, and for its penetration into community and family. Finally, in a small number of cases the people contended to keep their lord. The reasons here were mixed: not only was he the devil they knew but what the future had in store now was not just a new lord but a whole new system. And in this mixture, along with the continuity of repertoire, we can see the essence of contention in the Meiji era: new motivational wine in old behavioral bottles.

Creators of Contention

In the gap between context; individual calculations of interest, opportunity, and resources; and catalytic stimuli, on the one hand, and contentious behavior, on the other, stand leaders. In some cases they were only barely necessary. Where prior gatherings brought together numbers of people sufficient to provide a sense of safety and potency, and where the action taken required little organization or direction—for example, in a riot—one can ignore leadership and still approximate an explanation of contention (Bercé 1990: 41ff.). But in most instances leaders were necessary to focus the activist potential of the people, to define the relevant popular collectivity, to articulate the interests and intentions of this collectivity, and to represent publicly the justice of the people's cause (Yasumaru 1975: 198ff.). That is, even if they were unnecessary for the inception of contention, they were certainly essential to effective contention.

Still, a sort of "generic" approach to leadership may still suffice. James Coleman (1990: 198ff.) implies a highly individualistic aproach to leadership, arguing that the inception of collective behavior lies in individuals' decisions to transfer control over their own actions to someone else. I would say that in early modern Japan the community, in the persons of its leaders, was already in institutional control of a variety of individual behaviors and that the transition from individual calculation to collective contention lay in the decision of those in control to act. Alternatively, Robin Hood types like Bansuke were sought out by people who had already decided to obey him; in this case the transition to action lay not in the participants' decisions but in the discovery of a willing leader. In other words, we may simplify by hypothesizing that popular contention in early modern Japan occurred through the primary agency of one of two factors—

institutional context and rational choice—and evaluate the relative importance of the two by examining the leadership of contentious events.

In the leadership of popular contention the lower but secure orders such as shopkeepers and artisans, the gainfully employed, family men in their thirties and forties, rustic or plebeian "intellectuals" with some education, community leaders and marginal elites, and doctors and priests surface repeatedly.[4] In almost three-quarters of the recorded cases (73 percent) leaders came from the ranks of village or town leaders, and in another 8 percent of the cases supracommunity officials or elites were the leaders.[5] Other types of leaders are little in evidence across the era as a whole. Lesser but propertied elements in village and town took the lead in 10 percent of the cases; members of specific occupational groups came to the fore 6 percent of the time; and the poorest elements of rural and urban society appear to have provided leadership only 4 percent of the time.[6] The poor included tenant and landless farmers, servants, and historically servile groups; occupational groups producing contentious leaders included firemen, freight shippers, coolies, fishermen, salt workers, artisans, merchants, doctors, day laborers, and priests—and also gamblers and *ninkyō*, which is less an occupational category than a social element comprising crooks, self-styled Robin Hoods, and others on the shady edge of the law.

Thus during the era as a whole, institutional leadership predominated, although plebeian—and more often anonymous—leadership is almost surely underdocumented. But leadership was not static: it moved down the social ladder during the era (Aoki M. et al. 1981 3:67; Vlastos 1986; Scheiner 1973: 585), as Table 32 demonstrates. Between the seventeenth and nineteenth centuries supracommunity and elite leaders fell from 15 percent of the leadership to 3 percent, and the community leadership presence, while retaining its salience through the eighteenth century, eventually declined by 32 percent. The poor came out of nowhere to become leaders in 9 percent of the documented incidents, and occupational groups produced leaders in 10 percent of the nineteenth-century cases and the lesser orders went from 2 percent to fully 24 percent of the leaders. Together these three groups' representation increased tenfold—from 4 percent to 43 percent—and, as before, we may rest assured that the lower social

---

[4] Gurr 1980: 100–101; Mousnier 1970: 320ff.; Scott 1976: chap. 5; Bercé 1980: chap. 3, 1990: 80; Tilly et al. 1975. For Japan, see inter alia, Beasley 1972: 341–42; Hyakushō Ikki 1980: 94–95; Morris 1975: 153; Fukawa 1976: 345ff.; Fukaya 1983: 128–29; Aoki M. et al. 1981 3:67, 1:128–31. My own data leave much to be desired: in only 316 cases do Aoki's data include information on socioeconomic or administrative characteristics of the leaders of contentious events. Thus strong patterns must be found in the data before we put any faith in them.

[5] Terms for such community leaders include *kimoiri, shōya, nanushi, kumigashira, osabyakushō, toshiyori* and *sō-toshiyori, mura* or *machi yakunin,* and *hyakushōdai.* Supracommunity leaders include local samurai, *dogō,* and *gōshi; ōjōya;* and domain or bakufu officials.

[6] Terms for such lesser elements include generic *hyakushō, honbyakushō,* and *chōmin,* plus richer (*gōnō*) and smaller holders (*kobyakushō, komae, shomin, hirabyakushō, wakibyakushō,* etc.). The poor are referred to variously as *genin, hikan, hinnō, saimin, nago, kosaku, mizunomi, mutaka, gesaku,* etc.

Table 32. Evolution of leadership

	17th-century contention	18th-century contention	19th-century contention
Elite or supracommunity leaders	15%	9%	3%
Community leaders	81	82	55
Lesser social elements	2	3	24
Occupational groups	2	4	10
Poor and servile orders	0	3	9
	100%	101%	101%

elements were even more active than these data suggest, since they were far less likely to be fingered by either the state or historians. The peers of Hachiemon and Hyōsuke were superseded by the likes of Bansuke and Miura Meisuke, leader of the Sanhei incident in Nambu domain in 1853. Son of a headman, Miura was big and strong and well-traveled as a miner and transport worker; he had some education and urban experience and had by dint of his own efforts achieved a modest status as a creditor and employer by 1853. He had become a village leader, seemingly less because of his family background than because of his own actions. He had enjoyed a physical, occupational, and psychic freedom that was not rare, if not typical, in the culture of late Edo society (Fukaya 1979: 233ff., 1983: ii–v, 40ff.). He was more reputable than Bansuke, but no less the product of a society in economic and social flux, and the receptiveness of the people to both of them was also perhaps a product of the times.

A clear relationship can be proposed, even from these fragmentary data, between the changes of the era and the pluralization and proletarianization of leadership. It also takes little imagination to picture the relationship between leadership and the forms and magnitudes of contention. We find those higher in the social and political hierarchy leading more political, more organized, and more deferential forms of contention. More plebeian types come to the fore in social conflict and in more amorphous and aggressive contentious events.

And this pattern is what we see in Table 33. Supracommunity and elite elements and community leaders were far more likely to lead protest; poor and occupationally based leaders are found almost exclusively in the forefront of social conflict; and urban and rural smallholders—presumably with the resources and sophistication necessary to utilize political channels if need be—were likely to lead both social and political conflicts, backing off only from the dangerous forms of open protest which, I contend, required institutional pressure to induce leadership.

The behavioral repertoire corroborates these data. Supracommunity elements may have been most likely to lead coercive appeals; community leaders, however, were clearly in the lead in flight and end-run appeals, both of which were highly deferential and highly organized, and also in intracommunity disputes, many of

Table 33. Leadership and form and magnitude of contention

	Type of contention		
	Social conflict	Political conflict	Political protest
Supracommunity officials and elites	2%	10%	9%
Community officials	53	68	79
Property owners	19	17	6
Poor and marginal groups	9	2	3
Occupational groups	18	2	3
	101%	99%	100%

	Contentious repertoire			
	Flight end-run appeals	Coercive appeals	Riots	Community disputes
Supracommunity officials and elites	9%	11%	5%	5%
Community officials	85	73	46	80
Property owners	4	6	20	10
Poor and marginal groups	0	6	7	5
Occupational groups	2	4	22	0
	100%	100%	100%	100%

	Number of types of aggressive or violent behavior in event			
	None	One	Two or more	Total
Supracommunity officials and elites	88%	8	4	= 100%
Community officials	79%	11	10	= 100%
Property owners	63%	13	23	= 99%
Poor and marginal groups	69%	15	15	= 99%
Occupational groups	39%	6	56	= 101%

Note: For all tables, n = 316 and p < 0.0000.

which pitted one village's leadership against another's or one community faction against another. They were far less likely to play a role in rioting. The other groups—especially occupational ones—were far more likely to provide riot leadership, to the complete exclusion of organized protest and flight (in the case of the poor) and community disputes (in the case of occupational groups). What political actions the poor did lead were coercive appeals; the middling strata appear to have led such appeals occasionally, and also end runs and abscondences, but they too were much more likely to surface in riots and community disputes.

As one goes down the status hierarchy the magnitude and aggressiveness of contention increased. Supracommunity elements led the most deferential events, which scored an average of 3.6 on my 10-point scale of magnitude, and in 88 percent of them no aggressive behavior was recorded. Events led by community leaders averaged 3.4 in magnitude, and 79 percent were aggression free. The poorest groups produced leaders in events that may have been slightly smaller-scale (4.8 average magnitude) and moderate (69 percent nonaggressive) than those led by property owners (5.0 and 63 percent). Perhaps those at the base of society were more easily intimidated than their commoner betters, but both were outshone by events led by representatives of occupational groups, which averaged a dramatic 7.6 in magnitude and involved aggressive behavior over 60 percent of the time. This pattern parallels others' findings that artisans, journeymen, boatmen and dockworkers, and other occupational groups were singularly salient in contention in other early modern societies. My suspicion is that occupational representatives enjoyed the organizational resources of smallholders and the built-in constituency of community officials but had less of a stake in the economic, social, *or* political status quo than either; plus, they were exclusively consumers. And bear in mind that this category includes those whose "occupation" was Robin Hood.

Thus there were, I suggest, two mechanisms by which the leadership of contentious behavior emerged in early modern Japan. The first was institutional, to which community or other collectivities were key, and the constraints of community office created certain circumstances in which it was rational for officials such as Hachiemon and Hyōsuke to take the lead, even in protest (White 1988b). Office offered many opportunities for self-enrichment, favoritism, and prestige, but its imperatives and popular expectations of it were crystal clear: when the community was imperiled its officials were to take the lead. Ideally, of course, everyone would participate, thus enhancing the chances of success and reducing those of punishment. But even if they didn't, the leader was pressured to act.

Such priorities fly in the face of usual constructions of the preferences of rational people, but in fact, they are found in other times and places as well (Magagna 1991: 113ff.; Rudé 1964: 247). What they do, as long as communities remain cohesive, is in effect to shift our focus on inception from individual calculation to catalytic events, since we can predict calculation in the presence of catalysis. Indeed, institutional rules and norms could override the better judgment of officials, most of whom really felt that contention was wrong (Yasumaru 1975: 154ff.).

The problem for this rather simple model of leadership is that community cohesion declined during the early modern period, but contention did not. Therefore, we must look more closely at those who took up the slack as community institutional leaders became less willing and able to mobilize their people. These leaders were primarily of two types: first, the representatives of occupational and other social groups, who formed a subset of both the "lesser social elements" and "occupational groups" included in Table 32, and second, the Robin Hoods. The first group lay somewhere between the community officials and the Robin Hoods: they were in some sense beholden, either objectively or subjectively, to some reference group, and they probably had a personal economic or other stake in the contemplated contention, but they also must have had a higher risk-taking propensity than those who could rely on formal office for influence with the authorities. There was probably a continuum of them running from members of old and respected families to individuals who faced disaster along with their neighbors but had an extra soupçon of something which enabled them to take the lead. Their rationality was probably not norm driven or rule driven but instrumental. If they won, they or their families would at least survive; if they did not act, they faced ruin.

Beyond the *soupçonniers* lay a leadership type that was equally rational in a quite different way. Variously described as strong (or headstrong), chivalrous and brave, irrepressible, presumptuous and forward, sly and crafty, stubborn, and persuasive or silver-tongued,[7] such individuals emerged sometimes from the farming class but more often from outside the established orders (Yasumaru 1975: 175), from the status turbulence characteristic of the times. Bansuke, Meisuke, Tatsuzō (leader of the massive Kamo Uprising of 1836), and others were less the representatives of any occupational group than the marginally respectable or wholly disreputable in a wide variety of occupations new to Tokugawa society.[8] Brokers and entrepreneurs of conflict, they were equally willing and able to mediate or instigate a quarrel.

This social marginality is the key to their attitude toward leadership. They expected little material benefit and seem to have responded more to a self-image than to normative constraints or instrumental goals. Like community leaders, they hoped to lead a unified collectivity and thus defy authority, enjoy the exhilaration of the moment, and face good odds of material success (and popular esteem, however fleeting) and a low probability of apprehension. Also like the officials, they were apt to act alone, attracted to this path by enjoyment of defiance and anticipation of social esteem. Inaction, regardless of whether others mobilized or not, was less attractive to them, despite the probability of punishment, for if they did not act, they would miss out on a thrill, a challenge, and a chance to take a whack at the establishment and win a bit of respect into the bargain. In other words, the leadership types we see are equally rational, but in quite different ways. The community officials were rationally following the collectively determined dictates of their role; leaders from the lesser but propertied strata pursued instrumental relief; and the Robin Hoods followed what Max Weber has called "value rationality," acting primarily on strongly held personal attitudes.

As noted, such individuals were the product of socioeconomic change, and it is not impossible that the greater frequency of contention in the later years of the Tokugawa era was to some extent due to the presence of more potential

[7] Words used to describe them include *otokodate, shitatakamono, kozakashikimono, kyōseisha, kuchikikumono,* and *kyōki.*
[8] Yasumaru 1973: 111; Fukawa 1976: 200ff.; Fukaya 1978: 185ff., 335; Hasegawa 1977: 147ff. Such persons were not unique to Japan: see Weller and Guggenheim 1982: 101; Wolf 1969: 33; Naquin 1976: 78, 87–88, 111; Chesneaux 1972: 33; Cohn 1961: chaps. 3, 10; Chaliand 1978.

entrepreneurial leaders (after Fukaya 1978: 330ff.). Absolute material deprivation may have diminished, as did community solidarity, but contention grew, perhaps because the lower orders had gained access to leadership from their own ranks (Fukaya 1978: 329ff.). Many of the Robin Hood leaders had well-established prior reputations as troublemakers *and* arbiters (Aoki M. et al. 1981 4:216ff.). Of course, for establishment leaders the two were the same, as one official is said to have commented of the selection of Bansuke for leadership, "There's never been an ikki leader who hasn't been executed. It's too bad, but Bansuke will be, too. So at least he won't be around to bother the local village officials" (Yasumaru 1975: 206). By and large, the people seem to have recognized leadership talent. Hachiemon, for instance, had his ups and downs, but the villagers kept coming back to him, and Kanno Hachirō, leader of a protest in northern Aizu in 1866, had already spent five years in exile for an earlier petition (Vlastos 1986; Shōji et al. 1981: 428, 449ff.). In any case, when social tension rose in the later years of the era, Robin Hood leaders emerged from the wings, not from nowhere (Fukaya 1983: 75).

The Process of Precipitation

The data thus present a mildly discomfiting picture. The inception of contention appears almost mechanical. Within a given context, grievances, opportunities, and resources make it rational for people to contend; given a catalyst and leadership (sometimes the same thing), contention ensues. And leadership seems almost ubiquitous, although it cannot have been. Or can it? Intuitively, it seems likely that there were cases of people "objectively" close to contention, or even eager to protest, who did not because no one would take the first step. Such cases were probably far more common than action. On the other hand, perhaps people did not act because they had not been pushed over the edge; that is, perhaps precipitating events are the key. Both precipitation and leadership may simply have been unpredictable, and I must then admit the weakness of my theories in the face of Fortuna.

One of the reasons that precipitation is hard to pinpoint is that manifest action was often the result of lengthy planning: a catalytic event might precede mobilization by weeks, months, or even years (Aoki M. et al. 1981 3:66). Plotters traveled about collecting funds, spreading tales of other actions, inviting or pressuring participation, organizing participants, circulating petitions, and setting dates and places of and signals for mobilization (Shōji et al. 1981: 394–95; Yokoyama 1977: 198ff.; Kokushō 1971: 26). Mobilization itself was often an extended series of events, moreover. After a policy change or a climatic aberration that threatened popular livelihood the first response was usually a legal petition or plea; if refused, it was followed first by desultory grumbling and then by increasingly structured discussions of options and nighttime meetings (Walthall 1986: 20ff.). The atmosphere became manifestly charged—over and over, the runup to a contentious event included references by local officials to an insurrectionary mood—and simultaneously, explicit discussion of action became more secretive as it approached the ever-vague limits of legality.

But these limits could be skirted. One facilitating factor was the large number of occasions on which the people came together in the daily order of things. Village assemblies, markets, and festivals were frequent and provided opportunities to recruit, connive, agitate, and even initiate contention (see also Bercé 1990: 20ff.). In 1719–1721 sequential poor harvests plagued Mito domain, and the people won no tax relief with their petitions. On the tenth through the twelfth of the tenth month of 1721 an annual temple ceremony was scheduled, with relief to be provided for the poor on the twelfth. By prior plan, the relief recipients turned the event into a riot in which several people were killed or injured; one of the leaders of the event was also executed (Yashiro 1989: 114ff.).

But even when there was no purposive use of such events, one cannot avoid a certain mechanistic impression, visible in contention in other times and places as well: given a tense situation, any large gathering seems to have been likely to explode.[9] Crowds reduced the probability of arrest to near zero (Yamada 1984: 255–56). In such a situation any probability of success at all could, with the addition of a rumor, a leader, or a provocation have set the people off (Bercé 1980: 127).

Contentious events once under way had three characteristics. First, they tended to snowball. Regardless of the extent of planning, it was rare for large events to mobilize all at once (Rekishi Kagaku 1974: 41). Once in motion, the community-based components of a movement usually maintained their independence, even on occasion carrying their own flags. Such aggregation was difficult, given the multiplicity of interests involved. The Mito protest of 1708 was able to maintain not only two large coalitions of villages, but an all-domain movement that managed to produce a single (albeit quite extensive) petition of grievances and demands (Nagasu 1986: 45ff.). Most events, however, were far more modest. As noted, some three-quarters of Aoki's events involved only a single village, and fewer than one in ten involved as many as ten; only some 5 percent overflowed the borders of a single county.

This snowball pattern also occurred in reverse. As contentious events wound down they tended to do so gradually, as one constituent community after another quit and went home. This was the case even when major government concessions were won (because no single concession need have met everyone's demands) or when contention was suppressed (because in such cases the troops had to chase down and disperse the constituent groups one at a time).

Second, contention tended over time to become increasingly multitactical. The stereotypical event—infrequent in the overall constellation of contention but looming large in the historical record and especially in the cities—combined a riot by the lower orders with simultaneous petitions (Toyoda 1962: 269ff.). At times these tactics worked at cross-purposes; at others, they were two

[9] Lewis 1990; Bercé 1990; Uesugi and Ishitaki 1988: 102; Kitazawa 1982: 62–63.

coordinated prongs of a single movement. More often than not, however, it seems that such tactical complexity resulted from social differentiation and *disor*ganization rather than from organizational sophistication.

Third, contention was interactive. The people acted autonomously, but their actions were after the very first move largely determined by the response of their antagonists, whether officials, neighbors, or rich merchants. Quick relief and concession could completely preempt contention; inflexible rejection seems almost inevitably to have provoked more popular action. It would be nice to have better records of initially rejected petitions that went no farther. But where contention *did* occur it was almost always an iteration in an extended interaction between contenders.[10] The problem for the rulers was eternal: Will concessions conciliate the people or simply encourage them in their insubordination? To the extent that interests govern contention one would expect people to be appeased; if opportunities are key, then concessions should exacerbate rebellion. The historical record contains many examples of both, although the later in the process they occur, the less dampening effect concessions seem to have.

For example, in the town of Ōmi Hachiman the popularly elected elders were in late 1786 at odds with the town administration and the intendant over alleged corruption. The elders demanded to see the town books; initial refusals were followed by extended negotiations and the reluctant divulging of information. Eventually the elders had all the material they demanded, but still could not figure out the use to which a considerable sum of municipal money had been put. By this time word of the negotiations had spread; tension was rising, as was pressure on the intendant to do something.

On the sixteenth day of the tenth month the intendant did something he must have thought rather radical. He extracted the disputed sum from the relatives of the two officials under attack, put both of them (plus five other town officials and two merchant financiers) in domiciliary confinement, and turned municipal government over to the elders. On the twenty-fifth, however, the intendant got his reply: a demand for the reduction and partial restitution of taxes and adoption of a new basis for rice-cash exchange. He entered into negotiations with the new town government, and in the first month of 1787 a domain elder arrived to join the talks. He offered to have the old officials formally resign, institute the election of town officials, and reduce taxes, but the town elders countered with a request for the forgiveness of unpaid taxes and the right to petition Edo directly without going through the intendant.

At this the domain erupted. The town elders were summoned and excoriated and five neighborhood representatives were arrested. But the people had the bit in their teeth. They attacked the homes of the merchants, whereupon those who had been arrested were released and the elders spent the next few days cooling things down. At the end of the month two new town officials were elected, the intendant ratified the choices, and the episode came to an end (Harada 1982:

[10] Mousnier 1970: 1ff.; McKean 1981: chap. 3; Harada 1982; Waddington et al. 1989: 9.

chap. 9). The authorities had tried obduracy, minimal response, conciliation, and intimidation; the people and their chosen leaders had persistently pushed their interests, escalated their demands in response to flexibility, responded in kind to coercion, and eventually settled for what looks like more than half a loaf. Interests drove them, but opportunities appear to have determined specific tactics and dictated an opportune time to resolve the situation.

Thus, I can attempt to describe and explain the contentious process. I cannot capture specific cases with my theory, since the steps in the minuet of rulers and ruled were reciprocally contingent. Still, certain types of situations broadened the opportunities for contention, and the people showed themselves capable of taking advantage of them. In the Mito protest of 1708 the people took full advantage of the death, during their activities, of the shogun. Mito, being a branch house of the Tokugawa family, was already in a swivet over the death, and with the feudal lords converging on Edo, the time was perfect for a public appeal that would cause the Mito house maximum embarrassment (Nagasu 1986: 70).

The people of Mito were successful. Yet the simple fact of sudden opportunity did not guarantee success. In Tsuyama domain in 1726 the death of the heirless lord prompted rumors and fears among both rulers and ruled, and the people, rose to demand cancellation of debts and miscellaneous taxes, a significant cut in the basic rice tax, and the dismissal of certain local officials (Hayashi 1976a: 78; Sasaki 1974: 136ff.; Bix 1986: chap. 3). Despite official concessions, the protest blew up into a full-scale uprising against domain authority and was ultimately crushed by domain troops with some fifty executed and over a hundred imprisoned. The domain suffered also, from a shogunal reduction in size of 50 percent, but this was probably of little comfort to the people.

Nevertheless, interregna were times of intense anxiety in the domains, since they were opportunities for the shogunate to alter the size, location, or even the ruling family of the fief. This uncertainty increased the odds that the clan elders would do anything in their power to avoid the impression that they were less than competent, and the odds that the people (quite apart from taking the opportunity to capitalize on long-standing grievances) would agitate against any administrative change. This tendency was clear on both the domain level and nationally. Internal contention rose opportunistically at both the beginning and end of the Tokugawa era (see also Kimmel 1988: 90; Tilly 1986: 25ff., 191ff.). At the end, for example, in Aizu popular contention broke out within ten days of the Restoration (Vlastos 1986: chap. 7).

A final aspect of the historical record which bears upon the inception of contention is the notion that contention in one locale stimulated it nearby. In some cases the links are unmistakable. In the Gunnai dispute in which Hyōsuke played a part, it was the entry of the Gunnai people into the Kuninaka Basin which incited the people there to rise. And in 1825 when Iwakidaira domain imposed a forced loan on its territory in Mino province, one village protested and was exempted, whereupon the rest of the area blew up (Yashiro 1989: 197). More often, however, it is my impression that physical contiguity per se was less important than common economic or political conditions and the spread of news of contention across broad areas, catching on only here and there.

For example, the massive Demma Uprising of 1764 spread along the Nakasendō Road as the result of the increased corvée imposed on the villages there (Hayashi 1976a: 170). We have seen, as well, how great cycles of contention swept the country on several occasions. It appears to be the commonality of causal factors—especially grievances—rather than the epidemiological spread of contention itself which is at work. We have already seen how small was the scale of most contentious events. Moreover, Aoki records only 2–3 percent as having been either the overflow from nearby events or the continuation of earlier events in the same locality, and most of Aoki's events lasted but a single day. Thus the image of infection of villages by their neighbors is less striking than that of simultaneous response to common underlying conditions. To appropriate a Japanese metaphor, it looks more like bamboo shoots popping up all over after a rain.

I began this chapter with an admission of "error," that is, with the acknowledgment that my structural predictors of popular contention would be forever unable to explain the phenomenon fully, that examination of individual agency is essential to a complete explanation. We are left still facing a significant explanatory lacuna. My data and overall approach are simply more attuned to a structural than a voluntaristic model of contention. I can address agency in part, and I can try to finesse the problem, but it will not go away.

I can address the problem directly in two ways. First, my examination of the rationality of leadership suggests that structural analysis can provide macrolevel explanations that could be addressed, at least in principle (Little 1991), on the individual level. Certain structural conditions rendered it rational for individuals in different positions in the socioeconomic structure both to lead and to follow. And there were individuals in such structural positions in every community; indeed, over time, their numbers seem to have increased. My data have indicated that there were three positional types of leaders: community officials; the poor and marginal or occupationally defined; and property-owning citizens in between. The first and second groups are easiest to explain; the third—10 percent of all recorded leaders and 24 percent in the nineteenth century—are the most problematic and least accessible. To some extent they are those of whom Thomas Smith (1959) spoke: generally prospering freeholders with more to lose from crises and more to gain from contention as the era wore on. And the economic origins of their interests are suggested by the nature of the events they led: social (either as producers or consumers), not political; largely within the community; and neither obsequiously deferential nor explosively intense in magnitude. But without extensive examination of individuals such as Miura Meisuke, just which such individuals might take the lead, when, and why we cannot know.

There is another direct approach to the problem. The "why" of contention is visible in putative causes and popular demands. That intracommunity reasons were cited most frequently is slightly counterintuitive, given the stress in most histories on state-aggravated misery and oppression. Granted, the complexity of reasons makes such generalizations weak, but the fact that economic, fiscal, and especially political reasons appear farther down the list does not confirm the conventional wisdom. The evolution of reasons, on the other hand, does reflect both the political and economic changes characteristic of the era and the devolution of leadership roles over the same period. But again, although we can estimate that there were more lower-strata potential leaders in the nineteenth than the seventeenth century, and we can suggest what issues they were willing to take the lead on, where they might come from, and how big the events they led might be, we cannot predict when any one of them might have emerged. There may have been many more Sherwood Forests than Robin Hoods, and the general existence of the forest does not explain the specific emergence of the hero.

My examination of catalysis and mobilization also tantalizes. It offers some indications of the interaction of leaders and authorities. Early concessions seem to have dampened contention, whereas later ones seem to have had the opposite effect; overall, a carrot-*and*-stick approach seems to have worked best from the establishment's point of view. In particular, the people appear to have been mollified by early concessions, but if contention continued, they appear to have become increasingly sensitive to repression, especially if some gains had already been made. Their view seems to have been: Ask for something; if you get it, either go home or ask for more; if, you ask for more and your antagonists become increasingly angry (even if they continue to concede), be prepared to settle for whatever you have already received and hope that they do not renege after the dust has settled.

But *what* determines whether initial concessions will be accepted or rejected? To some extent it was probably the depth and variety of the grievances that initially led to contention. To a significant extent it must have been leadership as well. There are half-a-loafers and aggrandizers, and nothing but a case-by-case approach can suggest why one emerged now and another then. My look at catalysis is similarly frustrating: sudden grievances, sudden opportunities, and the dynamics of interaction can all explain contention, but not so generally as to help much in building a theory.

Thus the temptation to finesse the question. For purposes of parsimony one can assert that potential leaders existed always and everywhere and, given appropriate structural conditions, either institutional or personal incentives would bring them into prominence. Therefore, a microlevel approach to the problem is unnecessary if our structural data are good enough. And, indeed, the existence of catalytic events does seem much more fortuitous than the existence of potential leaders, which can be partially inferred from structural data. For example, we find more leaders coming from the traditional source, community officials, in regions characterized by lower levels of economic development and social flux, and more poor and occupationally defined leaders in highly developed and differentiated regions. On each of six separate measures, the proportion of events led by officials diminishes (monotonically in four instances) from the least to the most developed and differentiated regions.[11] And it is not the propertied nonofficial stratum that took up leadership roles: there is no consistent relationship between development and differentiation and their involvement. Rather, it is the poor and marginals and occupational representatives who increased in salience—by anywhere from two-thirds to 300 percent—on five of six measures.

But such findings beg the question of whether community officials would lead or not. Most were surely opposed to contention in principle, and we have no data on the frequency with which they dissuaded their people from contending. The less-developed, less-differentiated regions saw less contention, but was it entirely because of structural factors? Of course not: that is what the unexplained variance in magnitude of contention tells us. But to what extent is it because of officials who prevented contention? We cannot say. Thus my approach can do no better than a *deus ex machina* interpretation of the inception of contention: the *machinae*—community institutions and socioeconomic structure—are always there and so are institutional, propertied, and Robin Hood *dei*. Given certain antecedent conditions, the *dei* will simply emerge. Or at least there is some likelihood that they will appear. This is not an entirely welcome outcome, but there it is. One hopes that historians of a more microscopic bent will go where my data do not and generalize about what they find there.

---

[11] For this analysis I used three measures of development—proportion of commercial crops in county agricultural production, extent of commercialization of provincial agriculture, and nongrain products as a proportion of provincial agricultural production. I used two measures of social differentiation—county urbanization and extent of tenancy. I dichotomized each of these five measures and created six measures of socioeconomic flux by combining nongrain products and urbanization, nongrain products and tenancy, and so forth.

PART IV

CONSEQUENCES AND CONCLUSIONS

13

IMPLICATIONS AND INTERPRETATIONS

Having addressed the basic questions of what? and why? I find myself faced with the last question: So what? The people of early modern Japan contended among themselves and with the state in a wide variety of ways, but who cares? Were all these alarums and excursions of any moment for society, for the state, or even for those involved? The protagonists certainly did not move mountains. Did they move even molehills?

Some say that the idea that popular contention "produced important social change [is] easy to reject" (Rozman in Jansen and Rozman 1989: 502). Others disagree by definition, claiming that the very act of contention signifies heightened mass consciousness and self-actualization and supports assumptions of the teleological progress of history. I have found along my way abundant evidence that popular contention had both direct and indirect effects on the political, economic, social, and ideological context of early modern Japan and that it influenced the interests, opportunities, and resources of the people. It certainly influenced the authorities' immediate responses and, arguably, their long-term posture and behavior as well. I would guess at this point that it probably influenced the subsequent behavior of the people and future events such as the Meiji Restoration and forms and frequencies of popular contention during the Meiji period as well.

At this point I want to recap some of this evidence and adduce new evidence by which to evaluate my impressions. I shall also consider contrary evaluations. I do not say that popular contention affected everything in sight, but neither do I shrink from speculation.

Contention and Context

The aspects of the political context most directly affected by popular contention were policy, personnel, and structure. Japanese commoners were able, through contention, to limit and redirect fiscal policy, gain rights to common lands and to the disposition of property (Elison and Smith 1981: 13), and even to determine macrolevel government policy in the areas of finance and social control. Such revelations did not surprise me. Popular contention in other early modern societies led to stronger guarantees of justice, institutionalization of peasant power, protection against enclosure, and enhanced relief measures; it also limited the prerogatives of the state, hindered national war efforts, and significantly reduced state revenues (Blickle 1981: 182, 187; Manning 1988: chap. 7; Bercé 1990: 150ff.). Indeed, it has been proposed (Kierman 1980) that the very emergence of the early modern state was promoted by a fear of the people which pushed the nobility toward a compact with the monarch. We have seen the same thing, to a less complete degree, in Japan, where the bakufu made ever more frequent common cause with the lords in the face of endemic popular contention, and where lords, faced with the options of pacifying the people and losing face and revenue or resisting and possibly intensifying contention and ending up punished by the shogunate, increasingly chose conciliation.

I need do little more here than reiterate some of the policy changes that followed from popular contention. Quite apart from successful attempts to repeal specific taxes, exchange rates, and land surveys, the long-term effects of contention included the standardization of tax media and rates and growing reliance on revenues other than the basic land tax, with consequent reductions in both the arbitrariness and the capacity of policy (Aoki M. et al. 1981, 1:133, 2:229–34); and bakufu demands for just and able performance by local administators and for the smooth processing of popular petitions (Aoki M. et al. 1981, 5:183ff.). Certain of the specific consequences—disaster relief, tax cuts, and price controls, for example—have been rightly described as ephemeral (see, e.g., Sasaki 1974: 59). But others, such as the shogunate's rescission of its order to transfer the lord of Shōnai, were not (Kelly 1985). The cumulative effect of policy change included such gross anomalies as the once-unthinkable impoverishment of large numbers of the samurai (Kaikyū Tōsō 1981: 239). Perhaps the final triumph of early modern popular contention occurred in the 1870s when the Meiji government rolled back the rate of its new land tax from 3 percent to 2.5 percent as the result of popular protest (Hayashi 1976b: 244).

Nevertheless, popular contention did not make the policy context unequivocally more beneficent. Unknown numbers of commoners paid with their lives, freedom, and property for their actions, and the severity of punishments grew over time.[1] More and more behavior became illegal; more violent repression was ordained; more channels of articulation were closed; and repeated attempts were made to keep protest away from the capital. Practice, as I have noted, drifted if anything in the opposite direction. Nevertheless, by the end of the era the state enjoyed unquestioned preeminence in social control policy, which cannot but have smoothed the transition to a modern state in this particular policy arena.

---

[1] Yamada 1984: 86; Rekishigaku Kenkyū 1985: 92; Hayashi 1976b: 219ff.; Aoki M. et al. 1981, 2:235ff.

But politics cannot be assessed apart from its practice. At the uppermost levels of the system, both bakufu officials and lords were occasionally sacked in the aftermath of widespread contention (Hayashi 1976b: 200ff.). It is quite clear that the lords feared the bakufu's wrath, and the people played upon this fear, realizing that an end-run petition to the state was often more effective than a direct appeal to their own lord (Rekishi Kagaku 1974: 38). This fear penetrated down the administrative hierarchy, too, not without reason. After one prolonged protest in Bingo province in 1786–1787, the peasant participants were amnestied, while thirteen officials were punished (Bix 1986: chap. 10). After the Sanhei incident of 1853 in northern Nambu domain over two hundred domain officials were disciplined (Fukaya 1983: 144). In 1751 Tamura Hanemon, an official of Matsushiro domain, decreed a 15 percent tax increase, and some two thousand persons from seventy-two villages marched on the castle town to demand a tax rescission and Tamura's skin. The domain gave in; Tamura, noting this vote of no confidence, fled to Edo, where he was arrested and thrown in prison; he later died there (Yashiro 1989: 170–71).

In 1755 Akita domain issued silver certificates. Local merchants, opposed to the measure, withheld goods from sale, stimulating inflation. Pro- and anticurrency groups were in conflict within the domain government, but a townsmen's appeal to the shogunate moved the domain to crack down on the "pro" faction, of which one leader was executed. The petitioners were also punished, thirteen of them subjected to death, exile, or confinement, and nine samurai suffered too: eight were ordered to commit suicide and one was expelled from the nobility (Yashiro 1989: 16ff.).

My data on this score, unfortunately, rely almost solely on such anecdotes. The Aoki data record only 210 incidents of punishment of officials, and I have no clue as to the accuracy of this figure. It may be that these anecdotes account for all those rare and noteworthy times when officials were in fact punished, but I doubt it. The incidents in the data were certainly not only slaps on the wrist: 41 percent of them involved relatively light disciplinary action such as transfers, dismissals, and forced retirements and resignations, but 29 percent included domiciliary confinement or imprisonment, exile, or property confiscation. And another 29 percent involved demotion, transfer, forced retirement, expulsion from the samurai class of lords, or the execution of officials. One could of course dismiss such actions as cosmetic and insignificant in the larger political context. But the awareness that such degrading and career-ending actions were possible (Sasaki 1972: 35ff.) had (I suggest) a material effect on the conduct of the authorities.

It was not simply that an individual official or two was scapegoated. In the course of the early modern period the political context also changed structurally in response to popular contention. The popularly detested position of overheadman was eliminated by the bakufu (see also Harada 1982: 152ff.), and parts of domains were on occasion transferred from one jurisdiction to another in response either to manifestly inept rule or to positive entreaty from the people there (Yamanashi-ken 1978: 32ff.). The increasing adoption of election as the method for choosing village headmen and the broadening "electorate" significantly changed the political milieu of the village (Tozeren 1981). Informally, the growth of the petitioners' inns in Edo, and the changing role of their quasi-lawyerly owners, increased the channels of remonstration available to the people.

Still, popular contention in early modern Japan never challenged or altered the basic status quo. The authorities repeatedly gave in to popular demands, but never recognized the legitimacy of contention. Over and over, concrete concessions were accompanied by reiterations that the authority of the state was absolute and the rights of the people nil. Even episodes such as the Demma Rebellion of 1764, with its hundreds of thousands of participants, could be described as "an explosion," an "atheoretical struggle, [not] a decisive force able to advance history" (Kitazawa 1982: 164–65). The question rests on the subjective evaluation of significance. How significant is a village reform that substantively expands the political space of a few newly enfranchised villagers but leaves the rest of the institutional or policy universe untouched?

I assert that popular contention in early modern Japan had a modest and indirect but substantial effect on the economy in two ways. The first was the overall monetarization, marketization, and commodification of the economy driven by the evolution of revenue from kind to cash, a process largely brought about by popular resistance to in-kind exactions and by the state's increasing reliance on nonagricultural taxes in its efforts to avoid popular resistance. The second effect came through peasant capital accumulation, which resulted from successful resistance to extraction and laid the basis for rural economic development (Rekishi Kagaku 1974: 306–7; Fukaya 1979: 213–14, 303, 334ff.). One cannot suggest that contention was some sort of omnipotent economic influence, but it is a fact that the retreat of the *fisc* left an increasing portion of a growing "GNP" in the hands of the people, and this capital founded countless enterprises. It also led to social differentiation, which in turn contributed to contention.

Thus, the indirect effect of contention on the social context was meaningful. Directly, of course, hitherto servile elements strove through contention for full hyakushō status during the seventeenth century, and small farmers strove to commute or cast off corvée obligations (Kaikyū Tōsō 1981: 223). In later centuries commoners contended for social and political rights commensurate with their enhanced economic situations (Smith T. 1959) and then created new bases of solidarity in a "reformed" community leadership structure (Aoki M. et al. 1981, 2:264).

Contention brought social change from the top down also. Increasing levels of contention during the era led the authorities to attempt to co-opt popular leaders, to make them a more effective instrument of social control. They exacerbated the resulting alienation by turning popular elites into a source of revenue. Rather than directly tax a populace that was prone to resist, the state gave commoner elites new commercial privileges and offices and extracted a portion of the fruits of privilege in the form of "loans" (Yokoyama 1977:

119–27; Aoki K. 1966: 88). By the nineteenth century many commoner elites had been completely compromised and, indeed, had in their own eyes ceased to have much in common with the unwashed beneath them. Thus, while some villages developed new bases of solidarity, others fragmented and fell to squabbling.

Popular contention during the era had a certain influence on high philosophy. Such thinkers as Motoori Norinaga, Aizawa Seishisai, and the Mito School saw social disorder as a commentary on the state, and a number of philosophical writers used popular contention as a justification for criticizing the Tokugawa system.[2] In the more plebeian mental—"intellectual" seems a bit pretentious—context of contention, there are four areas in which popular contention influenced the popular mind.

The first was cathartic. Despite my assertions of the rationality of contention, contention also—especially when it took the form of popular judgment—served to appease indignation, if not rage. The exaction of justice was more rhetorical than real. In one event the surviving record attributes to the leaders the declaration, "Take Kamiyama and Tsuchiya [the local villains], beat them to death and cut them to shreds; the farmers will slake their hatred by eating their flesh" (Yasumaru 1973: 103). But there is no evidence that anyone was actually killed. Still, there was an orgiastic air about some events (Yasumaru 1973: 247), especially the later stages of urban riots, when hangers-on turned to wholesale looting and destruction.

But even those episodes marked by expressions of hatred were usually characterized by the second aspect of context, that is, a powerful popular judicial consciousness (Aoki M. et al. 1981, 4:46). The prevalent sentiment in the aftermath of contention was often probably "justice is done." The later stages of a riot may have been anarchic, but the social and normative function was still "to punish the heartless as an example to the world" (Yasumaru 1975: 238). The rioters themselves often discriminated neatly between those deserving of punishment and those—such as the main house of Hachiemon's family—who avoided attack because they had a reputation for lending at reasonably low interest (Fukaya 1978: 19–20).

Thus contention was, third, a ratification of the "social contract," the normative umbrella under which everyone lived (Sasaki 1974: 76–143). The line between acceptable and unacceptable taxation was never clear, but the common people were always close (or had an interest in appearing close) to the line, and as the era wore on they became increasingly quick to assert that the line had been crossed. The state, for its part, never acknowledged any such contract. In its actions, including the punishment of its own minions, it admitted its existence, but such clarifications required popular initiative.

Finally, this increasing willingness to challenge authority signified that popular consciousness had been raised by contention. Through contention the people

[2] Najita and Koschmann 1982: 43ff.; Harootunian 1970, 1988; Hall 1991; Jansen 1989.

became able to conceive of change, improvement, alternative living conditions, and even alternative rulers, at least on the local level. The era saw a "general trend away from . . . humble deference" (Walthall 1986: 206) which led all the way to the outrageous effrontery of the farmers of Sanhei who, upon returning home after a successful protest against the Nambu domain, announced that if things had not improved in seven years they would do it again (Fukaya 1983: 142). Even the samurai were at wits' end, bemoaning commoners who "don't even bow, and go around with insolent expressions on their faces" or who "walk into a liquor shop and say, 'Lend us some sake or we'll wreck the place'" (Yasumaru 1975: 181–82). Such effrontery was occurring in a policy context of increasing formal repressiveness. But the institutional context was in decay, as was the will of the samurai. One may hypothesize a spiral of contention and consciousness, one feeding the other until, by the end of the era, popular awe of the samurai had largely dissipated.

The effect of contention on interests, opportunities, and resources was both direct and indirect. Indirectly, the role of political interests in contention seems to have declined: the increasing relative salience of social conflict reflects the retreat of the political from the center of popular attention (albeit with a revival at the end of the era). The economic context had a mixed effect: prosperity raised increasing numbers of people above subsistence, but it and development made increasing numbers of people vulnerable to the market, and it proliferated economic interests, increasing the chance of random—much less systematic—collision among them. My data suggest that if prosperity diluted grievances, this effect was far outweighed by both the contentious implications of development and the sudden shock of economic reversal.

The social context had a less mixed impact on interests: social differentiation and urbanization were clearly related to contention of all types. And consciousness also seems to have contributed to popular interest in contention. One constant throughout the era was use of the government's own ideals against it. But mentality was changeable as well: consciousness rose and precedents accumulated over the era, as did examples of state vulnerability.

As time passed, opportunities were revealed and seem to have increased. Political decay invited challenge and reduced the cost of contention. The opportunity structure was predominantly part of the political context. Economic change worked far more powerfully on the interest component of the equation than on opportunities, and although social change in the form of urbanization brought ever larger numbers of people into proximity with moneylenders and merchants, the social context, too, had its primary impact elsewhere. Ideology affected opportunities only insofar as the intellectual vigor and self-confidence of the samurai decayed.

Popular resources for contention were marginally augmented by political factors, specifically, by the enhanced political status of previously lower-status groups who rose through the agency of economic development. Economic change, however, had a greater influence on resources (which, politically, were legally nil throughout the era). Larger numbers of people, now above the subsistence line, were able to think of other things than survival, more people had more to lose, and more people had the wherewithal, for example, to take off for Edo to press a case that might take months to resolve. The social context was also a major resource. Throughout the era villages, or cohesive groups within villages, constituted the primary units of mobilization for contention. One might have expected that social differention would erode this resource; instead, it appears that the units of mobilization shrank in size but multiplied in number, as economically defined groups within the village began to coalesce for contentious purposes. It is possible that levels of popular contention would have been higher in early modern Japan if social differentiation had not progressed so, but it seems to me that the influence of social change in general on grievances, and of the proliferation of intravillage groups with unifying economic interests on resources, outweighed this possibility.

The effects of contention on contention were both indirect, through context, and direct, in that government response to contention affected popular behavior immediately. I shall return to the effects of government behavior in the context of official responses; at this point the remaining question is what connection popular contention had to the Meiji Restoration.

This question is surrounded by debate. Some historians see popular contention as the vanguard of the bakufu's fall and a revolutionary force propelling Japan toward a higher stage of historical development. Others see an indirect contribution to the Restoration: popular contention drained state coffers, dispersed state armed forces, and manifested the ineptitude of government.[3] And Yoshio Sugimoto, in a quantitative exercise (1975, 1978a), found that domains with *little* contention were free to act on the national stage. The implication is that contention in the shogunal lands robbed the state of economic and political strength and thus contributed to the Restoration.

Other observers are less impressed. Conrad Totman (1980) has written an authoritative treatment of the last years of the shogunate with almost no reference to popular contention and William Beasley, in a work of similar scale, acknowledges the fiscal impact of contention and the philosophical critique of Tokugawa rule generated from contention but does not see contention as a "primary determinant" of elite actions anywhere along the way (1972: 417; see also Wilson 1992; Borton 1938: 120–21). Many Japanese scholars (see, e.g., Aoki M. et al. 1981, 5:45–48) share this view. My own position is that popular contention occurred largely independent of the Restoration, and insofar as my data permit me to address the question, they support this expectation.

Specifically, simple associations between intradomain contention and domain roles in the Restoration reveal no significant linear relationships at all.[4] Pro-Tokugawa domains appear clumped in the least *and most* contentious categories,

---

[3] Borton 1938: 19–20; Sasaki 1973: 104; Aoki M. et al. 1981, 2:295; Norman 1965.
[4] The data on domain role were taken from Sugimoto 1975.

and the domains that led the Restoration are characterized by moderate levels of contention of all types. It is not that *none* of my data help explain domain roles in the Restoration: bigger, economically stronger, effectively governed and well-regulated Western outer domains were far more likely to be part of the anti-Tokugawa camp. But I suspect that these characteristics (which, one must note, *were* associated with relatively low levels of contention), and not contention per se, played the direct role in explaining domain activity in the upheavals of the late 1860s.

Impact and Interpretation

If one's interest is in systemic transformation, popular contention in early modern Japan did not amount to much. But there are more modest perspectives. I have said that contention did matter on the contextual level, and one can say as well that it mattered very much to individuals, families, and communities. It might have been in vain; indeed, some have asserted that contention only made a "miserable condition yet more miserable" (Walthall 1986: 39). I maintain that *even if* individual events did not succeed or work lasting change on the system, their aggregate effect on the context was significant (Scott 1985: 29–30). There is every reason to expect that taxes would have been heavier, relief would have been less, government would have been more arbitrary, merchants would have been more rapacious, and officials would have been more corrupt.

But we need not stay on the contextual level to make an argument for significance. Individual lords would have been extraordinarily obtuse to ignore the extirpation of lordly families and obliteration of domains that did not govern acceptably (Aoki M. et al. 1981, 5:223). And the people demonstrated, even in unsuccessful contention, that they were in no way mystified by the status quo. As we have seen, actual contention was rare, occurring in less than 5 percent of all the county-years of Tokugawa Japan. And success was rare also. Harada Tomohiko (1982: 386) estimates that no more than one in ten incidents succeeded, and my own data take specific note of successful or amicable settlement in only 12 percent of all events. But word of contention was ubiquitous among elites and people, and substantive concessions—even if denied and accompanied by draconian punishment (Sasaki 1974: 35ff.)—can be examined. Even one of the more critical assessors of popular contention, Herbert Bix (1986: 137), notes that the people were able to force the state to "modify or rescind altogether those policies that peasants would not tolerate."

We may examine the payoff of popular contention in two different ways: as "success" generally defined, and as substantive settlement. I shall consider punishment separately; since it was often anticipated, punishment does not indicate that an event did not achieve its aims.

As noted, only some 12 percent of all of my events were recorded as having been amicably or successfully settled. Neither magnitude nor type of contention suggests why one event failed and another did not, but time, deference, and regime type do. During the middle 150 years of the era (1700–1850) roughly 14 percent of the incidents ended successfully, as opposed to 10 percent during the first century and only 6 percent under the Meiji regime. Deference helped: 14 percent of the contention that avoided threatening, aggressive, violent, or destructive action ended successfully or amicably, whereas none of the events in which all occurred succeeded. The political locus of contention was important too: 15 percent of the events occurring in Tokugawa territories and hereditary domains ended amicably but only 11 percent of those occurring in the outer domains. The type of contention least likely to meet with success was the riot. Others have noted the importance of organization to success (Rudé 1971: 339ff.; Fukawa 1976: 188; Blickle 1981: xv), but we should recall that without organization there were no concrete demands that could be successfully fulfilled. And riots combined maximum amounts of coercive behavior and disorganization.

One also notes a variety of what look like constructive outcomes of events not explicitly categorized as successful. The number eventuating in some sort of positive outcome is 18 percent of the total, which I suspect is an underestimate. We have already seen many of the sorts of resolutions recorded: most commonly, taxes were reduced, eliminated, reallocated, or postponed; village administration was reformed procedurally and structurally; village officials were fired, transferred, or forced to resign; and aid was given. On fewer occasions land surveys and development projects were halted or redone; currency was withdrawn, exchanged, or redeemed; prices were cut, hoarding was banned, and trade was freed; workers and tenants received wage and rent concessions; and certain groups either won new status or had traditional prerogatives withdrawn.

Again, overall magnitude of contention is not associated with constructive outcomes, but deference is: 19 percent of the least aggressive events but *none* of the most aggressive elicited some positive response. Type of contention bears little connection to outcome either. Nor does time, at least at first glance, except that the proportion of events constructively resolved drops precipitately to 8 percent after the Restoration. But when one looks at social conflict and political protest separately, the implied efficacy of social conflict appears to have *declined* over time—going from 23 percent of events in the seventeenth century to 18 percent in the nineteenth. That of political protest reached 22 percent during the eighteenth century, whereas previous and subsequent centuries saw resolution rates of only 15 percent. At first glance this finding seems counterintuitive. Almost all the resolutions recorded here involved political intercession, and as the polity weakened one would have expected it to become increasingly concessionary. The social data seem more comprehensible, since such contention often (and, one may expect, increasingly) did not seek governmental redress. But protest is less tractable. Perhaps there is a connection to the occurrence of the major systemic consequences of contention during the eighteenth century, when both the private economic sector and the government fiscal apparatus were restructured as the direct and indirect consequence of contention. Still, one expected less official intransigence in the nineteenth century. Perhaps by that time the government's capacity to pay off was declining.

The final aspect of note regarding the resolution of contention involves regime type, and here, again, there is a slight indication that the outer lords were the least responsive: 19 percent of the events occurring in Tokugawa and hereditary domains elicited a constructive response, compared to only 15 percent of those occurring in the outer domains.

Thus, on these two dimensions at least, popular contention had an impact. On the microlevel, in at least one of five cases the authorities responded in ways that redressed the demands of the people at least temporarily. One may rest assured that additional unrecorded or unofficial remedies were extended as well, not to mention the concessions of merchants and moneylenders, who must have been a bit sobered by having their shops and homes sacked, their goods seized or destroyed. Did all this go on within the unquestioned context of the Tokugawa status quo? Of course. And was this status quo unquestionably autocratic, exploitative, and arbitrary? Of course. Does this mean that these remedies were epiphenomenal froth lapping the foot of a towering crag of oppression? Only if one dismisses the economic, political, and even physical survival of thousands of common people.

On the systemic level, I have speculated that long-term structural changes, which could at the very least be described as reformist, derived in part from contention. Sometimes these changes resulted from contention, as we saw in the Temmei and Tempō periods (Fukawa 1976: 151–52; Walthall 1990: 21; Ooms 1975: 73–76). In others—notably the Kyōhō period—extractive reforms led to contention (Aoki M. et al. 1981, 5:212ff.; Maruyama 1974: 251; Rekishi Kagaku 1974: 64), which as often as not brought the reforms to an abrupt halt (Shōji et al. 1981: 467ff.). When one overviews the era as a whole it is difficult to dismiss the argument that the broad outlines of the political, social, and economic context were intimately and significantly interrelated with popular contention.

This argument neither demands revolutionary actuality nor implies it. By hamstringing the regime fiscally and dissipating its coercive forces, contention played a progressive role (Fujitani 1982: 115–29). And as we have seen, a great many popular aspirations and demands were *incompatible* with the presuppositions of the Tokugawa state. Nevertheless, the word "revolutionary" simply does not seem to apply.[5] The absence of revolution does not constitute failure in any way. Revolution was not what the people sought; it was not necessary to what they sought; and what they sought through contention they often got.

---

[5] Harada 1982: 387; Sugimoto 1978: 26; Wilson 1992. This is especially so when Japan is looked at comparatively (Shōji et al. 1981: 416ff.; Skocpol 1979: chap. 2; Tilly 1993: 10, 49), although the changes made *later* under the Meiji regime might well have been revolutionary: Wilson 1992: 129; Tilly 1993: 240.

Contention and Retribution

But what they got, they got at a price, which was not small. Indications are that the people accepted this price, but I cannot simply adduce indications. I must consider official measures of retribution before offering any final thoughts about the individual or collective rationality of contention or about the probable effect of punishment on subsequent behavior. My assumptions of rationality are supported by my data on the substantive resolution of contention. In the great majority of cases, outcomes came swiftly enough that the people would have been able to see a clear cause-and-effect relationship between contention and concession.

Repression nevertheless remains, and Tokugawa law prescribed a range of sanctions grisly enough to deter any thinking person (Kitazawa 1982: 174ff.). A rising in Shikoku in 1600 against a new lord, by retainers of the old, resulted in several hundred executions, and a protest against misrule in Dewa province in 1638 was followed by thirty-five crucifixions (Yashiro 1989: 55ff.; Aoki M. et al. 1981, 5:176ff.). Between 1622 and 1633 the people in Shiraiwa domain petitioned eight times over high taxes, heavy exploitation, and popular misery; finally thirty-eight representatives did an end-run appeal to Edo while people back home stormed the castle and killed one domain elder. All thirty-eight representatives were executed. It was probably small popular comfort that the lord was also expelled from the samurai class and his fief confiscated by the shogunate (Yashiro 1989: 190–91).

Punishments were easy to effect. Frequently local officials were ordered to quell local disturbances and then were punished themselves. Sometimes the authorities complied or temporized until the people simmered down, then sent agents through the countryside to grab alleged leaders. These people were commonly released and told to stay in their villages; the real investigation would begin later, on the scene or in Edo or both, and sometimes run for months (Fukaya 1978; Sippel 1977: 315). With exceptions such as Hyōsuke, for the most part, people stayed put until the investigators came around or summoned them to Edo. With livelihood, property, family, and social identity locked into a community, flight was not an option for most, and knowing that one's relatives and neighbors might well be punished for one's own escape must have deterred others. After contention subsided and the people returned to their homes, there was really no way they could protect themselves, and so they waited in apparent docility for the axe to fall (Aoki M. et al. 1981, 4:224).

But the axe did not always fall. Indeed, official preference was always for private settlement, or *naisai*, which was in fact frequently ordered by the authorities (Aoki M. et al. 1981, 4:57–58). If things were settled with a minimum of upheaval, the people reavowed their basic loyalty and submissiveness thereafter, and the shogunate didn't hear of the affair (Yashiro 1989: 99–100), amnesty was by no means out of the question (Hayashi 1976a: 111–12). A protest against new taxes in Shirakawa domain in 1720 involved over fifteen thousand participants, who at one point interdicted a main highway. The officials responsible for the taxes—but none of the participants—were punished (Sasaki 1974: 85ff., 94–95). And in Fukuchiyama domain in 1860 over twenty thousand people laid waste to shops and offices and fought with domain troops over a variety of trade controls, monopolies, and merchant miscreancies. The domain gave in, one samurai was ordered to commit suicide, several more were dismissed or exiled, the lord's family was demoted, and two merchants were imprisoned. None of the participants was prosecuted (Harada 1982: 215ff.).

But as important as frequency or severity is pattern. Do official punishments provide us with any indications of either the cause or the effect of popular contention?

The answer, I believe, is yes. The pattern of retribution that emerges from my data is one of heavy-handed but inconsistent response followed by severe but also inconsistent punishment, which disproportionately focused on political protest but diminished dramatically over time. In other words, neither initial response nor ultimate punishment was calculated for effective deterrence (although punishment may well have made *social* conflict relatively attractive), and the predictable cost of contention declined substantially during the era.

The initial official response to popular contention is measured here by whether the authorities initially placated or repressed the people or did something ambiguous, and by the number of persons arrested.[6] Placatory responses—which occurred in 31 percent of the cases in which an initial response was recorded—included official apologies, extension of relief, persuasion of the people to go home, mediation of disputes, or acceptance of a petition. Repression—occurring in 40 percent of the cases—included arresting or capturing participants or attacking or dispersing them forcibly or violently, or forcibly returning absconders. In-between responses included official reprimands, warnings, or threats; holding an inquiry or dispatching officials; obstructing some popular action; and rejecting a demand or petition. Exactly how repressive this pattern is, is arguable. In 60 percent of the cases the regime either appeased the people or equivocated, although many of the in-between responses presaged later coercion. Clearly the risks at this point were substantial.

But they were not consistent. Repressive responses varied directly with the magnitude and aggressiveness of contention: 72 percent of the most intense incidents, and 86 percent of the most coercive, were met with repressive responses. Yet so were 17 percent of the mildest incidents and 32 percent of the completely nonaggressive ones. If the odds of repression were one in three no matter how assiduously one avoided aggressive behavior, then perhaps aggression was not worth avoiding. And the same pattern is visible in arrests: fewer than five individuals were arrested in 60 percent of the events recorded, with more than twenty arrests in only 20 percent of the cases. And, although the number arrested varied with magnitude and aggressiveness, fewer than five arrests were recorded in 38 percent of the highest-magnitude events and 31 percent of the most aggressive. It appears that one could hope to get away with even serious infractions of the civil order.

This seems to have been the case even in political protest. The most repressive responses and the most arrests followed social conflict, not protest. Repressive responses were made to 53 percent of the incidents of social conflict, in comparison to 35 percent of protests. It may be that the authorities initially took a kid-gloves approach to protest because it was more threatening.

The punishments ultimately imposed reveal a similar pattern. They were heavy: death, life imprisonment, and distant exile were imposed in fully 50 percent of the cases for which punishments were recorded (n = 832). Light penalties such as domiciliary confinement, fines, pillory or manacles for a definite period, reprimand, and dismissal from office were imposed in only 9 percent of the cases. The other 41 percent of the cases involved penalties of intermediate degree such as banishment from locality or province, flogging, imprisonment (with or without torture), and confiscation of property. Thus visions of draconian treatment are not off the mark, especially because torture was a standard interrogatory technique whether or not any punishment was ultimately imposed.

But was punishment sufficient to deter a rational person? Here there is room for doubt. Both the severity of punishments and the number of persons punished varied directly with the magnitude and aggressiveness of contention, but the punishment did not closely fit the crime: heavy penalties were the rule across the board, following 64 percent of the highest-magnitude events and 60 percent of the most aggressive, and also 41 percent of the mildest and 48 percent of the completely noncoercive ones. The relationship between magnitude and aggressiveness of contention, on the one hand, and severity of punishment, on the other, was surprisingly inconsistent[7]—a situation that some have argued *maximizes* the probability of subsequent contention. A riot in Ōsaka in 1768 which lasted for several days resulted in seventy-four arrests; the heaviest penalty imposed was one banishment (Sasaki 1974: 279). In 1798 over ten thousand persons rose in Takada domain in opposition to heavy taxes and unresponsive rule; they wrecked the shops and homes of the rich and attacked government offices, and twenty-six were killed and over a hundred wounded in the conflict. One person was executed, two were jailed, and a number of participating villages were fined—a rather modest response to an event of this magnitude (Yashiro 1989: 23). Although over eleven thousand persons in 239 villages were punished in the aftermath of the massive Kamo Uprising of 1836, only two were executed and four banished (Fukawa 1976: 366).

The regime did deal with protest as expected: sixty percent of the protest events, versus only 37 percent of the social conflict, elicited heavy punishment,

---

[7] The correlations (*tau-b*'s) between severity of punishment and number of persons punished, and magnitude and aggressiveness, ranged between 0.09 and 0.19.

and more persons were punished in the aftermath of protest than after social conflict, despite the significantly greater aggressiveness of the social conflict events. In other words, protest was met—and, it was hoped, defused—with a soft hand, but it was ultimately followed with an iron fist. Overall, nevertheless, it looks as if one ran almost as good a chance of being hanged for a nonaggressive, socially squabbling sheep as for a violent, protesting goat. In 53 percent of the events for which punishments were recorded (n = 655) no more than three punishments were handed down; in another 26 percent of the cases between four and ten people were punished, and even in roughly 40 percent of the highest-magnitude and most aggressive incidents ten or fewer people were punished. Thus in only about one event in five were more than a dozen people punished. The regime seems to have been carrying out exemplary punishments, but one wonders if the example had the desired effect.

This doubt becomes stronger when one looks at the temporal evolution of punishment. On the surface the authorities seemed to get tougher: repressive laws and responses and arrests went up as the era wore on. But these were responses to the growing magnitude and aggressiveness of contention. Actual punishments, moreover, reveal one possible reason for the rising tide of contention: the number of people punished decreased slightly over time and the proportion of events eliciting heavy punishment dropped monotonically, from 82 percent in the first sixty years of the period to 25 percent in the period 1850–1867. The state went from a stream of repressive edicts in the mid-eighteenth century to preventive measures of relief and price control in the mid-nineteenth (Hyakushō Ikki 1980: 379–80). It seems to have lost its grip, its teeth, and its resolve, and it would be surprising if the people did not notice. Social contention, in particular, may have owed some of its increase to the relatively mild way it was dealt with—and urban contention also (Harada 1982). We have already seen that leadership was relatively difficult to discern in the more tumultuous (and more often social) urban contention, and this difficulty may be why only 18 percent of the urban disorders were followed by heavy punishments, as opposed to half of all incidents.

The rational response of the people to sanctions can also be inferred from the abrupt turnabout of the Meiji Restoration. The level of contention was at an all-time peak in the first year or two of the Meiji era, but fell away quickly (Jansen 1989: 367). One reason, we may infer, was the new state's no-nonsense attitude (Tozeren 1981; Yashiro 1989: 71ff.): 62 percent of the recorded events between 1868 and 1877 were met with repressive responses, only 8 percent with placatory responses, and the number of arrests surpassed anything seen under the Tokugawa. Heavy punishments were meted out in 80 percent of the cases, and the number of persons punished also increased sharply.

The benefits of contention (as measured by the "positive" outcomes already discussed) thus seem to have decreased over time, but the costs (as measured by punishment) went *way* down (until the Restoration), and the expected increase in contention did in fact occur. As noted, the people paid a price for contention, but between the opening years of the shogunate and the Restoration the price was not predictably high or certain, and if you were likely to pay the same price for either a big or small "investment" in contentious behavior, why not really go for it?

Retribution and Contention, Contention and Contention

Thus retribution did not follow inevitably upon contention. Let us consider the relationship in reverse. What sorts of effects did either contention or its repression have on subsequent levels of contention? I have already suggested that there may have been "cultures of contention," areas in which a legacy of contention in the popular consciousness became a resource that contributed to higher magnitudes of contention in later years. I have said, too, that repression quite likely did *not* serve a deterrent purpose. It also seems clear to me that any feedback effects of past contention had limited effect across systemic changes. The temporal demarcation of the era seems justified because the repertoire and causation of popular contention became quite different in the Meiji period, although popular contention during the early modern era may have influenced local magnitudes of contention after the Restoration.

Our first item of interest is contention per se. Clearly, in some areas of early modern Japan contention was endemic. Of 631 counties, 22—representing 3 percent of all counties and only 9 percent of the country's total agricultural productivity—saw over fifty incidents apiece, accounting for 25 percent of all contentious events and 21 percent of the total magnitude of contention during the era. At the other extreme, 74 counties recorded no incidents whatsoever during the era. The question is whether this distribution is attributable to the local legacy of either somnolence or sedition, or to the effects of the sorts of structural factors I have already noted?

In some instances collective memories are clear. One example is the shogunal village of Sekimae (Sasaki 1972: 132ff.), where in the 1770s the headman Chūzaemon borrowed a sum of money, using the villagers' land as collateral, and lent it out at interest. A group of villagers led by Sadaemon protested; Chūzaemon counterprotested; and both leaders were punished. Chūzaemon died, and the intendant ordered his son Chūbei to repay his father's debt, with interest; Chūbei in turn called in all the other loans his father had made and hailed those who could not repay before the intendant. Sadaemon's group paid off these debts to Chūbei, and grateful farmers petitioned to have Sadaemon named headman. Now Chūbei remonstrated, and the shogunate divided the village into two parts, or *kumi*. Uneasy peace followed, but by 1867 the "Chūzaemon-gumi" and the "Sadaemon-gumi" were at odds again over the original division of village land between the two kumi. This time a conference of village headmen intervened and an apparently satisfactory restitution was made. To the best of my knowledge this put an end to the conflict—after ninety years. And in an example of vindictiveness which the Hatfields and McCoys might have

Table 34. Conjunctural characteristics of the most and least contentious counties

	Average of 631 counties	Average of 22 most contentious counties	Average of 22 most contentious counties (631-county average = 100)	Average of 74 least contentious counties	Average of 74 least contentious counties (631-county average = 100)
Agricultural product per capita (1–4 scale)*	3.0	3.5	117	2.9	97
Food supply per capita (1–5 scale)*	3.0	3.0	100	2.9	97
Urbanization (1–4 scale)	1.8	2.6	144	2.2	122
Agricultural vulnerability (1–4 scale)	2.1	2.8	132	1.6	75
Commercial-ization of agriculture (1–4 scale)	2.3	2.6	112	2.2	95
Administrative fragmentation (1–4 scale)	2.4	3.5	147	1.9	80
County tax rate (1–5 scale)	3.0	2.0	67	3.4	113
Communications links (1–5 scale)	2.6	3.5	135	2.1	81

*These two scales are coded in reverse, i.e., 1 represents *many* calories per capita and koku of agricultural productivity per hectare.

admired, the family of one headman dismissed in 1784 for misrule was ostracized by the rest of the village until 1927 (Yokoyama 1986: 182–83).

But a conjunctural/interest and structural/opportunity explanation of the pattern of contention must supplement a *mentalité*/resource explanation. We have already seen that county contention in any given year varied inversely with the total contention over the previous five years. Moreover, the conjuncturally distinctive seventy-four cycle years I have identified (26 percent of the entire era) witnessed 47 percent of the events and 55 percent of the total magnitude of contention. In addition, when one looks at the two extreme groups of counties, conjunctural and structural factors stand out. As Table 34 shows, in the high-conflict counties the mean values of eight of the nine most explanatorily powerful variables we have were on the contention-prone side of the mean for all counties, and in three instances—administrative fragmentation, tax rate, and urbaniza-tion—they were far beyond it. Extreme concentrations of contention are found in counties that were administratively fragmented, lightly taxed, urbanized, and plugged into national communications networks. They were not at a disadvantage with respect to food, but overall their agricultural sectors were relatively commercialized, relatively unproductive, and quite vulnerable.

But reality is hardly neat and clean, as we see in Taki county in Tamba province. Part of the Sasayama domain, Taki county was the locus of sixty-eight contentious events during the era, despite being coherently ruled and taxed at an average rate, not particularly commercialized or vulnerable agriculturally, relatively isolated, and very well fed. Three of its incidents were of a magnitude of 10, and extreme punishments were visited upon the county on three different occasions, with little apparent effect. In 1869, however, demands for tax cuts and loan extensions followed a poor harvest. The demands were made manifest in a riot in which sixty-one buildings were destroyed; the new regime riposted with a number of punishments including one execution, and that was that for popular contention in Taki county.

That Meiji repression was of a different order we have already seen. The question here, however, is what kept contention going during the early modern period. And this we do not fully know. Sasayama was a medium-sized hereditary domain ruled by the Matsudaira family until 1749, when the lord—a man of rapacious and oppressive reputation—was transferred following a series of popular uprisings (Kodama 1979: 277–78). His successor, Lord Aoyama, continued his heavy-handed ways and eight more outbursts occurred during the 1750s and 1760s. A 1771 tax hike amid poor crop conditions led to a protest involving perhaps 70 percent of all the households in the entire domain and forty-nine sentences, including one execution. Far from deterring the people, however, this retribution was followed by some two dozen more incidents before the end of the era.

Certainly, the people of Taki had vivid memories of contention—a generation did not go by without it. But politically also it seems to have been a place conducive to contention. Ultimately we cannot sort out the two, and in all likelihood both factors contributed to the tumultuous history of the place.

A look at the seventy-four counties where no contention occurred—also seen in Table 34—fleshes out the picture. The quiescent counties were less distinctive than the turbulent ones, but again conjunctural and structural factors—a relatively unstressed economy and a firm political hand—appear to play a role. These counties were significantly more coherently ruled and heavily taxed, and they lay relatively off the beaten path, although they were relatively urban—the one exception to my prediction. They were also agriculturally less commercial and less vulnerable than the average county, and their food and productivity situations are slightly better than the average.[8]

---

[8] One should keep in mind that the differences between the most and least contentious counties and the 631-county average are greater than these tables indicate, since the 631-county average includes the most and least contentious.

This group of counties offers more anomalous cases like Taki county, perhaps unsurprisingly, especially if one is inquiring after local cultures of contention. It is easier to conceive a tradition of insubordination than one of quiescence. Moreover, I suspect that to the extent that legacies of contention are significant, they are so on a supracounty level. Communications were sufficiently effective in early modern Japan that people throughout the country were familiar with such hero-martyrs as Sakura Sōgorō, and neither the village nor the county may be the proper level on which to investigate the role of such traditions and collective memories. I must also confess the limitations of this analysis, which is not the best one for approaching such questions. In locating high concentrations of contention in particular areas, I have only provided the raw material for those more inclined to probe local cases.

What I can fruitfully investigate is the possible repressive effect of contention on later conflict. Amakusa county was the scene of the Shimabara Rebellion of 1638, the biggest and most sanguinary uprising of the entire era. It was also the scene of over fifty other contentious events in the years after 1638 (Hyakushō Ikki 1982: 138), compared to the national average of eleven events per county. In 1609 the people of Mito domain rose in protest over heavy taxes, killing an intendant in the process (Yamada 1984: 15). The domain, in retaliation, obliterated the offending village. Nevertheless, the domain was the scene of thirty-five contentious events during the early modern era, of which that of 1609 was simply the first. And of the later incidents, six scored a maximum of 10 on my scale of magnitude. Kuji county, moreover (where the unfortunate village had been located), saw fifteen additional incidents after 1609, with the next one occurring in 1624.

A final example can be found in Dewa Murayama county. There had been two previous conflicts there by 1638, when, as we have seen, thirty-five leaders of a protest were lured to the castle, arrested, and immediately executed (Yamada 1984: 19–20). No further episodes occurred until 1720 in Murayama county, suggesting that the events of 1638 had at least this much effect. Subsequently, however, the county witnessed a flood of conflict: 113 events in the years after 1720, four of which entailed the heaviest of penalties. Repression may have worked the first time, but after 1720 nothing sufficed to keep the people of Murayama county off the streets.

A more systematic look corroborates these anecdotes. Of the 86 counties in which contention was countered by light penalties, unsurprisingly, only 12 saw none thereafter. But of the 142 counties that were the scene of a single contentious event followed by heavy penalties, only 20 saw no further contention. In other words, 86 percent of the lightly punished counties were subsequently undeterred, but so were 85 percent of those heavily punished.[9] Moreover, of the 97 counties in which more than one contentious event

_____

[9] This terminology is admittedly loose: counties were, of course, not actually punished. Most counties were, however, quite small, and it is highly unlikely that a death penalty imposed in one village went

was followed by heavy punishments, 79 percent saw additional contention later in the era. The inconsistency we have seen may well explain why even draconian punishments such as these had an apparently minor effect on popular behavior.

When one puts together all the 238 counties scourged at least once by heavy penalties for contention, one finds that they had an average of nineteen contentious events apiece, against the national average of eleven. That is, the most heavily punished 38 percent of the 631 counties saw 65 percent of the contentious events in the era. Repression seems to have had little deterrent effect: most of the heavy punishments came early in the era, but the people appear to have gone right on contending, and gradually the regime seems to have lost its taste for repression.

Up until the Restoration, that is. Contention followed by harsh punishment after the Restoration was much less likely to be followed by further contention than it had been been under the Tokugawa. I have found forty cases in which severely punished contentious events were the last to be recorded in the counties where they occurred. Of these, 58 percent occurred during the ten years following the Restoration, and only 42 percent occurred in the 268 years of the Tokugawa era. To be sure, any given event occurring under the Tokugawa had many more years following it (in which contention might occur) than an event occurring after the Restoration. Moreover, the level of popular contention began to rise again later in the Meiji period. But in the short run, the Meiji regime's uncomprising attitude toward contention seems to have significantly constricted the opportunity structure of conflict.

Thus the Meiji Restoration seems here too to constitute a watershed, the end of the early modern era and of its characteristic patterns of popular contention. At first forms and loci remained as they were under the Tokugawa, but gradually, contention moved toward the lowlands and the cities, and especially into factories and tenanted farmlands, and the forms of contention known as ikki were eclipsed. Nevertheless, as we saw in Chapter 9, there was a very general continuity between contentiousness past and future, quite consistent with the notion of contentious subcultures. Social conflict perhaps contributed more to future levels of contention than did political conflict or protest, but the resemblances among all three and subsequent contention are more striking: those regions high in contention under the Tokugawa did indeed tend to remain cantankerous under the new state. And this tendency seems to have continued almost up until World War I. The dramatic changes in political and social structures, and in levels and distributions of economic development, make it highly unlikely that structural factors explain much of this continuity. Few alternatives to the "contentious tradition" or "contentious subculture" come to mind, and it is extremely unlikely that such traditions or subcultures did not exist—and influence behavior—far back into the early modern era.

---

unnoticed by any other village in that county, and probably neighboring ones as well.

It is thus my conclusion that popular contention in early modern Japan was not simply sound and fury. It is more than conceivable that it sapped the strength and will of the state and simultaneously enhanced its growth. Diminishment of the state, which increased subsequent opportunities for contention, took place directly, as the state simply caved in to insubordination, and indirectly, as revenues declined and state coffers emptied. Enhancement of the state primarily took the form of centralization. In the area of civil order state prerogatives, and their general acceptance, grew throughout the Tokugawa era in direct response to popular contention. One might expect the opportunities for conflict to have been constricted in consequence, but in fact, the Tokugawa state came to resemble a growing shell, overreaching itself even as its resources dwindled. The people understood this situation full well.

Another reason that growth of the state did not diminish popular opportunities to contend was that it did not take care of its own. The samurai were close to poverty by the end of the era, and their morale is easy to imagine. One of the key reasons they were so poor is that lords found it easier to cut their stipends than to risk confrontation with the people over increased taxes.

Finally, popular contention—without ever seriously questioning the status quo—ameliorated popular conditions. I speculate, moreover, that this improvement was not limited to those villages actually contending. Domains sometimes made concessions only to those immediately involved, but this strategy invited invidious comparisons by other villages. As a rule, it seems unlikely that a domain, sobered by conflict, would alter its general posture only locally. Within the village, meanwhile, the reforms of administrative practice and leadership selection emerging from popular contention led not to anything resembling democracy but certainly to broadened participation in many areas. One might expect such improvements to reduce popular grievances and interest in contention. Perhaps so, but any such reduction was countered by the effects of economic change which derived in turn from contention.

Specifically, I have maintained that the commercialization of the economy and the capital accumulation that facilitated protoindustrialization indirectly resulted from the popular contention that left an increasing share of production in the hands of the people. Such changes also generated jealousies and feelings that economic morality had been violated and made an increasing proportion of the population vulnerable to the vagaries of the rural market economy or the urban food supply. To the extent that money and leisure were essential to contention, economic change enhanced the necessary resources. It is my view, however, that economic change was primarily a source of grievances and that such grievances grew over time.

Grievances grew because the agency through which economic change acted was social change, and the social context of the Tokugawa commoner changed significantly and contentiously during the early modern era. Movements for equality of hitherto hierarchical groups within the village drove contention in both the beginning and later decades of the era, resulting, early on, in the creation of the hyakushō class and, later, in reformed villages. Also in the later years of the era, the village integration that might have enhanced the potential for contention was countered by the co-optation of local elites by the temptations of wealth and the efforts of the state, which meant to incorporate them into its own structure of social control. Thus, the social consequences of contention had mixed implications for further contention. Village integration increased resources but probably reduced grievances; social differentiation and village disintegration probably had opposite effects. I suspect that differentiation and disintegration dominated, but that differentiation outweighed disintegration, that the village or the supravillage area simply became a stage on which larger numbers of separately aggrieved groups contended. As long as people such as Bansuke were around— and I have said that their presence increased during the era—the co-optation of the village leadership did not deprive the people of leadership resources.

The process that produced people like Bansuke was primarily economic but also psychological. Contention demystified authority for the people; by the late Tokugawa period consciousness had risen and deference had decayed, largely because the vulnerability of the regime to contention had been demonstrated time and again. Certainly in the short run contention could have a depressive effect on interests in contention: it was cathartic; it gave expression to popular concepts of justice; and it ratified the social contract as ordinary people saw it. But over the long run, as the discovery of subcultures of contention suggests, popular consciousness most probably became a resource for further contention. One can make a similar argument on the elite level: contention, as evidence of disarray in the realm, was one force behind the development of philosophical schools critical of shogunal rule. But the link here is too distant for us to make much of it.

The same is the case with the Meiji Restoration. Certainly the straitened circumstances of the shogunate—fiscal decay due partly to contention—made it difficult to resist the Restoration alliance. But I have found no real link between contention and Restoration. Whatever link may appear between domain turbulence and participation in the Restoration is quite possibly spurious. I suspect that certain conditions in certain domains led both to differential levels of contention *and* to different roles in the Restoration.

The impact of popular contention in early modern Japan was substantial vis-à-vis the context, the interest-opportunity-resource constellation influencing later contention, and the lives of the people themselves. In a significant number of cases the outcome of contention was positive, if not actually successful. Such outcomes were infrequent, to be sure, but when the people were careful to organize, to be deferential and perhaps to focus on the shogunate rather than the domains, their successes were more numerous. Of course, many social conflicts brought both short-term benefits—the redistribution of the property of the unjust and the unbenevolent—and in all likelihood the long-term remolding of merchant consciousness. Yet these eventualities were never recorded as the "successful" prosecution of a coherent set of demands.

In other words, contention had benefits, and contention invited more contention—until the Restoration. After 1868, positive outcomes of all sorts diminished rapidly as the new regime cracked down. Contention dwindled, too, as would be expected from my assumption that the Japanese people were rationally calculating the costs and benefits of their actions.

As benefits invited contention, moreover, so did declining costs. Punishment was cruel but inconsistent and increasingly lax. Protest was indeed punished more heavily than social conflict, and aggressive contention more heavily than deferential, but protest and aggression sometimes went unpunished and social squabbles and obsequious supplications sometimes brought death. Urban contention—the most destructive of all—tended to escape retribution altogether. Punishment, in other words, did not fit the crime; although the benefit of contention seems to have declined during the era, the cost thereof dropped dramatically, thus relatively increasing popular attraction to contention as a means of goal attainment. At the same time, dwindling punishments represented a more open opportunity structure for contention, and contention, unsurprisingly, grew.

Until, again, the Restoration, when the payoff to contention shrank drastically and its cost rose precipitously. One might imagine that resultant popular hostility would lead to more contention, but the opposite was true: conflict faded abruptly in the early 1870s.

In confirmation of my previous findings—that punishment does not seem very deterrent—I also found that draconian punishment of popular contention did not eliminate it. Severely sanctioned localities kept right on contending. Indeed, contention seems to have fed itself. There are extraordinary regional concentrations of popular contention in early modern Japan. The notion of subcultural resources acting over time, while it must be considered in concert with structural factors, is attractive beyond the anecdotal evidence.

The notions of both rational deterrence and nonrational memories derive additional strength when we look at them in the early Meiji era. Repression imposed inconsistently and decreasingly by the shogunate did not deter. Repression imposed consistently and regularly by the Meiji regime did deter. The people did not cease to contend, but they seem to have laid back until new developments during the Meiji era brought new grievances, opportunities, and resources. And then, in more modern ways, they began to contend again.

But even though the forms, repertoires, vehicles, and channels of contention changed in Meiji Japan in ways that I feel justify the periodization of this book, the traditional or subcultural inclination of certain regions to contend did not, at least not nearly so quickly. Even under the Meiji state, as overall levels of contention declined nationwide, some areas remained more obstreperous than others. In this instance structural factors, which were drastically altered by the Restoration and subsequent events, do not seem adequate to explain what transpired. Along with reasoned calculation of the utility of contention, the Japanese people seem to have acted also on the basis of psychological resources drawn from years long past. Even with the insensitive, impersonal sorts of data used here I can see inklings of a tradition of contention as mediated by individuals' minds.

14

CONCLUSION

"The root is man. . . . The end is man." So began and ended Heinz Eulau's (1964: 3, 133) pioneering advocacy of the "behavioral persuasion" in social science research. I have tried to take his advice to heart, looking at people, insofar as possible, on their own terms—sometimes individually, sometimes in groups— as people in action, rather than as mathematical abstracts, vehicles of history, or reified institutions. I have not always succeeded, speaking often of the Farmers or the Authorities, but I have also spoken of Hachiemon, Hyōsuke, and Bansuke, and of the people of Mito, Tsuyama, Niigata, and many other places. And where I have focused on the aggregate characteristics of times and places, I have tried to indicate how the phenomena could plausibly be expected to influence popular behavior through their influence on the thoughts of individuals either individually or collectively.

Explanation has been my primary goal. I have tried to describe and interpret but, most of all, to understand why contention—in this place, for this reason, by these people, at this time, in this manner—occurred as it did in early modern Japan. I have tried to generalize and, for this reason, have couched my study in theoretical terms. I have also used theory to organize my data so as to see if a comprehensible shape results. If I have in the process illuminated theory, all the better, but I have not really tested any one theory. My goal is to understand the real more than the theoretical world, and it is my view that this world is a causally eclectic place. Attempts to test rival models of popular contention in early modern Japan (Nomiya 1992) and elsewhere (Rule 1988) have found that *all* are helpful to some extent. The past provides us with few data that uniquely measure a single concept. Many of my variables have been configurational; that is, they have implied various values of a variety of different variables. Such things as taxes, economic development, and urbanization can be measured, but they imply multiple social, political, and economic phenomena, some of which have contrary implications for contention. In this book I have capitulated to the interwoven complexity of the real world; nevertheless, used in this modest way, theory has helped me to understand popular contention with only a limited number of anomalies.

Thus the primary question I pose here is, Has theory served us—and the contentious people of early modern Japan—well? Do we now understand them and their contention better than we did? And has contention served us in our efforts to understand early modern society in Japan? In answering these questions I refer back to Figure 1, which guides my response. I have tried here to assess the relevance—separately and in tandem—of the political, social, economic, and "ideological" contexts of early modern Japan; their implications for the interests, opportunities, and resources the reasonable (if not Rational) consideration of which led people toward or away from contention of different types and intensities; the catalysis, mobilization, protagonists, and contours of contentious behavior; and the outcomes of contention for those involved, for those above and around them, and for our understanding of early modern society in Japan and elsewhere. I have tried to weigh the relative influence of some of these factors: context versus voluntarism, emotions versus hard calculation, individual versus collective considerations, politics versus economics, popular initiative versus reaction to adversaries, and payoff versus punishment. In most cases I have found that many things matter, but that rigorous attribution of unique causes is impossible.

Still, my strategy has not served me badly. The conceptual integrity of the era seems clear. The new system that emerged around 1600 produced multiple new types and processes of popular contention, which evolved along with that system and faded from view shortly after it expired in 1868. There was some repertorial carryover at both ends, but novel contexts, actors, interests, opportunities, resources, and repertoires became clear in a short period of time. And I would say that I have managed to capture this repertoire adequately. Examining popular contention in terms of its legality or illegality, its aggressive or confrontational posture, its locus in the politicosocial structure, and its magnitude has generated types of contention which vary systematically with significant aspects of the institutional and individual contexts of contention and which in turn lead toward systematically different state responses and effects on future structures and individuals. Thus, the concepts adopted here have enabled me to describe, interpret, and understand contention in discrete cases and as a totality.

Patterns of Contention

On the grossest level, there are suggestions that the frequency of popular contention was lower in Japan than in other early modern societies. I have attributed this relative quiescence not to a Japanese cultural predilection for harmony but to the separation of the nobility from the populace, to the secularism of contention, and to the low profile of the Tokugawa state. Contention took basically three forms: there was a major (and, in my data, underestimated) current of low-key social contention, a small but increasing number of large-scale and belligerent eruptions (again primarily social), and a significant but variable current of middling contention, mostly political but deferential. Overall, social contention tended to be smaller in scale but more aggressive than political protest; as I have noted, both the deference of protest and the safety of numbers would recommend themselves to any rational commoner faced with the prospect of confronting the Tokugawa state.

Patterns of contention corroborated my suggestions that commercial and protoindustrial change, consequent social change, and political decay conduced to contention. Levels of contention rose through time and then fell after the Meiji Restoration, but the composition of contention varied inversely. Overall, contention was least but protest was relatively most frequent when the government was most salient. As government moved into the background it was social conflict, not protest, which rose in response. This trend was clearest during the cycles of contention, which supported my suggestion that sharp reversals also caused contention: the cycles coincided with periods of severe dearth and other economically based stimuli, and the peaks of contention during the cycles were accounted for primarily by social, not political, contention.

Cycles and trends combined in the decades after 1720. The frequency and average magnitude of events increased, and they became more consistently nonpolitical. The eighteenth century was in fact the most distinctive period of the era. Contention increased most rapidly on a per capita basis, and both the size and the aggressiveness of contention peaked. The repertoire of contention became more variegated, with flight and end runs decreasing and coercive appeals increasing, along with village disputes, diffuse grumbling, and riots—all forms typical of more plebeian leadership and participation and less organization. And the century ended with the Temmei period, the first nationwide wave of contention, which I have said reflected not only widespread dearth but also nationalization of economic and social processes and of political problems and strategies, both elite and mass.

The spatial distribution of contention was consistent with these patterns. Total contention and social contention were greatest in the economically advanced central core, both the mountains and the Kinai economic heartland; the mountainous central core, developing but ecologically vulnerable, was a turbulent region all during the era, and over time, the greatest increases were seen in the metropolitan Kantō and Kinai, also economically and socially fluid and also home to large populations highly vulnerable to failures in the food supply. Actually, it was the hinterlands of the metropolitan areas, rapidly developing but exploited by the cities, drained of population, and more loosely governed than the core, which were the most contentious.

The general pattern, however, was one of greater contention and more social conflict in more urban areas and less contention but more political protest in the countryside. This pattern was reproduced on the national level. The periphery, less developed and more domain-governed, saw less contention but more political protest, especially the more confrontational coercive appeals, even though the domains were markedly more harsh in their response to contention. The lower magnitude of contention was as expected, but at first glance, the relative frequency of protest amid tighter rule seemed anomalous. In fact, however, it is consistent with the temporal pattern. Overall contention varied inversely, but protest directly, with what I have called government salience—the potential of the authorities to put down contention but also to be seen as *either* cause *or* cure of popular grievances. My earlier finding that contentious cycles came amid periods of intense inferred grievance comes back to mind. It is possible that in early modern society interests outweighed opportunities in the causation of contention.

The only exception to this core-periphery pattern occurred at the regional level, where a curvilinear pattern was found. Contention was high in the urban core, low in intermediate areas, and highest in the urbanized portions of the periphery—economically developed but vulnerable on both producer and consumer dimensions and loosely governed either by multiple jurisdictions or by the shogunate. This last factor again suggests the importance of governmental salience: contention in general and protest in particular were most frequent in those domains that overreached their capabilities. Thus, my suggestion that interests outweigh opportunities in the calculus of contention might be simplistic. Contention was especially frequent where both interests generated by government taxation and regulation and opportunities created by governmental weakness were high.

The possibilities of both of these situations are demonstrated in the stories of Hachiemon, Hyōsuke, and Bansuke. All three lived among people with intense grievances: the region in which Higashi Zenyōji village lay was in decline, chronically drained and disorganized by its proximity to Edo and afflicted by a tax increase at a time of dearth; Gunnai was also a poor region, beset by rapacious merchants and unresponsive rulers, albeit possessed of a high degree of social mobilization; and rugged Nanzan was afflicted by repeated changes in its administrative position and fiscal obligations. But Hyōsuke and Bansuke had some room for maneuver: in Gunnai there was little regulative force in evidence, and in Nanzan the very administrative instability that provoked the people led to elite temporizing and laxity. Hachiemon, by contrast, had few opportunities: Kawagoe domain had been unresponsive to the whole series of appeals which preceded his own, and in fact, his own role in the incident was designed to minimize its risks. Nevertheless, he acted, and he was quite possibly unsurprised at his fate. The thing to note is that despite this apparently closed opportunity structure, Hachiemon was by no means the only person willing to contend with the state.

Context and Causation

Thus, the broad patterns and specific cases of contention appear capturable with the concepts—such as context—I have adopted, and consistent with my earlier hypotheses about the influence of context on popular contention. I disaggregated this concept—arbitrarily, to be sure—into political, economic, social, and ideological or intellectual components. Politically, institutions, ideology, policy, and performance seemed to be useful dimensions of the context, and indeed, I found systematic links between context and popular contention.

Institutionally, the early modern Japanese state was autocratic and centralized but also limited, fragmented, and indirect. Such a structure was quite capable of provoking the people but did not dispose of coercive instruments sufficiently coherent to deter rational people. Where fragmentation or direct shogunal rule predominated—as in Gunnai and Nanzan—and when, as in the later years, coherence deteriorated, contention was indeed greatest and also least political in content. Where rule was tighter, as in Higashi Zenyōji, protest was relatively likely. After the Restoration, the imposition of a centralized structure initially stimulated popular contention but then closed the opportunity structure with an effectiveness that was quickly reflected in levels of conflict.

Ideologically, there were constants that facilitated an interest in contention, such as the elite's own ideals of reciprocity and benevolence, or mitigated its intensity, such as the secularism of political culture and morality. There were also striking variations. The growing realm of shogunal authority gave the people an additional resource to use against their lords; physiocratic ideas guaranteed that grass-roots commercial and protoindustrial development would lead to friction with the authorities; domain autarky meant that both grievances and opportunities for contention would vary locally; and systemic fragmentation generated many instances of elite division, an opportunity for popular leverage of which people frequently took advantage. The Restoration changed things radically. The new regime unilaterally violated the social contract, voided earlier popular justifications for remonstration, and cast the people adrift ideologically, thus stimulating interest in contention but simultaneously stripping the people of ideological opportunities and resources. A priori, one might not be able to predict whether contention would increase or decrease; to the extent that ideology had an independent effect, it looks as if resources and opportunities dominated.

In the area of policy and performance, variations across political space and time appear to have influenced contention. The state's absolutist regulatory posture belied its actual openness. Harsh but inconsistent, the state largely left the people to regulate themselves; over time it tightened its formal control but became less able to enforce its will. This bifurcation prompted me to distinguish between state development, which continued until the 1850s, and state capability, which began to decay as early as the late seventeenth century. When and where these trends were most marked, the people contended more frequently and were punished less heavily, thus leading toward even more contention later on.

Similar trends were visible in extractive policy. Economic growth and fixed tax rates reduced government revenues (and enhanced popular resources) relatively, and this reduction was exacerbated by rising elite consumption. Initially the government tried to raise taxes, with brief success in the first half of the eighteenth century. Subsequently, a rising wave of contention blocked this path, and the government resorted to a wide variety of expedients, most of which tended either to provoke the people or to hurt the nobility or both. Fiscal disorder prompted measures that increased popular economic insecurity, but it also led to less effective extraction, and the increase in contention which I expected to follow from overreach—a discrepancy between ends and means and a cumulation of interests and opportunities—is indeed in evidence. The more general pattern was contrast between areas and times in which government was either aggressive and capable or passive and inept. An interpretation based on grievances would anticipate more contention under intrusive and effective government; an interpretation based on opportunities would predict more contention under inept, laissez-faire rule. My data showed a clear tilt toward the latter, although *amid* the lower levels of contention in tightly ruled times and places it is social conflict rather than political protest which decreases the most.

This finding also turned our attention toward leadership, since the more risky political protest is driven relatively more by agency than by structure. Policy and performance conduced toward certain patterns of leadership. Tokugawa institutions created leaders, and the harshness of rule suggested that they would be predominantly institutional leaders who had little choice in their roles. One might have expected that the co-optation of local officials by the regime over time would reduce contention. Instead, the increasing inconsistency of repression apparently offset this general trend and fostered the emergence of a wider variety of leaders, thus leading to what I found: increased contention, an increasing number of nonelite commoners in its van, and an increasing volume of the nonpolitical contention in which nonelites took a more prominent role.

Again, the Meiji Restoration was a watershed. What we see in the Restoration are a surge and decline, and a dramatic politicization, of contention—all corresponding to expectations. At a time of political upheaval followed by the establishment of an unprecedentedly intrusive state, contention was unsurprisingly politicized. The initial regulatory vacuum that accompanied the Restoration was rapidly filled by centralized state institutions and self-righteous statism. It was also filled by new extractions and the commodification of land and by consistently harsher repression. The rapid falloff in contention suggests that the contradictory implications of interest and opportunity were resolved in favor of rational individual perceptions of opportunity.

The four aspects of the economic context on which I focused were the economic structure and the political economy, processes of economic change, the "social economy" of popular living standards, and government-economy relationships. The economy itself was feudal in principle and political in fact. Exploitation was the rule, the freeholding hyakushō farmer the ideal, and commerce at the discretion of the state the necessary evil. This system augured popular contention against exploitation, farmer leadership of contention, and endless friction between elites opposed in principle to (but seduced by) commerce and commoners opposed to government interference of any kind. All these factors varied across time and space. Exploitation was less in shogunal lands, but contention (especially social conflict) higher, and exploitation decreased over time, while contention increased. At the beginning of the era, lower orders contended for hyakushō status; then, as expected, the farmers became the core of contention. As this stratum became differentiated with economic growth, contention increased between the new commoner elite (or *gōnō*) and other farmers, between less and more privileged farmers, between established and *arriviste* economic groups, and between the emerging stratum of tenants and the freeholders. And the relationships I have found between economic development and contention exemplify the way in which protoindustrial and commercial development influenced contention where and when they occurred.

The most prominent aspect of economic change in early modern Japan was this protoindustrial and commercial growth. Absolute growth and economic diversification both occurred, leading to increased popular resources, the accumulation and deployment of capital, the differentiation of social groups and interests, and a steadily increasing proportion of the population which was vulnerable to market fluctuations as either producers or consumers. Combined with the inevitability of reverses and the decay of the Tokugawa state, these changes led to higher levels of overall contention (in both the highland protoindustrial core and the metropolitan regions), to increased social contention, and to a diversification of reasons, repertoires, and participants.

But I have *not* linked economic change to contention through the mechanisms of immiseration and the polarization of the peasantry. Differentiation, yes; and the declining role of freeholding hyakushō and increasing roles of lower elements, both urban and rural, did not surprise me. But overall polarization, no. And general immiseration, also no. Life was austere for most, reverses were inevitable, and poverty was certainly common. But great vulnerability could coexist with prosperity; by-employments could keep alive a tenant's dream of regaining hyakushō status; the gross level of poverty in the poorer northeast has been overestimated; and the government's bite eased over time. And macrolevel economic growth on a great scale occurred without question. The upshot was that for most people, in most places, at most times, life must have been supportable if not improving.

But what, then, of increasing contention over time and higher contention in better-off regions? My data—especially those on cycles—suggest that short-term economic changes, and the long-term social implications of economic conditions, were more important than general economic conditions per se. Change I have tried to capture with price and wage fluctuations and the notion of vulnerability. Ecological vulnerability helps to explain the magnitude of contention in the northeast, the mountainous central core, and especially the contentious parts of southern and western Honshū, Kyūshū, and Shikoku, which were vulnerable even without high levels of natural disaster. Contention in the protoindustrially developed but rugged and otherwise hardscrabble central core is clarified by producer vulnerability to market fluctuations, and understanding of the increasing and disproportionately social, plebeian, and riotous contention of the urban regions is aided by the notion of consumer vulnerability.

Finally, government-economy relationships were characterized by increasing estrangement and inept management. The government's retreats from the land tax, its increasing reliance on extractions from merchants, the nobility, and (for the shogunate) the domains, and the burgeoning of the economy outside its control all led me to expect that its salience in the popular eye would decline, and with it the political proportion of popular contention. And so I found across time, although across space I also found that those regimes which countered this trend, which overreached extractively, faced higher levels of contention of all kinds. Moreover, elite attempts to recoup their finances often led to ill-considered new extractions, thus suggesting that the economic retreat of the state would not be accompanied by a decline in the overall level of contention.

I found confirmation of the rule of decreasing state salience and increasing social conflict in the Restoration. The salience of the state increased dramatically, and so did political contention. In the short run, overall contention grew as well, although the presumably greater popular interest in contending against the new fiscal structure ran headlong into the new (non)opportunity structure, with consequences seen.

The social context of popular contention in early modern Japan was determined by a process initiated by the national unifiers of the late sixteenth century, centered upon the village, and characterized by fixed classes and fluid stratification. The process involved the national survey of landholdings (or kenchi) and official assessment of the value of each parcel of land (its kokudaka) in terms of agricultural output; the allocation of land and tax obligations first to lords and then to retainers and finally to the newly created freeholding hyakushō; and the collectivization of tax obligations and common and individual rights and duties in the village (the murauke system). These four factors all influenced the shape of popular contention profoundly. They created contentious issues; a whole dramatis personae of actors, leaders, and targets; units of mobilization; physical loci of contention; and resources for use in conflict.

The two most noteworthy components of this process were the community and the hyakushō. The community was the key middle-level factor between macrolevel context and individual considerations; it was the locus of rights, identity, property, and mutual assistance; it was the basis of economic viability and social mobilization for the people and the major target of government extraction. With the removal of the samurai to the cities the village was left with considerable room for sub-rosa activity and limited local deterrents to contention. On the other hand, I believe that the absence of elite elements in the community accounts in part for the moderation of popular contention in Japan as opposed to other early modern societies.

What deterrents did exist were in the hands of the community's own officials, among whom the headman soon became the crucial nexus of state-society contact. Throughout the era, however, and especially in its first half, the headman was the predominant leader of contentious action. His superior, the intendant or (in the domains) the county magistrate, was in a similarly key position, but the headman's role was more ambiguous and he was more cross-pressured. We cannot know how many headmen dampened contention, like Hachiemon, or forestalled it, but it seems clear that to the extent that leadership was available early in the era, it resided in them.

Over time, however, headmen were increasingly co-opted by the state. The result might have been the decapitation of popular contention, but it was not; instead, I found an increase in contention, social rather than political, led by lesser elements in the community, in forms requiring less organization and sophistication. Apparently the diminution of village solidarity did not crucially reduce popular resources for contention.

But it did diversify them, largely through the agency of social differentiation. Objective differentiation began early on, after the homogenization of the hyakushō class in the seveteenth century, and was clear by the mid-eighteenth century. Subjective differentiation followed. A rural economic elite emerged; substantial numbers of middling farmers persisted; and tenancy appeared. But even this group, and the landless as well, were kept in the village, often in decent circumstances, by protoindustrial by-employments. The consequence was more contention, more social contention, more frequent targeting of community leaders, and less frequent leadership of contention by community leaders. But the consequences were also contingent on the issues involved. In Bansuke's region of Nanzan better- and worse-off farmers made common cause in the first round of contention, but the fruits of this episode benefited only the better-off. When the small farmers continued to pursue their distinct interests, their betters turned on them, and Bansuke paid the price.

Economic decency was less accessible to the lower orders in the city. Urban poverty and an amorphous urban lower class appear to have grown over time and increasingly frightened their betters. Yet the cities were also the locus of more elaborate social control and relief systems, thus presenting a contradictory scene: presumably, acute vulnerability and interest in contention, a major demographic resource, and spatial ease of communication and mobilization, on the one hand, and concerted official efforts to reduce interests and opportunities, on the other. What I found were somewhat higher levels of contention in the city, albeit disproportionately in forms that did not necessitate extensive leadership or organization and did not run the greatest risk of provoking the authorities. I also found indications that it was the metropolitan hinterland, where interests and resources were still high but coercive structures were less extensive, rather than the core, where contention flourished the most.

Overall, patterns of contention are consistent with the aspects of the social context upon which I have focused. Contention, especially its social component, increased in magnitude and repertorial heterogeneity over time; it was, at the same time, relatively tame. It tended to be more organized, deferential, and political in the village; more amorphous, aggressive, and social in the city. It focused predominantly on community officials, with their role as target increasing gradually relative to that of leader. As social differentiation pluralized participation and repertoire, it also diversified the pool of potential leaders, with Robin Hoods such as Bansuke coming to supplement institutional figures such as Hachiemon and Hyōsuke.

As I have noted, these two types of leaders came to contention with quite different mindsets. What is striking is that all three—and their compatriots—had little awe of their samurai rulers. All three of these cases, one must note, occurred in the mid-nineteenth century, when respect for the state was at an all-time low. Nevertheless, throughout this book my evidence indicates that the Tokugawa people were "mindful" rather than either mindlessly passionate or supinely mystified. They also look rational or, perhaps, economically rational and politically moral, and much of the time moral judgments or interests seem to precede rational consideration of opportunities and resources, risks and benefits. Attempts to disentangle the two are ill-advised.

The first aspect of popular consciousness I examined was the "culture of contention"—views of the proper place and form of conflict in society and of the propriety and process of transforming grievances into contentious intent. Nationally, this culture was moderate, not radical, and focused above all else on justice, on the upholding by both better-off commoners and the state of their end of the reciprocal and benevolent social contract. Over time the legitimacy of the contentious option grew, aided by several resources, including the nationalization of contention under the concept of "public authority" and the expressly activist posture of the shogunate and by the existence of multiple standards—in other real or imagined places and times—against which to compare the status quo. Locally, we have seen, certain regions were prone to contend, despite draconian punishment, and this tendency persisted after the Restoration. It is just as likely that there were local cultures of circumspection and endurance, and we do the people a disservice by ignoring the mechanisms they must have devised to get by. Here, however, my focus is behavior, and in its absence I am handicapped.

Popular conceptions of contention evolved during the era, with aggressive contention and repertorial variety growing. Referents also became increasingly national; it would be presumptuous to assert that this contentious consciousness significantly eased Japan's transition to a modern nation-state, but both elites and people do seem to have accepted, by the early nineteenth century, the primacy of the state in this area. And although popular consciousness was thrown into utter disarray by the Restoration, with such basic concepts as right, wrong, authority, reciprocity, obligation, redress, and contract all in flux, it did not take the people long to understand the new regime as both cause and cure of their complaints.

All of which is to argue once again for popular reason. Early modern popular contention was mythic, inspired and instructed by tales of martyrs and heroes, but not mystified. The causal analysis of structural factors I shall summarize is fully compatible with a society of individual agents fully capable of conceiving of a better world and of calculating the safest and most effective way to pursue it.

Their achievement merits our attention because it did not rely on two elements common in other early modern societies where consciousness was similarly on the rise: first, a supportive or nurturant elite ideology and, second, religion. Overall, religion during the Tokugawa era was a tool of social control, not a resource for popular contention. It is conceivable that herein lies one reason for what I have suggested was the relatively low level of popular contention in early modern Japan, and also for the relative bloodlessness of contention, with Shimabara being the exception that proves the rule.

Beneath these constants, nevertheless, lay change, the pluralization of consciousness which followed upon the other contextual changes I have discussed. By the end of the era there were probably—would that my data could reveal them—three different streams of popular contentious consciousness, the first typifying the commoner elites, a second typifying freeholding farmers and propertied townsmen, and a third typifying the land- and propertyless, the poor, the itinerant, and the marginal. In consequence, I expected, and found, heterogenization of contentious motives; more proactive contention; and larger-scale, more aggressive, less organized, and less political contention. These "streams of consciousness" must not be thought of as coherent schools of thought or even organized sets of ideas; but it is not unreasonable to conceive of common interests and calculations flowing from more or less equivalent positions vis-à-vis power, property, and the productive process. I skirt the Scylla of reification here, but I also wish to avoid the Charybdis of reductionism. The clarity of roles as target or participant, the difference in motives, and the repertorial distinctiveness of these three broad groupings does not, I hope, do injustice either to individual thoughts or to collective patterns of contention.

Interests, Opportunities, and Resources

As the preceding discussion indicates, I have largely inferred popular interests, opportunities, and resources from the contextual positions of social groups, supplemented by the imputation of tendencies toward rationalism and indignant response to (contextually implied) injustice. Interests could be either hotly emotional or coolly calculated and could derive from considerations of defense and protection, gain and improvement, or moral or institutional propriety or imperative. They revolved primarily around the weight of extraction or administration, the performance of officialdom, and the economic fluctuations to which all were subject, as seen through the cultural and institutional lenses of individual, familial, and community economic viability, autonomy, and status. And often they commingled, as the multiplicity of demands made in contentious incidents makes clear.

But they also commingled with opportunities, in the complete absence of which they probably remained inert. Indeed, some have suggested that they were of minor explanatory import because they were constant in an exploitative, autocratic society; thus, only opportunities and resources are at issue. I have found little support for this view, but opportunities have still loomed large, whether as lax coercion, loose administration, elite vulnerability, or structural alternatives such as petition boxes, itinerant inspectors, and courts. And resources, although least amenable to quantitative analysis with the data at my disposal, have by all indications counted greatly, in the form of numbers and potentially contentious crowd formations, organization and unity, ritual and symbol, and leadership of various types.

Acknowledging that quantitative analysis does not do justice to resources, I proceeded, and found many of my contextual inferences confirmed. Economically, dearth, vulnerability, development, and the reversals implied by natural disaster and price fluctuations all contributed to contention—primarily through the agency of grievances, I suspect. Politically, administrative fragmentation and shogunal rule, administrative institutionalization and control, high levels of extraction, and governmental overreach all contributed—primarily by influencing the opportunity structure, I suspect. Social differentiation, mobilization, and memory seem linked to contention also, in the form of urbanization, economic development, communication links, and prior levels of contention. Social differentiation initially appears anomalous but is not: differentiation often occurred—as in sericultural regions—in a context of continued community cohesion, and where it did not, it appears to have led not to the atomization of communities but to their disaggregation into multiple groups, each with common interests and, more important, access to potential leaders. Urbanization, too, may seem anomalous given the greater coherence of social control structures in cities. Apparently, the vulnerability, density, and mobility of the city frustrated the repressive aspirations of the government.

When I combined my measures of interest, opportunity, and resources, I found support for the argument that all three count, and a more ambitious analysis of interests and opportunities alone, across both time and space, corroborated this finding. Three conclusions have emerged, however. First, some of the relationships I have found are contingent. Better-off domains found it necessary to tax their people less, and they reaped tranquillity; the most administratively stable domains taxed more heavily but also had greater warrior populations; they too reaped tranquillity; but larger, poorer, less stable, and less well policed domains extracted eagerly but ineptly and reaped turbulence. Second, political protest appears to be more the result of interests, and social conflict, of opportunities, perhaps accounting for the finding that political protest was relatively most frequent in those times and places where the opportunity for contention was apparently least; the key, I have already said, is the obtrusiveness of the polity in society and not the irrationality of protesters. Third, political protest appears to be less structurally explicable than social or political conflict. It seems to me that protest, which is less promising, more dangerous, less simply opportunistic, relies more on agency, organization, planning, and leadership—all factors poorly measured here.

Analysis not of gross magnitudes of contention but of its composition suggests further conclusions. Social conflict appears relatively frequent amid economic development, urbanism, prosperity, and short-term fluctuations, whereas protest is more the product of poor, underdeveloped, and rural places and times. In the case of social conflict, reverses appear key; in that of protest, chronic dearth. Politically, administrative fragmentation, low taxes and low regulative capacity, and governmental overreach seem to lead disproportionately to social conflict, and heavy taxes and tight, domainal rule seem to conduce to protest. Lower levels of social mobilization are correlated with higher levels of protest also, suggesting once again that protest is characteristic of those regions of the country where traditional forms of community organization and leadership remained stronger. In the areas where protest was relatively frequent, life was tough and so was the government, but the influence of economic factors in general seems greater than that of the political. Social conflict, by contrast, seems more equally influenced by both sets of factors. Still, in light of these findings and my observations on cycles of contention, I believe that in early modern society popular contention in general is initially caused more by grievances, as inferred from the conjuncture of economic factors, than by the opportunities provided by the political context.

The Contentious Process

I have broken down the contentious events actually observed into three headings: grievances, demands, and other stated reasons; the cast of leaders, participants, and targets; and the course of contention itself—all of which feed back into the descriptive and causal arguments I have made. The single most frequent type of reason involved intracommunity interests, but the most frequent broad categories of reasons and demands were economic and fiscal, with political and administrative reasons next, and other types of social and communal reasons last.

Intracommunity reasons revolved around village administration, and the demands made were for changes in officials or in their decisions; other social reasons involved status and the rights and spaces of communities themselves. In both cases the usual result was low-key social conflict. Fiscal reasons and demands almost always involved taxes, and led to medium-intensity political conflict and protest; economic reasons focused on poor harvests, food shortages, high prices, and dearth, and demands were made for relief, assistance, and the regulation of prices and trade. We can also see in the dynamic of economics and fiscality the rhythm of the agricultural calendar: autumn and winter periods of crop assessment, harvest, and tax payment saw the highest frequencies of contention, but it was primarily deferential political protest; the greatest intensity of contention came in summer, in the form of food riots.

Indeed, contention with economic roots was the most intense of all, according well with my data on cycles of contention, in which economic interests appear to have been key, in which social contention rose disproportionately, and in which the average magnitude of events increased. But there was an exception, unsurprisingly, when economic reasons led to political demands, in which case the people, as ever, tailored their tactics to their adversaries and moderated their tone. In specific incidents the tendency was for demands to proliferate. Partly this pattern resulted simply from the incorporation of different groups in the movement; partly it was a negotiating tactic; and partly it was responsive to the actions of adversaries. Popular mindfulness is quite clear: regardless of reasons or demands, contention among the people was more aggressive than when the people confronted the state.

My data on reasons and demands generate other conclusions when placed in the flow of time. Economic reasons rose but then leveled off during the era, once again suggesting that poverty was not, overall, on the rise. Intracommunity reasons fell with the homogenization of the hyakushō class and then rose with differentiation, whereas political reasons fell with the retreat of the state and later rose amid the politicization of the end of the era. Fiscal reasons fell throughout the era as the state gradually backed off from extractions from the people. Although the repertoire of contention did not change immediately with the Restoration, reasons and demands did. What we see in the early Meiji era is new motivational wine in old behavioral bottles.

I have said that leadership in early modern Japan can be treated as a natural feature of the social landscape: where there were communities, there were institutional leaders such as Hachiemon and Hyōsuke; where there was socioeconomic flux, there were rapscallions such as Bansuke. In neither case do we have to explain extraordinary circumstances that might make leadership rational: it was *ordinarily* rational. Recognizing that it was permits us to delve more deeply into catalysis—the stimuli that brought leaders and followers together—but leadership deserves attention also.

In the first place, the very proposition that institutional leadership was a constant confronts the fact that, over time, it was *not* constant. Co-optation drew community officials away from their people, and differentiation drew the people away from them; nevertheless, contention increased. My response is that differentiation spawned a multiplicity of occupational and socioeconomic groups within and crosscutting the community, that solidarity within these groups was possible, and that they had access to leaders. Further, this evolution of participation and leadership influenced patterns of contention: institutional leaders were much more likely to lead low-intensity, deferential, organized forms of contention, especially political protest. Lower-strata and occupational group leaders—whose numbers rose over time—were, by contrast, more likely to lead aggressive, less organized forms of social conflict. Sometimes, of course, the leaders, like the unfortunate Hachiemon, were simply following their followers, but it is unlikely that they did not influence tactics at all.

In general, however, there are parallels between leaders and followers. Three-fourths of the recorded leaders, throughout the era, were community officials; roughly 60 percent of the recorded participants, throughout the era, were either landholding farmers or propertied townsmen. Both imply the mainstream conventionality of contention and the importance of calculated interests and rights and sophisticated organization, not misery, desperation, or impulse. And both were deferential and political in their actions. The lower social strata, while involved much more in social conflict, also had a predilection for low-magnitude contention. When social organizations contended, conflict tended to be more intense; in particular, they tended to start with litigation and, if unrequited, end up in coercive appeals. It was the social extremes, though, that were both most political and most aggressive. At the beginning of the era warrior groups fought violently against the establishment of the new regime, and in its later decades marginal social groups became the core of both coercive appeals and riots. The gradual downward movement of the social center of contentious gravity makes it clearer why the average magnitude of incidents increased over time and why less organized forms of action increased also.

In fact, when we combine data on the targets of contention with those on participants, what we see is a general depoliticization of contention in early modern Japan. In the years before 1750, 26 percent of the contention involved lesser orders among the commoners opposing their betters; after 1750 the proportion rose to 43 percent. In contrast, 35 percent of the events before 1750 involved mainstream commoners contending with the authorities; after 1750 this proportion fell to 14 percent. Throughout the era, lesser commoners tended to contend with their betters; the betters, however, became less eager to contend with the state: such contention accounted for 56 percent of the mainstream groups' contention before 1750 but only 31 percent thereafter. As time passed, the frequency with which commoner political and economic elites were the targets of contention increased, while that of samurai officials declined. Partly the trend may have resulted from the increasing role of groups less inclined to contend with the state, but even more, I think, it came from the reduced salience of the state.

In consequence, contention stayed closer to home as the era wore on. Targets of contention who were within the community tended overwhelmingly to be commoners, and almost all such contention was social. Extracommunity targets were overwhelmingly samurai officials, and the accompanying actions were overwhelmingly protest. Thus the act of going beyond the village and that of confronting the state were largely one and the same. In either case the decision was a major one, and the farther people went, the more careful they became: political protest against intracommunity targets was deferential, but not so deferential as that against extracommunity ones, and the higher up the administrative ladder the target was situated, the more deferential the protest. Social conflict, whether in or out of the community, was more aggressive. Perhaps both deference to authority and the indignation brought to bear on commoners were calculated estimates of what the contentious market would bear.

In any case, the notion of calculation reemerges. I have assumed that such calculations tended to be rational, based on the pursuit of "public goods," dependent on predictions of the behavior of both allies and adversaries, and governed by community and cultural rules and popular memory. These assumptions have served us well, for in their light, the inception of contention is not difficult to understand. It *is* difficult to predict. And my attempts at prediction have been far more general than I like, making contention look distastefully automatic: where people with an interest in contention can gather in sufficient numbers to suggest both safety and efficacy, where the context permits such gatherings and the planning thereof, and where potential leaders are present—there we will find contention.

My model is a bit more nuanced than this schematic. In early modern Japan it looks as if group mobilization and defiance, although reciprocally causal, were most often linked as cause and effect, and leadership—the presence of persons for whom leading was a rational course of action—preceded both but was more often preexistent rather than called forth by the stimuli that prompted the contention. Sometimes groups formed and then seized upon this leadership; sometimes leaders generated the groups. The size of the initial gathering was determined primarily by community size; that of the eventual movement, less by organization and communication than by the geographical scope of the stimuli.

But we still face the question of catalysis. Whence comes the event that brings leaders, plans, and people together? Here the actions of elites are key. It is sudden changes in interests, opportunities, or resources, or in the number of people with certain interests, opportnities, or resources, which catalyze contention, and such changes are usually elite-generated. Elite responses to dearth, to fiscal exigency, and to popular indignation at official misbehavior or incompetence are hard to predict, and popular responses to them are equally so. We can "postdict" that there was more contention in shogunal lands than in the domains, but we cannot say if it is because the shogunate was more provocative or less competent or because within the relatively open opportunity structure of the house lands mild provocation sufficed to rouse the people. Assumptions of contextualized rational consideration of interests, opportunities, and resources help us to understand both leadership and participation; examination of the reasons and demands behind contention help us understand its motivations and goals; and context helps us understand why which regimes might in general do the things they did, but where and how and why a sufficient catalyst appears remains inaccessible. Fortuna has frustrated us.

Catalysts there were, nonetheless and contention did occur, in ways that do not defy understanding. After its inception, it took shape in explicable ways. Most of the events I have examined unfolded within the span of a single day; even so, I have found extraordinary preparations, with careful organization, multiple tactics, and contingencies taken into account. The overall pattern was interactive and complex. The influence of interests, plans, leaders, and mainstream social elements seems to have been relatively greatest at the outset of contentious events, giving way relatively to opportunities, quick response to official actions, spontaneous popular actions, and lower social strata. Initial demands tended to fade, and new demands to emerge, often in response to elite actions. Detailed plans unraveled quite soon, replaced by contingent flexibility: the people tended to adapt quickly to the actions of their adversaries. They were less chess players— mapping long sequences of contingent moves—than "garbage can planners" (March and Olsen 1989) making do quickly with whatever the evolving opportunity structure presented.

A conciliatory structure seems to have worked if adopted early on. A repressive structure seems to have intensified contention when used early in the process but always worked ultimately. Early conciliation, with the later threat of repression, seems to have been the most effective strategy for inducing popular compliance. Put differently, I hypothesize that initial response to the interests that were initially relatively important worked, whereas once an event was under way, interests faded in relative importance and the officials had to tighten the opportunity structure in order to restore order. In any case, however, very soon in the process it became difficult for any one leader or group of leaders to maintain control: people in different places, faced with different opportunities amid a fragmented political structure, began to go their own ways. Partly leaders were eclipsed because lower, less disciplined social elements often joined contentious events in progress, as happened in Gunnai. Partly it was because the pluralization of opportunity, in tandem with popular opportunism, led to tactical proliferation. The different leadership types were not infinitely flexible: institutional leaders tended to prefer disciplined, deferential political tactics; leaders from lower social strate preferred less organized and more aggressive social tactics. Sometimes the two proceeded in parallel, as in Nanzan; sometimes the lower swamped the higher, as in Gunnai.

In any case, some combination of spontaneous fatigue or disintegration and official repression or concession put an end to the event. Sometimes participants wreaked havoc on miscreant merchants and returned home in moral triumph; sometimes they lost in court or official audience, simply drifted away, or fled from government troops. Such demobilization usually took the same snowball form as the initial mobilization—communities and groups of communities joined and withdrew as units—but the result was the same. With a few exceptions, such as the fugitive Hyōsuke, the people then waited in their communities for the government to reveal the denouement of the drama.

This act was not long in coming. It was difficult to predict, because the authorities were often initially placatory, especially in the face of deferential contention and political protest. Substantive concessions were made with significant frequency, especially when the people were deferential or when they confronted the shogunate rather than the domains. But punishment was frequent too—especially in response to aggressive contention and protest—and often cruel, and the authorities almost never recognized the legitimacy of popular contention, even if they acknowledged the merits of a complaint. Even successful contention did not set an official precedent.

Nevertheless, subjective popular precedents accumulated: examples of inconsistent punishment, official responsiveness or even timorousness, successful evasion of retribution, and successes so crucial that even their sanguinary aftermath did not deter emulation. Such precedents increased in number over time, and the regime lost the will and ability to enforce its rules and prerogatives. It put on an initially more threatening face in response to contention, and the people seem to have won fewer payoffs with time, but the punitive cost of contention went way, way down, and one need not presume a very great degree of popular rationality to foresee that contention would spread, or that it would fade quickly once the Meiji regime reversed the posture of the Tokugawa state.

I have therefore maintained that contention contributed something positive to the popular condition in early modern Japan. It did so directly, through government concessions, and also indirectly, through its impact on the system. Indirect effects are hard to demonstrate and must remain speculative. Still, I have found evidence that popular contention influenced the political context: public policy moved away from the basic land tax and toward the impoverishment of the samurai, and it increasingly diverged from government practice. The increasing harshness and increasing inconsistency of punishment reflected the contradiction between state growth and state capabilities and were but one manifestation of the decay of the Tokugawa state.

Contention also influenced government personnel—clearly, when officials were punished, and ambiguously, when officials were sobered by the knowledge that colleagues had been forced to commit ritual suicide. It influenced political structure as well. Both the coercive and the judicial apparatuses of the Tokugawa state were elaborated in order to cope with contention; domain boundaries were redrawn in consequence of contention; and villages were restructured either from above or by themselves in response to popular challenge.

The economic context, too, was shaped by contention. Specifically, I have suggested that commercialization, monetization, and capital accumulation were all encouraged by the changes in fiscal and economic policy prompted by contention. And these changes in turn influenced the social context, contributing to social mobility and differentiation, to the emergence and estrangement of commoner elites, to the proliferation of interests, and to the contention that ensued.

Finally, one may speculate that the Japanese people both reaffirmed the legitimacy of traditional consciousness and developed new images of themselves, of the state, and of contention through their own behavior. They were neither blind to the decay of the state nor forgetful of the contententious precedents set by others nor cowed by repression—at least until the Meiji era. The early modern era was for them a time of learning by doing, since the state was hardly inclined to facilitate their remonstrations.

What they learned was that both grievances and solutions were less and less political. But their overall interest in contention did not decline, since both chronic and short-term economic problems, the mysterious but often malign workings of the market, the inequities of status and wealth, and a host of other factors were always with them in varying degree. Over time, opportunities to contend both among themselves and with the state grew, partly as the result of prior contention itself. Among the long-term results of contention were enhanced resources for contention: a raised consciousness and a rich memory made contention increasingly thinkable, and social differentiation, while unquestionably destroying the unity of many communities, seems to have led not to a decline in the overall mobilization potential of society but to an *increase* in *smaller* social, economic, and occupational units of mobilization.

Finally, the aftermath of contention reaffirms my conviction that the clearest view of popular contention is through the lenses of structure or context, culture or memory, and agency or choice. I have found great local differences in the magnitude of contention, which can be largely but not completely explained by the conjuncture of structural factors. I have also found that contention endured there and elsewhere regardless of repression, suggesting both the ongoing influence of conjuncture and the ongoing ability of the people to calculate the link between ends and means. And I have found a continuity of contention across the structural and conjunctural chasm of the Restoration, which bespeaks powerful memories and cultures of contention as well as enduring structures of preferences and strategies of choice.

Thus the question of significance has been addressed. Contention in early modern Japan was popularly significant. It made a meaningful difference in the minds and lives of the people and, more than likely, on balance, a positive one. Hachiemon might not have agreed with this assessment; Hyōsuke might have agreed that his odyssey was at least a learning experience; and Bansuke might have felt the whole thing was worth it, even his ill-advised provocation of the poorer peasants.

I am a bit less certain that contention was systemically significant, though it does appear that meaningful systemic changes are at least consistent with the aggregate effect of contention over many years, and this aggregate outcome may well have included modification of the relationship between state and society. Again, contention has much to teach us about the politics, economy, society, and culture of early modern Japan.

It is also theoretically significant. It seems to me that such notions as indignation and calculation, agency and structure, state growth and capability, institution and choice, interest, opportunity, and resource, and magnitude and repertoire are useful tools in the understanding of contention. Finally, I assert the methodological significance of quantitative analysis as a fruitful tool in the understanding of contention, even in ages long past with records of dubious nature. I have abstracted and aggregated Hachiemon, Hyōsuke, Bansuke, and thousands like them and made sweeping generalizations about their times, their home places, their neighbors and overlords, their political and economic circumstances, and their ideas. I have done so with abandon but not arbitrarily, and I have tried to bring my arguments back to them, arguing in principle from my numbers and in fact from historical cases. Originally, they led small lives; with the help of a variety of data, I have tried to make them larger than life. I began with them and end with them. They contended, against great odds, with the political and economic forces of their age, and it is the least we can do for them—even for Bansuke.

APPENDIX 1

THE AOKI KŌJI DATA

The data included in Aoki Kōji's *Hyakushō Ikki Sōgō Nempyō* (1981) were compiled from a wide variety of national and local sources, each documented along with the entry for each event. These documents are being separately collected and published by the Azekura Publishing Company as *Hennen Hyakushō Ikki Shiryō Shūsei*, under the editorial direction of Hosaka Satoru. To date, volumes containing materials through the 1830s are complete. The data in this file, however, are coded from Aoki (1981).

The Aoki data are not directly comparable with the data used in most other quantitative studies of collective behavior. Other studies have emphasized deaths from political violence as a measure of magnitude of contention, whereas the types of conflict analyzed here resulted in recorded deaths (not including government-inflicted deaths) in only 2 percent of cases. Another difference is the use of number of participants as an inclusion criterion in many studies; the Aoki data set includes all events found in local histories, official records, diaries, and other sources, regardless of size. Moreover, since many events in the set represent the acme of a movement rather than the entire movement, there was, in all likelihood, a background of low-level contention and dissent significantly greater than that indicated here. Much of it, however, was routine and legal, and I do not wish to include it here.

Indeed, many events comprised a sequence of multiple separate incidents. I have focused on the events, first, because my goal is explanation and in one sense all an event's component incidents have the same causes and, second, because many preliminary incidents didn't amount to protest, though the acme of the event may have. Thus, overreporting would be a much greater problem if the focus were on single incidents (Tong 1991: 28–29). Still, one of the major problems in conflict studies—incommensurable data sets—is not overcome in this book; it handicaps my attempts to test different theories from the field.

My primary goal is the understanding of empirical phenomena, for which in their own right the Aoki data are far better than anything else available. They are, in the opinion of specialists in the field (Aoki Michio, Fukaya Katsumi, personal communications), accurate as far as they go. It appears to be agreed that Aoki included nearly all the political protest that occurred during the period covered. It is felt that he substantially underrepresented social conflict: it is unlikely that any of Japan's sixty thousand to seventy thousand villages went for almost three hundred years without any open social conflict. Aoki has not, however, apparently been biased regionally or temporally (beyond the improving documentation over time [Aoki K. 1966: 63]) in his underrepresentation. The one data set against which Aoki may be checked, Harada Tomohiko's (1982: 360–63) on urban protest and riots, indicates substantial underrepresentation but very close parallels in geographical and temporal distribution (compare with Aoki K. 1981: 32–33). Thus one should treat the data as a sample of social and political conflict and protest during the era rather than the universe of contention. It underestimates conflict during the seventeenth century more than subsequently, and it underestimates social conflict relative to political protest. But although Aoki's data must be used with care for description, the explanatory patterns, changes over time, and interregional differences do not appear seriously biased.

Previous quantitative studies of popular contention in Tokugawa Japan—all using Aoki's data (Yokoyama 1977; Sugimoto 1975, 1978)—have been done at the provincial level. Given the statistical problems noted (Tong 1991) and the great disparities within the seventy-four provinces in both economic conditions and levels of contention, it is preferable to approach the subject on a smaller scale (Nakamura 1964b: 190). Popular contention in that era was most commonly collective, the unit of mobilization of which was the village, but there are almost no nationwide village-level data sets. Even within counties there is more economic heterogeneity than is desirable (although the average county was only some 180 square miles), but the county is still closer than the province to the ideal unit of analysis. In my search for mutually corroborative findings with data from different sources, however, I conduct my analyses on the domain and provincial levels also.

APPENDIX 2

MAGNITUDE AND TYPE OF CONTENTION

The primary dependent variable in this study is the magnitude of contention, calculated both for different types of contention and for the total amount of contention occurring in each of the spatial units (631 counties, or *gun*; 74 provinces, or *kuni*; 363 feudal domains, or *han*; and 46 prefectures, or *ken*) and temporal units (288 years) included in the Aoki data described in Appendix 1. Thus, two variables are needed: a typology of contentious events and a measure of the magnitude of each. Such typologies are not hard to find for popular contention in early modern Japan, but all of them are based either on the causes of conflict or on categories such as petition, protest, village dispute, and riot— often official legal terms with little relation to the magnitude of the events described.[1] Some typologies derive only from the legal terminology of the time— for example, for the Tokugawa authorities the most important aspects of contention were deliberate concert (*totō*), display of any weapons (including farm implements), and contravention of regular, legal channels of remonstrance. These distinctions were made without any regard for cause, magnitude, participants, or quality of contention, in the same way that a "riot" in early modern England was simply a legal category, a contentious assemblage whose participants, after having had the Riot Act read to them, still refused to disperse. At the other extreme are merchants' appeals (kokuso or kuniso) and millenarian movements (yonaoshi), which imply specific actors, targets, and objectives. In other cases the derivation of the categories is even less helpful: two of Aoki's major types are urban contention (toshi sōjō) and village disputes (murakata sōdō), the criteria for which are simply locational.

---

[1] Aoki K. 1981; Yokoyama 1977; Borton 1938; Kokushō 1971.

Measures of magnitude are rarer; to date only two quantitative studies of Tokugawa-era protest have been made, and both weighted events according to the formal categories used by Aoki (Yokoyama 1977; Sugimoto 1978). These categories cannot be ignored, since supplementary data on the magnitude of conflict are missing for many of the events in the Aoki *Nempyō*. The fact that many events actually combine types of contention (e.g., a village dispute followed by a petition, or a petition accompanied by a riot) and the tendency for categories of intensity to be assigned according to the form of activity rather than its duration or intensity make a more elaborate typology and measure of magnitude advisable.

The first step was to code as many of the events in the Aoki *Nempyō* as possible according to Aoki's own categories. These categories, and additional categorical descriptors appearing in the entry for each event, were used for a maximum of two descriptors per case. The result was sixty-nine different types of events; 7,370 of the total 7,664 events in the *Nempyō* (96 percent) had at least one such descriptor assigned to them. This raw taxonomic resource far surpasses in detail the six to eight types of events used by Aoki and other historians to date. Some of these types, however, represented overlaps in judgment by coders and some represented the content or objectives of contention (e.g., "tax strike") rather than its form; consequent refinement of types reduced the number of types to fifty-two.

The next step was to impose some theoretically meaningful order on the types derived from the *Nempyō*. Three intuitively important dimensions of contention appear repeatedly in the literature on popular protest: (a) whether a form of collective behavior was legal or illegal; (b) whether behavior was nonviolent or violent; and (c) whether contentious behavior was within the commoner class or was directed at the warrior nobility or formal or informal agents of government.[2] The rationale for this dimensionality is threefold. First, both legality and "verticality" reflect the assumption that whether or not contention impinges upon the (coercive) state has powerful implications for its consequences (including the state's response) and, hence, for the individual and collective calculus that precedes it. Moreover, we would expect both illegal and "vertical" action to reflect more intense interests, greater resources, and wider opportunities than legal contention between commoners.

Second, intra- or interclass nexus reflects the assumption that the extent to which groups of commoners contend among themselves as equals, against their betters, or directly against the state reflects context: class structure, the salience of the state in society, the cohesion of communities, economic structures and the

---

[2] The dimension of legality draws on, or was considered important in light of, Zimmermann 1983: 12; Muller 1979: 4–6; Bohstedt 1983; and Manning 1988. The dimension of violence draws on Barnes, Kaase, et al. 1979; Gamson 1975; Tarrow 1994; Sanders 1981; Oberschall 1973; Tilly et al. 1975; Gurr 1980: 2ff.; and Piven and Cloward 1979. The dimension of verticality draws on Gurr and Duval 1976; Tilly et al. 1975; Tilly 1978a, 1981; Perry 1980; Hobsbawm 1959; and Rudé 1964.

course of economic change, and popular attitudes about the justifications and limits of dissent and the obligations of government and one's fellows. Third, aggressiveness hypothetically reflects the quality of both intraclass and state-society relationships and, again, has far-reaching implications for impact and state response (DeNardo 1985). I wish to see *who* acted vis-à-vis *whom*, and *how*, on the assumption that variation on all three of these dimensions will result from different contextual circumstances, different mixes of interests, opportunities, and resources, different catalytic phenomena, and different decisional calculi; will involve different mobilizational processes and trajectories; and will entail different consequences.[3]

Therefore these three themes, somewhat elaborated, were adopted, and each of the fifty-two types of contention was categorized as:

1. Legal or ambiguously legal (1) *or* illegal (2);
2. Nonviolent/nonconfrontational/nonchallenging of the status quo/deferential (1) *or* disorderly, challenging (by its very disorderliness), but weak or unfocussed in its objectives, targets, and degree of dissatisfaction (2) *or* aggressively, purposively, actively, directly confrontational and challenging (3) *or* violent toward persons and/or property (4);
3. Horizontal, among individuals or groups of the commoner class (1), *or* vertical, between individuals or groups within the commoner class unequally situated in the socioeconomic or political hierarchy (2), *or* vertical, between groups of commoners and members of the ruling class or the institutions or agents of government (3).

The result of this categorizaton is the typology presented in Table A.

The next step was to create three indices based on these three dimensions and to see if these dimensions in fact bore any relationship to the empirical reality of the magnitude of the events so described. The coefficients (gammas) presented in Table B indicate that, indeed, the theoretically derived dimensions do bear substantial relation to this reality, the only surprise being that horizontal social conflict appears to have been more aggressive and destructive than vertical political protest. Communal contention may be smaller in scale but more intense (because the contenders were more equally matched in coercive resources?),

---

[3] What these categories do *not* imply is objectives or goals held by either the challengers or their targets. For one thing, many actions had multiple objectives: commoner manifestoes of twenty or thirty separate grievances were not rare. Therefore, for example, the "political" in political protest refers to actors, not objectives. That is, the approach of this study is both structural and voluntaristic, and the initial assumption is that different groups living within certain structures, under different circumstances, will adopt different contentious means to pursue similar goals; *and* that different groups may choose the same means to pursue different goals. In many instances the class composition of the actors, the circumstances under which they act, and their stated demands permit inference of their motivations, but the relationship of objectives to categories of contention is an empirical question, not part of the categories themselves.

Table A. Categories of conflict based on three dimensions

Legal/ illegal	Deferential/ violent	Horizontal/ vertical	Type of event	Category of conflict
1	1	1	1. *Yoriai* (meeting)	Societal
			2. *Murahachibu* (intravillage social ostracism)	Societal
			3. *Kyōron* (village boundary dispute)	Societal
			4. *Suiron* (dispute over water rights)	Societal
			5. *Noron* (dispute over fields)	Societal
			6. *Sanron* (dispute over village rights to mountain land and rights to forest products)	Societal
			7. *Gyoron* (dispute over fishing rights)	Societal
			8. *Irefuda* (village election dispute)	Societal
			9. *Zaron* (dispute concerning shrine-related village group)	Societal
1	1	2	10. *Yōkyū* (unspecified request or demand)	Societal
			11. *Funsō* (quarrel or dispute)	Societal
			12. *Deiri* (quarrel or dispute)	Societal
			13. *Murakata sōdō* (inter- or intravillage conflict)	Societal
1	2	2	14. *Kosaku/hikan sōdō* (tenant dispute)	Societal
			15. *Hyakushō sōdō* (dispute among or disorderly behavior by farmers)	Societal
			16. *Fushinnin* (vote or decision of no confidence in village official[s])	Societal
			17. *Kyūdan* (accusation of, e.g., village official malfeasance)	Societal
			18. *Gishin* (expression of suspicion, accusation)	Societal
1	1	3	19. *Shūso* (orderly petition or complaint)	Litigation
			20. *Hakoso* (petition placed in official petition box)	Litigation
			21. *Kuniso* (merchants' plea for commercial respite or advantage)	Litigation
			22. *Soshō* (litigation)	Litigation
			23. *Negai* (plea, petition)	Litigation
			24. *Uttae* (plea, petition, litigation)	Litigation
1	2	3	25. *Fuon* (disorderly or contentious gathering)	Political
			26. *Tonshū* (disorderly or contentious gathering)	Political
			27. *Shōshū* (disorderly or contentious gathering)	Political
2	1	3	28. *Chikuden* (flight)	Political

continued

Table A. *continuing*

Legal/ illegal	Deferential/ violent	Horizontal/ vertical	Type of event	Category of conflict
			29. *Chōsan* (flight)	Political
			30. *Hariso* (complaint, plea, demand posted about or on wall or gate of relevant office)	Political
			31. *Suteso* (complaint, plea, demand scattered about the streets or before relevant office)	Political
			32. *Rempan* (circular, usually of signatures, demands, or action plans)	Political
2	2	2	33. *Kome sōdō* (rice conflict or riot)	Societal
			34. *Yonaoshi* (attack on rich merchants or farmers)	Societal
			35. *Gōdan* (parley held under coercive conditions)	Societal
			36. *Toshi sōjō* (urban conflict or riot)	Societal
			37. *Sutoraiki* (labor strike)	Societal
2	2	3	38. *Kagoso* (complaint, plea, demand presented to official in his palanquin)	Political
			39. *Jikiso* (complaint, etc., presented to official above official of first jurisdiction, end-run appeal to higher office)	Political
			40. *Osso* (another term for end run)	Political
			41. *Kadoso* (complaint, etc., left at gate of official's office or residence)	Political
			42. *Kakekomiso* (complaint, etc., lodged after entering office without permission)	Political
			43. *Rōjō* (shutting up or fortifying group in defiant position)	Political
			44. *Suwarikomi* (sit-in, sit-down strike)	Political
			45. *Totō* (conspiracy; gathering with apparently specific intent to protest)	Political
2	3	3	46. *Gōso* (complaint, etc., lodged aggressively, confrontationally, in defiance of proper procedures)	Political
2	4	2	47. *Uchikowashi* (destructive riot)	Societal
2	4	3	48. *Sōran* (riot or insurrection)	Political
			49. *Hanran* (riot or insurrection)	Political
			50. *Dogō ikki* (insurrection)	Political
			51. *Buryoku tōsō* (armed insurrection)	Political
			52. *Hōki* (insurrection or rebellion)	Political

Table B. Correlations (gammas) between three dimensions of conflict and measures of magnitude of conflict

	Three dimensions of conflict		
		Type of action	
	Legal or illegal	Deferential or violent	Horizontal or vertical
Action involves			
Threatening behavior	0.78	0.79	−0.10 (n.s.)
Aggressive behavior	0.83	0.81	−0.21
Destruction of buildings or property	0.94	0.86	−0.71
Duration of event in days	0.52	0.56	0.03 (n.s.)
Number of villages involved	0.57	0.57	0.63
Number of participants	0.67	0.67	0.30

Varimax rotated factor analysis of six measures of magnitude of conflict		
	Factor 1: Scale of event	Factor 2: Aggressiveness
Action involves		
Threatening behavior	0.09	0.95
Aggressive behavior	0.08	0.95
Destruction of buildings or property	0.20	0.80
Duration of event	0.68	0.04
Number of villages involved	0.85	0.07
Number of participants	0.80	0.24

whereas political protest may be larger in scale but relatively deferential (people couldn't outgun the government, but they could outnumber it).

Given three empirically and theoretically meaningful dimensions of contention, the next step was to reduce the fifty-two types of contention according to them. Therefore a new index was created in which each event was given a three-digit code in accordance with its values, for the first descriptor given for it, on the three dimensions of contention. For example, an at-least-probably legal, politically nonchallenging, horizontal intervillage dispute would be coded 111 on this index, as suggested by the first three columns of Table A. This index, as one may gather from the twelve groupings of event types in Table A, has twelve categories (N.B., this is a categorical variable).

Next, I investigated whether or not these categories differ empirically, in two steps. I looked at the mean score of all events in each category on each of the six measures of contention shown in Table B. (To make sure that these groups were relatively homogenous, especially on the horizontal-vertical dimensions, I examined the relative social position and political status of actors and target groups/individuals/institutions for each major type of event.) Since factor analysis of the six measures (see Table B) indicated two clear dimensions of contention—scale or

Table C. Ranking of event categories in terms of measures of magnitude of conflict

Category of Events[1]	1 Average of means of cases in category on 3 measures of aggressiveness of behavior	2 Average of means of cases in category on 3 measures of size of incident	3 Sum of averages	4 Sum of averages converted to 10-point scale	5 Summary magnitude score	6 Mean of cases in category on factor-score-based measure of aggressiveness of behavior	7 Mean of cases in category on factor-score-based measure of size of incident	8 Sum of means	9 Sum of means converted to 10-point scale	10 Summary magnitude score
1-2-2	-14	-52	-76	1.00		-23	-24	-47	1.22*	
1-1-2	-33.7	-31.3	-65	1.27	1	-34	-21	-55	1.00*	1
2-1-3	-32.7	-21.7	-54.4	1.54		-34	-12	-46	1.24	
1-1-3	-39	-6	-45	1.75		-46	23	-23	1.86*	
2-2-3	-38	-5	-43	1.80		-44	18	-26	1.78*	
1-2-3	-9.3	-3.3	-12.6	2.53	2	-9	0	-9	2.24	2
2-3-3	14.3	47	61.3	4.33		13	41	54	3.94	
2-2-2	97.7	-21	76.7	4.72	5	110	-40	70	4.37	5
1-1-1	30	58.7	88.7	5.01		30	45	75	4.50	
2-4-2	226.7	65.3	292	9.95		239	35	274	9.87	
2-4-3	135.7	158.7	294.4	10.00	10	123	156	279	10.00	10

1. See Table A.
* These two pairs of event types do not follow a strict low-to-high progression

Table D. Qualitative classification of events in cases of multiple descriptors

The secondary descriptor indicates a form of	The primary descriptor indicates that the event is a form of		
	Litigation or legal plea	*Social conflict among commoners*	*Remonstration or protest behavior*
Litigation or plea behavior	Litigation/ petition	Political conflict	Political protest
Social conflict among commoners	Political conflict	Social conflict	Political protest
Remonstration or protest behavior	Political protest	Political conflict	Political protest

size (duration, number of participants, and number of villages involved) and aggressiveness (presence or absence of threatening or overtly aggressive behavior and number of structures destroyed or damaged)—the mean of the means of the events in each code category for each group of three magnitude measures was calculated and the two means were summed; the sums and the ranking of each category of contention on a 10-point scale are presented in Table C, columns 3 and 4. To corroborate this calculation and produce an interval measure of magnitude, the two factors emerging from the six measures of magnitude were also used to create two factor-score-based variables, "aggressiveness" and "size." The mean score of each category of events on each of these two variables was calculated and the categories again ranked on a 10-point scale (Table C, columns 8 and 9). On each scale, four natural groupings of the same categories appeared with only the two slight, asterisked, within-group discrepancies noted in column 9; the spacing of these clusters suggested the creation of a single new variable, "magnitude of contention," with values of 1, 2, 5, and 10. Each of the 7,370 typed events was therefore coded 1, 2, 5, or 10 on the basis of the category in which its first descriptor placed it. If missing on the primary descriptor (i.e., if the Aoki *Nempyō* did not formally classify it but described it with one of the accepted descriptors in the body of the entry for the event), then the secondary descriptor was used. For events that bore two descriptors, the larger (in magnitude) was used; thus, a communal conflict (murakata sōdō) that became a full-blown insurrection was coded as 10, not 1. The total conflict magnitude score for a given spatial or temporal unit then became the sum of the number of events of each type occurring in that unit multiplied by the magnitude of each event.

On the basis of the literature and examination of the social, economic, and political relationships between actors and targets shown in the *Nempyō* data, the fifty-two types of contention were divided into three categories—litigation, pleas, and petitions; social contention between groups of commoners; and political protest by commoners against the state—as shown in the last column of Table A. If only one descriptor was given or if both descriptors were in the same category, then that became the event's category. Combinations of descriptors were coded as shown in Table D, producing four types of contention: litigation and petition, social conflict, political conflict, and political protest. The "political conflict" category comprises events that (a) began as social conflict but resulted in political action not in the form of antigovernment protest but for purposes of seeking adjudication, restitution, compensation, or punishment; or that (b) eventuated in protest as the result of an official response to some contentious social event; or that (c) consisted of litigation or petitioning the focus of which was some social conflict. In the analyses presented here, magnitudes of contention in each spatial or temporal unit are calculated and analyzed for the totality of conflict and for three of the four types of contention.

Popular contention itself is defined for my purposes as a gathering in public or in a publicly accessible place in which people collectively state demands, grievances, or other claims outside of accepted, legal, conventional channels of interest articulation, claims that, if realized, would affect the interests of people outside the group.[4] "Claims" range from direct (verbal or physical) attack on a person or object to laying out a program to statements of opposition or petition; and "outside the group" includes the state, although a contentious event need not actually include interaction between contenders. One contender may be a target without being an active participant. Indeed, one type of event used here is *fuon*, "unrest" or "disquiet," which refers to gatherings at which grumbling and murmuring were the extent of activity. Contention excludes at one extreme clandestine conspiracies (although the secret planning that preceded many a contentious event did not disqualify it) and routine meetings of public bodies at which claims vis-à-vis others which overstep the conventional authority of the body do not occur.

Contention thus excludes fully institutionalized, routinized, conventional, and legal means of asserting claims such as lawsuits and petitions, except when such actions led to, resulted from, or were otherwise part of a more disruptive and unconventional sequence of events. Therefore, unless otherwise specified, events categorized as "litigation and petition" (n = 530) are excluded from my analyses. This exclusion also brings my data more into line with reality. Yokoyama Toshio (1986: 11) maintains that the number of recorded events in a region varies to some extent with the number of active local historians there and that the number of minor incidents recorded is especially responsive to their industry. Thus, by excluding the events most sensitive to artificial regional variation, I can restrict myself to types of contention the record of which is most nationally valid.

---

[4] This definition closely follows that of Tilly 1981: 12–14, 24; 1980: 11; and Tarrow 1994: 2. It is broader than the explicitly political forms of contention defined in Muller 1979: 4–6; Gurr and Duval 1976: 140ff.; Sugimoto 1978: 274–75; and Gurr 1980: 2ff.

BIBLIOGRAPHY

Akita, George. 1967. *The Foundations of Constitutional Government in Modern Japan.* Cambridge: Harvard University Press.

Almond, Gabriel, and G. Bingham Powell. 1966. *Comparative Politics.* Boston: Little, Brown.

Anderson, Barbara. 1980. *Internal Migration during Modernization in Late Nineteenth-Century Russia.* Princeton: Princeton University Press.

Anderson, Perry. 1979. *Lineages of the Absolutist State.* London: Verso.

Aoki Kōji. 1966. *Hyakushō Ikki no Nenjiteki Kenkyū.* Tokyo: Shinsei Sha.

———. 1968a. *Meiji Nōmin Sōjō no Nenjiteki Kenkyū.* Tokyo: Shinsei Sha.

———. 1968b. *Nihon Rōdō Undō Shi Nempyō.* Vol. 1. Tokyo: Shinsei Sha.

———. 1981. *Hyakushō Ikki Sōgō Nempyō.* Tokyo: Sanichi.

Aoki Michio et al. 1981. *Ikki.* 4 vols. Tokyo: Tokyo Daigaku Shuppan Kai.

Aono Shunsui. 1988. *Daimyō to Ryōmin.* Tokyo: Kyōiku Sha.

Arakawa Hidetoshi. 1964. *Saigai no Rekishi.* Tokyo: Chibundō.

———. 1967. *Kikin no Rekishi.* Tokyo: Chibundō.

Asher, Herbert, et al. 1984. *Theory-Building and Data Analysis in the Social Sciences.* Knoxville: University of Tennessee Press.

Baerwald, Hans. 1974. *Japan's Parliament.* Berkeley: University of California Press.

Barnes, Samuel, Max Kaase, et al. 1979. *Political Action.* Beverly Hills: Sage.

Beasley, William. 1960. "Feudal Revenue in Japan at the Time of the Meiji Restoration." *Journal of Asian Studies* 19.

———. 1972. *The Meiji Restoration.* Stanford: Stanford University Press.

Beloff, Max. 1962. *The Age of Absolutism, 1660–1815.* New York: Harper and Row.

Bendix, Reinhard. 1977. *Nation-Building and Citizenship.* Berkeley: University of California Press.

———. 1978. *Kings or People.* Berkeley: University of California Press.

Bercé, Yves-Marie. 1980. *Révoltes et Révolutions dans l' Europe Moderne.* Paris: Presses Universitaires de France.

Note: Japanese names are given below in Japanese word order—surname first—except when the source cited is in English.

——. 1990. *History of Peasant Revolts*. Trans. Amanda Whitmore. Ithaca: Cornell University Press.

Berejikian, Jeffrey. 1992. "Revolutionary Collective Action and the Agent-Structure Problem." *American Political Science Review* 86.

Berry, Mary Elizabeth. 1986. "Public Peace and Private Attachment: The Goals and Conduct of Power in Early Modern Japan." *Journal of Japanese Studies* 12.

——. 1987. "Mass and Hauser, eds., *The Bakufu in Japanese History*." *Journal of Japanese Studies* 13.

Bianco, William, and Robert Bates. 1990. "Cooperation by Design: Leadership, Structure, and Collective Dilemmas." *American Political Science Review* 84.

Bird, Isabella. 1880. *Unbeaten Tracks in Japan*. New York: Putnam.

Birt, Michael. 1985. "Samurai in Passage." *Journal of Japanese Studies* 11.

Bix, Herbert. 1978. "Miura Meisuke, or Peasant Rebellion under the Banner of 'Distress.'" *Bulletin of Concerned Asian Scholars* 10.

——. 1986. *Peasant Protest in Japan, 1590–1884*. New Haven: Yale University Press.

——. 1987. "Class Conflict in Rural Japan." *Bulletin of Concerned Asian Scholars* 19.

Blalock, Hubert. 1984. *Basic Dilemmas in the Social Sciences*. Beverly Hills: Sage.

Blickle, Peter. 1981. *The Revolution of 1525*. Baltimore: Johns Hopkins University Press.

Bloch, Marc. 1964. *Feudal Society*. 2 vols. Trans. L. A. Manyon. Chicago: University of Chicago Press.

Bohstedt, John. 1983. *Riots and Community Politics in England and Wales, 1790–1810*. Cambridge: Harvard University Press.

Bolitho, Harold. 1974. *Treasures among Men*. New Haven: Yale University Press.

Borton, Hugh. 1938. "Peasant Uprisings in Japan of the Tokugawa Period." *Transactions of the Asiatic Society of Japan*, 2nd ser., 16 (May).

Bowen, Roger. 1980. *Rebellion and Democracy in Meiji Japan*. Berkeley: University of California Press.

Brameld, Theodore. 1968. *Japan*. New York: Holt, Rinehart, and Winston.

Bright, Charles, and Susan Harding, eds. 1984. *Statemaking and Social Movements*. Ann Arbor: University of Michigan Press.

Brinton, Crane. 1965. *The Anatomy of Revolution*. New York: Vintage.

Brown, Philip. 1991. "The Central-Peripheral Balance of Authority in Early Modern Japan." Paper prepared for the annual meeting of the Association for Asian Studies, New Orleans, April.

Brustein, William, and Margaret Levi. 1987. "The Geography of Rebellion: Rulers, Rebels, and Regions, 1500–1700." *Theory and Society* 16.

Burton, Donald. 1978. "Peasant Struggle in Japan, 1590–1760." *Journal of Peasant Studies* 5.

Calhoun, Craig. 1982. *The Question of Class Struggle*. Chicago: University of Chicago Press.

——. 1983. "The Radicalism of Tradition." *American Journal of Sociology* 88.

Chaliand, Gerard. 1978. *Revolution in the Third World.* New York: Penguin.

Chalmers, James, and Robert Shelton. 1975. "An Economic Analysis of Riot Participation." *Economic Inquiry* 13.

Chamberlin, John. 1974. "Provision of Collective Goods as a Function of Group Size." *American Political Science Review* 68.

Chambliss, William. 1965. *Chiaraijima Village: Land Tenure, Taxation, and Local Trade, 1818–1884.* Tucson: University of Arizona Press.

Chesneaux, Jean, ed. 1972. *Popular Movements and Secret Societies in China, 1840–1950.* Stanford: Stanford University Press.

Chong, Dennis. 1989. "All-or-Nothing Games in the Civil Rights Movement." Paper prepared for the annual meeting of the American Political Science Association, Atlanta, August.

Choucri, Nazli. 1974. *Population Dynamics and International Violence.* Lexington: Lexington Books.

——, ed. 1984. *Multidisciplinary Perspectives on Population and Conflict.* Syracuse: Syracuse University Press.

Cohen, Youssef, et al. 1981. "The Paradoxical Nature of State Making: The Violent Creation of Order." *American Political Science Review* 75.

Cohn, Norman. 1961. *The Pursuit of the Millennium.* New York: Harper.

Colburn, Forrest, ed. 1989. *Everyday Forms of Peasant Resistance.* Armonk, N.Y.: Sharpe.

Coleman, James. 1990. *Foundations of Social Theory.* Cambridge: Harvard University Press.

Collcutt, Martin. 1985. "Zen in the Meiji Restoration." Paper prepared for the annual meeting of the Association for Asian Studies, Philadelphia, March.

Cornelius, Wayne. 1975. *Politics and the Migrant Poor in Mexico City.* Stanford: Stanford University Press.

Coser, Lewis. 1956. *The Functions of Social Conflict.* New York: Free Press.

Craig, Albert. 1961. *Chōshū in the Meiji Restoration.* Cambridge: Harvard University Press.

——, ed. 1979. *Japan: A Comparative View.* Princeton: Princeton University Press.

Craig, Albert, and Donald Shively, eds. 1970. *Personality in Japanese History.* Berkeley: University of California Press.

Dahl, Robert, and Edward Tufte. 1973. *Size and Democracy.* Stanford: Stanford University Press.

Davies, James, ed. 1971. *When Men Revolt and Why.* New York: Free Press.

Davis, David. 1974. "*Ikki* in Late Medieval Japan." In *Medieval Japan*, ed. John Hall and Jeffrey Mass. New Haven: Yale University Press.

De Grazia, Sebastian. 1948. *The Political Community.* Chicago: University of Chicago Press.

DeNardo, James. 1985. *Power in Numbers*. Princeton: Princeton University Press.

DeVos, George, and Hiroshi Wagatsuma, eds. 1966. *Japan's Invisible Race*. Berkeley: University of California Press.

Dion, George. 1986. "Collective Action as Conventional Behavior." Master's thesis, University of Minnesota.

Donoghue, John. 1977. *Pariah Persistence in Changing Japan*. Washington, D.C.: University Press of America.

Dore, R. P. 1984. *Education in Tokugawa Japan*. Ann Arbor: University of Michigan Press.

Dorn, Walter. 1963. *Competition for Empire, 1740–1763*. New York: Harper and Row.

Dower, John. 1982. "The Yoshida Boom: Rethinking 'Prewar' and 'Postwar' Japan." Paper presented to the Triangle East Asia Colloquium, Research Triangle Park, N.C., October.

——, ed. 1975. *Origins of the Modern Japanese State: Selected Writings of E. H. Norman*. New York: Pantheon.

Duby, Georges. 1974. *The Early Growth of the European Economy*. Ithaca: Cornell University Press.

Dunbabin, J. P. D. 1974. *Rural Discontent in Nineteenth-Century Britain*. London: Faber and Faber.

Easton, David. 1965. *A Framework for Political Analysis*. Englewood Cliffs, N.J.: Prentice-Hall.

Elison, George, and Bardwell Smith, eds. 1981. *Warlords, Artists, and Commoners*. Honolulu: University Press of Hawaii.

Elster, Jon. 1989. *Nuts and Bolts for the Social Sciences*. Cambridge: Cambridge University Press.

Emerson, Richard. 1983. "Charismatic Kingship." *Politics and Society* 12.

Esherick, Joseph. 1987. *The Origins of the Boxer Uprising*. Berkeley: University of California Press.

Eulau, Heinz. 1964. *The Behavioral Persuasion in Politics*. New York: Random House.

Evans, Peter, et al., eds. 1985. *Bringing the State Back In*. Cambridge: Cambridge University Press.

Feeny, David. 1983. "The Moral or the Rational Peasant?" *Journal of Asian Studies* 42.

Feierabend, Ivo, and Rosalind Feierabend. 1966. "Aggressive Behaviors within Polities, 1948–1962: A Cross-National Study." *Journal of Conflict Resolution* 10.

Finkel, Steven, et al. 1989. "Selective Incentives and Collective Political Action." Paper prepared for the annual meeting of the American Political Science Association, Atlanta, August.

FitzGerald, Frances. 1972. *Fire in the Lake*. Boston: Little, Brown.

Fraser, Andrew. 1981. "Local Administration, 1860–1890: Structure and Costs." Paper prepared for the Tokugawa-Meiji Transition Workshop, Quail Roost, N.C., September.

Frohlich, Norman, Joe Oppenheimer, and Oran Young. 1971. *Political Leadership and Collective Goods*. Princeton: Princeton University Press.

Fruin, Mark. 1973. "Farm Family Migration: The Case of Echizen in the Nineteenth Century." *Keio Economic Studies* 10.2.

——. 1980. "Peasant Migrants in the Economic Development of Nineteenth-Century Japan." *Agricultural History* 54.

Fujimoto Toshiharu. 1976. *Kinsei Toshi no Chiiki Kōzō*. Tokyo: Kokon.

Fujitani Toshio. 1982. "*Okagemairi" to "Eejanaika*." Tokyo: Iwanami.

Fujiwara Masato, ed. 1964. *Meiji Zenki Sangyō Hattatsu Shi Shiryō*. Annex 1–5. Tokyo: Meiji Bunken Shiryō Kankō Kai.

Fukawa Kiyoshi. 1976. *Nōmin Sōjō no Shisōshiteki Kenkyū*. Tokyo: Mirai Sha.

Fukaya Katsumi. 1978. *Hachiemon, Hyōsuke, Bansuke*. Tokyo: Asahi Shimbun Sha.

——. 1979. *Hyakushō Ikki no Rekishiteki Kōzō*. Tokyo: Azekura.

——. 1983. *Nambu Hyakushō Meisuke no Shōgai*. Tokyo: Asahi Shimbun Sha.

Fukuzawa, Yukichi. 1969. *An Encouragement of Learning*. Trans. David Dilworth and Umeyo Hirano. Tokyo: Sophia University Press.

Fuse, Toyomasa. 1975. *Modernization and Stress in Japan*. Leiden: Brill.

Gagliardo, John. 1967. *Enlightened Despotism*. New York: Crowell.

Gamson, William. 1975. *The Strategy of Social Protest*. Homewood, Ill.: Dorsey.

Garon, Sheldon. 1987. *The State and Labor in Modern Japan*. Berkeley: University of California Press, 1987.

Gerth, H. H., and C. Wright Mills. 1981. *From Max Weber*. New York: Oxford University Press.

Gilbert, Felix, ed. 1975. *The Historical Essays of Otto Hintze*. New York: Oxford University Press.

Goldstone, Jack. n.d. "Origins of the English Revolution: A Formal Model." Unpublished manuscript. Northwestern University.

——. 1991. *Revolution and Rebellion in the Early Modern World*. Berkeley: University of California Press.

Grafstein, Robert. 1989. "The Evidential Decision Theory of Political Behavior." Paper prepared for the annual meeting of the American Political Science Association, Atlanta, August.

Graham, Hugh, and Ted Gurr. 1969. *The History of Violence in America*. New York: Bantam.

Granovetter, Mark. 1978. "Threshold Models of Collective Behavior." *American Journal of Sociology* 83.

Greenstein, Fred, and Nelson Polsby. 1975. *Handbook of Political Science*. Vol. 1. Reading, Mass.: Addison-Wesley.

Gunning, J. Patrick. 1972. "An Economic Approach to Riot Analysis." *Public Choice* 13.

Gurr, Ted. 1968. "A Causal Model of Civil Strife." *American Political Science Review* 62.

——. 1970. *Why Men Rebel*. Princeton: Princeton University Press.

———, ed. 1980. *Handbook of Political Conflict.* New York: Free Press.

Gurr, Ted, and Raymond Duvall. 1976. "Introduction to a Formal Theory of Political Conflict." In *The Uses of Controversy in Sociology*, ed. Lewis Coser and Otto Larsen. New York: Free Press.

Gurr, Ted, and Herman Weil. 1973. "Population Growth and Political Conflict." Unpublished manuscript. Northwestern University, November.

Haga Noboru. 1973. *Yonaoshi no Shisō.* Tokyo: Yūzankaku.

Hah, Chong-do, and Christopher Lapp. 1978. "Japanese Politics of Equality in Transition: The Case of the Burakumin." *Asian Survey* 18.

Hall, John. 1955. *Tanuma Okitsugu, 1719–1788.* Cambridge: Harvard University Press.

———. 1966. *Government and Local Power in Japan, 500–1700.* Princeton: Princeton University Press.

———, ed. 1991. *The Cambridge History of Japan.* Vol. 4. Cambridge: Cambridge University Press.

Hall, John, et al., eds. 1981. *Japan before Tokugawa.* Princeton: Princeton University Press.

Hall, John, and Marius Jansen, eds. 1968. *Studies in the Institutional History of Early Modern Japan.* Princeton: Princeton University Press.

Hane, Mikiso. 1982. *Peasants, Rebels, and Outcastes.* New York: Pantheon.

Hanley, Susan. 1983. "A High Standard of Living in Nineteenth-Century Japan: Fact or Fantasy?" *Journal of Economic History* 43.

Hanley, Susan, and Kozo Yamamura. 1977. *Economic and Demographic Change in Preindustrial Japan, 1600–1868.* Princeton: Princeton University Press.

Hara Akira. n.d. "Bakuhan-sei Shakai no Gaikan." Unpublished data, photocopied.

Harada Tomohiko. 1982. *Kinsei Toshi Sōjō Shi.* Kyoto: Shimonkaku.

Harafuji, Hiroshi. 1978. "*Han* Laws in the Edo Period." *Acta Asiatica*, no. 35 (November).

Hardacre, Helen. 1985. "Creating Shinto: The Great Promulgation Campaign and the New Religions." Paper prepared for the annual meeting of the Association for Asian Studies, Philadelphia, March.

Hardin, Russell. 1982. *Collective Action.* Baltimore: Johns Hopkins University Press.

Hardy, Melissa. 1979. "Economic Growth, Distributional Inequality, and Political Conflict in Industrial Societies." *Journal of Political and Military Sociology* 7.

Harootunian, Harry. 1970. *Toward Restoration.* Berkeley: University of California Press.

———. 1988. *Things Seen and Unseen.* Chicago: University of Chicago Press.

Hasegawa Noboru. 1977. *Bakuto to Jiyū Minken.* Tokyo: Chūō Kōron Sha.

Hauser, William. 1974. *Economic Institutional Change in Tokugawa Japan.* Cambridge: Cambridge University Press.

Hayami Akira. 1973. *Kinsei Nōson no Rekishi Jinkōgakuteki Kenkyū.* Tokyo: Tōyō Keizai.

———. 1982. "A 'Great Transformation.'" Paper prepared for the Third International Studies Conference on Japan, The Hague, September.

——. 1988. *Edo no Nōmin Seikatsu Shi*. Tokyo: Nihon Hōsō Shuppan.

Hayami, Yujiro, and Masao Kikuchi. 1982. *Asian Village Economy at the Crossroads*. Baltimore: Johns Hopkins University Press.

Hayashi Motoi. 1976a. *Hyakushō Ikki no Dentō*. Tokyo: Shinhyōron.

——. 1976b. *Zoku Hyakushō Ikki no Dentō*. Tokyo: Shinhyōron.

Hibbs, Douglas. 1973. *Mass Political Violence*. New York: Wiley.

Hirsch, Herbert, and David Perry, eds. 1973. *Violence as Politics*. New York: Harper and Row.

Hirschman, Albert. 1970. *Exit, Voice, and Loyalty*. Cambridge: Harvard University Press.

Hirschmeier, Johannes. 1964. *The Origins of Entrepreneurship in Meiji Japan*. Cambridge: Harvard University Press.

Hirshleifer, Jack. 1987. *Economic Behavior in Adversity*. Brighton: Wheatsheaf.

Hobsbawm, E. J. 1959. *Primitive Rebels*. New York: Norton.

Hoffer, Eric. 1951. *The True Believer*. New York: Harper and Row.

Honjo, Eijiro. 1935. *The Social and Economic History of Japan*. Kyoto: Institute for Research in Economic History of Japan.

——. 1972. *Honjō Eijirō Chosaku Shū*. Vol. 5. Osaka: Seibundō.

Horie Eiichi. 1960. *Meiji Ishin no Shakai Kōzō*. Tokyo: Yūhikaku.

Huang, Philip. 1985. *The Peasant Economy and Social Change in North China*. Stanford: Stanford University Press.

Huber, Thomas. 1981. *The Revolutionary Origins of Modern Japan*. Stanford: Stanford University Press.

Huntington, Samuel. 1968. *Political Order in Changing Societies*. New Haven: Yale University Press.

Hyakushō Ikki Kenkyū Kai, ed. 1980, 1982. *Tempō-ki no Jinmin Tōsō to Shakai Henkaku*. 2 vols. Tokyo: Azekura.

Iida Bunya. 1979. "Tempō Jusannen Kōfu Kami-Fuchū Kyūmin Gokyū Sangyōshiki to sono Haikei." *Shinano* 31. 6 (June 1).

Iinuma Jirō. 1991. *Tokugawa Zettai Ōsei Ron*. Tokyo: Mirai Sha.

Ike, Nobutaka. 1950. *The Beginnings of Political Democracy in Japan*. Baltimore: Johns Hopkins University Press.

Inglehart, Ronald. 1977. *The Silent Revolution*. Princeton: Princeton University Press.

——. 1990. *Culture Shift*. Princeton: Princeton University Press.

International Society for Educational Information, ed. 1974. *Atlas of Japan*. Tokyo.

Irokawa Daikichi. 1966. *Kindai Kokka no Shuppatsu*. Tokyo: Chūō Kōron Sha.

Ishida Takeshi. 1970. *Nihon no Seiji Bunka*. Tokyo: Tokyo Daigaku Shuppan Kai.

Ishii, Ryosuke. 1978. "Japanese Feudalism." *Acta Asiatica*, no. 35 (November).

Iwahashi Masaru. 1981. *Kinsei Nihon Bukka Shi no Kenkyū*. Tokyo: Ōhara Shinsei Sha.

Jannetta, Ann. 1987. *Epidemics and Mortality in Early Modern Japan*. Princeton: Princeton University Press.

Jansen, Marius B. 1961. *Sakamoto Ryoma and the Meiji Restoration*. Princeton: Princeton University Press.

——, ed. 1989. *The Cambridge History of Japan*. Vol. 5. Cambridge: Cambridge University Press.

Jansen, Marius B., and Gilbert Rozman, eds. 1986. *Japan in Transition*. Princeton: Princeton University Press.

Johnson, Chalmers. 1964. *Revolution and the Social System*. Stanford: Hoover Institute.

Kagaku Gijutsu Chō Shigen Chōsa Kai. 1967. *Santei Nihon Shokuhin Hyōjun Seibun Hyō*. Tokyo: Ōkura Shō.

Kaikyū Tōsō Shi Kenkyū Kai, ed. 1981. *Kaikyū Tōsō no Rekishi to Riron*. Vol. 2. Tokyo: Aoki.

Kajinishi Mitsuhaya. 1978. *Chiso Kaisei to Chihō Jichi Sei*. Meiji Shi Kenkyū Sōsho, vol. 2. Tokyo: Ochanomizu.

Kano, Tsutomu. 1973. "Peasant Uprisings and Citizens' Revolts." *Japan Interpreter* 8.

Kaplan, Abraham. 1964. *The Conduct of Inquiry*. New York: Harper and Row.

Katō Takashi. 1990. "Edo no Shihai to sono Tokushitsu." Paper prepared for the Conference on Edo and Paris in the Early Modern Period, Tokyo, June.

Katsumata Shizuo. 1982. *Ikki*. Tokyo: Iwanami.

Keirstead, Thomas. 1990. "The Theater of Protest." *Journal of Japanese Studies* 16.

Kelly, William. 1985. *Deference and Defiance in Nineteenth-Century Japan*. Princeton: Princeton University Press.

Kerbo, Harold. 1982. "Movements of 'Crisis' and Movements of 'Affluence.'" *Journal of Conflict Resolution* 26.

Kertzer, David. 1988. *Ritual, Politics, and Power*. New Haven: Yale University Press.

Keys, Charles. 1983. "Introduction." *Journal of Asian Studies* 42.

Kierman, V. G. 1980. *State and Society in Europe, 1550–1650*. New York: St. Martin's.

Kimmel, Michael. 1988. *Absolutism and Its Discontents*. New Brunswick, N.J.: Transaction.

Kimura Motoi, ed. 1954. *Kyūdaka Kyūryō Torishirabe Chō*. Tokyo: Kondo.

Kitajima Masamoto. 1966. *Bakuhan-sei no Kumon*. Tokyo: Chūō Kōron Sha.

Kitazawa Fumitake. 1982. *Meiwa no Dai-Ikki*. Tokyo: Bunka Shobō Hakubun Sha.

Kitō Hiroshi. 1983a. "Edo Jidai no Beishoku." *Rekishi Kōron* 19.

——. 1983b. *Nihon Nisennen no Jinkō Shi*. Kyoto: PHP Kenkyū-jo.

——. 1985. "Seijuku Shakai no Jinkō." *Sekai to Jinkō* (June).

Kobayashi Hiroshi. 1978. *Kaidō: Ikite iru Kinsei*. Vol. 2. Kyoto: Tankō Sha.

Kodama Kōta. 1967. *Chihōshi Dainempyō*. Tokyo: Jimbutsu Ōraisha.

——. 1979. *Hanshi Sōran*. Tokyo: Shin Jimbutsu Ōraisha.

Kokushō Iwao. 1971. *Hyakushō Ikki no Kenkyū, Zoku Hen*. Tokyo: Dōhō Sha.

Kornhauser, William. 1959. *The Politics of Mass Society*. New York: Free Press.

Korpi, Walter. 1974. "Conflict, Power, and Relative Deprivation." *American Political Science Review* 68.

Koschmann, J. Victor. 1987. *The Mito Ideology.* Berkeley: University of California Press.

Koschmann, J. Victor, ed. 1978. *Authority and the Individual in Japan.* Tokyo: University of Tokyo Press.

Krantz, Frederick, ed. 1988. *History from Below.* New York: Blackwell.

Krauss, Ellis. 1974. *Japanese Radicals Revisited.* Berkeley: University of California Press.

Krauss, Ellis, et al., eds. 1984. *Conflict in Japan.* Honolulu: University Press of Hawaii.

Krieger, Leonard, ed. 1967. *The German Revolutions.* Chicago: University of Chicago Press.

Kriesberg, Louis, ed. 1978. *Research in Social Movements, Conflicts, and Change.* Greenwich, Conn: JAI.

Kriesi, Hans-Peter. n.d. "Research Design for the Project on the Development of New Social Movements in the Eighties." Unpublished manuscript. University of Geneva.

Kubota, Akira. 1972. "Some Survey Findings on Political Protest in Japan." Paper prepared for the annual meeting of the American Political Science Association, Washington, D.C., December.

Kuhn, Philip. 1970. *Rebellion and Its Enemies in Late Imperial China.* Cambridge: Harvard University Press.

Kurasawa Susumu. 1968. *Nihon no Toshi Shakai.* Tokyo: Fukumura.

Lakatos, Imre. 1970. "Falsification and the Methodology of Scientific Research Programmes." In *Criticism and the Growth of Knowledge,* ed. Lakatos and Alan Musgrave. Cambridge: Cambridge University Press.

Lanternari, Vittorio. 1963. *The Religions of the Oppressed.* New York: Knopf.

Leavell, James. 1981. "The Police in Transition." Paper prepared for the Tokugawa-Meiji Transition Workshop, Quail Roost, N.C., December.

Lee, Ronald, ed. 1977. *Population Patterns in the Past.* New York: Academic Press.

Lenin, V. I. 1952. *The Collapse of the Second International.* Moscow: Foreign Languages Publishing House.

Lerner, Daniel. 1958. *The Passing of Traditional Society.* New York: Free Press.

Levy, Marion. 1966. *Modernization and the Structure of Societies.* Princeton: Princeton University Press.

Lewis, Michael. 1990. *Rioters and Citizens.* Berkeley: University of California Press.

Lichbach, Mark. 1987. "Deterrence or Escalation?" *Journal of Conflict Resolution* 31.

———. 1989. "An Evaluation of 'Does Economic Inequality Breed Political Conflict?' Studies." *World Politics* 41.

———. 1991. "The Rebel's Dilemma: Social Order, Collective Action, and Collective Dissent." Unpublished manuscript. University of Colorado, August.

Lifton, Robert, et al. 1979. *Six Lives, Six Deaths.* New Haven: Yale University Press.

Lipsky, Michael. 1968. "Protest as a Political Resource." *American Political Science Review* 62.

Little, Daniel. 1989. *Understanding Peasant China.* New Haven: Yale University Press.

———. 1991. *Varieties of Social Explanation.* Boulder, Colo.: Westview.

Magagna, Victor. 1991. *Communities of Grain.* Ithaca: Cornell University Press.

Manning, Roger. 1988. *Village Revolts.* Oxford: Oxford University Press.

March, James, and Johan Olsen. 1989. *Rediscovering Institutions.* New York: Free Press.

Markoff, John. 1986. "Contexts and Forms of Rural Revolt." *Journal of Conflict Resolution* 30.

Marsh, Alan. 1977. *Protest and Political Consciousness.* Beverly Hills: Sage.

Maruyama, Masao. 1974. *Studies in the Intellectual History of Tokugawa Japan.* Trans. Mikiso Hane. Princeton: Princeton University Press.

Maslow, Abraham. 1954. *Motivation and Personality.* New York: Harper.

Mason, T. David. 1984. "Individual Participation in Collective Racial Violence: A Rational Choice Synthesis." *American Political Science Review* 78.

Mass, Jeffrey, and William Hauser, eds. 1985. *The Bakufu in Japanese History.* Stanford: Stanford University Press.

McCarthy, John, and Mayer Zald. 1977. "Resource Mobilization and Social Movements: A Partial Theory." *American Journal of Sociology* 82.

McClain, James. 1988. "Failed Expectations: Kaga Domain on the Eve of the Meiji Restoration." *Journal of Japanese Studies* 14.

McClain, James, and John Merriman. 1990. "An Overview of Edo and Paris." Paper prepared for the Conference on Edo and Paris in the Early Modern Period, Tokyo, June.

McEwan, J. R. 1962. *The Political Writings of Ogyū Sorai.* Cambridge: Cambridge University Press.

McKean, Margaret. 1978. "Citizen's Movements in Japan: Rural Revivalism or Modern Democracy?" Paper prepared for the annual meeting of the Association for Asian Studies, Chicago, April.

———. 1981. *Environmental Protest and Citizen Politics in Japan.* Berkeley: University of California Press.

Mendels, Franklin. 1982. "Proto-Industrialization: Theory and Reality." In *Eighth International Economic History Congress, Budapest 1982, "A" Themes,* ed. International Economic History Association. Budapest: Akademiai Kiado.

Midlarsky, Manus. 1982. "Scarcity and Inequality." *Journal of Conflict Resolution* 26.

———. 1988. "Rulers and the Ruled: Patterned Inequality and the Onset of Mass Political Violence." *American Political Science Review* 82.

Migdal, Joel. 1988. *Strong Societies and Weak States.* Princeton: Princeton University Press.

Miller, David. 1985. "The Geography of Discontent in Pre-famine Ireland." Paper prepared for the annual meeting of the American Committee for Irish Studies, Tacoma, April.

Minami Kazuo. 1978. *Bakumatsu Edo Shakai no Kenkyū.* Tokyo: Yoshikawa Kōbunkan.

Miyamoto Matarō and Kōzō Yamamura. 1981. "Ryō-Taisenkanki Kosaku Sōgi no Sūryō Bunseki e no Isshikiron." In *Senkanki no Nihon Keizai Bunseki,* ed. Nakamura Takafusa. Tokyo: Yamakawa.

Miyata Noboru. 1970. *Miroku Shinkō no Kenkyū.* Tokyo: Mirai Sha.

Mombushō, ed. 1980. *Nihon Kyōiku Shi Shiryō.* Vols. 8, 9. Kyoto: Rinsen.

Moore, Barrington. 1978. *Injustice: The Social Bases of Obedience and Revolt.* White Plains: Sharpe.

Moore, Will. 1989. "Rational Rebels: Overcoming the Free-Rider Problem." Paper pre-pared for the annual meeting of the American Political Science Association, Atlanta, August.

Morikawa Hiroshi. 1962. "Meiji Shonen no Toshi Bumpu." *Jimbun Chiri* 14. 5.

Morris, Ivan. 1975. *The Nobility of Failure.* New York: Holt, Rinehart, and Winston.

Mosk, Carl, and Simon Pak. 1977. "Food Consumption, Physical Characteristics, and Population Growth in Japan, 1874–1940." Working Paper 102, Center for Japanese and Korean Studies, University of California.

Motoyama Yukihiko. 1962. "Bakumatsu Ishin-ki ni okeru Shomin no Ishiki to Kōdō." In *Meiji Ishin Shi no Mondaiten,* ed. Sakata Yoshio. Tokyo: Mirai Sha.

Mousnier, Roland. 1970. *Peasant Uprisings.* New York: Harper and Row.

Muller, Edward. 1979. *Aggressive Political Participation.* Princeton: Princeton University Press.

———. 1985. "Income Inequality, Regime Repressiveness, and Political Violence." *American Sociological Review* 50.

Muller, Edward, et al. 1991. "Discontent and the Expected Utility of Rebellion: The Case of Peru." *American Political Science Review* 85.

Muller, Edward, and Karl-Dieter Opp. 1986. "Rational Choice and Rebellious Collective Action." *American Political Science Review* 80.

Muller, Edward, and Erich Weede. 1988. "Cross-National Variation in Political Violence: A Rational Action Approach." Unpublished manuscript. University of Arizona.

Murakami Tadashi. 1965. *Tenryō.* Tokyo: Shin Jimbutsu Ōrai Sha.

———. 1983. "Edo Bakufu Chokkatsuryō no Chiikiteki Bumpu ni tsuite." *Hōsei Shigaku,* no. 25 (February).

Murakami, Yasusuke. 1984. "Ie Society as a Pattern of Civilization." *Journal of Japanese Studies* 10.

———. 1985. "*Ie* Society as a Pattern of Civilization: Response to Criticism." *Journal of Japanese Studies* 11.

Nagasu Toshiyuki. 1986. *Osso.* Tokyo: Sanichi.

Najita, Tetsuo. 1974. *Japan.* Chicago: University of Chicago Press.

Najita, Tetsuo, and Irwin Scheiner, eds. 1978. *Japanese Thought in the Tokugawa Period.* Chicago: University of Chicago Press.

Najita, Tetsuo, and J. Victor Koschmann, eds. 1982. *Conflict in Modern Japanese History.* Princeton: Princeton University Press.

Nakai, Kate. 1988. *Shogunal Politics.* Cambridge: Harvard University Press.

Nakamura Satoru. 1964a. "Hōkenteki Tochi Shoyū Kaitai no Chiikiteki Tokushitsu." *Jimbun Gakuhō,* no. 20.

———. 1964b. "Meiji Shonen ni okeru Nōgyō Seisanryoku no Chiiki Kōzō." In *Burujowa Kakumei no Hikaku Kenkyū*, ed. Kuwahara Takeo. Tokyo: Chikuma.

———. 1968. *Meiji Ishin no Kiso Kōzō*. Tokyo: Mirai Sha.

Nakamura Takafusa, ed. 1981. *Senkanki no Nihon Keizai Bunseki*. Tokyo: Yamakawa.

Nakane, Chie, and Shinzaburo Oishi, eds. 1990. *Tokugawa Japan*. Trans. Conrad Totman. Tokyo: University of Tokyo Press.

Naquin, Susan. 1976. *Millenarian Rebellion in China*. New Haven: Yale University Press.

———. 1981. *Shantung Rebellion*. New Haven: Yale University Press.

Nelson, Joan. 1969. *Migrants, Urban Poverty, and Instability in Developing Nations*. Cambridge: Harvard Center for International Affairs.

Nihon Rekishi Daijiten Henshū Iinkai, ed. 1979. *Nihon Rekishi Daijiten, Bekken: Nihon Rekishi Chizu*. Tokyo: Kawade.

Nihon Tōkei Kyōkai, ed. 1982. *Tōkei Shūshi*. Vol. 2, no. 5 (pp. 9–22), no. 8 (pp. 97–107). Tokyo: Yūshōdō.

Nishikawa Shunsaku. 1979. *Edo Jidai no Poritikaru Ekonomii*. Tokyo: Nihon Hyōron Sha.

———. 1985. *Nihon Keizai no Seichō Shi*. Tokyo: Tōyō Keizai.

Nishiyama Matsunosuke, ed. 1972–78. *Edo Chōnin no Kenkyū*. Tokyo: Yoshikawa Kōbunkan.

Nomiya, Daishiro. 1992. "Rebellious Peasants: Japan in the Nineteenth Century." Ph.D. diss., University of North Carolina.

Norman, E. Herbert. 1965. *Soldier and Peasant in Japan*. Vancouver: University of British Columbia Press.

Oberschall, Anthony. 1973. *Social Conflict and Social Movements*. Englewood Cliffs, N.J.: Prentice-Hall.

———. 1980. "Loosely Structured Collective Conflict." In *Research in Social Movements, Conflicts and Change*, ed. Louis Kriesberg. Greenwich, Conn.: JAI.

Ōkawa Kazushi, ed. 1976. *Chōki Keizai Tōkei*. Vol. 6. Tokyo: Tōyō Keizai.

Olson, Mancur. 1963. "Rapid Growth as a Destabilizing Force." *Journal of Economic History* 23.

———. 1971. *The Logic of Collective Action*. Cambridge: Harvard University Press.

Ooms, Herman. 1975. *Charismatic Bureaucrat*. Chicago: University of Chicago Press.

Ostrom, Elinor. 1991. "Rational Choice and Institutional Analysis: Toward Complementarity." *American Political Science Review* 85.

Ōtomo Atsushi. 1979. *Nihon Toshi Jinkō Bunpu Ron*. Tokyo: Taimeidō.

Ōuchi Tsutomu. 1980. *Nihon ni okeru Nōminsō no Bunkai*. Tokyo: Tokyo Daigaku Shuppan Kai.

Parsons, James. 1970. *Peasant Rebellions of the Late Ming Dynasty*. Tucson: University of Arizona Press.

Parvin, Manoucher. 1973. "Economic Determinants of Political Unrest." *Journal of Conflict Resolution* 17.

Pennington, Jean, and Helen Church. 1980. *Bowes and Church's Food Values of Portions*

Commonly Used. Philadelphia: Lippincott.

Perry, Elizabeth. 1980. *Rebels and Revolutionaries in North China, 1845–1945*. Stanford: Stanford University Press.

——. 1981. "Popular Unrest in China: The State and Local Society." Paper prepared for the Conference on the Role of the State in Change and Development in China, 1880–1980, George Washington University, December.

Pharr, Susan. 1990. *Losing Face*. Berkeley: University of California Press.

Piven, Frances, and Richard Cloward. 1979. *Poor People's Movements*. New York: Vintage.

Pollack, David. 1985. *The Fracture of Meaning*. Princeton: Princeton University Press.

Popkin, Samuel. 1979. *The Rational Peasant*. Berkeley: University of California Press.

——. 1985. "Colonialism and the Ideological Origins of the Vietnamese Revolution." *Journal of Asian Studies* 44.

Powell, G. Bingham. 1981. "Party Systems and Political Performance: Participation, Stability, and Violence in Contemporary Democracies." *American Political Science Review* 75.

——. 1982. *Contemporary Democracies*. Cambridge: Harvard University Press.

Pye, Lucian. 1966. *Aspects of Political Development*. Boston: Little, Brown.

Ragin, Charles. 1987. *The Comparative Method*. Berkeley: University of California Press.

Rahder, J. 1935. "Record of Kurume Uprising." *Acta Orientalia* 14, pt. 2.

Ravina, Mark. 1992. "The Amoral Economy of the Tokugawa Peasant." Paper prepared for the annual meeting of the Association for Asian Studies, Washington, D.C., April.

Rebel, Hermann. 1983. *Peasant Classes*. Princeton: Princeton University Press.

Reich, Michael. 1982. "Public and Private Responses to a Chemical Disaster in Japan: The Case of Kanemi Yusho." Paper presented to the Triangle East Asian Colloquium, Research Triangle Park, N.C., February.

Rekishi Kagaku Kyōgi Kai, ed. 1974. *Nōmin Tōsō Shi*. Rekishi Kagaku Taikei, vol. 23. Tokyo: Azekura.

Rekishigaku Kenkyū Kai, ed. 1985. *Kōza Nihon Shi*. Vol. 6. Tokyo: Tokyo Daigaku Shuppan Kai.

Richardson, Bradley, and Taizo Ueda, eds. 1981. *Business and Society in Japan*. New York: Praeger.

Rikugun Sambō-bu, ed. 1880. *Kyōbu Seihyō 1880*. Tokyo: Rikugun Shō.

——. 1976. *Kyōbu Seihyō 1875*. Tokyo: Seishi Sha.

Rogowski, Ronald. 1974. *Rational Legitimacy*. Princeton: Princeton University Press.

Rohlen, Thomas. 1976. "Violence at Yoka High School." *Asian Survey* 16.

Root, Hilton. 1987. *Peasants and King in Burgundy*. Berkeley: University of California Press.

Rostow, W. W. 1975. *How It All Began*. New York: McGraw-Hill.

Roth, Jack. 1980. *The Cult of Violence*. Berkeley: University of California Press.

Rothbaum, Fred. 1980. "Childrens' Clinical Syndromes and Generalized Explanations of Control." *Advances in Child Development and Behavior* 15.

Rowe, William. 1989. *Hankow*. Stanford: Stanford University Press.

Rudé, George. 1964. *The Crowd in History*. New York: Wiley.

Rule, James. 1988. *Theories of Civil Violence*. Berkeley: University of California Press.

Rummel, Rudolph. 1966. "Dimensions of Conflict Behavior within Nations." *Journal of Conflict Resolution* 10.

Runge, C. Ford. 1981. "Common Property Externalities: Isolation, Assurance, and Resource Depletion in a Traditional Grazing Context." *American Journal of Agricultural Economics* 63.

——. 1984a. "Strategic Interdependence in Models of Property Rights." *American Journal of Agricultural Economics* 66.

——. 1984b. "Institutions and the Free Rider: The Assurance Problem in Collective Action." *Journal of Politics* 46.

Russett, Bruce. 1964. "Inequality and Instability." *World Politics* 16.

Saitō Osamu. 1973. "Nōgyō Chingin no Sūsei." *Shakai Keizai Shigaku* 39.

——. 1975. "Ōsaka Oroshi-uri Bukka Shisū, 1757–1915-nen." *Mita Gakkai Zasshi* 68.

——. 1983. "Population and the Peasant Family Economy in Proto-industrial Japan." *Journal of Family History* 8.

——. 1985. *Puroto-Kōgyōka no Jidai*. Tokyo: Nihon Hyōron Sha.

——. 1986. "Changing Structure of Urban Employment and Its Effects on Migration Patterns in Eighteenth- and Nineteenth-Century Japan." Discussion paper no. 134, Institute of Economic Research, Hitotsubashi University, March.

——. 1987. *Shōka no Sekai, Uramise no Sekai*. Tokyo: Riburopōto.

——. 1988. "Jinkō Hendō ni okeru Nishi to Higashi." In *Bakumatsu-Meiji no Nihon Keizai*, ed. Odaka Kōnosuke and Yamamoto Yūzō. Tokyo: Nihon Keizai Shimbun Sha.

Sanders, David. 1981. *Patterns of Political Instability*. New York: St. Martin's.

Sartori, Giovanni. 1970. "Concept Misformation in Comparative Politics." *American Political Science Review* 64.

Sasaki Junnosuke. 1972, 1973. *Murakata Sōdō to Yonaoshi*. 2 vols. Tokyo: Aoki.

——. 1979. *Yonaoshi*. Tokyo: Iwanami.

——, ed. 1974. *Hyakushō Ikki to Uchikowashi*. Tokyo: Sanseidō.

Scheiner, Irwin. 1973. "The Mindful Peasant: Sketches for a Study of Rebellion." *Journal of Asian Studies* 32.

Schelling, Thomas. 1978. *Micromotives and Macrobehavior*. New York: Norton.

Schick, Frederic. 1984. *Having Reasons*. Princeton: Princeton University Press.

Scott, James. 1976. *The Moral Economy of the Peasant*. New Haven: Yale University Press.

——. 1985. *Weapons of the Weak*. New Haven: Yale University Press.

Scott-Stokes, Henry. 1974. *The Life and Death of Yukio Mishima*. New York: Farrar, Straus, and Giroux.

Sekiyama Naotarō. 1948. *Kinsei Nihon Jinkō no Kenkyū*. Tokyo: Ryūgin Sha.

——. 1958. *Kinsei Nihon no Jinkō Kōzō*. Tokyo: Yoshikawa Kōbunkan.

————. 1959. *Nihon no Jinkō*. Tokyo: Chibundō.

Sen, Amartya. 1967. "Isolation, Assurance, and the Social Rate of Discount." *Quarterly Journal of Economics* 81.

Sheldon, Charles D. 1958. *The Rise of the Merchant Class in Tokugawa Japan, 1600–1868*. Locust Valley, N.Y.: Augustin.

Shigematsu Kazuyoshi. 1986. *Edo no Hanzai Hakusho*. Tokyo: PHP Kenkyū-jo.

Shimbo Hiroshi. 1978. *Kinsei no Bukka to Keizai Hatten*. Tokyo: Tōyō Keizai.

Shimbo Hiroshi and Saitō Osamu, eds. 1989. *Kindai Seichō no Taidō*. Tokyo: Iwanami.

Shingles, Richard. 1987. "Relative Deprivation and the Inclination to Protest." Unpublished manuscript. Virginia Polytechnic Institute, March.

Shōji Kichinosuke. 1970. *Yonaoshi Ikki no Kenkyū*. Tokyo: Azekura.

Shōji Kichinosuke et al., eds. 1981. *Minshū Undō no Shisō*. Tokyo: Iwanami.

Sippel, Patricia. 1977. "Popular Protest in Early Modern Japan: The Bushū Outburst." *Harvard Journal of Asiatic Studies* 37.

Siverson, Randolph, and Harvey Starr. 1990. "Opportunity, Willingness, and the Diffusion of War." *American Political Science Review* 84.

Skinner, G. William. 1979. "Social Ecology and the Forces of Repression in North China." Paper prepared for the ACLS Workshop on Rebellion and Revolution in North China, Harvard University, July.

————. 1987. "The Historical Geography of Population Processes in China, Japan, and France." Paper prepared for the Social Science History Seminar, Miami University, April.

————. 1988. "Nobi as a Regional System." Paper prepared for the Nobi Regional Project Workshop, Nagoya, January.

Skocpol, Theda. 1979. *States and Social Revolutions*. Cambridge: Cambridge University Press.

Smelser, Neil. 1963. *Theory of Collective Behavior*. New York: Free Press.

Smethurst, Richard. 1986. *Agricultural Development and Tenancy Disputes in Japan, 1870–1940*. Princeton: Princeton University Press.

Smith, Henry D. 1981. "From Edo to Tokyo: The Provincial Interlude." Paper prepared for the Tokugawa-Meiji Transition Workshop, Lake Wilderness, Wash., August.

Smith, Thomas C. 1959. *The Agrarian Origins of Modern Japan*. Stanford: Stanford University Press.

————. 1969. "Farm Family By-employments in Preindustrial Japan." *Journal of Economic History* 29.

————. 1977. *Nakahara*. Stanford: Stanford University Press.

Social Research. 1985. Vol. 52, no. 4.

Sorel, Georges. 1961. *Reflections on Violence*. New York: Collier.

Staggs, Kathleen. 1985. "Meiji Buddhist Reformers and the State in the Later Meiji Period." Paper prepared for the annual meeting of the Association for Asian Studies, Philadelphia, March.

Steiner, Kurt, et al., eds. 1980. *Political Opposition and Local Politics in Japan.* Princeton: Princeton University Press.

Steinhoff, Patricia. 1978. "Political Dissent and Psychosocial Conflict." Paper prepared for the annual meeting of the Association for Asian Studies, Chicago, March.

———. 1980. "Group Process, Isolation, and Cultural Models as Factors in Recanting by Japanese Terrorists." Paper prepared for the annual meeting of the International Society of Political Psychology, Boston, June.

———. 1981. "The Radical Left in the Postwar Student Movement." Paper prepared for the annual meeting of the Association for Asian Studies, Toronto, March.

Stevenson, John. 1979. *Popular Disturbances in England, 1700–1870.* London: Longman.

Sugimoto, Yoshio. 1975. "Structural Sources of Popular Revolts and the Tōbaku Movement at the Time of the Meiji Restoration." *Journal of Asian Studies* 34.

———. 1978. "Peasant Rebellion and Ruling Class Adaptation at the Time of the Meiji Restoration in Japan." Paper prepared for the World Congress of Sociology, Uppsala, August.

Suzuki Hisashi. 1962. "Tokugawa Bakushindan no Chigyō Keitai." *Shigaku Zasshi* 71. 2.

Takagi Shunsuke. 1983. *Eejanaika.* Tokyo: Kyōiku Sha.

Takekawa Yoshinori. n. d. "Yamanashi Nōmin Sōdō Shi, sono 1." *Kai Shigaku,* no. 10.

———. 1961. "Yamanashi Nōmin Sōdō Shi, sono 6." *Kai Shigaku,* no. 15.

Tarrow, Sidney. 1981. "Cycles of Protest and Cycles of Reform: Italy (1965–1979)." Proposal submitted to the National Science Foundation, March.

———. 1983. "Struggling to Reform: Protest and Policy Innovation in Advanced Industrial Democracies." Unpublished paper. Cornell University.

———. 1989. *Democracy and Disorder.* Oxford: Oxford University Press.

———. 1990. "Political Opportunities, Cycles of Protest, and Collective Action: Theoretical Perspectives." Paper prepared for the Conference on Social Movements, Cornell University, October.

———. 1994. *Power in Movement.* New York: Cambridge University Press.

Taylor, Stan. 1984. *Social Science and Revolutions.* New York: St. Martin's.

Tezuka Toshio. 1962, 1963. "Tempō Sōdō no Gunnai Kyokumen." *Kai Shigaku,* nos. 16, 18.

Thompson, E. P. 1966. *The Making of the English Working Class.* New York: Vintage.

Thrupp, Sylvia, ed. 1970. *Millennial Dreams in Action.* New York: Schocken.

Tilly, Charles. 1968. "Collective Violence in Nineteenth-Century French Cities." Paper presented at Reed College, February.

———. 1978a. "Collective Violence in European Perspective." Center for Research on Social Organization, University of Michigan, June.

———. 1978b. *From Mobilization to Revolution.* Reading: Addison-Wesley.

———. 1980. "How (and, to Some Extent, Why) to Study British Contention." CRSO Working Paper no. 212, University of Michigan, February.

———. 1981. "Britain Creates the Social Movement." CRSO Working Paper no. 232, University of Michigan, March.

——. 1982. "Proletarianization and Rural Collective Action in East Anglia and Elsewhere, 1500–1900." *Journal of Peasant Studies* 10.

——. 1983. "Flows of Capital and Forms of Industry in Europe, 1500–1900." *Theory and Society* 12.

——. 1986. *The Contentious French*. Cambridge: Harvard University Press.

——. 1989a. "History, Sociology, and Dutch Collective Action." *Tijdschrift voor Sociale Geschiednis* 15.

——. 1989b. "The Geography of European Statemaking and Capitalism since 1500." Unpublished manuscript. New School for Social Research.

——. 1990a. "State and Collective Action in Japan and France, 1600–1800." Paper prepared for the Conference on Edo and Paris in the Early Modern Period, Tokyo, June.

——. 1990b. *Coercion, Capital, and European States, A.D. 990–1990*. Cambridge, Mass.: Blackwell.

——. 1990c. "Mobilization and Contention in Great Britain, 1758–1834." Unpublished manuscript. New School for Social Research, September.

——. 1993. *European Revolutions*. Cambridge, Mass.: Blackwell.

——, ed. 1975. *The Formation of National States in Western Europe*. Princeton: Princeton University Press.

Tilly, Charles, et al. 1975. *The Rebellious Century, 1830–1930*. Cambridge: Harvard University Press.

Tilly, Louise, and Charles Tilly, eds. 1981. *Class Conflict and Collective Action*. Beverly Hills: Sage.

Tōkei-in, ed. 1968. *Kai no Kuni Genzai Ninbetsu Shirabe*. Tokyo: Hōbunkaku.

Tokyo Hyakunen Shi Henshū Iinkai, ed. 1973. *Tokyo Hyakunen Shi*. Vols. 1, 2. Tokyo: Tokyo-to.

Tong, James. 1991. *Disorder under Heaven*. Stanford: Stanford University Press.

Totman, Conrad. 1967. *Politics in the Tokugawa Bakufu, 1600–1843*. Cambridge: Harvard University Press.

——. 1980. *The Collapse of the Tokugawa Bakufu, 1862–1868*. Honolulu: University Press of Hawaii.

Toyoda Takeshi. 1962. *Nihon no Hōken Toshi*. Tokyo: Iwanami.

Tozeren, Selcuk. 1981. "Takaino Village and the Nakano Uprising of 1871." Ph.D. diss., Columbia University.

Trimberger, Ellen Kay. 1978. *Revolution from Above*. New Brunswick, N.J.: Transaction.

Tsebelis, George. 1985. "Prisoner's Dilemma and Dependency." Paper prepared for the annual meeting of the American Political Science Association, New Orleans, September.

Tsuchiya Takao and Ōno Michio. 1931. *Meiji Shonen Nōmin Sōjō Roku*. Tokyo: Namboku.

Tsuda Hideo. 1977. *Bakumatsu Shakai no Kenkyū*. Tokyo: Kashiwa.

Tsukahira, Toshio. 1966. *Feudal Control in Tokugawa Japan: The Sankin Kotai System*. Cambridge: Harvard East Asian Monographs.

Tussing, Arlon. 1966. "The Labor Force in Meiji Economic Growth: A Quantitative Study of Yamanashi Prefecture." *Journal of Economic History* 26.

Uesugi Satoshi and Ishitaki Toyomi. 1988. *Chikuzen Takeyari Ikki Ron*. Fukuoka: Kaichō Sha.

Umemura Mataji. 1961. "Kenchikugyō Rōdōsha no Jisshitsu Chingin, 1726–1958." *Keizai Kenkyū* 12.

———. 1965. "Tokugawa Jidai no Jinkō Sūsei to sono Kisei Yōin." *Keizai Kenkyū* 16.

Upham, Frank. 1976. "Litigation and Moral Consciousness in Japan." *Law and Society Review* 10.

van der Woude, Ad, et al., eds. 1990. *Urbanization in History*. Oxford: Oxford University Press.

Vaporis, Constantine. 1986. "Post Station and Assisting Villages: Corvée Labor and Peasant Contention." *Monumenta Nipponica* 41.

Vlastos, Stephen. 1981. "Conflict in Rural Japan in the Early Meiji Period." Paper prepared for the Tokugawa-Meiji Transition Workshop, Quail Roost, N.C., September.

———. 1986. *Peasant Protests and Uprisings in Tokugawa Japan*. Berkeley: University of California Press.

Vogel, Ezra. 1979. *Japan as Number One*. Cambridge: Harvard University Press.

Waddington, David, et al. 1989. *Flashpoints*. London: Routledge.

Wakeman, Frederic. 1977. "Rebellion and Revolution: The Study of Popular Movements in Chinese History." *Journal of Asian Studies* 36.

Wakita, Osamu. 1975. "The *Kokudaka* System: A Device for Unification." *Journal of Japanese Studies* 1.

———. 1982. "The Emergence of the State in Sixteenth-Century Japan." *Journal of Japanese Studies* 8.

Wallace, Anthony. 1956. "Revitalization Movements." *American Anthropologist* 58.

Wallerstein, Immanuel. 1974. *The Modern World-System I*. New York: Academic Press.

Walthall, Anne. 1983. "Narratives of Peasant Uprisings in Japan." *Journal of Asian Studies* 42.

———. 1986. *Social Protest and Popular Culture in Eighteenth-Century Japan*. Tucson: University of Arizona Press.

———. 1990. "Edo Riots." Paper prepared for the Conference on Edo and Paris in the Early Modern Period, Tokyo, June.

———. 1991. *Peasant Uprisings in Japan*. Chicago: University of Chicago Press.

Walton, John. 1984. *Reluctant Rebels*. New York: Columbia University Press.

Weber, Eugen. 1976. *Peasants into Frenchmen*. Stanford: Stanford University Press.

Weber, Max. 1947. *The Theory of Social and Economic Organization*. Trans. A. M. Henderson and Talcott Parsons. New York: Oxford University Press.

———. 1977. "Basic Sociological Terms." In *Understanding and Social Inquiry*, ed. Fred Dallmayr and Thomas McCarthy. Notre Dame, Ind.: Notre Dame University Press.

Weede, Erich. 1988. "A Utilitarian Approach to Mass Rebellion, Violence, and Revolution." Paper prepared for the annual meeting of the American Political Science Association, Washington, D.C., September.

Weiner, Myron, and Samuel Huntington, eds. 1987. *Understanding Political Development*. Boston: Little, Brown.

Weller, Robert, and Scott Guggenheim, eds. 1982. *Power and Protest in the Countryside*. Durham: Duke University Press.

Westney, D. Eleanor. 1981. "An Organizations Approach to the Tokugawa-Meiji Transition." Paper prepared for the Tokugawa-Meiji Transition Workshop, Quail Roost, N.C., September.

White, James. 1973. *Political Implications of Cityward Migration: Japan as an Exploratory Test Case*. Beverly Hills: Sage.

———. 1984. "Protest and Change in Contemporary Japan." In *Institutions for Change in Japanese Society*, ed. George Devos. Berkeley: Institute of East Asian Studies.

———. 1988a. "Social Conflict and Political Protest in the Nobi Region, 1600–1868." Paper prepared for the Greater Nobi Region Project Workshop, Nagoya, January.

———. 1988b. "The Rational Rioters: Leaders, Followers, and Popular Protest in Early Modern Japan." *Politics and Society* 16.

———. 1988c. "State Growth and Popular Protest in Tokugawa Japan." *Journal of Japanese Studies* 14.

———. 1989. "Economic Development and Sociopolitical Unrest in Nineteenth-Century Japan." *Economic Development and Cultural Change* 37.

———. 1992a. "Core, Periphery, and Popular Contention in the Tokugawa City." *Meijō Hōgaku* 42, special issue (May).

———. 1992b. *The Demography of Sociopolitical Conflict in Japan, 1721–1846*. Berkeley: Institute for East Asian Studies.

———. 1993a. "Cycles and Repertoires of Popular Contention in Early Modern Japan." *Social Science History* 17.

———. 1993b. "Political Opposition." In *Postwar Japan as History*, ed. Andrew Gordon. Berkeley: University of California Press.

Wigen, Karen. 1990. "The Geographic Imagination in Early Modern Japanese History." Asian/Pacific Studies Institute, Duke University.

Williams, E. N. 1970. *The Ancient Regime in Europe*. New York: Harper and Row.

Wilson, George. 1992. *Patriots and Redeemers in Japan*. Chicago: University of Chicago Press.

Wolf, Eric. 1969. *Peasant Wars of the Twentieth Century*. New York: Harper and Row.

Wong, R. Bin. 1982. "Food Riots in the Qing Dynasty." *Journal of Asian Studies* 41.

Wortman, C. B., and J. W. Brehm. 1975. "Responses to Uncontrollable Outcomes." In *Advances in Experimental Social Psychology*, ed. Leonard Berkowitz. New York: Academic Press.

Wylie, Lawrence. 1964. *Village in the Vaucluse.* New York: Harper and Row.

Yamada Tadao. 1984. *Ikki Uchikowashi no Undō Kōzō.* Tokyo: Azekura.

Yamamura, Kozo. 1981. "The Meiji Land Tax Reform: An Economic Transition to a Modern State." Paper prepared for the Tokugawa-Meiji Transition Workshop, Lake Wilderness, Wash., August.

Yamanashi-ken, ed. 1978. *Yamanashi Kensei Hyakunen Shi.* Vol. 1. Kōfu.

Yashiro Kazuo et al., eds. 1989. *Nihon Sōdō Jiten.* Tokyo: Sōbun Sha.

Yasumaru Yoshio. 1973. "Minshū Hōki no Sekaizō." *Shisō*, no. 586.

———. 1975. *Nihon no Kindaika to Minshū Shisō.* Tokyo: Aoki.

———. 1984. "Rebellion and Peasant Consciousness in the Edo Period." In *History and Peasant Consciousness in South East Asia*, ed. Andrew Turton and Shigeharu Tanabe. Ōsaka: National Museum of Ethnology.

Yokoyama Toshio. 1977. *Hyakushō Ikki to Gimin Denshō.* Tokyo: Kyōiku Sha.

———. 1986. *Shinano no Hyakushō Ikki to Gimin Denshō.* Matsumoto: Gōdo Shuppan.

Yoshihara Kenichirō. 1980. *Edo no Machi Yakunin.* Tokyo: Yoshikawa Kōbunkan.

Yoshinaga Akira. 1973. *Kinsei no Sembai Seido.* Tokyo: Yoshikawa Kōbunkan.

Yoshizumi Mieko. 1967, 1968. "Tetsudai-fushin ni tsuite." *Gakushūin Daigaku Bungakubu Kenkyū Nempō*, nos. 14, 15.

Zagorin, Perez. 1982. *Rebels and Rulers, 1500–1660.* 2 vols. New York: Cambridge University Press.

Zimmermann, Ekkart. 1983. *Political Violence, Crises, and Revolutions.* Cambridge, Mass.: Schenkman.

Zuckerman, Alan. 1991. *Doing Political Science.* Boulder, Colo.: Westview.

INDEX

absolutism, 31–33, 40
actors. *See* contention: social composition
administrative fragmentation, 211, 297
agrarianism, 37, 64, 78
appeals, 47, 49, 143, 155–61, 164
aristocracy. *See samurai*

bakufu. See shogunate
bakuhan system. *See* shogunate
Bansuke, 4–6, 11, 15, 167, 255, 257, 291, 296, 302
benevolence. *See jinsei*
bushi. *See samurai*

cities, 51, 67, 75, 81, 84–85, 96, 103, 160, 167, 171, 206, 214–15, 219, 301
  growth of, 64–65
  organization of, 94–95, 99
  poverty in, 93–94
coercion. *See* repression
coercive appeals, 144, 147, 155–61, 258
commerce, 43, 64–68, 85, 90, 207–8, 219, 274, 290, 295
community. *See* villages
Confucianism, 36, 44, 70
consciousness, popular, 11–12, 36, 56–58, 64, 107–13, 130, 285–89, 297, 302
conspiracy, 2, 5, 47, 50
contention
  aggressiveness in, 104, 135–38, 178–79, 258
  composition of, 145–55, 177–81, 187, 195, 217–19, 222–35, 242–44, 258–59, 304–5, 321–23
  context of, 8–12; cultural, 107–22; economic, 63–82, 298–99; political, 27–62; social, 83–105, 300–301
  correlates of, 178, 181, 203–4, 222–33, 286–88, 295; economic, 204–10; political, 210–14; social, 214–19 (*see also* disasters, natural; contention: spatial distribution of; contention: temporal

distribution)
  data on, 22–23, 313–14
  defined, 6, 323; dimensions of, 19, 140, 147, 184–85, 320; typologies of, 140–41, 315–19
  elite. *See samurai*
  frequency of, 56, 80, 93, 126–29, 172–77, 193–94, 198, 294; in other societies, 127–29, 231, 233, 294
  impact on: disaster relief, 272; domains, 273, 290; economic growth, 274, 310; farmers, 274; headman, 274; interests, 276; judicial system, 250–53; land surveys, 272; lords, 278; Meiji state, 272; myths and tales, 20–21; national learning, 275; officials, 273, 310; opportunities, 276; popular rights, 275; protoindustrialization, 274, 290; punishment, 272, 285; resources, 276–77; *samurai,* 272; shogunate, 20, 272, 290–91; social control, 49–54, 272; state, 272, 290, 310; subsequent contention, 20–21, 166, 217, 276, 285, 288–89; taxation, 272; villages, 290
  inception of, 17, 82, 261–67, 308–9
  interests and, 12–13, 15–16, 55, 59, 80, 99, 104, 204–10, 218–19, 233–38, 303–5
  magnitude of, 53, 121, 135–38, 146, 168, 179, 194, 198, 242–44, 279, 283, 295–96, 315–22
  official response to, 20, 48, 97–98, 170–71, 310 (*see also* punishment; repression)
  opportunities and, 13–16, 55, 59, 80, 210–14, 218–19, 233–38, 303–5 (*see also* administrative fragmentation)
  reasons for, 240–45, 266, 305–26; economic, 249–50; during Meiji era, 253–55; fiscal, 250–52; political, 252–53; social, 245–48 (*see also* contention: interests and
  role in Meiji Restoration, 277–78

345

www.ingramcontent.com/pod-product-compliance
Lightning Source LLC
Chambersburg PA
CBHW021808270326
41932CB00007B/95